FREE GIFTS

Free Gifts

CAPITALISM AND THE POLITICS
OF NATURE

ALYSSA BATTISTONI

PRINCETON UNIVERSITY PRESS
PRINCETON & OXFORD

Published by Princeton University Press
41 William Street, Princeton, New Jersey 08540
99 Banbury Road, Oxford OX2 6JX

press.princeton.edu

GPSR Authorized Representative: Easy Access System Europe - Mustamäe tee 50, 10621 Tallinn, Estonia, gpsr.requests@easproject.com

All Rights Reserved

ISBN 978-0-691-26346-5
ISBN (e-book) 978-0-691-26348-9

British Library Cataloging-in-Publication Data is available

Editorial: Rob Tempio and Chloe Coy
Production Editorial: Jenny Wolkowicki
Jacket design: Chris Ferrante
Production: Erin Suydam
Publicity: William Pagdatoon
Copyeditor: Maia Vaswani

Jacket image: Frans Snyders, *Draped table laden with game, fruit, vegetables and a boar's head*, 1609–1657, oil on canvas, 46½ × 52½ in.

This book has been composed in Arno Pro

Printed in the United States of America

10 9 8 7 6 5 4 3 2 1

For Betsy Ritz and Rick Battistoni
and for Simon

CONTENTS

Introduction

IN THE ENDLESS expanse of the universe, every living thing we know of exists within a thin layer, spanning just a few hundred meters, of a single planet—Earth. This space of life, sometimes termed the critical zone, is as large, relative to the Earth, as an apple's skin to its flesh.[1] If this zone is small relative to the vastness of space, however, it nevertheless supports an astonishing array of life: sea stars at the sunless, frigid bottom of the ocean and pikas in the upper altitudes of the Himalayas; over a thousand species of ant in the Amazon rainforest alone. Or at least, it has. Today, many of the Earth's beings are not doing well. One million species presently stand at risk of extinction; the last forty years alone have seen the loss of an estimated 50 percent of vertebrate wildlife. The vast majority of vertebrates living on Earth today are domestic animals bred in factory farms for human consumption: livestock now constitute 60 percent of mammals and 70 percent of birds.[2] Plant life, too, has been drastically remade: vast forests have been felled for timber; plains and marshlands have been steadily converted to monocrop plantations and pasture, or cleared to make way for roadways and suburban sprawl. Others face more oblique dangers. As global temperatures warm, bristlecone pines that have stood for millennia are threatened by the migration of unfamiliar pests and increasingly frequent wildfires. As Arctic snow melts earlier each year, the eggs of the birds that breed on Siberian tundra hatch too late to feed on the insects that emerge from the frozen ground, decimating their populations. Artificial lights disorient insects and turtles; artificial noise disrupts the communication of birds and whales.[3]

Catastrophic climate change is, of course, the most pressing and obvious ecological challenge we now face, though hardly the only one. Global temperatures have already risen an estimated 1.1°C from preindustrial temperatures, and this rise is projected to reach 2.5°C or more by the end of the century.[4]

While as recently as a decade ago climate change was still viewed as a problem of the distant future, its effects are increasingly obvious in the here and now: in the punishing heat waves that have swept through India and Europe; wildfires in Australia and flooding in Pakistan; megadroughts in the American West and the Horn of Africa; cyclones striking Mozambique and hurricanes devastating Caribbean island states. The acceleration of its underlying causes, too, is an astonishingly recent phenomenon: more carbon has been emitted since the fall of the Berlin Wall—or, as David Wallace-Wells observes, since the premiere of *Seinfeld*—than in all previous human history.[5]

This is not a crisis only for nonhuman beings; nor even for self-proclaimed nature lovers or environmentalists. It is a crisis for everyone presently living on Earth—though it affects some far more immediately and severely than others. Millions of people around the world, including most Indigenous peoples, rely directly on wild plants and animals for sustenance. Billions more rely indirectly on other species: wild insects that pollinate crops, marshes that filter water, root systems that ward off erosion.[6] Every single one of us relies on other beings to keep the planet habitable: on the microbes in the soil, plankton in the oceans, and forests spanning huge swathes of the globe, without which the Earth's atmosphere would not support plant and animal life. The planet once seemed to exist beyond us, offering a stable background against which human lives and dramas could unfold. The mounting evidence that this is no longer the case—that, in fact, it has never been the case—has prompted a reckoning in many quarters. In political discourse it has become routine in recent years, to the point of cliché, to describe climate change as an "existential threat." Scientists have proposed naming a new geological era, the Anthropocene, marked by the entrance of human activity into the fossil record. Humanists and social scientists, once content to leave nature to environmentalists, have called for a dramatic rethinking of the precepts of Western thought, and perhaps for abandoning them altogether.[7]

In economics, however, the astonishing transformations of our planet are frequently attributed to a surprisingly narrow cause: the absence of price. As the economist Nicholas Stern observed in his landmark paper on the economics of climate change, "Greenhouse gas emissions are externalities, and represent the biggest market failure the world has seen."[8] In other words, the effects of accumulating greenhouse gases are not factored into the prices of market goods, and as a result, are not taken into account in economic decisions. The use of the Earth's atmospheric and water cycles as an emissions sink, similarly, is typically costless, despite their nearly infinite value to human and nonhuman life. So too are biodiversity and ecosystem loss traced to the literal priceless-ness of many nonhuman species, ecologies, and organisms. The economist Pavan Sukhdev, for example, argues that the "economic invisibility of nature" has serious consequences, insofar as no one pays to preserve the Amazon's "rain factory" or for insects' pollination services.[9] Although it is the likes of "peat bogs and bees" that keep life "possible and bearable," the economic jour-nalist Jonathan Guthrie notes in the *Financial Times*, "we have not typically attributed any value to them." This, he adds, "seems like a mistake."[10]

The gap between these two discourses—the language of existential threat and that of economic error—is vertiginous. The idea that the end of the world might come about as the result of an accounting blunder tilts into absurdity. Is it really possible that this "mistake" could bring an end to life on Earth as we know it? And if so, why hasn't it been corrected? For if this is a mistake or a failure, it is one that has proven enduringly difficult to rectify. The paradox of nature's nonvalue is a persistent one in political economic thought. Similar observations have been made for decades, even centuries: by the classical political economist Jean-Baptiste Say and the feminist economist Marilyn Waring, by the neoclassical economist Arthur Pigou and the ecological econo-mist Herman Daly, and by many more beside.

At the same time it is perplexing to regularly encounter claims that nature is endangered because it does not appear in the market. After all, capitalism fa-mously puts a price on everything: it is notoriously merciless in its disregard for moral value, religious belief, sentimental attachment, family ties, and cultural practice. The realm of the market perpetually expands, stripping ever wider swathes of the world for parts; markets regularly destroy the things that are bought and sold, such that everything precious must be protected from them— or at least so generations of critics have claimed. But if capitalism is character-ized by relentless commodification, then its continual failure to value many kinds of nature is puzzling. It suggests a different question than the one usually asked: not why *shouldn't* these incredibly useful activities be commodified— but rather, why *haven't* they been?

This problem, I argue, is much more profound than has typically been acknowledged, and deserves more careful critical attention than it has received. That is what this book is about: capitalism's persistent failure to value nonhu-man nature, and what it means for politics—as well as for our collective future on this planet. Capitalism, this book argues, systematically treats nature as a "free gift": something that can be taken without payment or replenishing; something that is materially useful but that tends not to appear in exchange.

This is not an accident or an oversight; rather, it is foundational to how capitalism works.

The Politics of Nature

To name capitalism as the driving force of contemporary ecological transformations is typically to invite the charge of reductionism. Capitalism is important, many acknowledge, but it is only a subset of a much deeper problem with human relationships to nature.[11] The climate crisis, it's often said, requires us to rethink the basic frameworks with which we interrogate the world, including the relationship between politics and nature itself. Indeed, for much of the history of modern political thought, the very idea of a politics of nature might have seemed unintelligible. Politics is usually understood to be a distinctly human activity, perhaps even *the* defining human activity, while nature describes the world as it operates independently from human action. Politics concerns the realm of decisions about how things will and ought to be, while nature names that which simply is and cannot be changed. Politics describes the actions of human subjects; nature, the passive backdrop against which they play out. Nature is most present in political thought as landscape or metaphor, resource or territory.[12] The driving force of much Enlightenment thought was the imperative to separate the natural from the political—to debunk superstition, deflate myths, disenchant the world.[13] The distinction between nature—how things are—and politics—how things are made—has stood, G. A. Cohen argues, as "the foundation of all social criticism": only if something could be otherwise, after all, do we have grounds to challenge it.[14]

Yet the distinction between nature and politics has also long been questioned from the vantage point of Indigenous ontologies and feminist phenomenologies—and in the past few decades, by ecological thought. Ecologists remind us that human beings are part of nature, dependent on and unavoidably connected to other kinds of life. In recent decades, the reality of interdependence has been brought into ever starker relief by the worsening climate crisis. And yet the crisis has also scrambled our coordinates for what a politics of nature might be.

On the one hand, anthropogenic climate change has crowned a growing suspicion of the category of "nature" itself. In 1989, Bill McKibben famously declared the "end of nature," claiming that human modification of the atmosphere meant that a world standing apart from human beings had ceased to exist. "We have ended," he argued, "the thing that has—at least, in modern times—defined nature for us: its separation from human society."[15] Many argued in response that nature had never really been separate from human society at all. Environmental scholarship has long interrogated the idea of nature, scrutinizing its representation in culture and language, science and discourse, art and politics. Nature has been thoroughly dissected and deconstructed, debunked and defanged. Time and time again, it has turned out that those invoking "nature"—scientists included—have imported their own social values into their arguments, whether intentionally or accidentally; all too often, the invocation of "nature" has conveniently justified the status quo. At times the idea of nature has seemed not only the most complex in the English language, as Raymond Williams once suggested, but so complex as to be unusable altogether: too liable to act as ideological cover, too imbued with moral and cultural expectation, too rooted in Cartesian dualism or Baconian domination.[16] The one thing it certainly is not is *natural*: the idea of nature, scholars have concluded, was a thoroughly human construction long before climate change appeared on the scene. Climate change, then, simply confirms that nature is political all the way down.[17]

On the other hand, the worsening climate catastrophe has also been received as the *return* of nature: this time as an autonomous world of inhuman matter unvanquished by human fantasies of control and indifferent to human perceptions. The climate crisis, Dipesh Chakrabarty argues, "is about waking up to the rude shock of the planet's otherness." It is about remembering the force of an "inhuman nature" that exists beyond our representation and manipulation.[18] If the *idea* of nature is no longer viable, in other worlds, actually existing nature—the physical force of the material world—is as lively as ever. The environment, in turn, is not just a passive medium that surrounds us, but something actively made by living beings—ourselves included. Our human world is populated by countless nonhuman agents, from the billions of carbon molecules accumulating in the atmosphere to the microbes that circulate in our food and guts.[19] Climate change therefore forces us to confront the aspects of our world that we have not made and do not control; it reveals that the modern project of bending nature to our will has failed once again. When Chakrabarty, like McKibben, confronts the end of an assumed separation between nature and society, he is beset by the opposite anxiety: that climate change signifies not the end of nature but the end of the social; the end of a distinctively *human* history. Climate change reminds us that the achievements we attribute to human action and ingenuity rest on material conditions that we have often taken for granted, but no longer can. Perhaps what we have called "civilization" is really just the contingent stability of the Holocene era; perhaps what we moderns have called "freedom" is really just the product of fossil fuels.[20] To understand the world today, some charge, we have to look more closely at this other nature—not nature as idea but as vibrant matter, nature as the multitude of nonhumans that make up our shared world. We must turn from the global to the planetary, Chakrabarty argues; we must come down to Earth, Bruno Latour insists.[21]

Taken together, these revelations seem to point in opposite directions. On the one hand, we live on a human planet, and thus on a thoroughly *political* planet.[22] Yet on the other, we live on an inhuman Earth replete with agencies we do not control or even understand. The implications are often dizzying. To make sense of this predicament, we are called on to interrogate our received wisdom, challenge our assumptions, revise our concepts: freedom, responsibility, action. William Connolly, for example, argues that we must "rethink old ideals from the ground up" in light of what we now know about planetary forces; Cara New Daggett, that "the ontological shift forced upon us by the Anthropocene also upends our understanding of politics."[23] "We inherit a world that no available political category is designed to manage," Pierre Charbonnier declares, "and therefore we are faced with a seemingly impossible task."[24]

If climate change is transforming our planet in unprecedented ways, however, the reflections it has prompted are not as unprecedented as we tend to imagine. We do confront a set of novel and daunting challenges—but so too have all political thinkers past. The project of political theory is fundamentally one of coming to terms with a world in flux.[25] The political categories we now see as mundane—mass politics, democracy, the modern state—were once unprecedented in their own right. For that matter, even the ecological challenge to political thought is less novel than it might seem. For decades, work in environmental political theory has asked whether ecological precepts are compatible with core traditions and concepts of modern political thought, and considered how they might be reconciled.[26] The growing relevance of these analyses only reiterates their fundamental point: that nature cannot stand apart as a set of issues or ideas to which political theory can simply be applied.

Rather than cordoning nature off from politics or abolishing the distinction altogether, this book starts from the premise that "nature" pertains to politics of all kinds—not only those issues we tend to think of as "environmental." Instead of treating "politics" as the organization of human life, to be distinguished from the scientific or technical organization of nonhuman matter, it holds that to organize human life is always also a material enterprise, and hence a natural one. All of our actions play out in a material world, whether or not they are explicitly posed as environmental or consciously take the more-than-human world into account—and this means that decisions about how to relate to other human beings are always, inevitably, decisions about how to arrange the world around us.

This premise does not mean, however, that nature and politics are *identical*. As ambiguous as it has often turned out to be, whether because we have smuggled politics into our ideas of nature or hidden the material foundations of our politics, some distinction between nature and politics remains essential to the latter. Denaturalization remains a bedrock of critique, vital for interrogating seemingly immutable phenomena and locating their political dimensions. But efforts to denaturalize institutions and relationships often run the risk of *dematerializing* them: of detaching politics from the material world we call nature altogether. Political thought, then, must undertake *denaturalization* alongside *rematerialization*: it must attend to the physical reality of the world while critically assessing the social relations in which it is situated. We do not need a new idea of nature to motivate care for the more-than-human world, or a conception of nature set apart from human artifice that we can protect from our interference. What we do need is a sense of what we can make of the world we are given; of what we can hold ourselves and others responsible for; of what must be as it is, and what can be otherwise. We need a better sense, too, of how the more-than-human world works, and how, precisely, we are remaking it: through what kinds of relationships and practices, institutions and structures. We don't need to re-think political theory from the ground up, in other words—we simply need to look at it aslant, so as to better glimpse the places where the politics of nature already appear, and the tools we already have to make sense of it.

A central claim of this book is that one of the densest sites of interaction between nature and politics is in the material realm we call the economy.[27] While historians of political thought have often written of "industrialization" or "capitalism" or "modernity," they have too rarely attended to the transformations of the more-than-human world that these phenomena entail.[28] But it is in the economy that the matter given by nature is transformed into human artifacts, that wild flora become crops and fauna become livestock, that minerals become resources and long-decayed organisms become fuel. These interactions are structured, moreover, by a particular kind of economy, at present the one that encompasses nearly all the world: capitalism. Capitalism is now *the* political economic system upon which nearly all human beings now rely for our livelihoods and for our lives, how we obtain food and clothing, shelter and comfort; how we attend to our wants and needs.[29]

We are used to thinking about capitalism as a particular way of organizing economic production and exchange, perhaps even as a way of ordering social life writ large.[30] But capitalism inadvertently orders, and reorders, relationships among human beings along many dimensions, beyond even the space of the workplace or market. It reorganizes, too, the relationships of the more-than-human world—all the way down to the molecular makeup of the atmosphere itself.[31] Its emergence is perfectly correlated to the steady rise of carbon emissions; its more recent triumph over the globe, to the near-total decimation of other species. In the course of constructing vast factories, excavating massive mines, and monocropping fields, capitalism has also reconstructed the very biosphere.

Capitalism, in other words, is not only a system for making and exchanging goods, nor even for making the social world in which we live. Today, it is the dominant worldmaking force—and more than that, the dominant *planetmaking* force.[32] To understand the politics of nature today, then, we must understand how capitalism both represents nature socially and makes use of it materially. This is what the free gift of nature can help us apprehend.

The Free Gift of Nature

I take the description of nature as a "gift" from the classical political economists who wrote in the eighteenth and nineteenth centuries amid the rise of the industrial capitalism that has so transformed the modern world. To thinkers like Adam Smith and Jean-Baptiste Say, the role of nonhuman elements in production was evident and frequently remarked upon. Nature, the physiocratic thinker Anne Robert Jacques Turgot argued, makes a "pure gift" to production.[33] Elements like water, air, and light, Say observed, are "spontaneous gifts of nature" to human consumption.[34] Smith made note of the work that nature does in agriculture; David Ricardo lauded the abundance of "natural agents" that "perform their work gratuitously."[35] Elements ranging from trade winds to soil fertility, they noted, alternately enhanced, combined with, and substituted for human labor. Nature, these thinkers agreed, clearly made useful and necessary contributions to nearly all forms of production—even if they did not always agree on how these contributions should be characterized.

These depictions of nature as a gift echo a broader tradition of Western thought in which nature is a gift from God—ostensibly to all of humanity. Jean-Jacques Rousseau mused on natural man, who enjoyed the "gifts Nature offered him" without a thought of extracting them; even John Locke noted that the gift of the earth, and of the fruits and beasts "produced by the spontaneous hand of Nature," belong to everyone—at least before those fruits are plucked by an industrious laborer.[36] As these examples suggest, the gifts of nature have often had different valences even within the Western tradition. Sometimes they are understood as a recognition of human superiority: Locke, for example, claims that God gave "inferior creatures" to humanity for the express purpose of our use.[37] For Kant, too, human beings have "an equal share in the gifts of nature"—yet the sign of truly *human* reason, that which raises man above the animals, comes in our realization that wool was given to the sheep not for its use but for ours.[38] Others have insisted that the gift of the Earth must be treasured: the "gift of good land," for the agrarianist Wendell Berry, must be stewarded with care; for Pope Francis, the Earth that has been given to us must be preserved for others yet to come.[39] What is common to these interpretations, however, is that they are unidirectional: there can be no real reciprocity for a gift from God. This is illustrated most clearly in the philosophy of Georges Bataille and Jacques Derrida, for whom the gift consists in a pure and absolute form of generosity that exceeds the possibility of return altogether—and thereby stands outside the logic of exchange.[40]

Another tradition understands the gift differently: not in terms of unilateral or unconditional generosity, but as something that carries the expectation of reciprocity. Many Indigenous peoples, too, describe the land and its fruits as gifts: the Anishinaabeg, Winona LaDuke writes, describe wild rice as "a gift from the Creator"; the Potawatomi botanist Robin Wall Kimmerer writes of wild strawberries as "gifts from the earth."[41] But true gifts, Kimmerer observes, "are not free": they must be replenished and returned.[42] Gifts form lasting relationships; they create social obligations and demand responses. For anthropologists like Marcel Mauss and Karl Polanyi, it is the fundamentally *reciprocal* nature of the gift that illustrates the possibility of exchange *without* the commodity form: the gift stands as the central social relation of noncapitalist societies.[43]

For all their differences, both of these accounts of the gift—as an expression of pure generosity on the one hand, and a relationship of radical reciprocity on the other—posit the gift as an alternative to the commodity. Gifts either defy the possibility of return and thus the logic of market exchange, or require a kind of ongoing response that is antithetical to commercial transactions. Gifts are often taken to reflect an ethic rather than a calculation, an emphasis on altruism or community rather than individual gain; they are said to be of a different order than the commodity and the market. Whatever gifts are, after all it is clear that they are *not* bought and sold.[44]

The peculiar, paradoxical kind of gift addressed in this book, however—the *free gift of nature*—is different from either of these. This term—*free gift*—is an odd one. Relative to common meanings of the gift, it seems either redundant or oxymoronic. If a gift is understood as pure generosity, then to call something a *free* gift is superfluous. If gifts are never really free, by contrast, then the phrase seems like a contradiction in terms. In fact, the modifier *free* is telling: it provides a clue that the free gift is not timeless or universal, but rather a category defined in relation to the market. The free gift of nature is free in the sense of costless, gratuitous: it denotes that something is priced at *zero*. The *free* gift, then, is not an alternative to the capitalist commodity at all. Rather, the free gift is a distinctively capitalist social form, no less central to capitalism than more familiar concepts like the commodity and the wage. Key to the free gift of nature is the disjuncture between its obvious usefulness, even its seeming invaluableness, and its utter lack of value in economic terms. The paradox is that the free gift is valuable *because* it is free: because it provides something materially useful without cost. It is *this* feature, this dual character, that gives coherence to the wide variety of concrete activities that the free gift names. What unifies steam power, sheep organs, soil fertility, and other "natural agents" as a category is not their qualitative features, which are remarkably different in both material function and anthropocentric use, but rather, their nonappearance in the form of value. The free gift is the form nature takes in societies in which commodity exchange is generalized as the primary means of acquiring and distributing the goods necessary for subsistence.

The free gift is also the commodity's shadow. Following its spectral trace can take us into dimensions of capitalism often left unexplored. While capitalism is associated with commodification, the free gift reveals commodification's limits—limits set not by a society seeking to protect itself from the market, but by the market itself. It serves as a reminder that capitalism may be operative even where its telltale signs—exchange value, wages—are not immediately in evidence. It draws our attention to activities that have clear effects in the material world but do not seem to register in the sphere of "the economy." It foregrounds concrete processes often neglected by analyses of the abstract realms of value and money, finance and exchange, and shows how physical qualities figure into even these abstractions. It reminds us, in other words, of the material content that always attends social forms.

Nature, as Theodor Adorno insists, always remains nonidentical with the terms we use to describe it: "Objects do not go into their concepts without leaving a remainder."[45] This book is fundamentally interested in these remainders: in the aspects of the world that overspill the bounds of capitalist social form, that are not easily contained within capitalist labor processes, that appear as aberrations in both the physical organization of the world and the concepts used to make sense of it.[46] It is about the things that are left over when capital has commodified what it can, in what capital abandons or abdicates rather than absorbing. It is about the unwanted "residuals" of production, forms of surplus matter whose negative effects go unreflected in exchange value.[47] It is about the gifts that give too freely to be expropriated, and the kinds of nature whose qualities and capacities, however extraordinary, are surplus to capital's needs. It is also about the kinds of *human* labor that can't easily be organized by the wage and the boss, and that persist in seemingly anachronistic forms—or that even seem to be free gifts themselves. Looking at the free gift, in other words, not only gives us a new perspective on nature, but casts capitalism itself in new light. The analysis of capitalism can help us understand the current state of the natural world—and so, too, can the analysis of nature help us understand capitalism.

My analysis of nature and capitalism makes three interventions in particular. The first is to offer a theory of the free gift of nature as a capitalist social form, attending to its dual character: its concrete reality as physical substance, and the way that this substance appears within capitalist social relations. The second is to offer a critique of capitalism's treatment of nature rooted not only in capitalism's environmental consequences, but also in what those consequences indicate about our ability to act freely. The third is to follow the free gift into the world, showing what happens when social relations hit the literal ground—tracking the unusual phenomena that result from this collision, the conceptual apparatuses developed to make sense of them, and the political struggles that have erupted around them.

Theorizing the Free Gift

The first project of this book—to theorize the oft-overlooked free gift of nature and its place within capitalism—joins a growing number of works addressing capitalism's relationship to nature. Such analyses have flourished in recent years, whether tracing capitalism's reliance on fossil fuels and its pursuit of growth or condemning its extractivism and drive to dominate nature.[48]

This book approaches the question from a different angle. It does not track capitalism's effects on "the environment" per se, detail its ravenous use of resources, or calculate its material throughput. Instead, it looks at how nature appears in capitalism's fundamental social relations, and how it factors into its core operations. It charges that to understand contemporary ecological problems, we have to understand why some things come to have value under capitalism as a particular organization of economic and social life, and why others do not. While scholars have shown that ideas about "nature" always reflect specific social views and cultural values, critical theorists of "nature" have too rarely attended to the way that the social and natural are defined and ordered by capitalism's particular, and now dominant, system of value. We have to bring the question so often posed in environmental thought—What is nature?—together with one posed by Marx: What is value under capitalism?

Marx's own ecological relevance is much disputed. While he has long been criticized as an anthropocentric Promethean, as enamored with the mastery of nature as any capitalist, he has also been recovered, of late, as a proto-ecological thinker.[49] Indeed, Marx's critique of how the gifts of nature figure in classical political economy is a vital starting point for my own analysis: the "free gift of nature," he claims, is a gift only to capital. Where the means of production are privately owned, capitalists alone benefit from nature's contributions; they alone lay claim to the wealth that nature bequeaths. But these remarks on the free gift are brief. Instead of looking to Marx substantively or reading him exegetically, I draw on him methodologically. For the relationship between the natural and the social is not only present in Marx's explicit discussions of soil fertility and "robbery agriculture"; rather, it is at the heart of his thought about the commodity, value, and other core concepts in his critique of political economy. Marx makes a crucial distinction between the material content of objects and activities, from labor to goods, and their social form: their significance within the set of relationships that govern human social life. Marx's method, in other words, confronts one of the core questions of ecological thought—the relationship between nature and society—while situating it within capitalism as a particular form of social organization.

"Political economy has indeed analyzed value," Marx writes in *Capital*. "But it has never once asked the question why this content has assumed that particular form."[50] For all that classical political economists purported to study the meaning and source of economic value, they had not really asked what value *is* or what is specific about capitalism's definition of it. Marx is particularly interested in the status of human labor: Why, he asks, are so many different human activities classified under the simple category "labor" and recognized only in accordance with their ability to produce value?[51] Why is labor organized as it is, and how might it be organized differently? How is wealth defined in capitalism, and how might it be understood otherwise?

This is itself a denaturalizing move, one which aims to show that capitalism is a specific rather than eternal form of society. All human societies, after all, have *some* form of organization that structures which kinds of work are done and who does them; all have *some* way of meeting needs, satisfying wants, and distributing both surplus and burdens. If there were no possibility that society might be organized differently, then there would be no basis for critique, and no possibility of change. When we ask why production is organized as it is under capitalism, in other words, we recognize that there are many ways that it might be organized otherwise—that we are not fated by nature to live this way. Elements of human collective life that classical political economists treated as necessary, Marx argues, are in fact contingent to capitalism and therefore changeable. This is why *Capital* is a *critique* of political economy.[52] The critique of political economy, I argue, also offers a vital basis for a political critique of ecology. For in posing the question of why human labor is expressed in terms of value, Marx implicitly poses another—why nonhuman nature is *not*.

To address the free gift, then, this book flips Marx's central question. Why does such an enormously wide range of "content"—material capacities ranging from animal digestion to steam power—tend to take the *same form*: the "free gift of nature"? Why does capitalism draw such a stark distinction between human labor and other forces of production? If nature contributes materially to production, why is it not valued in the terms that capitalism counts? Why is the more-than-human world we call *nature* organized in the way that it is?

It also connects a value form analysis of capitalist logics to the nonidentical and irreducible logic of the concrete world—what we might call the logic of nature. For while the critique of political economy aims to denaturalize capitalism, sometimes it also dematerializes it in its own right. Analyses of value typically emphasize the triumph of capitalist social forms over material content, the way that capitalism abstracts away from the concrete world in pursuit of wealth assessed in quantitative terms. Capitalism comes to appear as *entirely* abstract: a system comprising solely abstract labor, abstract time, abstract value. The physicality of production, the concrete dimension of labor, and the specific qualities of use value tend to fall by the wayside. While the analysis of abstraction is undoubtedly vital, to understand the role of the useful but costless gifts of nature, it is also essential to *rematerialize* capitalism as a concrete form of social production.[53] Instead of countering the Marxist focus on abstraction with a swerve to understand vibrant matter in itself, however, as new materialists often have, I take seriously the *dual* character of capitalist forms, understanding material and social qualities as two components that are distinct but necessarily *tethered* to each other, and drawing attention to their interaction.[54] Attending to the materiality of the world in a physical sense does not require jettisoning an account of the social or collapsing the difference between the two, as is sometimes suggested. It simply means recognizing that the world is always both: it is composed of many kinds of material agencies that capital has not made and cannot do without; *and* it is organized primarily, if always partially and imperfectly, by specifically capitalist social relations in which the material world is figured as a means to a single abstract end.

This analysis, in turn, opens up political questions that reach beyond the scope of "the environment" or even "nature": Why *do* we value things as we do, and could we choose to value them differently? What, if anything, is wrong with this system of valuation—and what would it mean to genuinely transform it?

The Critique of Capitalist Unfreedom

To diagnose the free gift as a distinctively capitalist social form is to state that this is not a *necessary* relationship to nature, and therefore to open the space for politics. But this alone doesn't tell us what's *wrong* with treating nature as a free gift.[55] Although the project of denaturalization is vital, it stops short of a critique. The book's second project, then, is to offer a critique of capitalism's treatment of nature—one rooted not in claims about nature itself, but in capitalism's limitation of *human* freedom.

The grounds for an ecological critique of capitalism can seem obvious. Capitalism has long been shadowed by charges that its satanic mills have ravaged the natural world, while its calculative logic has disenchanted it. A longstanding strain of ecological thought embraces nature as a wholesome antidote to capitalist exploitation, artificiality, and alienation.[56] More generally, a wealth of environmental philosophy has brought normative questions to bear on the more-than-human world, whether debating nature's intrinsic value or expanding the sphere of moral concern to include nonhuman beings.[57] Environmental political theory, too, has often been explicitly normative, considering how various political traditions and regimes have neglected or actively harmed nature, investigating how environmental goods and bads are unjustly shared among human beings, and reflecting on how human societies might live more sustainably.

I share the concerns articulated by many of these thinkers, and recognize the dismay that attends their judgments. The problem, however, is that many ecological critiques of capitalism take the normative status of nature itself for granted. They hold up nature as the standard against which we might measure human society—and threaten to reify nature as the "thing without politics" that can be used to justify political stances.[58] Many environmental philosophies, meanwhile, theorize ethical obligations detached from real conditions and construe our failings in strictly moral terms. They challenge anthropocentric hierarchies of moral status as if they were matters of thought alone—and fail, as a result, to address *why* we act as we do.

The problem with capitalism, in my account, is not just that it destroys nature or unjustly distributes the material harms and benefits of production. Rather, these problems stem from another, second-order problem: that capitalism limits our ability to treat nonhuman nature as something *other* than a free gift. It constrains our ability, individually and collectively, to make genuine decisions about how to value and relate to the nonhuman world, and to take responsibility for those decisions. Put simply: capitalism limits our freedom.

While my analysis joins a growing body of work criticizing capitalism on the grounds of unfreedom, it departs from the republican framework that underpins many contemporary arguments in this vein. I look instead to the existentialist tradition of Jean-Paul Sartre and Simone de Beauvoir as an unexpectedly useful resource for a denaturalized ecological critique. For Sartre and Beauvoir, values are given neither by God nor nature: they are only what we assert and actively commit ourselves to in the world.[59] This antifoundationalist view of value is a particularly crucial resource in resisting two frequent tendencies in ecological thought: moral naturalism on the one hand, and naïve materialism on the other. It suggests that the meaning and value of more-than-human beings cannot be taken for granted or derived from the world as given, but, rather, must be consciously asserted and enacted. What is so troubling about capitalism, in my argument, is the way that its singular form of value restricts the fundamental human project of determining values for ourselves—not as individuals, but collectively. To treat climate change as a genuinely *existentialist* challenge, then, would mean taking it as a charge to reevaluate our collective ways of life and the values they reflect. It would require changing not only our lightbulbs or even our energy sources, but our way of recognizing the worth of things, activities, beings.

In developing this critique, I diagnose capitalism as a form of rule, with two particularly significant aspects: class rule and market rule. *Class rule* describes capitalism's constitutive division of social power among human beings, rooted in disparate control over productive assets, and the curious form of the rule of the few that results. *Market rule,* meanwhile, describes how decisions and actions are structured in societies fundamentally organized around market exchange. As I show, an existentialist account of freedom is better suited than a republican one to confront market rule in particular, and to address the unusual kinds of unfreedom that characterize capitalist societies—the kinds of actions that seem to happen "behind our backs," unfolding without our conscious intent.

This critique of capitalism does not pertain only to nature: my claim is that capitalism limits our freedom more broadly. A critique of the rule of class and markets, however, offers a new angle on environmental problems typically described in terms of justice or harm. The paradox of the free gift of nature also proves to be particularly productive for exploring broader questions of action and responsibility within capitalist societies. It is precisely because the "free gift" is such an odd category that it draws attention to questions of capitalist value that typically lie hidden within prices. We are used to accepting the judgment of the market as a measure of worth, after all. We may grumble about prices, but we usually have no choice but to pay them. When something is unpriced, however, we're left without a measure of what it's supposed to be worth. We have to think for ourselves about how we should assess it. The absence of price, in other words, leaves a vacuum that politics can fill. This is why, as we'll explore in greater depth, controversies about nature's intrinsic value tend to occur around the frontiers of commodification, where capitalism seems to be expanding into hitherto untouched areas.

More interesting than the question of whether any given element of nature "should be" commodified, however, is what these debates tell us about the nature of capitalist value itself. They point to the real problem, which Sianne Ngai describes as the "mismeasurement of wealth" at capitalism's heart.[60] Ngai explores this mismeasurement through the figure of the "gimmick." Gimmicks, she says, are "overrated devices" whose exchange value is obviously inflated and "flagrantly unworthy" relative to their usefulness, like a banana slicer or an automatic carving knife—but which we want, and perhaps buy, anyway.[61] When we judge something to be a gimmick, Ngai observes, we register "the discrepancy between an overprized object's false claim to value and what we take to be its true worth."[62] The gimmick appears valuable, but turns out to be a swindle.

The free gift of nature also points to a disquieting ambiguity around value—but the discrepancy between its usefulness and value runs in the opposite direction. Where the gimmick may be proclaimed "worthless" even though it is expensive, the free gift comes cheap even as it is said to be priceless. Indeed, where the classical political economists describe the gifts of nature with gratitude and even wonder, the free gift is now more often described with concern. There seems to be something *wrong* with the fact that the gifts of nature are free: Why is an obviously valuable thing not valued? How can a centuries-old redwood tree be worth less than a "smart refrigerator"; how can the things most necessary for life—clean air and water, a stable atmosphere—be worth less than the junk we buy and sell every day? The free gift reflects the contradictions at the heart of capitalism—and can illustrate our ambivalence about this way of organizing our lives. Questions about the gap between what nature's value *should be* and what it *is*, I argue, index a critique of capitalist valuation even where it isn't articulated as such.

While this book offers both an analysis and critique of capitalism's devaluation of nature, it does not offer an account of how nature *ought* to be valued otherwise. This is in part because we have an abundance of resources already: many debates about how we ought to relate to nonhuman nature are effectively debates about the values a noncapitalist world should have. They are oriented toward a world in which assessments of ecological function or cultural significance play a meaningful role in decisions about the production and allocation of things deemed beneficial to human and nonhuman flourishing; toward a world governed by more than one standard of value. We do not, at present, live in such a world. But ultimately, the question of how we, as human beings, should relate to the more-than-human world can't be outsourced to a set of inherent qualities or calculated by an ethicist. The critique of capitalist value can't tell us how a noncapitalist world ought to assign value—and in my view, it isn't the place of political theory to decide.

Instead of asserting values of my own, then, I aim to tease out the latent values and judgments that might challenge capitalist valuation, even where they are not articulated as such. I attend to collective intuitions that something is wrong when people are forced to breathe toxic air, when caregiving is largely unpaid, when species are driven to extinction, and attempt to spell them out more clearly. In highlighting the distance between these diagnoses and the actual state of affairs in the world in which we live, I aim to provide an account of that distance: in a world where capitalism reigns, the accumulation of abstract value is what drives decisions about production and distribution, as actively made by a subset of people who own and control the means by which goods are produced. Rather than simply envisioning how the world might be, I hope to identify the possibilities that might emerge from the world as it is.

Getting Concrete: Rematerializing Capitalism

The projects outlined above seek to develop a conceptual armature for thinking about politics, nature, and capitalism via the lens of the free gift of nature. Its third project is to make these concrete, showing what happens when capitalism's social form of value encounters the qualities of a material world that exists over and above it. For the self-valorization of capitalist value can never be frictionless: it must always pass through the material world. I therefore show how capitalism's social relations remake the material world, both within and beyond the formal space of production—but also how the material world often enables, sometimes resists, and always exceeds those forms.

One of the book's broader methodological interventions is to read ostensibly different sites—the "hidden abode of production," the polluted environment, the reproductive household, the regenerative ecosystem—as differently situated aspects of the same core process: the same *collision of abstract value with a material, more-than-human world*. My account doesn't posit an "inside" or "outside" to capitalism, nor a "background" and "foreground." It doesn't center attention on the factory as the "point of production" instead of the household—or vice versa. Nor does it identify some spaces as untainted by capitalism, offering "innocent reservoirs" from which a challenge might be mounted.[63] It does not, in other words, assume that some parts of social and ecological life are "part of capitalism" while others are not. It simply asks how the material world—comprising among other things the various capacities of human and nonhuman beings—is organized by and in relation to the distinctive social relations that characterize capitalism as a mode of production. It shows, in turn, how categories often used to delineate boundaries between capitalism's inside and out—including "the environment"—emerge out of this interaction rather than preexisting it as separate spheres in their own right. This method can help us see familiar problems—the costlessness of carbon emissions, the low value of reproductive labor, the worthlessness of ecosystems—not as discrete issues in need of solutions, but as interrelated consequences of a common cause.

From this basic starting assumption, different chapters track how the free gifts of nature appear as machinery and cooperation, pollution and social cost, reproductive labor and housework, natural resource and natural capital—each associated with a distinct "site"—the factory, the environment, the household, the ecosystem. They reveal how capitalism connects people not only through social relations but also through the material traces of those social relations in the world—how pollution, for example, constitutes potential collectivities as much as the factory does—and suggest how those connections might be mobilized against their source.

Much of this study considers the period now understood as the Great Acceleration: the period since 1950, which has on the one hand seen the rapid increase of human activity of various kinds, including foreign direct investment, GDP, energy use, and population; and on the other, troublesome indicators of biospheric health, measured via levels of nitrous oxide, methane, and ocean acidification.[64] At the start of this period, nature was typically described in terms of cyclical, regular change. For Theodor Adorno and Max Horkheimer in 1944, nature was the realm of "inexhaustibility, endless renewal, and permanence"; for Hannah Arendt in 1958, an "unceasing, indefatigable cycle."[65] Yet this seeming regularity has been radically transformed and in some cases thoroughly disrupted by human activity, which is today the core driver of biogeochemical cycles. In the course of the Great Acceleration—so far—the number of motor vehicles on the planet has risen twentyfold; the annual production of plastics, three hundredfold. Most pressingly, nearly 85 percent of anthropogenic carbon emissions have been released since 1945, and more than half in only the past three decades.[66] This rapid change, the environmental historians J. R. McNeill and Peter Engelke argue, constitutes "the most anomalous and unrepresentative period in the 200,000-year-long history of relations between our species the biosphere."[67]

Nearly all of what we think of as contemporary ecological thought has developed amid this exceptional period—and nearly all of contemporary political thought too. Each chapter, then, also traces how economists, philosophers, activists, and others—including many not explicitly concerned with ecology—responded to these planetary transformations. While the book focuses on Western thinkers, many of the ideas it traces have had global influence. I examine, especially, how the problem of the free gift has been figured in twentieth-century political and economic thought; for although the language of the "gifts of nature" now sounds quaint next to the technical terminology of modern economics, the paradox it describes—usefulness lacking value—has persisted. It underpins many of the central frameworks for addressing environmental problems today, and many ways of thinking about political economy more broadly. The rapid intensification of production in the twentieth century drove many economists to recognize the ways that economic activity spills beyond its designated bounds, while the rapidly developing apparatus of social science generated novel ways of thinking about the problems once addressed glancingly by classical political economists. Collective action problems and seeming aberrations to the rules of commodity exchange occupied the attention of social scientists across the political spectrum, identified in terms of "externalities," "public goods," and the "tragedy of the commons."

Among a variety of twentieth-century thinkers, I therefore pay particular attention to economists like Arthur Pigou, Ronald Coase, Milton Friedman, Friedrich Hayek, William Baumol, and others. I read them as Marx read the classical political economists: with an eye toward understanding as well as critique.[68] Instead of simply rejecting them as economistic or neoliberal, I argue that their ideas illustrate something crucial about the predicaments we face, even as they often remain wedded to a model of analysis that cannot fully grasp the dimensions and depth of the problems they confront. I highlight tensions between these resources and those of social and critical theory—but also reveal surprising points of convergence among radically different thinkers.

Although in its broader arc the book begins with the abstract and gradually turns to the concrete, within each chapter it also shuttles between the two—a method that is vital for both clarifying ideas and testing them. The book's concrete analyses don't simply apply the ideas advanced in theory, but rather build on and develop theoretical insights with reference to empirical and descriptive work in the social and natural sciences. Tracking capitalism's transformations of the world alongside the development of the ideas developed to make sense of them, meanwhile, accentuates one of the book's core claims: that nature is integral even to modes of thought that claim only a social purview.[69]

Chapter Outline

Free Gifts begins by laying theoretical groundwork. Chapter 1 develops the core concept of the book—the free gift of nature—by way of classical political economy and Marx's critique of it. I show how Marx's analysis of the radical disjuncture between abstract exchange and concrete use value, in his discussion of the commodity, can illuminate the perennial nonvalue of nature under capitalism. In chapter 2, I articulate the book's critique of capitalist unfreedom as an alternative to moralized appeals to nature itself. Reading Sartre alongside Hayek, I show how an existentialist conception of freedom can clarify the dimensions of class and market rule, while insisting on the importance of choosing values for ourselves.

At this point, the book turns toward analyses of how the free gift appears in concrete ecologies and economies. Instead of looking "behind Marx's hidden abode," I begin there, examining how the free gifts feature in the heart of industrial production before turning to spaces often treated as peripheral or even external to capitalism's core operations—the environment, the household, the biosphere.[70] Chapter 3 follows Marx's descent into the site of commodity production, considering how capital puts both the free gifts of nature and the free gift of human cooperation to work within the quintessential site of the industrial factory—as well as in sectors where control is more elusive. It introduces the idea of subsumption, describing the way that capitalist social relations reorganize physical production itself, while also highlighting its limits. Chapter 4 moves out from the factory, exploring the byproduction of waste that accompanies the production of commodities—often described by economists in terms of social costs or externalities. The social cost names the flip side of the free gift of nature—harmful physical effects that go unreflected in price. This chapter draws attention to capital's ability to costlessly impose surplus matter on others, and its power to remake the environment itself. Chapter 5 looks to the household, asking why certain kinds of *human* labor tend to be unpaid and unvalued—treated, in other words, as a free gift. Engaging the rich tradition of feminist debates about housework, it offers a sympathetic critique of dominant accounts of the parallels between the unpaid status of reproductive labor and nonhuman nature, and a new explanation for their similar position. Chapter 6 considers the regeneration of the biosphere itself, via the activities of a huge range of species, from plants that absorb carbon dioxide to microbes that break down soil contaminants. These activities present an exceptionally clear demonstration of the paradox of the free gift: they are vital for the continuation of both human and nonhuman life, but economically worthless. Despite years of effort, they have proved remarkably difficult to commodify. They illustrate that many kinds of nature can be valued only through political means.

The concluding chapter 7 steps back from the analysis of the free gift as it operates within capitalism to face the question: What happens if we *stop* treating nature as a free gift? In contrast to the recurring suggestion in contemporary political and social thought that human freedom is fundamentally tragic, premised on the destruction and domination of nature, I draw on Simone de Beauvoir's account of freedom as situated, embodied, and ambiguous in offering an account of freedom for a finite material world—and a way forward amid cascading disasters. A brief epilogue considers alternative relationships to nonhuman nature itself. I read contemporary calls to engage with the nonhuman world differently—with respect, with reciprocity—as expressions of hope for a world in which capitalism's treatment of nature as a free gift no longer dominates, and offer a closing hope of my own.

1

Theory of the Free Gift

THE IDEA that contemporary societies treat nature as a free gift is not hard to grasp on its face. If anything, it can seem all too obvious that nature gives, and we take. Nature provides a bounty, and we harvest it; nature overspills with abundance, and we gorge ourselves. Some version of this idea underlies each of the two dominant ways of characterizing capitalism's treatment of nature. One—what I call the worldview approach—focuses on the *idea* of nature as a free gift, charging that that capitalism has constructed an image of nature as an endlessly replenishable store of resources for human use, culturally and discursively representing nature in a way that justifies, sanctions, and ultimately enables its exploitation. The other, the expropriation approach, puts the emphasis on the violence of *taking*: it charges that capitalism has seized gifts of nature that once belonged to all, relentlessly extracted elements from the natural world, and torn human relationships to nature asunder. Neither is wrong, exactly. But neither quite captures how the free gift of nature emerges from capitalism's most foundational social relations.

The worldview approach typically understands capitalism as one element of a broader Western culture that places both nature and those human beings deemed natural at the bottom of a civilizational hierarchy. This way of thinking is often traced to René Descartes, charged with separating thinking human beings from soulless animals; to the Scientific Revolution, said to have converted the Earth from living thing to dead matter; and to the Enlightenment's disenchantment of the world amid the relentless drive toward rationalization.[1] Within this overall framework, there are different accounts of the precise relationship between capitalism and ideas of nature. In Carolyn Merchant's influential thesis, for example, capitalism's development of the productive forces drives changes in cultural perceptions of nature. The "organic worldview" of the Earth as a living being, Merchant claims, served as a fetter on capitalist development: only once the Earth was seen as a mere object could it be mined, its woods cut down for timber, its marshes drained; only with the death of nature could industrial production be unleashed.[2] Jason Moore's more recent analysis, meanwhile, suggests that capitalism has actively *constructed* nature as a free gift for the taking. Capitalism, Moore argues, has developed forms of scientific knowledge-making with the goal of "rendering nature external . . . the better that it could be subordinated and rationalized"; it has symbolically separated nature from society and "assigned" value to human labor alone.[3] At the same time, he argues, the modern "Nature/Society binary" has informed capitalism's own internal structure: Cartesian dualism is the ultimate "source" of other pernicious dualisms, including capitalism's own hierarchy of value; the divide between nature and society is "complicit in the violence of modernity at its core."[4] Capitalism, in other words, both relies on and actively reinforces the idea that nature and society are distinct.

The expropriation approach, meanwhile, points to the often brutal processes by which the gifts of nature originally bestowed upon all are converted to private property. Here, the touchstone is Marx's account of the enclosure of common lands that both dispossessed and proletarianized English peasants—the process of "so-called primitive accumulation."[5] The seizure of land that once served as a means of peasant subsistence, Marx charges, created a class of landless proletarians, left with no choice but to sell their labor. Capital thus comes into the world dripping with both blood and dirt—an evocative image that links the violence done to people and land alike. The separation of laborers from the land, many subsequent ecological critics claim, has also alienated people from the more-than-human world.[6] Relationships to land once rooted in dwelling or spirituality have been replaced by the *property* relation of ownership—and this conversion has continued as more and more elements of nature are claimed by private owners.[7] Accounts of "extractive" capitalism often focus not only on the violence by which class relations are constituted, but on violence done to the Earth itself, highlighting moments when capital actively rips elements of nature from the web of life, whether tearing up the soil to dig a mine, slaughtering animals by the thousands, or leveling entire forests. The expropriation account thus highlights the violent, coercive processes lurking beneath capitalism's ostensibly peaceful relations of exchange, claiming that these are its true reality.

These accounts have much to offer analyses of capitalism. They usefully historicize capitalism's development and add complexity to the portrait of capitalism as an actually existing social system. But neither quite explains how nature figures in capitalism's *own social relations*. They focus on ostensibly "extra-economic" processes—cultural and ideological representation on the one hand, coercion and violence on the other, a persistent duality that Søren Mau describes in terms of the "violence/ideology couplet"—rather than attending to the kinds of valuation, ideology, and brutality that are built into the processes we often describe as merely "economic" in their own right.[8] To see the free gift of nature as a *capitalist social form*, by contrast, is to take an immanent approach that locates capitalism's treatment of nature not in original or exceptional moments of violence or the ideological mystification of its "real" social relations, but in those very social relations themselves, unfolding in the course of its "ordinary" processes. It's not just that nature *appears* to be a free gift; in capitalist societies, it really *is* a free gift. Violence isn't just lurking beneath the surface of voluntary exchange; it's embedded *within* those seemingly bloodless relationships.

The Free Gift as Social Form: The Immanent Approach

My argument, by contrast, is that we treat nature as a free gift not because capitalism has tricked us into thinking that nature is worthless, distorted our ability to see it clearly, or alienated us from the land. (Although it may well have done these things too.) It is not simply a matter of our wrongheaded ideas or misguided culture; not something we can fix with greater awareness or more self-control. Nor is the violence we do to nature simply that which takes the form of overt brutality, rapacious extraction, or conscious spoliation. We treat nature as a free gift because of the way we relate to other human beings through wages and exchange—relations which structure our basic actions, and from which nonhumans are *constitutively* excluded.[9] Understood as a social form, the free gift of nature is not only a "world view," per Merchant, nor even a way of making the nonhuman world legible in the quantified scientific terms of "abstract social nature," per Moore, but rather what the philosopher Alfred Sohn-Rethel calls a "real abstraction"—a concept that structures action even in the absence of conscious intent.[10]

Not all abstractions are "real abstractions." The concepts of natural science, for example, are what Sohn-Rethel calls "thought abstractions," categories we use to organize our understanding of the world but which do not reliably structure our actions in it.[11] The "ecosystem," for example, is a thought abstraction that describes the relationships among a particular set of nonhuman entities, one consciously developed within a field of study to explain certain phenomena and order our knowledge about the more-than-human world. When we learn what ecosystems are, we learn how scientists have defined them: what counts as an ecosystem, how they function internally, how they relate to geological or atmospheric conditions. We might, in turn, use this knowledge to inform our decisions about how to act: evidence that a given ecosystem's health is declining, for example, might lead an environmental agency to set restrictions on its use.

The free gift of nature, by contrast, describes how human beings relate to the nonhuman world in capitalist societies by default—whether we choose to or not, whether we know it or not. We don't learn what these social relations are; we don't define them; we don't think about them. But we live them, every day. We enact them and reproduce them. And we do so even when we would prefer not to. Real abstractions are representations of the world that emerge not from conscious thought but from our actions. And the most basic action, in a society whose elementary form is the commodity, is the act of exchange. These acts of exchange reflect an underlying set of social relations that we engage in and reinforce without consciously recognizing. Exchange is not the *only* form of action in capitalist societies, of course, and far from the most esteemed. Nearly all of us prioritize *other* practices and relationships, and see exchange merely as a means to these other ends. But almost none of us live without engaging in this activity—and almost none of the other things we want to do are possible without it. At some point, we must pay for nearly all the things that we use to go about our lives, to meet our needs and satisfy our wants. We engage in exchange all the time: when we eat and drink, when we get on a train or fill our tank, when we go to a movie or read a book. When I buy a pair of jeans, I am implicitly deciding that X number of hours of my time, spent working to earn the money to buy them, is equivalent to Y number of hours of time that went into sewing them, growing and harvesting the cotton, and so on. When I do so, I'm also implicitly valuing the gifts of nature that go into making the jeans—the energy the cotton plant absorbs from the sun, the water drained from the reservoir, the nutrients sapped from the soil—at zero.

We see the real abstraction of the free gift in the way we constantly treat nature as valueless despite proclamations that it is "priceless," in the way we buy cheap things that we know are environmentally harmful. We'll look more closely, in the next chapter, at the constraints this structure of action-through-exchange places upon us, and the political dimensions of a society thus organized. But this chapter examines the underlying social relations themselves. For the real abstraction of the free gift is a corollary of the real abstraction of value—the shadow to relationships among human beings as they're ordered within capitalist societies.

One last piece of conceptual ground clearing is in order before we turn more squarely to the free gift. As we've seen, the terms *nature* and *society* are among the most contested in modern thought.[12] It is precisely because of this complexity that I approach each minimally. Value-form analysis provides what Rahel Jaeggi terms a "monistic social theory": a theory that does not separate out different "kinds" of social existence—economy, society, culture, and so on—for different kinds of treatment.[13] I understand "the social" in terms of capitalism's formal qualities; notably, its particular forms of value, labor, and wealth, and the relations of ownership and exchange that underlie them. This is not because these formal qualities are the sum total of social life under capitalism, or because other elements of sociality are irrelevant. To the contrary, it is because the richness of social life is far too complex and diverse to capture in its entirety.[14] By taking a formal approach I hope to provide a "thin" account of capitalism's tendencies and compulsions, which must always be concretely articulated with more specific patterns of social and cultural life. The critique of political economy laid out here, moreover, shows that the sphere of the "economic" is always deeply political in its own right—and that nature lies at its very heart.

My account is also materially monist in that I understand human and nonhuman beings, both living and non-, to be the same kind of substance, with the same physical reality. Although I sometimes use the term "nature" in a colloquial sense, to refer to nonhuman nature alone, one of the book's fundamental premises is that both humans and nonhumans are part of nature, understood as what the philosopher Kate Soper describes as "those material structures and processes that are independent of human activity (in the sense that they are not a humanly created product) and whose forces and causal powers are the necessary condition of every human practice, and determine the possible forms it can take."[15] At the same time, I understand human beings to have certain distinctive qualities—an ontology that Andreas Malm usefully describes as "substance monism, property dualism."[16] I don't attempt a definitive account of this distinction, and still less do I equate distinction with superiority. Here too, I follow Soper in seeing human beings as radically "underdetermined" by anatomy, physiology, and other biophysical conditions.[17] To be underdetermined means that although all human beings share basic features, we can make many different choices about how, and what, to be, both individually and collectively—as we will explore in greater detail in the next chapter by way of existentialism. This quality also has particular significance for how human labor is configured in capitalist societies, as this chapter shows.

With this, let's turn to the free gift itself. To understand how it operates within capitalist social relations, we must begin by returning to the locus of Marx's critique: political economy.

History of the Free Gift

The Natural Agents of Political Economy

It is in the realm of political economy that nonhuman nature has most explicitly entered into modern political thought, if typically in the guise of "raw material," land, and livestock. It is in the classical political economy of the late eighteenth and early nineteenth centuries, in particular, that the idea of the free gift of nature originates, amid now-obscure debates about the source of value. In the evocative language of "natural agents" and "gifts of nature"—the gifts being, of course, from God—political economists discussed how natural entities ranging from trade winds to the viscera of sheep made useful and necessary contributions to nearly all forms of production. This view of nature's gifts was a rosy one, colored by belief in divine providence and bolstered by European colonization of the Americas, which seemed to offer an inexhaustible source of natural bounty.[18] Nature seemed to give generously and in perpetuity, without expectation of return. Most seemed to have no doubt that it would keep on doing so—a faith that few today share. Yet returning to the classical political economists and their musings on the contributions of natural agents crucially allows us to open up the black box of economics and ask questions about the natural and social dimensions of value that modern economics is constitutively unable to pose. Tellingly, many of the most severe disagreements among these thinkers fall between those who locate the foundations of value in nonhuman nature on the one hand, and those who see it in human labor on the other. While the classical political economists' efforts to locate a single, substantial source of value stands as a conceptual limitation, it is one that Marx's critique can help us to understand, and to overcome.

For the first political economists, the eighteenth-century French physiocrats, it was "the earth which is always the first and only source of all wealth," as the physiocratic economist Anne Robert Jacques Turgot stated bluntly.[19] Nature, Turgot argued, makes a "pure gift" to production stemming from "her" own sheer generativity, one that neither expected a return nor accounted for human desires.[20] The physiocratic understanding of wealth was radically materialist: it held that the Earth generated physical elements that human beings could not, and which human labor merely rearranged.[21] On this basis the physiocrats concluded that agriculture was the only source of a *produit net*—a surplus above what was required to sustain the lives of the laborers who worked the land. All other sectors were unproductive, ultimately parasitic on agriculture.

The best way to encourage the production of wealth, then, was to let nature work free of human meddling—in particular, by liberalizing trade in grain. This was the source of the infamous doctrine *laissez-faire, laissez-passer*: let nature take its course.

While nature stood at the heart of the physiocratic theory of value, its contributions to production were perhaps most evocatively described by the French political economist Jean-Baptiste Say, who wrote extensively of "natural agents" at the dawn of the nineteenth century.[22] To use the language of "agency" in reference to nonhumans today is controversial—but to Say, it was simply obvious that nature played an agential role in economic production, in the sense that a contemporary theorist like Bruno Latour might invoke the role of "actants."[23] It was clear, in other words, that nonhumans produced effects in the world that went beyond those generated by human beings alone. Nature's role in agriculture was most obvious: "there is a process performed by the soil, the air, the rain, and the sun, wherein mankind bears no part, but which nevertheless concurs in the creation of the new product."[24] The sower of wheat obviously did not *make* the wheat, but "merely directs an operation whereby different substances previously scattered throughout the elements of earth, air, and water, are converted into the form of grains of wheat."[25] Other industries, like forestry and fishing, were similarly reliant on nature in obvious but often unacknowledged ways: "When a tree, a natural product, is felled," Say asked, "is society put into possession of no greater produce than that of the mere labour of the woodman?"[26]

If the contributions of natural agents were more obvious in some areas than others, however, Say thought them ubiquitous. They included not only biological processes, like the "action of the organs and viscera" that helped produce wool in a flock of sheep, or the "vegetative power of the soil" that generated crops, but the geophysical properties of the world itself—the tendency of heat to produce combustion in an engine, the wind that powered mills, the magnetism that directed a compass needle, even the pull of gravity.[27] These agents contributed not only to the production of familiar commodities like wool and wheat, he thought, but to "immaterial products." The likes of parks and gardens afforded pleasure, while trees improved public health by "absorb[ing] the carbonic-acid gas floating in the atmosphere we breathe, and which is so injurious to respiration."[28] Manufacturing, too, made use of natural agents not only as raw materials to be transformed into products, but as components of machinery and other instruments of production. They were present even in commerce, in the hemp of the sails and the wind that filled them—all,

Say claimed, "brought to concur in [the merchant's] purpose, with precisely the same view and the same result, and in the same manner too, as the agriculturist avails himself of the earth, the rain, and the atmosphere."[29]

Across sectors, the contributions of these natural agents were so "interwoven" with those of labor and capital, Say thought, that it was "difficult, or perhaps impossible, to assign, with accuracy, their respective shares in the business of production."[30] Because they existed independently of human activity, moreover, they were not subject to the usual principles of political economy, since they could not be produced or consumed like other goods. Indeed, for some thinkers it was precisely because nature was a divine gift—and therefore always-already available for use—that it was valueless. Locke famously claimed that the Earth, on its own, provided "almost worthless materials"; it was human labor that added "more than nature, the common Mother of all, had done."[31] For Locke it was precisely the *abundance* of natural gifts in the Americas that served as confirmation of the value of human labor: even Indigenous rulers, he argued, were poorer than English laborers despite the natural bounty they enjoyed.[32]

Adam Smith, although influenced by the physiocrats, similarly emphasized the role of human labor in value creation. Smith did not disavow nature entirely: he acknowledged that in agriculture "nature labors along with man; and though her labor costs no expense, its produce has its value, as well as that of the most expensive workmen."[33] While the work done by human laborers was necessary to direct natural fertility, he noted that "after all their labor, a great part of the work always remains to be done by her." Yet in manufacturing, he claimed, "nature does nothing, man does all."[34] Smith turned political economy resolutely away from the idea that nature itself generated wealth, and toward the view that human labor did. Later advocates of the labor theory of value recognized the contributions of natural agents, but insisted that they were irrelevant to the production of value. As David Ricardo observed, natural agents "are serviceable to us, by increasing the abundance of productions, by making men richer, by adding to value in use; but as they perform their work gratuitously, as nothing is paid for the use of air, of heat, and of water, the assistance which they afford us, adds nothing to value in exchange."[35] To the contrary, the use of natural agents tended to lower the exchangeable value of work, by reducing the amount of human labor required.

By the turn of the century, natural agents receded still further from political economic thought as the marginalist revolution dispensed with the debate over the foundations of value altogether.[36] They would return, late in the twentieth, via the heterodox branch of ecological economics, which charged economics with forgetting its material foundations and sought to restore nature to economic theories of value.[37] Indeed, what makes someone like Say so striking to read even today is that he articulates something that appears patently obvious: that human beings do not generate wealth alone. This basic observation is common in contemporary environmental scholarship. "The abundance that fueled Chicago's hinterland economy," William Cronon writes, "consisted largely of stored sunshine: this was the wealth of nature, and no human labor could create the value it contained."[38] Similar points are echoed in Richard White's account of the work done by the Columbia River, and Bathsheba Demuth's description of how the work of plankton and whales contributed to the blubber sought by whalers.[39]

It's true, of course, that much of what we think of as wealth is produced by beings other than ourselves. But what we think of as wealth is not necessarily what capitalism designates as value. What is immediately apparent to us is not necessarily false—but nor is it the whole. To understand it requires that we look beneath the surface, beyond the obvious. This is what Marx's critique of political economy insists, and what his own analysis seeks to reveal.

Critique of the Free Gift

Although he is often criticized for recognizing the value of human labor alone, Marx did not dispute that natural agents have effects in the world or even that they contribute to economic production. He was equally scathing toward his socialist contemporaries, who declared that human labor alone creates wealth, insisting that "*Nature* is just as much the source of use-values (and what else is material wealth?)."[40] The Earth often *does* produce a material surplus, Marx agreed, enough to feed the laborers and animals who work the fields and to plant the next year's crop, with an excess left over to sell or otherwise distribute. But the physiocrats had made the error of taking nature's role in production too much at face value. The physical fact of surplus grain, Marx observed, does not translate directly into the *social* category of surplus value.[41] The physiocratic view of nature as the source of value *in itself*, he argued, betrayed a naïve materialism, one that understood value as consisting of "material things—land, nature, and the various modifications." Their mistake was to consider these "material forms of existence—such as tools, raw materials, etc." separately from "the social conditions in which they appear in capitalist production."[42]

Natural agents had long been at work in the world. What was distinctive about their role in capitalism was not the simple fact of their physical agency but how they operated within the overall organization of production. It was necessary, in other words, to ask *why* material content (a surplus of wheat, say) appears in a particular *social* form (like a surplus of value). And if nature clearly played a role in generating material wealth and utility, capitalist value was a different entity altogether. This, Marx thought, was what the classical political economists had failed to recognize. *Capital* is famously a *critique* of political economy, one that holds that the classical political economists had failed to recognize the specificity of capitalism. In a society ordered by class, Marx argued, nature's gifts did not give to all, but to capital alone. "Natural elements entering as agents into production, and which cost nothing, no matter what role they play in production," Marx observed, serve as "a free gift of Nature's productive power to labour, *which, however, appears as the productiveness of capital, as all other productivity under the capitalist mode of production*."[43] Nature might, as Say had suggested, "do the work of eighteen persons"—but as long as the means of production were privately owned, the capitalist alone would capture the resulting wealth.[44] More than simply misapprehending the source or owner of value, Marx argued, to see the production of value in the production of grain itself had the effect of naturalizing capitalism, of rendering the "capitalist form of production" itself "an eternal, natural form of production," as if it too had simply emerged from the soil.[45]

Marx's comments on the free gift of nature are suggestive—but they are marginal in his work. Whereas volume 1 of *Capital*, the only one published in Marx's lifetime, begins with a long discussion of the commodity as capitalism's "elementary form," Marx's reference to the free gift of nature is buried deep in a discussion of rent in volume 3. Although the phrase is frequently referenced in passing, it remains remarkably undertheorized next to the likes of the commodity. If the concept itself occupies only a small place in Marx's own work, however, the peculiar term *free gift* nevertheless captures something vital not only about how surplus value is captured by capital but, more fundamentally, about the way that capitalism imbues some things with value—and simultaneously renders others valueless.[46] Put simply: Why are some things valuable and others not? Elaborating the significance of this peculiar concept requires that we connect Marx's brief but suggestive comments to his broader critique of capitalism.

The Free Gift and the Critique of Political Economy

Marx repeatedly emphasizes that "capital is not a thing, but a social relation between persons which is mediated through things."[47] One does not become a capitalist simply by owning elements of production, like machines or land;

rather, one becomes a capitalist only in relation to a class of people who are compelled to sell their labor. The "free gift of nature" is also not a thing—it is not simply a natural element or natural agent. Rather, the natural agent *becomes a free gift* only within capitalist social relations: only in relation to the division of human beings into the classes of capitalist and proletarian, in a situation of generalized commodity exchange and market dependence. It's under these conditions that the gift of nature meaningfully becomes *free*, in contrast to capitalism's elementary form—the commodity.

The Dual Character of Natural and Social Forms

Central to the critique of political economy is Marx's question: "why this content has assumed that particular form."[48] What are the particular social relations within which a given physical object or entity appears? This distinction between content and form is foundational to Marx's analysis of the commodity, and indeed to his analysis of capitalism writ large. Capitalism is for Marx a system of duality, of doubling, of appearances and what lies beneath.[49] The commodity, he argues, is defined by its "dual character": it has both "material content" and a "social form" (or alternatively both a "natural form" and a "value form"); it has both use value and exchange value.[50]

The natural form describes the material qualities of a good—whether a shoe is made from leather or rubber, for example; whether it is a stiletto or a galosh. Use value likewise reflects the physical properties and uses associated with entities in their natural form. The use value of a shoe, for example, is the protection it provides to one's foot or the stylish aura it gives to its wearer. These qualities may differ with the shoe in question—the use value of stilettos is primarily in their style; the use value of galoshes, their ability to repel water—but none is inherently superior to any other.

Social form, by contrast, describes the object's place within the social order of capitalism: the galosh is not just a shoe, but a commodity. Exchange value, in turn, reflects the measure of social forms in relation to one another— the number of shoes that can be exchanged for a coat, or a laptop, or a bottle of wine. Exchange value, Marx insists, is "purely social," having nothing to do with the physical characteristics of the good itself.[51] "Not an atom of matter enters into the objectivity of commodities as values," he warns, "in this it is the direct opposite of the coarsely sensuous objectivity of commodities as physical objects."[52] The social form, similarly, has nothing to do with the physical object's natural form: a rubber galosh and an electric car are very different as natural forms, but they are both commodities insofar as they can be exchanged.

As human beings, we see things in their natural form: we see the grain of a wooden table, for example, as "an ordinary, sensuous thing."[53] If it is of a particularly striking variety—mahogany, say, or teak—we might think of the tree that produced the wood. We recognize its use value—its suitability for eating meals or its sturdiness for holding books, or even its beauty. In this form, Marx observes, "there is nothing mysterious about it."[54] Things with use value simply are what they appear to be. But phenomenology doesn't serve well as an epistemic tool in a capitalist society. When we look at things as they are in physical form, we aren't really seeing them as commodities. For Marx, it is the presence of exchange value that famously makes the commodity a "very strange thing," something that is not quite what it appears. When a physical table takes the social form of the commodity, he argues, its value has "absolutely no connection" to its material qualities—its value is imperceptible to us, ghostly, phantomlike.[55] We can see, for example, that a table and a coat are not the same kind of thing—but we can't see *why* they are equivalent in value, what makes them exchangeable. It is this mystery, Marx argues, that requires attention.

All capitalist social forms have this dual character; all have both concrete and abstract aspects. Wealth, too, takes a particular form under capitalism: it is assessed not in terms of useful goods like food, clothing, and shelter, but as abstract value measured in monetary terms. Marx similarly distinguishes between the labor process in general and the labor process as it exists under capitalism. The labor process in general describes the concrete process through which people purposely act on and transform nature—alternately figured as "larder," "tool house," and "instrument"—to create things that are useful for human beings.[56] This, in other words, is production understood as a simple interchange between human beings and the nonhuman world. But the capitalist labor process is different. It is not *only* a labor process—it is also what Marx calls a "valorization" process, through which the capitalist realizes the value of the produced good in exchange.

The valorization process reflects capitalism's unusual form of sociality. People do not produce the things they need by themselves or within a community of people they know. Rather, they play a part in a vast interdependent web in which production is at once privately organized and socially coordinated through exchange. This sociality arises from capitalism's core features: private ownership of the means of production, production by means of wage labor, market dependence. Because the means of production are private, most labor takes place in isolation from other producers. People sell their labor power as individuals, and work as they are directed by their employer. They don't know what other workers are making or how. The moment when labor becomes social labor—when individual labor is connected to the overall organization of labor in society—occurs not in the moment of production but in the moment of exchange, when a good becomes a commodity by finding a buyer in the market. It is in this moment that workers, till then isolated in private workplaces, come into relation with one another via the exchange of the commodities they have made, and when they find out what their own labor is worth in relation to that of others. This means that labor, too, has a dual character. The "interchange with nature" that produces material goods necessary for human life is concrete labor. But "abstract labor" describes only labor whose product has been proven to be valuable in exchange, as measured in terms of "socially necessary labor time"—the amount of time that it takes an average worker to produce a given commodity at the general rate of technological development.[57] Because value is assessed in exchange, abstract labor is constituted only retrospectively, and includes only waged labor that produces commodities for sale— regardless of how useful or even essential noncommodified labor may be.[58]

If Marx's account of capitalist production sheds light on the multifaceted organization of human labor, however, it says nothing in particular about the organization of nonhuman nature. We can nevertheless extend his method to better apprehend the free gift.

The Free Gift as Social Form

What does the duality of capitalist social forms tell us about the free gift of nature? After all, at first glance the free gift does *not* appear to have the distinctively dual character of capitalism's other social forms. While Marx acknowledges that nature is a source of use value, even where it is not mediated by human labor ("air, virgin soil, natural meadows, unplanted forests, etc."), nature only ever seems to contribute use value.[59] It appears ordinary rather than mysterious, and hence irrelevant to the secret of capital accumulation. Indeed, in *Capital* Marx singles out the classical political economists' "dull and tedious dispute over the part played by nature in the formation of exchange-value" as illustrating the tendency at work in commodity fetishism: the tendency to mistake a thing's natural form for the social relations that make it strange.[60]

If the classical political economists had attributed too much weight to nature's physical powers, however, Marx's own treatment of natural forms and use value is too cursory. "Use value as such lies outside the sphere of investigation of political economy," Marx declares—and so, too, beyond the sphere of critique.[61] Subsequent analyses of value have largely followed suit: while claiming to analyze the *dual* nature of capitalist social forms, they have tended to present a one-sided view, focusing on distinctively capitalist abstractions while treating natural forms and use value as irrelevant.[62] Yet use value is more mysterious than Marx acknowledges, and more significant. The persistence of things with use value but *not* exchange value presses us to ask how, in constituting some things as having value, capitalism constitutes others as lacking it.

Let's look more closely at this peculiar phrase—the "free gift of nature." We should read the *free* in *free gift* in the economic sense—*free* as in without cost, without price, without exchange value. The very oddity of the term *free gift* indexes a collision between the relations of gift exchange often said to characterize noncapitalist societies and the relations of generalized commodity exchange that characterize capitalism as a mode of production. Only where most things have a price, after all, does it make sense to describe nature's gifts as free. Things that are not overtly bought and sold do not thereby escape the social form of exchange value, however: they are simply, if usually implicitly, priced at zero and assessed accordingly. In the process, their status within the overarching structure of a society primarily organized around the commodity is altered.

The free gift's lack of value, moreover, is fundamentally linked to capitalism's transformation of social relations among humans. The rise of a class division among human beings, which forces some people to sell their labor power to others, also gives rise to a new relationship between human beings and the nonhuman world. In representing a vast variety of human activities in the form of abstract labor, made equivalent by the process of exchange for a wage, capitalism simultaneously constitutes the still vaster variety of nonhuman life and capabilities as wage labor's opposite: the free gift of nature, *constitutively* wageless and unable to enter into the foundational relations of exchange that constitute capitalism's sociality. The social relation of value draws a stark line between human beings and all other entities.

Like the commodity, then, the free gift of nature captures the encounter, and disjuncture, between use and exchange value, matter and form, essence and appearance, natural and social form—but it inverts these relationships as they appear in the more familiar form of the commodity, pairing material usefulness with a *lack* of exchange value. This element of costlessness becomes particularly valuable in a class society in which one group of people purchase all inputs to production, including the waged labor of other human beings, and compete with other producers in the market. The pricelessness of the free gift, in turn, informs how natural agents are used in production, and thus refracts back into the material organization of production itself.

Indeed, the "free" aspect of the free gift of nature speaks only to one aspect of its dual character: its (non)appearance in the social form of value. Capitalism's social relations never *fully* dominate the material world; rather, matter retains an autonomous character with which economic and political systems must contend. Although capital is compelled by the pursuit of abstract value, the physical qualities of natural agents remain perpetually significant within concrete production processes. Although Marx holds that the commodity form has "absolutely *no* connection with the physical nature of the commodity," physical qualities *are* significant to how different aspects of nature appear within capitalism—to whether they are subsumed, commodified, alienated, owned.[63] Physical qualities affect the degree of control that capital can exert over production—and in turn, the control that can be exerted over human laborers. The relationship between content and form is more dialectical than is often acknowledged.

These two aspects of the free gift—cost as assessed in terms of exchange value, and control as mobilized through physical form—are typically treated as alternative explanations of nature's role in capitalism. Jason Moore argues that capitalism relies on the "cheapness" of nature, while Andreas Malm argues that the physical qualities of particular natural elements are more important than their cost.[64] (We will look more closely at both accounts later.) Rather than setting these in opposition, taking the dual character of the free gift of nature seriously requires attention to both the abstract nonvalue of nature and its concrete reality—and as well as to the ways that these aspects are interrelated. When we attend to both aspects of the free gift of nature, we can see capitalism's devaluation of nature more clearly—and we can also better understand capitalism's organization of *human* labor and social life.

Capitalism Is a Humanism; or, Why Capitalism Systematically Devalues Nature

To understand the nonvalue of nature within capitalist societies, I've argued, requires understanding social relations among human beings—and, in particular, the distinctive value afforded *human* labor. The challenge, for an ecological analysis, is to do this without affirming—or simply taking for granted—the exceptional character of human beings as such. Marx is often charged with both: he's often read as a humanist or anthropocentric thinker. Indeed, human labor is perhaps Marx's central object of investigation throughout his oeuvre, whether in his early investigation of human labor as foundational to species being or his later consideration of its value under capitalism. It is striking to note how frequently Marx explicitly identifies certain qualities, physical capacities, and so on as *human* ones; how often he compares humans to animals, whether marking similarities or differences. What, for Marx, is special about human labor? What distinguishes it from the elements of nature that also contribute to production? And what do the distinctive qualities of human labor mean for capitalism in particular?

Marx's own attention to human labor is typically read in one of two ways. The first, associated with the early Marx, is as a Hegelian commentary on the way that human spirit extends itself into the world, realizing itself in nature.[65] The second is as a statement of a "substantialist" labor theory of value, wherein the sheer physical expenditure of human energy somehow imbues things with value. There is evidence in Marx's writings to support both readings, as I discuss below. In my view, however, Marx is misread as a humanist. Rather, *capitalism is a humanism*—but not in the moral sense typically associated with the term. While human beings do, generally speaking, have certain capacities that can be distinguished from those of other species—as do *all* species—what makes human labor special under capitalism is the role of distinctively human consciousness in constituting capitalism's specifically *social* relations. Marx's critique of political economy, in turn, is also a critique of this particular way of figuring the human being. In other words, Marx is not himself responsible for privileging human beings over nonhuman nature (even if he likely did); rather, he points us to an ontological divide that capitalism draws and intensifies.

The Architect and the Bee

In considering what makes human labor distinctive, an obvious place to begin is with Marx's most famous statement about the difference between human and nonhuman labor, in which he compares the "worst of architects" to the "best of bees." This passage in *Capital*, in which Marx emphasizes the significance of human *purposiveness* in production, has often been read as a paean to the specialness of human consciousness in its own right. Marx recognizes that other kinds of beings engage in activities that "resemble" those of human beings, each effecting a change of form in the materials of nature to sustain their own form of life. The bee, like the architect, builds a home; the spider, like the weaver, constructs a web. While the resulting products have markedly different physical characteristics, corresponding to the needs of different life-forms— the finest cotton thread does not have the same tensile strength and stickiness as spider web; conversely, spider webs would serve poorly as material for human clothing—the products made by human beings are not always qualitatively superior. In some cases, the products generated by nonhuman activity may actually surpass those made by human beings. "A bee," Marx notes, "would put many a human architect to shame by the construction of its honeycomb cells."[66]

But what truly distinguishes the "worst of architects from the best of bees," Marx famously claims, is the purposive intent that directs human transformations of matter: "Man not only effects a change of form in the materials of nature; he also realizes his own purpose in those materials."[67] Human beings envision what they want to make, and labor in order to realize this vision. Only human beings, in other words, labor consciously; only they intentionally make the world in their own image. This is often read as part of Marx's Hegelian legacy: a celebration of spirit as it objectifies itself in the world, of a piece with the humanism articulated in the *Economic and Philosophic Manuscripts of 1844*, which posits labor as the defining quality of human beings.[68] This view has, in turn, been challenged by thinkers like Louis Althusser and looked upon skeptically by other critics of humanism. It has served as a central exhibit for ecological critics seeking to make the case that Marx is as anthropocentric as any other Enlightenment thinker, as well as for those who critique the Eurocentrism of his account of production.[69]

Yet this fable of the architect and the bee is *not* an account of what makes human labor valuable under capitalism specifically. Rather, it is a transhistorical account of what makes the activity of human beings distinctive from that of other kinds of beings that engage in nominally similar activities. It describes something about what we might think of as human beings' natural form. We might well want to contest the accuracy of this account of humanity, of course, or the portrait of nonhuman beings—Marx suggests here that nonhuman consciousness is basically nonexistent, while a large body of scientific research now clearly demonstrates otherwise.[70] But it is important not to confuse this account of human distinction per se with his account of how and why human labor is organized in the production of *capitalist value*.[71] And in fact, there is no obvious link between Marx's account of human labor as conscious, purposive activity and the status of human labor in the capitalist labor process. Workers on the assembly line are hardly consciously transforming the world according to their will, as in Marx's vision of the bee and the architect; rather, their activity is being directed by the owner of the factory.[72] As many subsequent theorists have observed, capitalism separates the conscious aspects of design from the work of execution, the work of thought from the work of construction, intellectual from manual labor.[73] In fact, Marx often emphasizes the *similarities* between the use of human labor power and nonhuman components of the valorization process directed by capital, as when he compares the human laborer to a horse: once hired, he notes, the capitalist has the right to use human labor power however he wishes, "just as much as the right to use any other commodity, such as a horse he had hired for the day."[74] What, then, is distinctive about human labor in the *capitalist* labor process?

"Congealed Quantities of Homogeneous Human Labour": The Substantialist Theory of Value

This brings us to the second reading of Marx's view of the specialness of human labor: the idea that human labor is the *substance* of capitalist value. Here recall the dual character of human labor under capitalism: labor has both concrete and abstract aspects, corresponding to the natural and social form of the commodity. To make a commodity as a use value requires a concrete labor process: to make, say, a table, someone has to actually hew pieces of wood into the right proportions and join them together in the right configuration. Making a table, in turn, is a totally different material process from making a ceramic mug, or a loaf of bread, or a microchip. This aspect of labor is concrete: it is specific to the use values it seeks to create; to the "natural form" of the commodity as a material good. Different kinds of labor, in turn, require different things from the human body—deft fingers in one case, upper body strength in another—and might, as a result, put differently embodied people to work.

As *commodities*, however, these radically different products are rendered equivalent in exchange. They aren't equivalent as use values (a table and a mug serve different purposes); nor is the labor that goes into them physically comparable (consider the difference between carpentry and pottery). This is the mystery of exchange value. The only common denominator across different commodities, Marx argues, is that some quantity of human labor has been expended to produce them. "What remains is its quality of being an expenditure of human labour-power," he writes. "Tailoring and weaving, although they are qualitatively different productive activities, are both a productive expenditure of human brains, muscles, nerves, hands etc., and in this sense both

human labour."[75] As he states bluntly, "The value of a commodity represents . . . the expenditure of *human labour in general*."[76]

What exactly does Marx mean by "human labor in general"? His repeated
use of physiological language often seems to suggest that "abstract labor" is a
category denoting the sheer quantity of human time and energy, unified by
the simple fact that it is performed by human bodies ("brains, muscles, nerves,
hands").[77] In these moments Marx *does* seem to suggest that human labor is
physically substantiated in the commodity itself, such that its value corresponds to the sheer amount of labor it "contains." He observes, for example,
that values "are merely *congealed quantities of homogeneous human labour*, i.e.
of human labour-power expended without regard to the form of its expenditure[;] . . . human labour-power has been expended to produce them, human
labour *is accumulated in them. As crystals of this social substance*, which is common to them all, they are values."[78] Upon reading such passages, it is not hard
to see why Marx is often thought to have a substantialist labor theory of
value—one that is by now widely discredited.

This view of labor as physically constitutive of value, however, seems incompatible with Marx's emphatic statements that value is "purely social"; in
these passages, value sounds like a physical thing, even as Marx elsewhere
insists that it is not.[79] It seems, in other words, to make precisely the mistake
Marx criticizes in the classical political economists—of conflating natural and
social form, treating the physical *substance* of human labor as the source of
value. What is specifically *capitalist* about the expenditure of human physiological power, which as Marx observes is common across all societies? Conversely, if the basis for seeing human labor as value generating is its status as
the sole common denominator between materially different goods, we could
just as easily posit—as some ecological economists have—an "energy theory
of value," in which the expenditure of energy, whether derived from human
labor power, horsepower, or fossil fuels, is the true basis of equivalence. Why,
ecological thinkers ask, if nature also contributes to use value, would only
human labor produce value?[80]

My argument, by contrast, is that human consciousness rather than sheer
physical exertion *is* key to the specialness of labor power and the category of
value—but not because it imbues "inert matter" with human purpose, because
nonhumans lack consciousness, or because human consciousness is superior.
Rather, it is because distinctively human consciousness underpins two core
elements of capitalism's social organization of production. First, human consciousness makes possible both the class relation of labor and capital and the

deployment of human labor in a wide variety of ways. Second, human conscious-ness underpins the social institution of wage labor and centrality of relationships mediated by the wage. This is key to the category "abstract labor": despite Marx's occasional use of physiological language, the concept of "abstract labor" refers to the *social* commensurability of human labor measured in units of time, purchased via the wage. While the way that these features of capitalism inform the organization of human social life has been much explored, they also have under-recognized implications for the status of the free gifts of nature.

Consciousness and Social Form

When it comes to the topic of human consciousness in the organization of cap-italist production, more illustrative than Marx's comment on the architect and the bee is Harry Braverman's meditation on the difference between human and nonhuman labor in *Labor and Monopoly Capital*. The significance of human con-sciousness, for Braverman, is not that human beings are uniquely able to make the world as they envisage it. Rather, the ability to organize production according to a conscious plan, however minimal or thwarted, is what makes the concept of social form significant at all: it means that there are many different ways that production *might* be organized. The ability to imagine and plan production, Braverman notes, and to communicate this plan clearly to others, is also what makes possible capitalism's particular organization of production. It is what per-mits human beings to separate "conception and execution": the bee constructs its own honeycomb cells, whether it imagines them in advance or not, but an architect designs a building for *others* to construct.[81] This separation, in turn, makes possible the separation of control over the means of production from the producers, insofar as one person can instruct others in what to produce and how.

This distinctive element of human consciousness is paired with a particular aspect of human embodiment—what Søren Mau describes, following Joseph Fracchia, as "human corporeal organization."[82] Most living beings can produce what they need to survive using only their own anatomy (although typically also in association with other beings). But humans depend on "extra-somatic tools," Mau observes—and this renders them uniquely vulnerable to the mo-nopolization, by others, of the tools necessary for survival.[83] Marx is emphatic that "nature does not produce on the one hand owners of money or commodi-ties, and on the other hand men possessing nothing but their own labor-power": people are not divided into the categories of capitalist and proletarian by nature.[84] But if class society is not *itself* natural, the division of the species into classes is thinkable only for human beings. It reflects something about the natural form of human beings—not necessarily something about "human nature," as it's typically understood, but the fact that only human beings have the *ability* to relate to one another in these terms.

For Braverman, moreover, it is not purposiveness in general but the *indeterminate* characteristic of human labor that renders it most fundamentally distinct from the contributions of nonhuman agents. When a producer "employs bees in the production of honey, silkworms in the making of silk, bacteria in the fermentation of wine, or sheep in the growing of wool," Braverman notes, "he can only turn to his own advantage the instinctual activities or biological functions of these forms of life."[85] He illustrates this point with the example, taken from the English engineer Charles Babbage, of a workshop that used caterpillars to manufacture lace: an engineer would use food paste to trace a pattern and the caterpillars would eat their way along it, spinning a strong but delicate web of lace as they went. Every natural agent can do things that human beings can't. But if their abilities are often extraordinary, their range is typically limited. A sheep can grow wool, but it can't knit a sweater or operate a loom. Bacteria can't be told to speed up fermentation, the way a worker on the assembly line can.

By contrast, recall here Soper's claim that the "natural form" of human beings is radically "underdetermined" by anatomy, physiology, and other biophysical conditions.[86] In the sphere of production, this indeterminacy means that human beings can engage in many different *kinds* of concrete labor.[87] Human beings can neither grow wool nor ferment grapes—but they can operate either a loom or a wine press. Human workers, in other words, can perform an immense variety of tasks, organized in almost countless ways. When a capitalist purchases labor power, then, they aren't just purchasing a single capacity—fermentation services or wool production. They are purchasing the ability to direct someone else's action; as Andrès Saez de Silicia puts it, the "right to command a certain amount of labour time."[88]

If the indeterminacy of human labor is what makes it so useful, however, that indeterminacy is also what makes political struggles over the labor process so acute within class societies. Human laborers *can* do any number of things—but it is not guaranteed that they will. "In purchasing labor power that can do much," Braverman observes, the capitalist "is at the same time purchasing an undefined quality and quantity."[89] Nonhuman factors of production by contrast—"buildings, materials, tools, machinery"—can generally be counted on to deliver reliably. Maximizing the potential of labor power therefore requires intensive management, generating struggles within the labor process itself. Whoever is able to squeeze the most time out of their workers will have an advantage over their competitors—which means that capitalists are constantly trying to organize labor more efficiently, usually by exerting greater control over workers' actions.

Braverman admittedly overemphasizes the instinctual elements of animal behavior, suggesting that animals act according to the "universal law" of nature rather than engaging in complex social relationships of their own.[90] But his basic point about the distinctive indeterminacy of human labor stands. A more important oversight lurks in his suggestion that nonhuman inputs to production simply *are* reliable, in contrast to unruly and disruptive human labor, and that they can therefore be used to channel and control human workers. Yet nature, too, has to be *made* reliable—and as we will see, this is not guaranteed.

The Anthropocentrism of the Wage

If human consciousness is important for the concrete organization of labor in production, it is also central to how labor power is obtained under capitalism, via the particular social form of the wage. Marx argues that human labor power is a "special commodity"—the only commodity whose use generates new value. The definition he offers of labor power, however, does not immediately tell us why: he describes it only as "the aggregate of those mental and physical capabilities existing in the physical form, the living personality, of a human being, capabilities which he sets in motion whenever he produces a use-value of any kind."[91] Thus defined, labor power seems to describe something about the "natural form" of human beings—about human beings qua human beings.[92] But what really makes labor power different from other elements of production is that human beings, and only human beings (at least so far), can sell the discrete and bounded use of their "mental and physical capabilities existing in the physical form" without selling themselves.[93] What is significant, in other words, is not only human *physiological* qualities but the cognitive ability of the laborer to distinguish their ability to labor from their physical self.

The useful qualities of nonhuman agents, by contrast, cannot be separated from their "person," the way that labor power can be distinguished from the laborer. It is this which makes possible capitalism's reliance on free labor (in the sense of freely offered in exchange for compensation, rather than "free" in the sense of unpaid, or "free" in the sense of unconstrained) rather than the obligatory or coerced labor of serfdom and slavery.[94] The point is not that wage labor alone defines capitalism: to the contrary, as we will see, capitalism

relies on many kinds of ambiguously free and nontraditionally waged relations. The wage, however, is capitalism's ideal form of labor, and the form that
structures human relationships writ large. It is reinforced by political and legal
instruments, like the recognition in rights of formal human equality that
marked the movement from status to contract. Abstract labor itself rests on
the assumed equivalence of human labor—the idea that one hour of human
labor is fundamentally the same as any other—underpinned by juridical
equality before the law. A certain structure of humanism, then, is both a pre-
condition for the exploitation of human labor—and a structure that defini-
tionally excludes nonhumans.[95]

It is through the wage, in turn, that people are connected to one another
under capitalism. People work not to produce anything in particular—indeed,
labor is often divided so intensely that they may not even know what they
themselves are making—but in order to earn the money with which they can
purchase the goods they need to survive, which someone else has made.[96] It is
from these foundational social relations that nonhumans are constitutively excluded. Nonhumans, of course, may receive food or shelter in exchange for the
work they perform; they may be entreated or cajoled into performing certain
tasks, or genetically modified to perform still others. But the wage, and money
more generally, represents a relationship between humans alone: paid not in
kind but in currency, measuring labor not in effort or effect but in time.[97]

This is a deceptively simple but decisive point: it is the basis of the argument
that value exists only as a relationship between human beings. Recognizing this
need not diminish the significance and variety of nonhuman consciousness:
differences do not necessarily imply hierarchy, and still less do they justify domination. Nor does it require a definitive account of the intelligibility of language
and symbolic communication across species. We don't need to take up Wittgenstein's dictum about the lion.[98] We can even accept that this kind of communication might one day be plausible—that chimps might learn to use money or that
artificial intelligence might make it possible to have conversations with whales
(though for their own sakes we should perhaps hope not). As things stand, however, only human beings seem capable of entering into the *specific* forms of symbolic value construction and interpretation that characterize a system organized
around exchange, mediated by the abstraction of money.[99]

If nonhumans are excluded from the wage, however, they are often still
organized *in relation* to it, even if indirectly. The wage, after all, reaches far beyond its recipients—as illustrated by Silvia Federici's concept of the "patriarchy
of the wage." Although many societies have some kind of gendered division of

labor, Federici observes, the introduction of the wage tends to convert difference into hierarchy. Those who receive a wage for their work are exploited—but they also gain the means by which to participate in the economy, and, effectively, in social life. By contrast, those who do not receive a wage—regardless of whether they make useful contributions to a household or community—become dependent on those who do. Where this division of labor is gendered, as it so often is, the wage serves to reinforce patriarchal power.[100]

A similar phenomenon occurs with respect to human wage labor and the contributions of "natural agents" to production. In all societies, humans and nonhumans have different capacities, which contribute to economic production and other kinds of social life in particular ways. But because nonhumans do not—and crucially, unlike Federici's housewives, *cannot*—receive a wage, they cannot engage in the kinds of interactions that structure social life under capitalism specifically. This inability also means that nonhumans cannot express their "preferences" in the market, or thereby acquire the things they need to survive. An orangutan, for example, cannot outbid palm oil producers to preserve the Indonesian rainforest as a home rather than a plantation. The orangutan and other rainforest dwellers are dependent, albeit often obliquely, on human beings who value the rainforest and are willing to pay to preserve it. I call this the *anthropocentrism of the wage*.

———

To say that capitalism is a humanism, then, is to say that capitalism is a system that organizes a set of distinctively human capacities: the ability to exchange labor power for a wage, and the relatively equal capacities of the human body to be put to work in a variety of ways. Its defining features—privately owned means of production, wage labor, and market dependence—rely on fundamentally human qualities and characteristics, with the result that its measure of value reflects human action and interests alone. Human beings are divided into capitalists and proletarians, and they relate to one another through the wage, through commodities they buy and sell. Nonhumans, by contrast, are wageless—and enter into these interactions only as goods to be bought and sold. In order to obtain human labor power, capital must purchase it; natural agents, by contrast, are freely available by default. The gifts of nature are therefore constituted as free in comparison to commodities, and assessed in relation to wage labor. Importantly, then, capitalism does not *intentionally* or *actively* devalue nature per se. Rather, nature's lack of value is the shadow of the value relation that connects human laborers; the shadow of relationships among people, which themselves unfold beyond our control.

The basic difficulty of reflecting the interests and needs of nonhumans in human social and political institutions is not a problem specific to capitalism. Other social and political orders must also face the challenge of representing nonhumans, and many have limitations in their own right. Nonhumans also cannot vote or participate in deliberative processes, to take two obvious examples.[101] For that matter, human societies cannot help but be anthropocentric to some degree, insofar as their decisions are always ultimately made by humans, in accordance with what we can know and think. But capitalism's dynamics render it particularly *unable* to take the interests of nonhumans into account.

How Matter Matters

So far we have largely attended to the abstract dimensions of the free gift as a social form, while considering the ways that the natural form of human beings structures the relationships at capitalism's heart. But as I've argued, an account that genuinely grapples with capitalism's duality can't remain in the realm of the abstract alone. It has to also attend to the concrete. Capital's simple logic is $M–C–M^1$: to convert money into more money through the production of commodities. In capitalist societies, this logic is the center of gravity, into which much of the world is pulled, and around which the rest of the world orbits.[102] But if $M–C–M^1$ begins and ends with abstract quantities, the intervening C means that accumulation is always underpinned by a qualitative transformation of the concrete world, as matter-energy is physically transformed in the production of the commodity itself. A tree becomes a log becomes a plank becomes a table; a sheep's coat becomes a ball of wool becomes a skein of thread becomes a woven cloth; a lump of ore becomes iron becomes steel becomes an automobile. The imperative of accumulation informs the material organization of commodity production—but so too do the material qualities of the concrete labor process affect the prospects for accumulation.

Capitalism is often portrayed as endlessly expansive, bringing everything within its scope. It can seem not only like a gravitational force but like a black hole. It has, indeed, been enormously successful in organizing much of the world in pursuit of accumulation—but not uniformly or universally so. Its ability to wring profit out of every entity, activity, and process on Earth has often been overstated. Although capital seeks to absorb what it can make profitable, it *abdicates* that which it can't. It doesn't only appropriate and exploit; it also abandons and expels. The material qualities of concrete production processes are an overlooked feature of how and why it does so.

For sheer costlessness is not the only aspect of the free gifts of nature that informs their use. While the basic qualities and abilities of human beings are, from one person to another, more or less the same, the material qualities of the vast array of nonhuman beings differ drastically across *kinds* of nature— across different organisms and species, across living beings and inanimate ones—and this affects both the manner and the degree to which they can be incorporated in capitalist production processes. While all of nonhuman nature is equally excluded from the wage, in other words, the physical diversity of various kinds of natural forms is enormously significant in whether and how they are utilized. In particular, crucial differences appear between the gifts of nature that can be subsumed and controlled, bought and sold—and those that (so far) cannot.

Subsumption and Alienation

Two aspects of the interaction between material qualities and capitalist social relations are particularly important, outlined here and discussed in greater detail in later chapters: first, the significance of material qualities within the concrete production process, which I discuss in terms of *subsumption*; and second, the significance of material qualities in constituting the property relations that govern the use of nature, which I discuss in terms of *alienation*.

The specific material content of natural agents is obviously significant in the concrete labor process. You can't make a table out of linen, or a coat out of wood; an ocean current won't heat a boiler and a caterpillar won't plow a field. But these qualities also remain more significant in the *valorization* process than is typically acknowledged. Control over nature, as Andreas Malm observes, often serves to facilitate control over labor.[103] In reorganizing the labor process according to its own social prerogatives, capital also physically reorganizes the material elements of production—what Marx describes in terms of subsumption. In some cases, it even reengineers the physical capacities of nonhuman beings themselves. Sheep might be bred to produce certain qualities of wool, for example; caterpillars, to produce new kinds of lace. Capitalist social forms thus directly alter the natural forms of nonhuman beings.

But control over nature is hardly automatic, and often elusive. Natural agents, too, have an autonomy of their own, one that often impedes their incorporation into production—even if only unconsciously. Just as the subsumption of human labor does not *obliterate* the "subjective, conscious, and collective aspects of human activity," which always remain grounds for political organization and action, even the successful subsumption of nature does not obliterate the qualities of the material world itself, or the autonomy of its many and variegated entities.[104] Subsumption is always accompanied by what I describe as *suprasumption*: the existence of matter in excess of its subordination to capital, which often constitutes obstacles to accumulation. The content of natural forms, in other words, feeds back into the appearance of social forms.

Material qualities also factor into the social relations of ownership that govern access to and use of nature's gifts. For the gifts of nature are not always *literally* free. Although natural agents can't appear in the market in their own right, they can be represented by a human being—and more specifically, by an owner. Rent, as Marx observes, is the "price paid to the owner of natural forces or mere products of nature for the right of using those forces."[105] Rents can't be said to represent nonhumans in any meaningful sense: as Paul Burkett notes, they are a "limp instrument" that only ever represent a tiny part of the vast array of capacities of natural agents, and they do not, of course, compensate the natural agents themselves.[106] Even so, it has long been proposed that nature's gifts will be valued where they are owned.

And yet many gifts of nature turn out to be remarkably difficult to represent even through the relationship of ownership. Their capacities can't easily be bought and sold; they seem to elude property relations. They are not, in other words, alienable. As we will see in later chapters, some kinds of nature are so inalienable that they resist even the imposition of rents—and thus remain free in perpetuity. Much of the violence done to the nonhuman world, in turn, is the result not of its forceful enclosure by private owners but of the operations of "ordinary" capitalism in a world, and on a planet, whose most fundamental processes *cannot* be privatized.

Capitalist Cyborgs

At a formal level, capitalism draws stark ontological divisions between human labor and nonhuman resources. The free gift of nature and waged human labor exist at opposite poles. But much of the world exists along a spectrum: capitalism creates cyborgs.[107] Human and nonhuman elements are substituted for one another and combined into novel entities altogether; together they generate and unleash previously unknown capacities—for better and for worse. This basic potential to make and remake the world is precisely the promise Marx sees in capitalism—and also the threat. Yet these novel entities are not well captured by social theory.

The terms of social theory—reification, naturalization, fetishism, second nature—typically seek to reveal the social lurking beneath the veil of the natural. They struggle to capture the interaction of human and more-than-human activity without eliminating the force of the latter. Recall Marx's claim that "capital is not a thing, but a social relation between persons which is mediated through things."[108] Too often in Marxist social theories which rightly enjoin us to attend to social relations, the *things* that for Marx necessarily mediate them drop out of the picture altogether—and so the materiality slips out of materialism. Similarly, Marx's analysis of commodity fetishism, central to many critiques of capitalism, addresses the way that relations among people often appear to be relations between people and things, observing that to see the likes of coats and shoes as mere objects is to obscure the ways in which they were made. Things, in this account, become mere camouflage for the social relations that actually make the world go round.

But if everything is actually a social relation *rather* than a thing—and ultimately the *same* social relation at that—why does this relation take such different physical forms? Why does capitalism look so different when, say, fossil fuels come into the picture, or plastics, and how does this in turn change how we, as human beings, relate to one another? The truth is that the likes of capital and the commodity are always both: thing *and* social relation; social relation *expressed through things*—things that have effects in their own right. Material qualities are always socially organized, and social relations are always materially mediated.

This is one of the key, and often overlooked, insights of Jean-Paul Sartre, whose thought we will examine more closely in the next chapter. Since human beings are "material organisms with material needs," Sartre writes, "we shall never find men who are not mediated by matter at the same time as they mediate different material regions."[109] Matter has its own disposition, which human action can reveal, channel, and reorient—but can't reconfigure entirely. It both reflects and refracts our own action. Sartre's analyses of *materialized praxes* and the *practico-inert* describe the ways that human social activity and relations are expressed in and through a material world that always exceeds them.[110] The material world channels and reflects human action (*praxis*), but never *only* human action: nonhuman nature always retains its nonidentical quality (the *inert*).[111] The *practico-inert*, then, describes the physical trace of human action;

the sedimentation of past projects in the form of material entities that shape, enable, and constrain future action. As Fredric Jameson observes, the *practico-inert* describes "objects which are not mere things and agencies which are not exactly people either."[112]

Sartre thus anticipates an idea that has animated more recent discussions of the Anthropocene, the age in which human activity has become the dominant force shaping the planet Earth, even as that activity has begun to spin out of our control. Like Jane Bennett's *heterogeneous assemblage*, or Bruno Latour's *hybrids*, the practico-inert reflects a view of matter as reactive but not perfectly malleable; unlike either, it resists the temptation to flatten differences between agents, instead retaining an account of distinctively human action at its core.[113] It is better understood in terms of what I call the *practico-actant*, in reflection of the dynamic and autonomous—rather than passive and compliant— character of the more-than-human world.[114] Like the Marxist concepts of alienation and reification, meanwhile, the practico-actant attends to the way that social relations come to appear as things—while taking *things themselves* more seriously, attending to the way that human actions and social relations manifest *physically*.[115]

Materiality without Morality

To recognize that the more-than-human world exists in excess of human projects is not to valorize the "unknowability" or "otherness" of nature as such. Matter's "unruliness" and "vibrancy" are often suggested to be morally significant forms of resistance to capitalist abstraction; nature's "dynamism" and "autonomy" are framed as forms of quasi-political rebellion.[116] The material world *does* exceed capitalism's forms of logic; it often *does* resist, impede, or otherwise fail to conform to capital's attempts to harness and reorganize it. But this is not the same as standing outside of capitalism. Even aspects of nature that resist subsumption and alienation do not necessarily escape the reorganization of the broader web life by capitalist social forms, as discussed in chapter 6 in particular. In any case, identifying the places where nature is or is not amenable to capitalist remaking should not, in itself, give cause for celebration or condemnation. The fact of physical resistance should not be conflated with political prescription. Our response to the troublesome mediation of capitalist social forms should not be the simple affirmation of an unmediated world of nature against *any* interpretation by the social—an impossible task, in any case. Capitalism situates nature in one way—but we never simply relate to nature directly, without the necessarily anthropocentric apparatus of meaning. The critique of capitalism, then, must focus specifically on *how* it assigns meaning, rather than criticizing the fact that it does so at all.

Indeed, nature's nonidentity—its existence beyond the concepts and practices we use to organize it—is not a challenge only for capitalism. All social orders must contend with, and rely on, a world they did not make and cannot control, comprising entities ranging from minerals deposited by asteroids that have randomly collided with the Earth to rapidly evolving microbes.[117] This basic fact is as likely to foil the social orders we think liberatory as those we think oppressive. It is vital, as I argue most directly in chapter 7, not to see the force of the nonhuman world *only* as a limit on human freedom: it is always simultaneously a condition of possibility and constraint. But as such, nature's recalcitrance must be assessed in relation to our projects and ends. Nature's autonomy is not just evidenced in the heartening examples of life that "rebels against the value/monoculture nexus of modernity" or charismatic organisms like mushrooms that seem to have eluded capitalist rationalization.[118] It lies, too, in more sobering reminders of the ways that the world really *isn't* under human control: the possibility, for example, that the monsoon might fail one year, or that climatic conditions could change drastically even *without* human alteration, as indeed they frequently have in the past hundred thousand years.[119]

Thus while I emphasize remainders and residues, excesses and superfluities— the "rough edges" of the physical world that capitalist discipline has failed to smooth—I do not see these sites as sites of noncapitalist social relations, political resistance, or moral value *in themselves*.[120] Rather, I see the sites where value snags on the material world as places where cracks in the seemingly smooth armor of value appear, and where different political possibilities appear more readily. The free gift is a site where the disjuncture between capitalism's form of value and other kinds is most visible, and where judgments about it are perhaps more easily made. But these judgments can't be outsourced to nature. Rather than simply affirming nature against capital, a *politics* of nature must instead attend to the values that diverge from capitalism's own, and seek to widen the cracks.[121] The next chapter takes up this challenge in more detail, considering how we might criticize capitalism without seeking refuge in nature.

2

Unfree to Choose

CAPITALIST RULE AND
EXISTENTIAL FREEDOM

THERE ARE MANY accounts of what, exactly, is wrong with capitalism. Critics charge it with stealing from the worker, degrading human relationships, generating inequality, exacerbating racial division, and reifying gender hierarchy. Others claim that capitalism is simply dysfunctional, doomed to repeated cycles of crisis until its eventual collapse.[1] When it comes to ecological issues, though, the problem can seem obvious: capitalism destroys nature. Variations on this theme abound. Capitalism has opened up a "metabolic rift" in the relationship between humanity and nonhuman nature; it has "alienated" human beings from nature, including our own.[2] Capitalism dominates nature, using it instrumentally rather than recognizing its intrinsic value or fundamental alterity.[3] Capitalism is degrading our earthly home—and the burdens of that destruction are borne unequally among human beings, just as capitalism's benefits are unevenly distributed.[4] Capitalism is generating new crises by undermining the "background conditions" of its own functioning—and perhaps even destroying itself in the process.[5] The problem with the free gift might seem to follow in this train, revealing that capitalism, as Marx claims, robs both the worker and the soil; that it doesn't pay its true ecological costs, just as it doesn't pay the worker the true value of their labor.[6]

These arguments are compelling. There is clearly something to them. The state of our planet is evidence enough that something is deeply wrong. But their foundations are unstable. Many ecological critiques of capitalism— perhaps most—are ultimately rooted in a morally significant but underspecified idea of "nature." To criticize capitalism's destruction, domination, or degradation of nature requires some idea of what nature is and why it should be protected—points often taken for granted. Perhaps they seem too obvious to elaborate. But upon some reflection, the simple idea of nature turns out to be complicated indeed.

If the nonhuman world is always in flux, as we have known it to be at least since Darwin, what exactly is the nature that capitalism is destroying? Metabolisms themselves are changeable things; what makes any given metabolism worth preserving? How can human beings destroy nature if we are *part* of nature, as ecological thinkers often remind us we are? What makes our transformation of the material world more destructive than the transformations wrought by termites or coral or bowerbirds? What would it mean to use or consume nature *without* destroying it, or to truly reciprocate nature's gifts? Can we even say that "nature" is being destroyed at all? After all, ash trees may be struggling, but ash borers are thriving. Why, for that matter, do the likes of forests and marshes count as "nature" while nonhuman elements of the built environment, like a skyscraper or a swimming pool, do not? Conversely, if nature has already come to an end, as many theorists of the Anthropocene claim, what is there left to protect, conserve, or defend? What makes nature worth protecting, defending, or restoring in the first place—and which natures do we have in mind?[7]

When we take a critical stance on nature itself, in other words, it is harder to know how capitalism has wronged it. The point isn't that doing so leaves us without resources for judgment or critique—far from it. If anything, it demands that we make the arguments underlying our judgments more explicit: why we should privilege the ash tree over the ash borer, or why we might justifiably intervene in human reproductive cycles but not in ecological metabolisms; why we think some aspects of nature must be protected to enhance human well-being, and why some might be worth protecting even at a cost to ourselves. The problem comes when critics of capitalism play a moralized nature as a trump card, one that disguises underlying judgments and assumptions.[8] In so doing they abdicate the truly challenging questions before us: questions about how we should live and why.

Many of the consequences that ecological critics of capitalism identify are indeed deeply troubling. But troubling consequences mark the beginning of critique rather than the end. Our judgment of capitalism can't lie only in empirical measurements of wealth or pollution, sheer statistics of poverty or biodiversity, as if these things speak for themselves. It has to lie in our assessments of what these indicators mean for our determination of whether the world we have made is a good one—and ultimately, whether we feel we have made this world at all. Instead of focusing on consequences *themselves*—on what "we" are "doing to nature," or what capitalism is doing to us; on metrics of economic growth or physical throughput—I follow the structure of action that produces them, and that places outcomes so out of our control.

The problem with capitalism, this book argues, is that it makes us unfree. This unfreedom distorts our ability to make decisions about how to relate to one another as human beings, as well as to the vast array of nonhuman beings that make up our world; and it thwarts our ability to take responsibility for those decisions. This is a critique rooted not in external standards for judgment, as given by nature, but in the belief that we ultimately should be able to make these decisions for ourselves. Where many recent critiques of capitalist unfreedom have taken inspiration from the republican principle of nondomination, mine looks elsewhere: to the freedom to choose, as articulated in the existentialism of Jean-Paul Sartre and Simone de Beauvoir.[9] To be human, for Sartre and Beauvoir, is to be faced with a choice about how to be; to even be able to conceive of such a choice. Freedom, in turn, consists in the possibility of choosing to be other than what we are, and taking responsibility for what we decide. It is precisely this kind of indeterminacy—the idea that human social life can be other than what it is—that underpins the critique of social forms, as we have seen. It is this indeterminacy, too, that drives the existentialist claim that our values are given neither by God nor nature nor custom, and must be grounded in our freedom alone.[10] The project of a human life, for Sartre and Beauvoir, is to be what one chooses, and to commit oneself to those choices through action in the world.

The freedom to choose is often dismissed as the slogan of neoliberalism, seen as the impoverished or even ugly freedom of the sovereign consumer.[11] The title of Milton and Rose Friedman's full-throated defense of capitalism, *Free to Choose*, could double for that of an existentialist manifesto. To some, this may seem troubling. Yet the freedom to choose is worth defending. Just as the formal institution of free and equal labor, however substantially limited and incompletely realized, has emancipatory elements, so too does the market's challenge to naturalized social values—however partial and often distorted—have liberatory dimensions, as Marx himself recognized.[12] Proponents of the freedom to choose are not wrong to reject the fixity of moral values or emphasize the importance of deciding what we think is most important. Rather than reading this resonance as the sign of a damning elective affinity, then, I show how existentialist accounts of the freedom to choose our values can reveal the *inadequacy* of capitalist accounts of freedom. Capitalist freedom, on this view, is a perversion rather than realization of existentialist freedom, insofar as it undercuts our ability to make genuine choices, and to take genuine responsibility for our decisions.

Capitalist unfreedom has two main components: what I describe as *market rule* and *class rule*. Rule is typically associated with the classic question—"Who rules?"—typically taken to be synonymous with the question "Who governs?"[13] Traced to the ancient Greek *archē*, it is generally thought to describe explicitly political systems of governance. My argument is not that capitalism is a political system in itself, in the manner of democracy or aristocracy: it is, primarily, a mode of production. But the way that capitalism structures economic decisions, although ostensibly distinguished from political ones, sets the terms for decision-making writ large. Each of capitalism's core dimensions—private control of the means of production and investment, and generalized dependence on markets, which serve as the primary mode of allocation and distribution—corresponds to a particular modality of rule, which together constitute capitalism as a system of unfreedom.

What I call *class rule* is a form of the rule of the few over the many, channeled through private ownership of the means of production and private power over investment. This form of unfreedom is often discussed in terms of the power that the capitalist holds over the worker. As I argue, however, class rule extends beyond workplace domination or even the class relation between labor and capital described by radical republicans and classical Marxists.[14] It consists in the concentration in private hands of power over investment—and hence over the ability to remake the world. Although critiques of consumption tend to point a finger at widespread "complicity" in environmental destruction, private control over production and investment means that decisions made by a tiny fraction of people—themselves subject to the competitive pressure of the market—fundamentally shape the world in which the rest of us live.

A second aspect of unfreedom—one that is less easily diagnosed—is what I call *market rule*. Market freedom is the mechanism on which capitalism's defenders tend to stake both pragmatic and moral arguments. In the market, it's said, people meet as formal equals, unmarked by status, buying and selling whatever they choose—including, vitally, their own labor power—to whoever will buy or sell from them. Markets allow us to decide for ourselves what is in our own interest and pursue it to the best of our ability. Markets offer a way to coordinate action through voluntary exchange rather than violent coercion, promising a social order to which everyone has consented—and which, it's often argued, produces benefits for all.[15] Skeptics have typically responded by debunking these principles of "freedom, equality, property, and Bentham" as illusory, pointing to the class relation that lurks beneath the seemingly equal surface of exchange.[16] My analysis instead looks more closely at the structure of market action itself, in order to diagnose the unfreedoms the market generates in its own right. What does it mean to live in a society in which markets mediate so many of our actions? If the market is the site of freedom, why does it so often leave us feeling helpless?

Market rule underscores the novelty of political life in a society where the vast majority of decisions are made and carried out through sheer agglomeration of individual choices, mediated by exchanges of goods. Our individual choices are limited not only as a matter of scale—not only, in other words, because they seem to be a minuscule drop in a massive bucket—but in their very structure, coordinated by an institution that simultaneously atomizes and aggregates our decisions in ways that defy both individual and collective control. The structure of market rule ultimately limits our ability to take responsibility for the world we have made, and to commit ourselves to the values we purport to hold. Just as we are frequently compelled to treat other people as workers and competitors, we are compelled to treat nonhuman nature as a free gift—regardless of our individual ethical assessments or moral values.

As I show in later chapters, these forms of rule illuminate drivers of environmental phenomena that are often described in terms of injustice or violence. Although injustice and violence are, indeed, often present, they tend to be downstream from these structuring features. Market and class rule do not apply only to our relationships to nature, however: they pervade life under capitalism more broadly. In fact, it's important that the critique of capitalism advanced in this book *isn't* specifically ecological. If, as I've argued, politics is inevitably bound up with the material world we call "nature," we can't separate out the ecological critique of capitalism from a social one. A Marxist-existentialist account of unfreedom is particularly apt in this regard. In its insistence that values must not only be stated but lived, it roots freedom in the material world, as we'll explore most significantly in chapter 7. While it echoes the classic Marxist critique of alienation in certain respects, moreover, it does so without essentializing either human nature or human relationships to the natural world. Rather than measuring capitalism's wrongness against a standard set by nature, it leaves open the question of how we understand ourselves in relation to the more-than-human world of which we are a part.

Class Rule and Class Power

Class rule is the most obvious form of capitalist unfreedom. While it appears easily legible in terms of the rule of the few over the many, it takes an unusual form.[17] The few aren't the well-born or the wise; their power isn't rooted in control of the organs of state power or channels of social influence. Their authority, rather, is conferred by sheer economic power, and often bypasses public decision-making processes altogether.[18] *Class power* names the distinctive forms of authority derived from privately held control over resources on which others rely to reproduce their lives. It is the power to command these resources as one pleases—and thus to command those who need access to them—with little accountability, except to the rule of the market itself.[19] And yet class rule is not *merely* the result of a maldistribution of wealth, of the sort that political theorists have long described—for capital isn't simply wealth. The few, in this instance, are capital personified. They don't simply use the public sphere to pursue their own personal interests, or even use their private wealth for their own advancement; rather, they act to regenerate capital in perpetuity.

Class rule is usually understood in terms of the domination of labor by capital. As Nicholas Vrousalis argues, capital is "just monetary title to control over the labour capacity of others."[20] Capital, in other words, is the power to purchase another's time and decide how it will be used; the ability of one group of people to command the activity of another, rooted not in any politically legitimated decision but merely in control over productive assets. It is this power that is typically seen as lurking beneath the mystifications of market freedom: Marx memorably descends from the realm of exchange, where relationships between persons merely *appear* to be equal, to the realm of production, where the foundational division in social power between owners of capital and proletarians is revealed.[21] Proletarians, he claims, are "doubly free": free to work for whomever they please, but also free of property—and thus free to starve if they can't find a way to trade their sole asset, their own bodily capacity, to those who control all the other things that reproduction requires. At the heart of capitalist production, then, is the expectation that some people will regularly submit to the will of others; that some people will regularly be able to command the will of others.

This dimension of class rule is largely comprehensible within the republican critique of domination. Within the workplace, both labor republicans and theorists of the firm observe, bosses and managers are entitled to exercise near-unrestricted authority, and have broad discretionary power over the terms of employment. Although workers enter into voluntary agreements to follow orders, the broader social relations of class leave them little choice but to accept the terms they are offered.[22] Class rule, however, extends much further than accounts of workplace domination suggest, and takes a wider array of forms than analyses of labor alone recognize.

For capital is not only title to command the labor of others, per Vrousalis, but the power to organize production and direct investment more generally. While this aspect of class rule—stemming from power over investment—has rarely been explored by political theorists, it is essential to the analysis of capitalism.[23] It is the power to decide what is produced and in what quantities, where and how—and hence to make decisions about many other aspects of social and ecological life. It is the title to quarry vast mines and build enormous factories; to drill deep into the Earth for hydrocarbons and convert ancient forests to plantations. Owners of capital thus have outsized power not only over the people whose labor they have purchased, or those with whom they enter into direct relationships of exchange, but over the conditions of life for many people who have entered into no formal agreement whatsoever—as when the owner of a factory that belches out smoke forcibly changes the conditions of life for those living in the neighborhood, the conditions of the local atmosphere, and even the global biosphere. Capital, then, is the power not only to produce commodities but to produce the physical world, without most people's consultation or consent.

Class rule also operates in more expansive ways than most existing accounts address. It is often depicted, especially in neorepublican accounts, in terms of the power to interfere with others, to actively direct or command their activity. The boss tells their employee to work faster or come in for an extra shift; or more egregiously, to change their behavior outside the workplace.[24] Similarly, class power, understood as power over investment, is most obvious when it takes the form of *active* direction of production: the decision, for example, to drain a wetland to build a housing development or build an energy-intensive data center. But class rule is equally evident in its seeming absences: in the ability to decide what *not* to produce, to *decline* to hire a worker, to *disinvest* from projects or regions, to *withhold* resources. It lies in the power to neglect those things that don't promise adequate returns, however needed they might be—and crucially, to do so without being held responsible for the outcomes that might result. Thus pharmaceutical companies invest in research on diseases that afflict the wealthy while neglecting those that affect the poor; real estate developers build luxury apartments rather than affordable housing; financiers invest in fossil fuels rather than renewable energy.[25] We might find this dismaying—but it's not obviously *wrong*, insofar as private actors are not expected to act for public ends.

To characterize capitalism as a system of class rule does not, emphatically, mean that capitalists rule as they please, nor that they rule alone. Although class power is capitalism's sine qua non, it is not the only kind of power that operates within it. It exists alongside, interacts with, exacerbates, and perhaps even generates forms of power and domination structured by other social categories like race and gender.[26] Although class rule operates primarily through control over economic rather than political resources, moreover, it can be reinforced or curbed by political institutions. States, too, have power to undertake investment, albeit rarely with total autonomy from private capital. And of course, class rule can be combatted and held in check by organization among those subjected to it.

Perhaps most fundamentally, however, the decisions that owners of capital, which shape the world that the rest of us live in, are themselves made under and indeed compelled by what I call market rule. Capitalists are subject, above all, to the law of value—a law made not by any conscious actor but emergent from countless individual decisions undertaken in competition—and as such it's the market, above all, that directs, disciplines, and even commands them. The market is capitalism's governing body; the institution that structures action on a daily basis, more than any other.

Market Freedom, Market Rule

It's fairly obvious what's troubling about class rule, at least in societies where people are supposed to be political equals. This kind of unequal power has few defenders as such. But it can also seem unsatisfactory as an explanation for the complexity of agency, power, and responsibility in modern capitalist societies. The transformation of our planet is simply too vast to attribute to any single company or even industry; to point a finger at capital can seem to imply a simplistic portrait of greedy villains acting to enrich themselves at the expense of others, one that conveniently shifts responsibility to a few bad actors rather than acknowledging widespread complicity.[27] Fossil fuel companies may drill for oil, but it's consumers who enjoy the benefits of burning it. Phenomena like climate change are the result of trillions of mundane choices: we each add some tiny amount of carbon to the atmosphere every time we eat or drive to work or buy a new outfit. "When we order products from Amazon, when we forget to turn off the air conditioning, or even when we buy a new item of clothing,"

Elisabeth Anker argues, "we damage the environment with thoughtless patterns of consumption."[28]

Such arguments about climate complicity follow in a long train of anxieties about responsibility for unintentional and often unwitting harms done to others through consumption, from "slave sugar" to "blood oil." They often carry a localized echo of Marx's critique of commodity fetishism, enjoining us to spot the relations of domination lurking within the mere things we buy every day.[29] Yet they rarely confront the institution that channels these actions—the market. Why is moral agency located so significantly in consumer choices? Why, even when we *know* that our purchases are problematic, do we often feel so powerless to do anything about it? And how might we understand responsibility differently if we attended more closely to the way action is mediated by the market?

The structure of responsibility in the market is challenging to grasp. It really *is* hard to see, on the surface, what is wrong with market choices.[30] Even their most negative effects tend to emerge from interactions that are, on their face, unobjectionable: the kinds of ordinary, legal transactions that we make unthinkingly every day when we willingly enter into arrangements with others, making exchanges we find mutually satisfactory. The outcomes that many people find troubling are ones that no one intends, arising from actions that no one in particular forces us to take. Some philosophers thus argue that despite our discomfort with these phenomena, there's actually no wrongdoing at all.[31] Others identify problems that they struggle to diagnose. Republican critics of domination often acknowledge the force of the market but bracket it to focus on forms of interpersonal domination more suited to the republican framework; accounts of "abstract" or "social" domination condemn the ways that markets appear out of our control but rarely articulate their specific normative dimensions.

My account of market rule thus addresses this form of unfreedom, and its mode of operation, more directly. The market has often been thought of as anarchic—as the *absence* of rule. Markets are infamously volatile; it's no coincidence that Mercury is the god of commerce. But market rule isn't only chaotic—it is also intensely orderly. Markets cultivate subjects and inculcate practices; they discipline and punish. They generate familiar, even lawlike, patterns of action and structures of relationships among people, even if it's never clear who exactly will end up on top. These laws aren't given by nature, of course: they emerge from interactions among human beings. In their patterned, even orderly nature, however, they aren't the same as the laws we consciously make either. Market rule is self-sustaining and self-organizing, generated by the structured actions of many

individual selves but exceeding the will or action of any individual self in particular: a "process without a subject," as Althusser put it, and also a political order
without a subject.[32] Market rule reflects, in a sense, what Niko Kolodny describes
as "rule over none": it does not require that anyone *in particular* is subordinate to
anyone else.[33] But market rule is not the democratic promise of ruling and being
ruled in turn. It is, rather, rule *by* each, simultaneously—and also by no one in
particular. It is rule by all *and* by none.

Market rule reflects the combined conditions of *market dependence*, wherein
most people must acquire most of what they need through market exchange,
and *market competition*, which makes success and even survival contingent on
contending with and besting others in the market. Market rule is oriented
around a singular form of value against which all goods and actions are
measured. It weighs on everyone: capitalists and workers, consumers and producers. In tandem with class rule, it becomes directional, oriented toward accumulation: each capitalist "obeys the immanent law, and hence the moral
imperative . . . to produce as much surplus-value as possible."[34] Capital flows
to wherever it can find returns; it allocates labor and other resources accordingly. Value comes to operate as a regulative principle for society writ large.
Market rule, then, is not anarchy but *axiarchy*—the rule of value.[35]

Market Freedom as Nonresponsibility

To develop the account of market rule, it's necessary to look more closely at the
claims made about market freedom. Markets are said to rely on uncoerced
choices and consensual agreement. In the market, we each pursue our own
self-interest, however we define it, making voluntary exchanges that we think
will make us better off, and so does everyone else. Markets aggregate our individual actions into collective outcomes. Crucially, our motives have no bearing
on these outcomes: markets are indifferent to our purposes, seeing only prices.
In other words, they detach intentions from consequences. As Eric MacGilvray
argues, then, the fundamental principle of market freedom is *nonresponsibility*.
People are able to choose among the options offered by the market "without
being publicly accountable for the consequences of those decisions, and thus
with the ability to impose certain costs on other people without their consent."[36] An avocado fad may send farmers' fortunes rising and plummeting; a
cultural propensity to save rather than spend may plunge the economy into
recession and workers into unemployment—but no one in particular is at fault.
No one is directly responsible for the prices of goods; no one is directly respon-

sible for the distribution of income. Even where markets bring about detrimental outcomes, it is no one's intent and no one's fault that they do so.

Condemnatory though it may sound, the charge of "nonresponsibility" is not a critique. To the contrary, the disconnect between intention and result has often been a point in markets' favor. Ideas like Bernard Mandeville's "private vices, public virtues" and Adam Smith's "invisible hand" take the optimistic view that individual actions motivated by self-interest turn out, however accidentally, to secure peace and prosperity for society as a whole. Markets do not require people to be wise, altruistic, or virtuous; they do not assume that people will take the common good into account or choose to act justly. Indeed, it is expected that they are not, and will not. Those who act with no thought of the general welfare will nevertheless advance it—perhaps *more* so than those who act with the common good in mind. This is why markets have often seemed to pose an answer to core problems of political thought—a form of order that takes people as they are and not as they might be; that realizes the common good treasured by the ancients while protecting the individual liberty prized by the moderns.[37]

If Smith and Mandeville had argued that the pursuit of individual freedom expressed via the market would redound to the benefit of all, however, markets' twentieth-century defenders—thinkers like Milton Friedman and Friedrich Hayek—make no such promises.[38] Instead, they suggest, there *is* no way to assess what is for the benefit of all; there is no such thing as society. There are only individuals and the choices they make about what would be best for them, according to their own judgments and values. If someone cares about preserving natural landscapes, they can choose to buy "green" products or donate to nature conservancies; what they cannot do is force others to contribute to these projects. Whereas states forcibly impose some people's preferences on others, in the market the individual is "the ultimate judge of his ends."[39] If those choices happen to upset the "patterns" we would prefer, per Robert Nozick, who are we to intervene?[40] This is, in other words, a stringent *inconsequentialism* rooted in the refusal of collective judgment altogether.

The market, in this view, is a way of acting socially but not cooperatively: people make free choices as individuals, and those individual choices are aggregated into what Hayek calls "spontaneous order." Spontaneous order also reflects a view of unintended consequences as felicitous, as Daniel Luban argues—but it strips away the explicit normative inflection of something like Mandeville's "public virtue," even as it naturalizes the idea of spontaneity itself.[41] Key to its realization is the fact that prices are a thin kind of knowledge, one that simply reflects information about supply and demand. When you buy a bunch of bananas, you don't need to know anything about the soil that nourished the trees on which they grew, or what kinds of noxious effects might have resulted from the process of farming them. It is not a problem, according to the theory of market freedom, that we don't know these things—to the contrary, it is a boon. It is precisely the limits of individual knowledge, for Hayek, that recommend the market as a way of aggregating the knowledge of all.[42] All you need to know is how much money you have, how much money things cost, and what your own priorities are. This, of course, is the *opposite* of the idea that we bear moral responsibility for the effects of our consumer purchases, that we could act rightly if only we did enough research. If you could know everything that went into your purchases and calculate the best outcome for everyone on Earth, we wouldn't need markets at all.

When Hayek proclaims that liberty and responsibility go together, then, this is not responsibility as many moral philosophers imagine it—responsibility for the effects of our decisions on other people, let alone for the direction or shape of collective life. His view of responsibility is perfectly compatible with the account of market freedom as nonresponsibility: we are not, according to Hayek, "accountable for our actions to any particular persons."[43] Freedom is only the freedom to allocate one's own resources as one chooses, toward the ends one prefers; responsibility is only for our own individual choices about how we will allocate the resources that belong to us, and for the results of those choices in our own lives. If someone chooses to spend their resources on entertainment instead of food, why should we stop them? If they choose to live near a smoky factory where rent is cheap, why should we prevent them? If they choose a hazardous job over a safer one because the pay is better, why should we prohibit them? They will have to bear the consequences—but that is their choice.[44] The same reasoning applies at the collective level: if we as a society have failed to value nature in the way that some people might prefer, it is simply because others have freely chosen to prioritize different things. If we are unhappy with the results, we must take a hard look in the mirror, and at our own "willingness to pay" for the things we claim to value. Our spending may turn out to reveal more about our commitments than our proclamations.[45]

Republican Limits

The optimistic view of unintended consequences, as articulated by Smith and Mandeville, is easily countered with evidence of more pessimistic outcomes, as we will consider shortly. But Hayek's account of market freedom is more challenging for contemporary advocates of freedom—particularly those drawing on the republican tradition—to refute. Early modern republicans were anxious that the rise of commerce threatened freedom, understood in a classical republican sense. Markets, they worried, introduced servile dependence while eroding common purpose and arrogating the sphere of self-rule.[46] Yet it is precisely the uncoupling of intention and result that has led many neorepublicans since to see the market as a potential counter to the arbitrary power of one person over another. If no one is responsible for the effects of their actions on anyone else, no one can impose their will on anyone else. The market, after all, does away with the qualities of impersonal and intentional action at the heart of the republican concept of domination. It disperses power and offers opportunities for exit. It is akin to a force of nature, Philip Pettit argues—and therefore not a source of domination.[47] Radical republicanism, so potent for diagnosing workplace power, has thus proved ill-suited to addressing market unfreedom, and hence to confronting the diffuse forms of compulsion, interdependence, and impotence that saturate daily life under capitalism.

The most robust defense of a republican account of domination *by the market* is offered by William Clare Roberts, who argues that capitalism institutes a form of domination that is *inter*personal even if *im*personal. The market, in its erraticism and unpredictability, constitutes "the exercise of an arbitrary power"; but the market itself is, as Roberts puts it, "just people," and so it subjects us to other people's wills, even if indirectly and unintentionally.[48] In dropping the requirement of intentionality, Roberts's account diverges significantly from the traditional republican view (at least, as articulated by Pettit)—and indeed stretches the republican concept of domination to the breaking point. As Roberts himself notes, the subjection of people to overarching, lawlike forces is a form of domination "novel to modernity"—one that a concept stemming from antiquity cannot quite grasp.[49] The republican critique of nondomination, moreover, doesn't adequately counter the account of the market given by its defenders. Indeed, Hayek's own insistence that one person must not be subjected to the arbitrary will of another is easily read in terms of republican liberty.[50] Hayek openly grants that the market is often out of our control—but nonetheless holds that the "impersonal and seemingly irrational forces of the market" are preferable to the "equally uncontrollable and therefore arbitrary power of other men."[51] This is more obviously consistent with the neorepublican view of nondomination than Roberts's account of domination as diffuse and impersonal, however more appealing we might find the latter.[52]

Critical theory offers its own diagnosis of capitalism's "abstract," "impersonal," or "social" domination—which Moishe Postone describes as consisting not "in the domination of people by other people, but in the domination of people by abstract social structures that people themselves constitute."[53] Although people appear to be free to invest, consume, and labor as they wish, this critique holds, they are compelled to act in ways that accord with the system's overall logic. What critical theorists describe as domination is therefore closer to a critique of alienation, describing the way that human activity comes to appear as an "alien power" out of our control, than to the republican critique of the arbitrary power of one person over another.[54] Yet this account of domination, as Roberts notes, is loosely defined, and its normative dimensions underspecified. Critiques of social domination typically stop short of spelling out what, exactly, human freedom consists in or how the market inhibits it.

Nor does this critique of domination quite land a blow against Hayek's defense of the market: for Hayek himself endorses market freedom on the grounds of something like self-determination. Markets, for Hayek, give us the freedom to choose what we as individuals value, to decide the direction of our lives for ourselves—and just as importantly, they force us to make choices about those values in the face of material constraints. We can assert any number of principles in the abstract, but the things we choose to devote our limited resources to reflect our *real* commitments, far more than any mere statement of belief. Precisely by virtue of its limitations, then, the sphere of market choice is "the air in which alone moral sense grows and in which moral values are daily recreated in the free decision of the individual."[55] The "opportunity to build one's own life," Hayek argues, "also means an unceasing task, a discipline that man must impose upon himself." This unceasing discipline, he argues, is why "many people are afraid of liberty."[56]

The resonance with Sartrean existentialism is striking. To choose, for Sartre, is to decide what we really value and what we want to be—and for Sartre, too, this is frightening. We alone are responsible for our choices, he emphasizes, and this responsibility is hard to face, insofar as it leaves us with no excuses for our actions. Freedom is anguish, which people constantly seek to deny—and yet it is ultimately inescapable. Sartre, too, emphasizes the necessity of realizing our choices in the finite world. Because human beings are at once embodied and conscious, subject and object—what Beauvoir describes as the condition of ambiguity—we cannot simply *think* about or articulate our values in the realm of ideas; we must commit ourselves to them in action, and attempt to see them through.[57]

This echo might seem suspicious. For Hayek, Alex Gourevitch and Corey Robin argue, the market provides "opportunities for existential choice"—but this is no compliment.[58] In fact, they argue, the market undercuts "those who take moral values as fixed points around which to organize some consistent shape of a life," instead driving us to treat values as "temporary, contingent, and as unfixed as yesterday's choice and tomorrow's preference."[59] Sartre's embrace of contingency might seem equally fickle—and overly compatible with Hayek's embrace of the market. In my view, however, it is precisely this resonance between Hayek's and Sartre's views of the freedom—and duty—to choose that makes Sartre's analysis of the constraints set on that freedom by the market a powerful *rejoinder* to Hayek. For what is most powerful in Hayek's view is precisely its intimation of an antifoundationalist approach to value, and its insistence that we have no choice but to choose. We *do* have to make choices about what we value, and we have to do so not only in word but in deed. We *should* look critically at appeals to a priori moral rules, communitarian virtues, or socially accepted norms.[60] It is crucial, in other words, to distinguish the market's role in undermining our ability to make genuine and lasting commitments from the idea that fixed moral values are a preferable alternative to "contingent" values altogether. It is only by recognizing that values *are* contingent rather than given, after all, that we can freely choose them; and only because they are *our values* that we care if they are overridden.

The problem lies in Hayek's view of how freedom might be realized. Against the specter of "society" as a morally unitary monolith whose values are enforced by the state, Hayek offers a view of the social as constituted through the mere aggregation of isolated individuals connected only through their own private consumer choices, which they cannot meaningfully communicate about or even understand.[61] This way of organizing both individual and collective action means not only that freedom is primarily expressed via the wildly unequally distributed medium of money, but also that even those with vast sums of wealth cannot really express the values they claim to hold. The market makes it almost impossible *even for* individuals to choose their own ends, as Hayek proclaims they must—and all the more so for collectives. The market, in other words, *limits* the power of each person to make decisions that reflect their own values, as Hayek insists we ought to be able to do.

Markets as Series

The Structure of Seriality

If the idea that we can be dominated by markets is an odd fit for republicanism and only loosely outlined by critical theory, its thrust is better captured by Sartre's concept of seriality, outlined in his *Critique of Dialectical Reason* (1964).

Sartre's effort, in this text, to reconcile his early individualist orientation with Marxism produces an unusual but generative theory of action as simultaneously atomized and social: undertaken by individuals who are at once isolated and connected by a socio-material structure, whose action is deeply constrained by the relationships this structure imposes, but which remains, in some sense, theirs.[62] This account, importantly, refuses a dichotomy between conscious agency and underlying structure. People's economic roles are largely conferred by the broader social order, and their options are curbed by its mechanisms—but they remain conscious agents making choices even within severe constraints. In other words, people's actions are not fully determined by an economic "structure" or a set of quasi-natural "forces," and they are not simply duped into acting irrationally—but nor are they really free.[63]

A series, for Sartre, is a loosely constituted collective of individuals aggregated around objects, structures, or practices to which all bear the same relation. People waiting for a bus, in his most well-known example, exemplify seriality: while individually different, each person bears the same relationship to the bus, as a potential passenger. Members of a series are typically aware of one another, but their relationships to one another are impersonal and detached. Their actions adhere to the practices and rules associated with the bus (waiting in line, buying a ticket), but they are undertaken in relative isolation. Insofar as members of a series act in relation to one another, they do so in anticipation that others are likely to act in just the same way that they themselves are. Because they are interchangeable with respect to the object or structure, members of a series typically view one another as potential competitors: each person who takes a seat on the bus threatens to block someone else from getting one. Because I expect the bus to be crowded at 5 p.m., I try not to take it until 7 p.m. Because I am anxious about getting a seat, I rush to board as quickly as possible.

As the example of the bus illustrates, seriality is not necessarily oppressive, and often it is insignificant. There is even something potentially liberatory about it, insofar as the feature of interchangeability reflects a condition of basic equality: people are not distinguished by status or personal characteristics. Seriality is always *dangerous*, however, in that it is an unconscious, habitual state in which we act in ways that reproduce familiar structures and relationships without interrogating or reflecting on them. It reflects a passive relationship to others as individuals, and to social structures as a whole—one in which we are not acting consciously, and thus one in which we perpetually risk falling into bad faith.

If the bus is Sartre's most famous example, his real interest is in more complex social formations.[64] Markets, for Sartre, are a prime example of "seriality as a force which is suffered in impotence."[65] The market "has an undeniable reality" that is "imposed on everyone," but which no one freely chooses.[66] This imposition is of a distinctive kind. Although sellers are in a competitive relationship to one another, theirs is not the antagonism of direct struggle, in which the winner gains the power to impose conditions directly on the loser. It is not, in other words, a Hegelian struggle between lord and bondsman, or a republican instance of the master who exercises arbitrary power over a slave, but rather a situation in which *everyone* is the abstract other *to everyone else*. People act in anticipation of others' actions, often hastening the effect they anticipate in the process; for example, when people dump stock that they fear will decline in price, they help to bring about its crash. This anticipatory relationship is in some ways reminiscent of that described by republicans, in which someone who is subject to the arbitrary power of another acts in servile expectation of the more powerful person's desires and commands—but the difference is that in the market, there *is* no actual person giving commands. The relationship between any given buyer and seller is conditioned by relationships among thousands, millions, even billions of other buyers and sellers, all expressed through the medium of price. We act in anticipation of the actions of anonymous others whom we do not know and will likely never meet; people who have no direct power over us, and never will—and who themselves are acting in anticipation of us.

Prices themselves are collective objects constituted through the actions of people composed as a series. Although they are generated by the "indirect" relationships among people, their strength comes from each individual's "impotence" relative to the collective. Prices in capitalist markets effectively hide decision-making—not only about the worth of individual goods, but about their worth *relative* to others. It's not really possible to evaluate one good in its own right: the price of any given good or service is determined only relative to the movement of the economy as a whole.[67] These anonymous, individual actions collectively generate outcomes that no one in particular intends, but which everyone must obey: prices are "realities which we are subjected to and which we live"; they convey "acts which we *have to do*."[68] The market thus appears as an "objective but alien necessity in every one of us"; its relations are what Iris Marion Young describes as "structured relations of alienation and anonymity that are felt as constraints on everyone."[69]

Decisions in the market are said to reflect our preferences—at least, the preferences of those who have the money to express them. Those who don't are largely invisible to the market; and in this, the poor, future generations, and nonhuman species are in more or less the same boat. Even those who *do* have money, however, can't simply choose what value they would like to attribute to different goods. I may think clean air is worth a great deal, for example, but in a true market I cannot pay what I think something is worth, or even what I negotiate with another individual. I can only pay what the market—the aggregation of millions of other buyers and sellers making transactions in competition with one another—decides it is worth, which may well be nothing at all. In the language of economics, as individuals we are all price takers, rather than price makers. If the ends to which we wish to commit ourselves include not only the fulfillment of our own personal desires but concern for the well-being of others, moreover—if we are committed to *not* consuming products made with child labor, or to *not* deforesting Indonesian jungles—we will find ourselves even more constrained, insofar as the principle of market freedom as nonresponsibility enshrines precisely the idea that we are *not* responsible to others for the effects of our actions.

Under capitalism, market rule is the dominant form of appearance of seriality.[70] Under conditions of near-universal market dependence, in turn, in which nearly all our decisions are market mediated, nonresponsibility is pervasive—and the freedom that consists in being responsible for our decisions is radically elusive. The strict *separation* of intent and consequences, the devolution of decisions to individuals alone, and the serial nature of those decisions means that the shape of the world is not one we have chosen in any meaningful sense. There is something perverse, then, about critiques of complicity that stop short of criticizing market freedom itself. We are thrown into a world in which we are enjoined to buy and sell the things we need to survive, told to think only of our own needs and leave coordination up to the market—then suddenly charged with responsibility for the harms we inadvertently perpetrate. However much we agonize over our consumer choices, the market is not and cannot be a site for the exercise of collective reason, dialogue, deliberation, or reflection.

Even decisions ostensibly made outside the market via expressly political and deliberative institutions, moreover, are often informed by market rule.[71] Governments at levels ranging from the municipal to the national exist in seriality in their own right, competing to attract private investment that can supply jobs for residents and sources of tax revenue to fund their own operations. To do so they may relax environmental regulations, fast-track permitting processes, or even actively entice polluting industries.[72] The more dire the straits of the political community in question—perhaps because they are suffering the aftermath of deindustrialization or deeply indebted following an externally imposed structural readjustment program or bearing the legacy of colonial rule—the worse the options will be.

Later chapters explore the configurations of market rule with other kinds of authority: from the *market subordination* that occurs where interpersonal domination is intensified by the market to the *market abjection* that comes with dependence on the market alone. Much of the book, however, focuses on the combination of market and class rule, which is intrinsic rather than contingent to capitalism. For as I've suggested above, capitalists, too, exist in seriality: they act in anticipation of what rivals will do, in the knowledge that they will ultimately be disciplined by the merciless rule of the market. Indeed, although market rule is most painful for the poor, it is typically most acute for capitalists. Consumers and workers are sensitive to prices, of course, often to the point that we neglect other kinds of preferences. We might take a job we dislike in order to make a higher wage, or buy a good we know is morally troubling—a car powered by internal combustion rather than electricity, perhaps—because the price is right. Roberts describes this tendency to respond to prices rather than act on one's own judgments in terms of *akrasia*.[73] But we can, so long as we're able to meet our basic material needs, forgo financial gain in hopes of realizing ethical values that we suspect aren't reflected in market valuations.

Capital, by contrast, has only one purpose—accumulation—to which all other considerations are subordinated. Private investment occurs only insofar as it is expected to be profitable, as determined in a competitive market. Competition, in turn, drives the adoption of labor-saving techniques and technologies, perpetually replacing human workers with nonhuman resources; it informs the very organization of production and underpins the kinds of workplace authority often described in terms of domination. It drives, too, capital's treatment of nonhuman nature: when one capitalist adopts a cost-cutting technology or technique, others must follow suit or risk ruin—even if those savings are achieved by dumping toxic waste in a river or working the soil to exhaustion. Because capital is oriented toward producing abstract value rather than meeting material needs, there is no point of abundance at which this process stops. What sociologists call the "treadmill of production" perpetually speeds up, and with it, the treadmill of material throughput.[74] Companies often gesture to competitive pressures as an excuse for why they simply *cannot* reduce carbon emissions or pay workers more, of course, and we should be wary of instances where such excuses are offered in bad faith. Conversely, laying blame with the individual investor or corporation can be politically potent. But overattributing responsibility to any given actor threatens to divert focus from the more fundamental nonresponsibility embedded in the overarching structure of decision-making, to which we are all subjected.[75]

An existentialist account of freedom, then, offers a necessary supplement to existing critiques of capitalist domination, articulating more clearly the freedom that capitalism thwarts: our ability to choose values for ourselves. By underscoring our inability to consciously, and collectively, decide what things are worth in a society organized around the law of value, enforced by the rule of the market, the existentialist account reveals that capitalism *frustrates* precisely the freedom it promises. The Hayekian view of the market as a forge of individual moral responsibility is a façade that obstructs a more genuine responsibility; the Friedmanian view of the market as the space where we as individuals are free to choose occludes the ways that it curbs our ability to make meaningful choices.

Materially Mediated Perversity: Counterfinality

Across different levels of action, then, markets constitutionally disaggregate intent and consequence, frequently compel us to act against our own better judgment, and limit our ability to choose values both individually and collectively. Perhaps this disconnect between intentions and consequences would be less concerning if we had faith in Smith's and Mandeville's optimistic view of markets' tendency to produce happy ends. But if the detachment of intentions from consequences has often seemed auspicious, the outcomes of a system founded on nonresponsibility can't be guaranteed. Already by the nineteenth century, Smith's optimism about unintended consequences seemed less well founded. Marx, Jon Elster argues, "stood Adam Smith on his head" by pointing to the perverse unintended consequences of market choices, arguing that capitalism's recurring crises were just as much the unintended product of aggregated market choices as its generation of wealth.[76] A century later, the critique of unintended consequences would rise to a crescendo, described in terms of "externalities" and "reflexive modernity," "free riding" and the "tragedy of the commons."[77] Warnings about the unintended consequences of human action became one of the most familiar refrains of twentieth-century environmentalism, often invoked as cautionary tales about human hubris or recklessness. Yet as we can see when we look at one of the most definitive documents of this discourse, Garrett Hardin's 1968 "The Tragedy of the Commons," they are only the most recent iteration of the debate about the unintended consequences of markets.

The central example in Hardin's tragedy concerns a group of herdsmen whose cattle graze a common field "open to all." It is in each herdsman's individual interest, Hardin argues, to add another animal to his herd since he will benefit from the eventual sale, while the impact of adding another grazer to the common pasture will be spread across all the herdsmen. But if each individual acted thus, the commons would soon be overgrazed and spoiled for everyone. "Freedom in a commons," Hardin concludes, "brings ruin to all."[78] His evocative description intentionally evokes the classical notion of tragedy as stemming from the inexorable logic of self-interested action in a world plagued by scarcity, even as it speaks to contemporary themes—namely, widespread anxiety about the status of the global peasantry in the aftermath of decolonization and racialized panic about overpopulation.[79] The basic scenario has often been abstracted into the model of the prisoner's dilemma, read as an ideal type of collective action problem that illuminates the behavior of human beings in general. It is widely invoked to describe environmental problems like pollution and overfishing in particular; climate change is cited as a paradigmatic example.[80]

Critics, meanwhile, have pointed out that people have often successfully collectively managed common resources through self-generated group rules, community norms, and social regulation.[81] Critiques of Hardin's tragedy sometimes take the form of moral tales in their own right, offering a romance of the commons as a crucial form of resistance to privatization. But to reject Hardin's analysis altogether is to turn a blind eye to the ways that capitalism has dissolved older ways of governing resources and put new pressure even on those that are still commonly managed. In fact, although Hardin's tragedy is styled as a timeless parable, the market is clearly visible around its edges. The herders he describes are not simply producing for their own benefit, but selling their animals somewhere offstage. Their action, which weighs benefits against harms on a purely individual level, is not motivated by sheer human nature, but by an assessment of market incentives, under what seem to be conditions of market dependence. The herders, in other words, are not self-sufficient subsistence farmers but market-dependent petty producers. Indeed, Hardin explicitly calls for "excorciz[ing] the spirit of Adam Smith," charging that Smith had failed to recognize that self-interested choices do not necessarily make everyone better off. Rather than exorcizing Smith, however, Hardin inverts him.[82] The tragedy of the commons describes precisely the structure of action that underpins the invisible hand—atomized individuals making choices with consequences that no one in particular intends—while taking a pessimistic view of the likely consequences.

As Steven Vogel argues, then, Hardin "accurately describes a problem endemic to market economies as such, whose (paradoxical) structure is exactly the structure that Marx described under the name of alienation."[83] Rather than alienation from nature, this is a problem of alienation from one's own action: a situation in which the things we do as individuals generate outcomes that appear as an "alien power" over and against us; where we are beset by problems we have caused, but which we can individually do nothing to alter. Its peculiar environmental dimensions are best captured by another Sartrean concept: counterfinality. Counterfinality is also a theory of unintended consequences as perverse rather than salutary, an inversion of Hegel's cunning of reason—itself also developed by way of Smith and Mandeville.[84] Yet Sartre's account emphasizes a crucial point that is only implicit in Hardin's: that human actions inevitably work through, and inscribe themselves in, the material world itself. Counterfinality is a version of the practico-actant, describing the realization, in physical form, of action that turns *against* our aims.[85]

The recalcitrance of matter is central to counterfinality: it describes how, as human action ripples through the physical world in unpredictable and uncontrollable ways, it can "become other" to us, such that our actions thwart our intentions.[86] Sartre's central illustration of counterfinality is, like Hardin's, agrarian, concerning a group of Chinese peasants who deforest a mountain in order to grow crops.[87] Their action is distinctively human: unlike a storm that randomly destroys trees, peasants systematically uproot them in order to clear the ground for planting. At the same time, their action is both conditioned and absorbed by the concrete reality of the soil, which has its own particular physical and chemical characteristics. The individual peasants are connected to one other through the medium of the soil itself, as the collective effect of their individual actions produces an emergent result that no one had intended: they inadvertently erode the soil, which the trees had kept in place, resulting in terrible and destructive floods. This is counterfinality: the peasant "produces the floods which destroy him."[88] The floods, crucially, are neither the result of the peasants' activity alone nor a sheer "act of nature." Rather, they reflect "*both* the strictness of physical causation *and* the obstinate precision of human labor": both intentional human action and the concrete materiality of the more-than-human world.[89] Thus it is "*in* and *through* labor," Sartre argues, that "Nature becomes both a new source of tools and a new threat."[90]

Like Hardin's parable, Sartre's story of counterfinality has a classically tragic quality in its suggestion that human freedom ultimately comes to ruin in a material world that perpetually foils our plans; Alberto Toscano reads it simply as the "tragedy of materiality."[91] Indeed, all social orders must contend with a world they did not make and cannot control; all kinds of action generate new material entities whose effects may thwart our intent. Read in tandem with analyses of class and market rule, however, counterfinality names the way that nature is not given but made—and made, increasingly, *by* capitalism. It can help us see how capital's social relations are not only mediated by but *instantiated in* the physical world itself. It's often said that "we" have remade the planet. But class rule means that most of us, most of the time, have very little say in what is made and how. We do not decide what buildings will be constructed or where, which products will be developed or why, which resources will be excavated or how. The decisions we do make are channeled by the market in ways that we can't predict or anticipate, and connected by the physical medium of the atmosphere, as the trillions of individually insignificant carbon molecules produced by our mundane daily actions combine to take on a terrible power. The likes of polluted air and threatened ecosystems, hurricanes and droughts, even the biosphere itself, are forms of the practico-actant, *material phenomena shaped and even made by social relations.*

Natural disasters have classically stood as *the* classic example of the difference between nature and politics: between misfortune and injustice, domination and accidental adversity, crises *for* a form of life and problems *with* a form of life.[92] However devastating the effects of a natural disaster, they are not caused by human social arrangements and so cannot indict them. But the blurring of this distinction is one of the most obvious and striking effects of the Anthropocene. A hurricane that destroys a village or drought that ravages a crop cannot, in light of the anthropogenic modification of the Earth's biosphere and climate, be understood as a blind force of nature, "act of God," or force majeure. These forces, acts, and disturbances clearly cannot be attributed to any single person; still less can they be traced to anyone's *intent*. But they are not random or merely natural. To treat them as such is to engage in what we might call, riffing on commodity fetishism, *nature fetishism*: to think that we are seeing the nonhuman world alone, or perhaps even human relationships *to* the environment, where we are really seeing social relations among people mediated *through* the environment. These phenomena, no less than intentionally constructed buildings and highways and pipelines, are aspects of the built environment, generated as the byproduct of decisions about investment; these public vices are the unintended consequences of our purchases, no less than Mandeville's public virtues. They are the unplanned—if often predictable—consequences of a form of social organization and coordination that fundamentally separates intention and effect, and constitutively devalues the material world—and that does so at progressively larger scales.

The problem, here, isn't that the world is increasingly made by rather than given to us. As Steven Vogel emphasizes, the environment, for human beings, is always a built environment; our "natural habitat" is always constructed as much as grown.[93] The problem is that our making of the world is so thoroughly out of our control. The world we live in is one we have constructed, but without any meaningful choice—and so the entire planet increasingly becomes an alien force standing over and against us.[94] The problem isn't rooted in "alienation from nature," but in alienation from ourselves, and from one another: from our practices, our actions, our responsibility, our freedom.

Countering Seriality: Constituting New Collectives

The passive, competitive relationship of seriality is, in a capitalist society, the default form of sociality. It can, however, be countered when people undertake more conscious forms of collective action oriented toward explicitly shared projects. To illustrate how consciously political groups might emerge out of seriality, consider again the simple example of riders waiting for the bus. At first they stand waiting in isolation, perhaps eyeing each other with suspicion that someone will cut the line. But perhaps eventually they begin to grumble about the bus's persistent tardiness, and the underfunding of the buses in poor neighborhoods. Perhaps they begin to meet regularly, not at the bus stop but at a local restaurant; they identify themselves as a group—maybe a bus riders' union—and start formulating a list of demands for more regular service. Perhaps they begin to work with the transit workers' union, whose members are also frustrated with stagnant wages and long hours, and begin to form a coalition representing working-class people of color in politics more generally.[95] Maybe they join forces with a group of climate activists seeking to reduce automobile use (for what is traffic but another form of seriality?). By taking conscious collective action, they regain some of the freedom they lose in seriality; by acting together they gain a power to alter the situation that they do not have alone.

Most social relations, of course, are more complex. Through simple acts like buying a T-shirt, we are connected to many other people who we'll likely never meet—those who grew the cotton, those who wove the fabric, those who sewed the shirt, those who staffed the container ship carrying garments across the world.[96] Most of the time, these relationships are represented only by the prices that emerge from the unconscious coordination of a huge number of buyers and sellers acting individually. Markets nevertheless connect people even as they atomize them; by making production deeply interdependent, they create the conditions for new forms of collective action. Actions that disrupt seriality can draw attention to the ways that markets are always also spaces of political power and disclose the material connections that markets generate. Indeed, many forms of political action under capitalism are efforts to do precisely this: to recognize the shared position that individuals hold relative to another institution or agent, and to confront it. Labor unions seek to interrupt the atomization of labor markets in which workers compete against one another, instead aligning them against the boss. Tenants' unions organize people who might otherwise compete for scarce housing units to challenge the landlord. Debtors' unions organize against the banks to which they all owe. Boycotts seek to disrupt perhaps the most atomized relationships of all—those of consumers, who are often connected only by the item they want to purchase.[97]

Attending to nonhuman nature introduces another way that people are passively connected: not only through social relations of class and market, wage labor and commodity exchange, but through the material traces that these relations leave in the world. In Sartre's example of counterfinality, the flooding caused by deforestation lays bare existing conflicts between peasants and landowners—themselves likely shaped by past struggles over access to fertile land—and may intensify them. At the same time, the floods generate new relationships among the people living in the plains below: the "universal" threat of flooding creates a common cause and forces them to decide whether and how to act collectively in response (for example, by building a dam). As capitalism remakes the physical world, from jungles reorganized as palm oil plantations to parts-per-million of carbon dioxide, the novel material entities it generates themselves also interpellate people as potential collectives.[98] Air and water pollution, for example, have often constituted the basis for organizing around the demand of environmental justice, as we'll examine more closely in chapter 4. In these instances, as much as in labor struggles, political actors must be actively composed out of the latent collectives generated by materialized social relations. Rather than exhaustively considering the ways that such groups might emerge and act together, as Sartre does in later chapters of his *Critique*, I locate moments and sites where the potential for conscious collective action is particularly significant, and identify steps—however tentative—toward more conscious group formation.

Conclusion: Resisting Bad Faith

When we refuse to countenance the possibility that things could be other than they are, or to examine the choices we make, whether alone or together, we are in what Sartre calls bad faith. Bad faith consists in the denial of our freedom, the disavowal of our responsibility. Sartre's most famous example of bad faith concerns the waiter who "play[s] at being a café waiter."[99] The waiter who performs their role a little too eagerly, he claims, shows that they are simply going through the motions of being a waiter. In fact, he argues, they are not *only* a waiter; they are a free person who is *choosing* to be a waiter—and who can always decide to stop playing that role. They can scowl at the customers, or throw the tray on the floor, or simply fail to show up to work at all. There may be consequences, but the waiter can choose to accept them: Sartre argues that the waiter has the choice "to get up each morning at five o'clock or to stay in bed, even if that gets [them] sacked."[100] Bad faith consists in denying that they are making a choice at all.

This will strike most readers as glib, and rightly so. What kind of a choice does the waiter really have? Read aslant, however, the instance of the waiter illustrates precisely the types of unfreedom I have described here. Instead of focusing on the waiter's inauthenticity, we might ask another question: why someone should have to spend so much time pretending to be a waiter in the first place. After all, the example of the waiter is revealing not only qua waiter but because Sartre could have made the same point with respect to any number of other jobs.[101] No one *is* their job, not even those fortunate few who see their job as a vocation. So why do so many of us play our roles so well? Why do we get up each day and go to work? More fundamental than the question of which *particular* roles we are compelled to perform—waiter, professor, miner, flight attendant—is the fact that nearly all of us have to work for wages in order to live, to submit to someone else's direction, and thus to spend a large part our lives acting as something that we are not. Sartre is right that the waiter has a choice each morning: they really can decide whether or not to go to work. The fact of class rule, however, means that they have a very good reason to go. As Sartre himself would later acknowledge, one might choose whether to be a waiter, but not whether to be a proletarian.[102] It's important, though, both to Sartre's social theory and to our understanding of capitalism, that some measure of freedom persists. As he writes in the *Critique* of the worker who sells his labor power at a pittance, "It is true that he has no other way out; the choice is an impossible one"—and yet his is still the action of a (doubly) free human being.[103] This is why it is so imperative to investigate the structures of choice itself.

It's not only class rule that compels the waiter. The overperforming waiter may be putting on a show for the customers, in hopes of a tip (admittedly less likely in postwar France), or for the manager, in anticipation of their reprimand.[104] The manager, meanwhile, may be under pressure from the café owner to increase revenue, who in turn is trying to keep the café afloat in a competitive industry with low margins and concerned about losing customers to the café down the street. Nobody *has* to do any of this, of course—the manager, too, could refuse to show up to work; the owner could sell the café—but then each will have to find some other way to make a living. The waiter's performance, in other words, is not simply a mark of individual inauthenticity, but a response to the authority of class power and the mute compulsion of market rule. The waiter usefully illustrates the way that we are compelled to play certain roles by virtue of our position within social systems, which themselves structure and constrain our relations to other people and to the nonhuman world; the way that our ostensibly free actions are channeled by, and unintentionally reinforce, structures we haven't consciously built.

Bad faith, crucially, is not only an individual condition. We are collectively in bad faith when we act as if we have no choice but to organize society in the way it is structured at present, when we treat what Iris Marion Young describes as "social-structural processes" as though they were "natural forces"—and so too when we treat social forms as if they were natural ones.[105] This pertains to nature itself: we are in bad faith when we treat our socially specific relationships to the nonhuman world as if they were themselves natural. A fish or a rock or a virus cannot be in bad faith in the way that a human being can—or if they can, we can't yet know it. But we, as human beings, can be in bad faith with respect to the more-than-human world, insofar as we accept that nature simply *is* what capitalism declares it to be. Just as we are frequently compelled to treat other people as workers and competitors, we are compelled to treat nonhuman nature as a free gift—regardless of our individual ethical assessments or moral values. We are in bad faith when we take these relations to nonhumans for granted, when we treat nonhumans as if they *are* the meaning our society has assigned them. When we look at a pine tree and see lumber, or at a bluefin tuna and see sushi, we are making the same error as we do when we look at a human being and see a waiter. We are in bad faith, too, when we conclude that the nonhuman world simply *is* a free gift across time—that all human societies would necessarily treat nonhuman nature as something that can be taken without return.

To be in bad faith, in other words, is to fail to recognize that we could see the nonhuman world differently, and to fail to recognize the existence of the more-than-human world in excess of *any* meaning we give it. Jade Schiff describes bad faith as a refusal to "cultivate responsiveness"—a denial of our capacity to respond to and be responsible to others—including, potentially, the more-than-human others on which we depend.[106] It is a failure to be responsive to the more-than-human world in its own right, even while grappling with the challenging fact that we can never fully stand outside of ourselves in doing so.[107] To say that the free gift of nature is a social form is, at the most basic level, to refuse bad faith by saying simply that this relationship could be other than it is.

We are usually in bad faith, insofar as the seriality of the market is the default modality in which we act. Most of the time, we pay what a price tag says something is worth, and accept that as, more or less, its value. It's precisely because the free gift of nature *fails* to appear in the form of price, however, that it can act as a wedge into the broader structure of capitalist valuation. When we start to wonder why an obviously valuable thing—clean air or a stable climate—isn't valued at all, we might start to wonder about value itself. The free gift, in other words, reveals the gap between how things are valued in the market and how they might be valued otherwise. With an eye to the project of what Martin Hägglund calls (following Nietzsche) the revaluation of values, I aim to tease out judgments that might challenge capitalist valuations, even where they are not articulated as such.[108] Instead of offering a set of principles according to which we might value nature differently, in other words, I attend to those that are already latent in thought and practice.

The freedom to choose is ultimately not an individual project; decisions about the collective transformation of our entire planet are not ones that can be made alone. We must reflect on the institutions and structures that organize our lives and the kinds of actions they make possible or prohibit, encourage or dissuade. We must consider whether they reflect the ways we want to live, the values we want to affirm, the choices we want to make—and if they do not, we must take it upon ourselves to change them.[109] This is what it would mean to take climate change seriously as an existential threat: to take it as a charge to genuinely reevaluate and revise our collective ways of life; to recognize our responsibility not only for some quantity of carbon emissions but for the world we have made and could make differently, if never fully as we please. We, as human beings, have to take responsibility for how we relate to the more-than-human world, because no one and nothing else can.[110] We will surely disagree about what this entails—and this is precisely why we can't simply gesture to a singular Nature to resolve such fundamentally political questions. We have to answer them for ourselves.

3

The Natural Machine

LABOR AND NATURE IN THE HIDDEN ABODE

IN 1958, the French manufacturer Péchiney hired the film director Alain Resnais, later to become a leading light of the nouvelle vague, to produce a short film on the production of the plastic styrene.[1] *Le chant du styrène*—a play on the siren song that tempted Odysseus—begins with a quote from Victor Hugo: "Man is served by blind matter. He thinks, he searches, he creates. With his living breath the seeds of nature tremble as a forest rustles in the wind."[2] Sprouts and flowers made of styrene blossom forth in primary colors: clearly artificial, yet mimicking the forms of the organic world. They are gradually replaced by a series of products with the abstract shapes, sharp lines, and right angles of industrial design, before the camera comes to rest on the image of a solitary red plastic bowl. The rest of the film traces the production of the bowl in reverse: beginning with the mold that "begets" it, then turning to vast inhuman landscapes of machinery, pipes, and circulating chemicals, before eventually contemplating "the raw matter, the abstract materials" of which styrene itself is made.

The film is a puckish celebration of modernity's triumphs over nature, of the genius of the (male) scientist, of what the American chemical company DuPont famously called "better things for better living through chemistry."[3] It is also a document of the so-called "golden age" of capitalism, the *trente glorieuses*—the three decades of growth and relatively shared prosperity that characterized life in western Europe and the United States after World War II, in which the "problem of production" seemed to have been solved.[4] Yet in references to the "raw matter" of which the plastic bowl is made, snippets of other worlds slip in. Styrene, the narrator notes, had once been extracted from benzoin, gleaned from the "Indonesian *styrax* bush," but now is produced artificially from the compound ethylbenzene—itself extracted from coal and oil.

Over the image of vast quantities of steaming coal, the narrator intones: "We could investigate further why both coal and oil exist. Does oil come from piles of fish? . . . Could oil be the fruit of plankton's labor?"

The narrator quickly abandons these lighthearted and offhanded questions as too "controversial" and "obscure." From the vantage point of the Anthropocene, however, they appear far more significant. Capitalism's worldmaking power once seemed to lie in its capacity for developing the forces of production, as epitomized by the vast factories of mass industry. And yet as *Le chant du styrène* itself notes, even the industrial sublimity of the factory ultimately relies on the heaping piles of coal generated by "plankton's labor." Even plastics, those iconic materials of artifice and alienation, are ultimately composed of prehistoric life forms compressed by the gravitational force of the planet over inhuman stretches of time. Within the film's celebration of industrial progress, then, seems to lurk a counternarrative about its persistent reliance on the natural world it claims to have conquered.

The factory is not an intuitive place to begin the study of the free gift of nature. Manufacturing is typically understood as the realm of quintessentially *artificial* production, characterized by inhuman machines. Since the Romantics, lovers of nature have looked aghast at the dark satanic mills that ravage the green countryside. In the twentieth century, the rapid acceleration of industrial production spurred the emergence of an antagonistic environmental movement. The suspicion of industry has often extended to industrial workers: environmental politics have frequently been construed in opposition to labor politics (typically assumed to be industrial), as evidenced by countless debates over "jobs versus environment."[5] Labor is said to belong to the realm of class politics, confronting capital at the point of production, while environmental politics are classified as "new social movements" oriented around ways of life rather than economic concerns.[6]

This chapter approaches the relation between labor and environment, nature and the factory, from a different angle. To understand how industrial production has remade the world, we need to understand not only how it affects nature outside the factory, but how it utilizes nature *within* it. Similarly, rather than seeing the politics of capitalism and nature in terms of conflicts between workers in the factory and the environment outside it, we have to understand the politics of how capital organizes labor and nature within the production process itself. For as Resnais's film suggests, the free gifts of nature are at work in even the most seemingly artificial spaces. In fact, in industrial production, there are *two* kinds of free gifts at work: those generated by natural agents deployed in novel ways through technology and machinery, and the free gifts that arise from cooperation among members of one species in particular—the gifts of social *human* labor, which increase with coordination. This chapter shows how capital exerts control over production to maximize both gifts, and foregrounds the oft-overlooked significance of natural agents themselves in realizing or obstructing that control. The factory is where capitalism's logic is most fully realized, instantiated in physical form—and enabled by certain kinds of natural agents. Yet although it is often taken to be the quotidian site of capitalist production, the factory is exceptional.[7]

———

Although industrial production lies in the backdrop of nearly all modern political thought, it is more often assumed than analyzed. Political theory has tended to treat production as a technical phenomenon, to be distinguished from the realm of the genuinely political. For decades, it was bracketed entirely by theorists of justice who identified the distribution of wealth produced as the relevant political question.[8] Many Marxists, for their part, have similarly treated the forces of production as "socio-neutral," equally compatible with either capitalism or socialism.[9]

More recently, however, political theorists have begun to identify production as a site of politics in its own right. Many have drawn on radical interpretations of the republican tradition, often rooted in nineteenth-century labor republicanism, to identify the operation of authority and arbitrary power within the workplace and offer compelling critiques of domination.[10] Yet these forays into the politics of production remain surprisingly immaterial. They say little about what goes on inside the hidden abode: about what workers actually *do* or *make*—let alone about how labor structures human relationships to nature, or vice versa. Labor appears not as a physical activity but a generic, even abstract phenomenon. The implication is that its particularities are irrelevant: what matters is the arbitrary power of the boss over the worker.

By contrast, this chapter argues that the material features of the concrete labor process have major consequences not only for "the environment," but for understanding the organization of production itself and the various forms of domination that pertain therein. To explore these questions, I draw on a body of thought that understands production to be fundamentally structured by capitalist social relations. Critical theories of production, technology, and the labor process have challenged the standard view of industrialization as a phenomenon of "neutral and inevitable technological change," offering in its place an account of how capital designs the very technologies and infrastructures required to achieve its ends.[11] On this account, there is a political content to the *physical* organization of production itself. Marx describes a key process in terms of subsumption: as capital absorbs and subordinates concrete labor processes, it exerts increasingly overt control over both human laborers and nonhuman components of production.[12] Subsumption is concerned with how capital makes the world in the most literal sense: how it orders tasks, designs technologies, and even engineers living organisms in service of its singular end.

Subsumption is typically seen as progressive: capital gradually integrates and more fully subordinates both human labor and nonhuman elements, culminating in the perfect order of the factory. Many critics of mass production have assumed, just as much as its boosters, that its hallmarks—standardization, rationalization, homogeneity—would continue to spread across the world. But if the factory represents the pinnacle of rationalized production, its form is far from universal. Capital's ability to achieve despotic control within it depends on an element typically taken for granted: the specific *qualities* of natural agents. In industry, capital relies on certain kinds of natures: inanimate energies and inorganic materials that can be precisely engineered to effectively channel its prerogatives, and to mediate its domination of the worker. Not all kinds of nature, however, are equally suited to this role.

While the chapter begins in the factory, then, it eventually turns to other hidden abodes. "Nature-based" sectors, in which nature is directly cultivated or extracted, remain perpetually reliant on biophysical processes, which operate according to their own logics, and which often preclude rationalization on the factory model.[13] These sectors have tended to deviate from the industrial rule. They are disproportionately marked by seemingly anachronistic forms of labor, from piecework to sharecropping. They have been understood as sites of underdevelopment or "stages" along the way to maturity, and explicitly excluded from statistical measures and labor regulations. Indeed, while the twentieth century is synecdochally identified with Fordism, it was the problem of the peasant as much as the proletariat that occupied many social and political thinkers, from the Chicago School to Marxist anthropology, ecological economics to subaltern studies.[14] The challenges of nonindustrial production spurred a remarkable number of the signature ideas of late twentieth-century social science: modernization and dependency theories, the tragedy of the commons, the resource curse, Dutch disease, human capital theory.

If the unusual dynamics of these sectors have often been cause for perplexity, they have also frequently been romanticized by thinkers across the political spectrum. On the one hand, nature-based production is sometimes characterized as peripheral to or "outside" of capitalism altogether—and even as a form of resistance to capital. Anna Tsing, for example, characterizes matsutake mushroom harvesting as an instance of "pericapitalist" production, in which capital creates value without controlling production overall.[15] Matsutake cannot be cultivated industrially; they grow wild in the woods, where they are foraged by independent pickers. Matsutake pickers thus work in "freedom," Tsing argues: they don't sell their labor for a wage, and no one tells them what to produce or how; they therefore stand at once inside and outside of capitalism. For Tsing, the persistence of these "pericapitalist" and even "noncapitalist forms" is a reason for cautious hope: they can be "sites for rethinking the unquestioned authority of capitalism in our lives."[16] Yet for others, the figure of the independent commodity producer connected to the land represents the opposite—capitalism's essence rather than its outside. From the ordoliberal idealization of the small farmer to Reagan's celebration of the cowboy, the right has often celebrated the small rural producer as the icon of capitalist freedom. For neoliberal thinkers of the twentieth century, the rancher and the farmer, beholden neither to bureaucrats nor bosses, seemed to offer alternatives to the unionized wage worker and the centrally planned firm. Agriculture, the economist John Brewster wrote in 1950, "is one of the last outposts of 'rugged individualism' with its creed of the 'self-made man.'"[17]

Both of these views of the independent producer contain echoes of the classical republican tradition, which exalts agrarian smallholders as bastions of independence against the dependence of wage slavery and trumpets the virtue of rural life over the venality of urban commerce.[18] Yet in truth neither the matsutake picker nor the rancher is self-sufficient in any meaningful sense—let alone free. Matsutake pickers may be able to forage when and where they please—but they must compete with one another to find mushrooms and sell them to powerful brokers with connections to wealthy consumers overseas. Ranchers may own their own land—but they must sell the calves they raise to industrial feedlots that set the price per pound at rock bottom (which themselves are squeezed by meatpackers, themselves under pressure from retail giants, themselves seeking to undercut competitors on prices).[19] These conditions typify those faced by many producers in nature-based sectors: they may operate on a small scale relative to the mass production of the factory, but they are integrated into global trade networks, disciplined by market rule, and subjected to class rule—here exerted not through the power of an employer but through the outsized market power of buyers and creditors. Capital's authority is ubiquitous in their lives—it simply operates at a distance.

As this chapter shows, the positions of the matsutake forager and the rancher exemplify a particular configuration of capital, labor, and nature. They reflect the peculiar conditions of sectors in which natural exigencies impede control of the labor process to the extent that capital *abdicates* control over production altogether. Abdication is not a defeat for capital but, rather, a strategy for capital accumulation under the conditions of high uncertainty that attend certain kinds of natural variability. Where nature is unreliable, such that investment is risky, capital leaves the coordination of production up to others—and intervenes at other points in the accumulation process.[20] Even where the parties never appear in the classical form of worker and employer who together descend into the sphere of production, producers in nature-based sectors are often subjugated by capital: by the coercion of buyers who set the conditions of exchange for small producers, by the merchant's monopsony power, by the bankers who extend credit on extortionate terms.[21] These relationships are not well captured by either labor republican accounts of domination in the workplace or visions of agrarian republican independence. An analysis of how class power operates beyond the direct labor-capital relation is vital for understanding the peculiarities of labor in nature-facing sectors—and those of the many other kinds of labor that deviate from the industrial norm.

Although this chapter begins in the industrialized, homogenized factory, then, it ultimately emphasizes the heterogeneity of forms that capitalist production takes. It provincializes the factory not in order to decenter capitalism, but the contrary: to show how capitalism structures even the kinds of production that do not appear in its image. It emphasizes the view from the "margins" of capitalist production not in order to champion the alternative ways of life found there, but to show that they, too, orbit around capital—and to show, for that matter, that they are not really marginal at all. As *Le chant du styrène* shows, they go to capitalism's heart.

The Gifts in the Machine

Two Free Gifts

Where, in the factory, are the free gifts of nature at work? One place is obvious: in the inhuman machines themselves, where they are enhanced through the application of scientific knowledge and channeled in new ways. The Industrial Revolution is often understood by both its critics and admirers as the result of what historian David Landes describes as the "rational manipulation" of nature, resulting in technologies that could replace and enhance the power of human labor.[22] Industry, the Abbé Sieyes held, consists in "perfect[ing] the gifts of nature," reorganizing them to unleash tremendous productive powers.[23] Classical political economists saw natural agents at work in the machines of the factory system: Jean-Baptiste Say argued that machinery "forc[es] into service of man a variety of natural agents" providing "gratuitous aid" to production.[24] As David Ricardo similarly observed: "The pressure of the atmosphere and the elasticity of steam, which enable us to work the most stupendous engines—are they not the gifts of nature? There is not a manufacture which can be mentioned, in which nature does not give her assistance to man, and give it too, generously and gratuitously."[25] To many critics, by contrast, industrialization has seemed to mark the domination and even death of nature, standing as the pinnacle of what Carolyn Merchant calls the "mechanical world view" which has rendered the more-than-human world fragmented, substitutable, mere dead matter to be molded for human interests.[26]

Marx is often thought to belong to the former camp, seen as an unabashedly Promethean advocate of industrial production.[27] He famously admired the technological wonders conjured up by the bourgeoisie, observing that capitalism had unleashed previously unimaginable productive forces through the "subjection of nature's forces to man"—even as he held that only communism could put those forces to work in service of truly universal abundance.[28] But Marx's view of industry is more complicated, and more ambivalent. Production, he thought, is fundamentally political, shot through with class struggle and social relations. If he did not always attend specifically to what we might today describe as the ecological effects of industrial production, his analysis of the interrelation of social and physical elements within it remains essential for understanding the role of nature—both in the social form of free gift and the natural form of matter—within the heart of the factory.

The core of production, for Marx, is the labor process, through which human beings act on and transform nature, in an interchange that both reveals the hidden potentialities of the nonhuman world and develops human capacities. Labor processes exist in all societies, insofar as people always have to make at least some of the things they need to survive, and they are always informed by the determinate features of the societies in which they exist. The capitalist labor process, however, is distinctive, as we have seen: it hitches the labor process to what Marx describes as the valorization process. The valorization process begins in the market, where the capitalist purchases all the necessary components—raw materials, tools, instruments, and the labor power of the worker—and then moves into the abode of production itself, where the capitalist alone organizes the labor process. The capitalist alone owns the product that results, which they go on to sell in the realm of exchange—beginning the cycle over again. Their goal in this process is not to produce use value, but to generate surplus value—and this end reverberates back through the means of production. It was this distinction that Marx thought the classical political economists effaced, and which led them to take the status of the free gifts of nature in production largely for granted.

Natural agents contribute to production not only by virtue of their sheer physical capacities—like the steam engine's ability to produce atmospheric pressure—but also the fact that they give this assistance, in Ricardo's phrase, "generously and *gratuitously*." The term neatly encapsulates the dual character of the free gift of nature: material capacities paired with an *absence* of exchange value. Their gratuitous quality is implicitly defined in relation to the costly human labor they are intended to supplement and replace. But as Marx notes, to attribute these qualities to natural agents per se is misguided: nature's gifts do not automatically work for capital any more than workers do. The elasticity of steam, for example—the way that water molecules spread out and become gaseous when heated—becomes a source of power only when harnessed by an engine built by human labor.[29] Although Marx observes that machines, once constructed, "do their work for nothing, like the natural forces which are already available without the intervention of human labour," he is emphatic that machines are only *like* natural forces. To understand how they operate within a given production process requires an analysis of how they are ordered by *human* labor. Thus Marx argues that in large-scale industry, "the product of . . . past labor" has been made to "perform gratuitous service on a large scale, *like a force of nature*."[30] While machines channel the forces of nature, in other words, they are not *themselves* free gifts of nature but, rather, objectifications of past human labor, deploying the knowledge of nature accumulated by human beings in general. While Marx rightly emphasizes the human role in bringing forth certain natural capacities, however, his description of machines as "objectifications" of human labor is curiously devoid of actual *objects*—of the sense of machines as entities that, however manmade, are nonetheless made up of nonhuman elements with qualities of their own. We'll return to this shortly.

A second, less obvious gift of nature is also at work in large-scale industrial production: the cooperation of human workers, which Marx sees as the "creation of a new productive power" in its own right.[31] When people work together, they divide tasks for greater efficiency, they share infrastructure and tools. They are invigorated by social contact, and perhaps even friendly rivalry. They coordinate across stretches of time and space that exceed the capacity of any individual. They develop new techniques and knowledge over time, which anyone else can use. Put simply, people working together are more than the sum of their parts. The element of *more*—the excess capacity that stems from coordination—is a gift of nature, a "natural force of social labor," in the sense that it stems from the distinctive capacities of human beings qua humans, engaging in distinctively human forms of social interaction.[32] As Marx notes, "When the worker co-operates in a planned way with others, he strips off the fetters of his individuality, and develops the capabilities of his species."[33] Just as machines reveal the hidden powers of nature—the ability of steam to drive a machine, for example—we might say cooperative labor reveals previously unknown capabilities of human beings, showing what's possible when human activity is arranged in particular ways. But in a capitalist society, Marx argues, this novel power, the "socially productive power of labour," develops—like all other gifts of nature—"as a free gift to capital." Although the capitalist pays each individual worker a set wage, their emergent collective capacity "costs capital nothing."[34] When cooperation increases, in other words, the capitalist alone captures the benefits.

The potential gains that come with increasing cooperation in turn drive the capitalist to exert intensive control over human labor. Within the factory, Marx is explicit, the "capitalist formulates his autocratic power over his workers like a private legislator."[35] The wage, the standard form of payment for labor power, measures time rather than output. The capitalist seeks to maximize use of that time, using various kinds of labor discipline and organizing workers in ways that maximize the free gift of cooperation. But the autocratic power of the boss doesn't exist in a vacuum. While capitalists themselves "acknowledge no authority other than that of competition," competition is a stern master.[36] The need to compete drives capital to continually restructure production in pursuit of greater efficiencies: to push workers to work faster and longer, reorganize the labor process so that workers cooperate more efficiently, and replace human workers with machinery. The valorization process, through which goods are sold as commodities such that capital receives a return on investment, feeds back into the concrete activities of labor; in other words, the labor process itself is changed by the social relations in which it takes place. It is the specific *unity* of production and exchange, then, the combination of market rule and class power, that gives the workplace its despotic character.[37] It is class power that permits the capitalist to direct the worker's activity after purchasing their labor power, and market rule that drives the capitalist to intensify it.

Subsumption and the Reordering of Nature

The concept Marx uses to describe this this unity is *subsumption*. As Andrés Saenz de Sicilia argues, subsumption "describes most directly what the specificity of capitalist domination consists in."[38] The term is a philosophical concept denoting the incorporation of the particular within the universal. Marx, however, deploys it to describe the process of progressive inclusion and absorption by which capital draws production more directly into its orbit, and subordinates the concrete labor process to its ends.[39] Subsumption therefore reflects the interaction between abstract and concrete, form and content: it reveals how, as capital exerts authority over production, it also incorporates and reconfigures the process by which human labor materially transforms nature. The social and material dimensions of this process are clearly articulated in Marx's account of the two major types of subsumption: formal and real subsumption.

Formal subsumption describes capital's assimilation of labor processes developed under noncapitalist modes of production through the imposition of capitalist social relations.[40] A capitalist might pay wages to a tailor, who uses her own tools to make shirts in the same way she always has, with the crucial difference that the capitalist now owns the resulting product. Capital has imposed a new social relationship on a process—introducing wage labor in place of independent production—without substantially modifying the process itself. The only way to increase production, in this arrangement, is to make workers work longer. But this has obvious limits in the capacity of the human body, and in the length of the day itself. Thus formal subsumption is typically understood as a transitional stage on the way to real subsumption— what Marx describes as a *"specifically capitalist mode of production"* in which the labor process *itself* is reorganized in order to achieve greater efficiency and productivity by intensifying and rationalizing, rather than simply extending, labor.[41]

Where formal subsumption transforms the social basis of production, in other words, real subsumption transforms it *physically*.[42] In particular, real subsumption aims to maximize—and even to produce—the free gift of human cooperation. First the capitalist encourages greater cooperation in the simplest possible way, by hiring multiple workers and bringing them physically together. The next step is the division of labor: the labor process is broken into discrete and simple tasks, which are distributed among workers. Here the tailors are assigned positions within a rough assembly line, so that one person cuts fabric, another stitches sleeves, another sews buttons, and so on. The apex of real subsumption, and of capitalist control over production, comes with the introduction of large-scale machinery, both as a supplement to and replacement for human labor. At this stage, it is the machines that perform the actions of cutting, stitching, and so on; the workers are simply auxiliaries. In the really subsumed workplace, epitomized by the vast Péchiney factory, both free gifts—those of human cooperation and the nonhuman forces channeled by machinery—are coordinated into a continuous, overarching process oriented toward valorization, generating a gift of cyborgian cooperation.[43]

Although formal and real subsumption are often discussed as two discrete moments, they are better understood as existing on a continuum. In actuality, instances in which the shift to wage labor is purely formal, having *no* effect on the material organization of labor activities, are rare; by the same token, so too are instances in which the labor process is *fully* under capital's control—as we'll examine in more detail. For now, two points in particular bear emphasizing. First is that capital tends to redesign natural agents for its specific purposes. The natural agents at work in production are, as Marx notes, channeled through devices built by human beings—and where they are owned by capital, they are built with the express purpose of maximizing surplus value. In real subsumption, we can see how capital's drive toward accumulation is expressed in and through the physical elements of production; how machines and shop floors are designed to instantiate capital's power in physical form; how nonhuman elements come to serve not only as tools, instruments, or resources, but as *mediators* of capitalist control. The second is that capital makes particular use of certain *kinds* of natural agents: those that facilitate its control over production. In other words, some material qualities are more suited than others to achieving the physical reorganization of production that real subsumption requires—and the significance of this fact has been radically underappreciated.

Natural Barriers

Because the shift from formal to real subsumption entails a wholesale physical reorganization of the labor process, it requires greater control over both human and natural agents involved in production. Marx's discussion of the regulation of the working day by the Factory Acts provides a clarifying illustration of the implications with respect to natural processes in particular. The industries that most vociferously opposed the regulation of working hours, he notes, were those that relied in some way on "organic, chemical, and physiological processes," on the grounds that the temporal exigencies of these processes would be misaligned with the rhythms of a regulated workday. Potters, for instance, claimed that their work would become impossible, because clay couldn't be made to dry on schedule. Such industries tended to rely on the "sweated labor" of cheap workers, usually women and children, employed for punishingly long hours. And yet when work hours were regulated by the Factory Acts, potters did not go out of business. Rather, they developed technologies that allowed production to continue within the new limits. The cost of pottery declined and the rate of output increased. Pottery production, in other words, was really subsumed.[44] Although capitalists had claimed that certain "natural barriers" were intractable, they had found a way to do the impossible when forced: as Marx concludes, "no poison kills vermin with more certainty than the Factory Act removes such 'natural barriers.'"[45] Appeals to the "natural barriers" to more efficient production were simply an excuse for the "waste of human life" in long hours spent at work; the implication is that they can, and eventually will, be overcome.[46]

The key to capitalism's extraordinary dynamism, this account suggests, lies not only in a general human "mastery" of nature; rather, the mastery of nature itself develops as a front in the ongoing class struggle. Where workers impose limits upon capital, capital responds by overcoming ostensibly natural limits, thereby revolutionizing production. In turn, theorists like Harry Braverman and Moishe Postone argue, the technologies designed by capitalists do not simply reflect growing human knowledge of nature in general, as standard accounts of innovation suggest. Rather, they are designed specifically in order to maximize control over the production process. Technology is not a politically neutral force, as socialists like G. A. Cohen have often claimed, but is, as Postone argues, "inextricably related to, and molded by, the basic social relations of that society."[47] Both labor processes and technologies themselves are fundamentally imbued with the imperatives of value production and shaped by past struggles between labor and capital. This suggests a major revision to dominant theories of both technological development and industrialization, one which sees the organization of nature and organization of society as fundamentally intertwined.[48]

A crucial political consequence of this account is often overlooked, however: technology is not only *molded by* social relations but *mediates* social relations. The domination of some people by others is often enacted *through* nonhuman agents reconfigured by capital. Real subsumption demands precise coordination of both labor and machinery; thus the second industrial revolution gave rise to what Alfred Chandler calls the "managerial revolution," in which capitalists deployed new practices of scientific labor management and new forms of supervisory authority. It is this *particular* form of "authority relation," wherein capital exerts direct and precise control over labor, that analyses of workplace domination have studied most carefully; it is the basis of what Elizabeth Anderson calls "private government" and Michael Burawoy describes as "market despotism."[49] But the natural agents at work in the physical organization of production itself have played a significant role in management in their own right. "Machinery," Braverman argues, "offers to management the opportunity to do by wholly mechanical means that which it had previously attempted to do by organizational and disciplinary means."[50] Although machines are widely understood as means of replacing costly human labor, equally important is their role in facilitating and even automating *managerial* labor, by objectifying the relations of production in the physical form of the machine. As the coordination of human workers and nonhuman elements of production becomes increasingly important, the machine—tireless, reliable, precise—becomes indispensable as a tool for regulating labor. The machine, as designed by the capitalist, tells the worker which task to perform (press this button, pull this lever); through its automated pace, the machine *itself* acts as a clock, enforcing time discipline directly by setting and speeding the pace of labor. As Sartre observes, "In a society in which one class owns the instruments of labor while others use them to produce commodities for a wage, it is precisely matter and the practico-inert object *which mediate between men*."[51] The machine *stands in* for capital; it is a practico-actant par excellence.

Where machines mediate control, the class power of the capitalist, the authority of the manager, and the immediacy of class struggle can recede from view. The manager doesn't need to shout at the worker to keep up the pace when widgets keep coming down the assembly line. Think here of the famous scene in *I Love Lucy* where Ethel and Lucy get a job in a chocolate factory.

While they are initially given instructions by a stern manager (a woman whose severity leads Lucy to address her as "Sir"), the manager then retreats from the scene, leaving the conveyor belt itself to set the pace—to famously comedic effect.[52] What the scene shows is how the machine channels market rule, class power, and managerial authority to command labor, while disguising these social relations as technical or objective qualities of matter. As Landes notes, "there is no overseer so demanding as the click clack of the machine"; the machine deployed by capital, Marx observes, is "not only an automaton but an autocrat."[53]

Crucially, however, for all the "natural barriers" that capital has overcome, not all natural agents are equally effective as material instantiations of the capitalist's will. The specific qualities of natural agents remain immensely important even in the heart of industry: Industrialization, it is widely recognized, substitutes inanimate forms of energy and inorganic matter for living and organic ones. This substitution is key to the process of real subsumption, and key to the subordination of labor to capital.

The Matter of the Machine

The significance of particular *material* qualities in extending control over the labor process is well illustrated by the transition, at the heart of the Industrial Revolution, from organic to inanimate sources of energy—and in particular, from water, wind, and muscle to steam power generated by coal. Coal is, we might say, is a gift of nature par excellence. It stores up the force of sunbeams, the only source of truly free energy, captured by the photosynthesizing power of plants long since deceased, compressed by what the political economist William Stanley Jevons called the "labor of natural forces"—the force of gravity and the geothermal energy radiating from the Earth's core. A ton of coal contains thousands of years' worth of sunlight, available for immediate use. Coal's usefulness, however, lies not only in the sheer quantity of energy it provides, but its physical *qualities*, which in the nineteenth century were widely recognized to be indispensable for the new age of machine production. As Jevons observed in *The Coal Question* (1865), published just two years before the first volume of *Capital*, the energy used to power the machinery of the nascent factory system had to be, above all else, "wholly at our command, to be exerted when and where and in what degree we desire."[54] Wind, tides, and flowing water were each inadequate in this regard, Jevons noted, either too temporally variable or too spatially fixed to be deployed whenever and wherever necessary.[55] Coal, by contrast, was a dense source of energy, easy to transport and easy to burn. Where water power threw up natural barriers to continuous production in the form of unpredictable and uncontrollable flows, coal could work around the clock, unaffected by seasonal cycles, geographic location, or the various other contingencies that beset wind and water. Thus, Jevons concluded, "the sun annually showers down upon us about a thousand times as much heat-power as is contained in all the coal we raise annually, yet that thousandth part, being under perfect control, is a sufficient basis of all our economy and progress."[56]

Coal was irreplaceable, in other words, because it enabled perfect control over the labor process. Where deployed under conditions of class rule, as Andreas Malm observes in *Fossil Capital*, it more specifically enabled capital to exert greater control over labor. The irregularity of water and wind, and the inability to deploy them on command, meant that capitalists could not reliably speed up production when necessary, or move factories elsewhere when they faced labor shortages or worker unrest. "If the autonomy of the working class is to be fought by a regiment of machinery," Malm argues, "the prime mover— the field commander—had better be reliable."[57] Water and wind were not. The failure of water to flow on schedule or wind to blow on time in turn enabled and emboldened the political resistance of workers. "Water, like workers, subverted capitalist authority," Malm claims—and in so doing lent support to workers' own subversion.[58] It was the regulation of the working day via the Ten Hours Bill that drove capital to overcome the "natural barriers" of wind and water energy, just as it had overcome the barriers posed by slow-drying clay. In order to maximize labor within the limited time of the regulated working day, capital had to exert tighter control over production, and hence over the energy that powered it. This required turning to coal—a form of energy that could be utilized exactly as capital required, unaffected by contingencies of time or place. Coal, Malm concludes, is a form of really subsumed energy, which enabled the real subsumption of labor.[59]

The switch to coal power highlights the essential difference that matter makes to production, illustrating how production is fundamentally structured by *content* as well as form. It makes clear, too, that capital does not "dominate nature" in any general or totalizing sense. Rather, it makes use of those *particular* natures that are suited to mediating the domination of some human beings by others. Malm's account thus provides an energetic supplement to Marx's story of progressive subsumption: water power is a "legacy" from the precapitalist era of concrete time, which is eventually superseded; really subsumed energies substitute for formally subsumed ones.[60] It is in keeping with most critical analyses of production, which similarly view subsumption as a progressively unfolding phenomenon—one that is now perhaps complete.[61] In these accounts, capital dispatches with one natural barrier after another: it gradually substitutes inanimate energy for muscle power and minerals for organic material; it banishes autonomous living natures and replaces them with dead matter, which, lacking a life or will of its own, does only its master's bidding.[62] Where once the patterns of labor were set by the seasons or rise and fall of the sun, capital imposes the abstract and regular time of the clock, with which it measures the working day to the second.[63] These accounts suggest, too, that machines can be made to *perfectly* express the will of capital—that matter is infinitely malleable, capable of being shaped in perfect accordance with the demands of valorization. They describe a world in which capital's drive toward abstract value has triumphed definitively over biophysical obstacles, and capital's despotism over the worker—enabled by its mastery of nature—is total.[64]

As descriptions of capital's tendential logic, these are largely accurate. Capital has succeeded, to an extraordinary degree, in overcoming natural barriers in the drive to control production. They categorically overstate, however, capital's success in making the world conform to its will. As Burawoy notes, the conditions in which capital achieves such total control over production are not the norm but rather "problematic, contingent, and indeed rare."[65] While the command that capital exerts over both nature and labor within the factory is taken to be the rule, it is better understood as the exception. There are many reasons for this, including workers' political resistance to capital's command. Yet one that has often been overlooked is *material* in the most literal sense—relating to the kinds of natural agents at work in the production process. In large-scale industrial production, capital channels its will through the exquisitely manipulable materials of coal and steel. (Even these materials are not *fully* controlled: Coal may facilitate continuous production pegged to the rhythms of abstract time—but coal itself, of course, is not actually abstract at all. Its useful qualities stem from its concrete form, and so too do its harmful ones—as we'll consider more closely in the next chapter.) But in types of production that require other kinds of natural agents, the problems that once attended pottery and wind power have persisted much longer. Natural barriers are reduced but never quite eliminated; perfect command remains elusive.

Suprasumption and Abdication

Subsumption is always accompanied by another process: what I call *suprasumption*. Where subsumption describes the ways that capital remakes both physical and social processes of labor in service of valorization, suprasumption describes the fact that both physical and social processes always exist in excess of that remaking. Whereas real subsumption denotes precise control over time, suprasumption is characterized by asynchronies and interruptions. Whereas subsumption describes the smoothing out of rough edges, the fitting of disparate components into a continuous and finely tuned whole, suprasumption describes the friction inevitably generated by speedup, the unintended byproducts that attend commodity production, the stubborn intrusion of the concrete into the smooth circulation of abstract value, the places where the material labor process spills beyond its containment by capitalist social forms.

Suprasumption occurs in all forms of production, even those that seem most perfectly controlled. In some instances, as we will see, it is significant enough to preclude the material transformations that real subsumption requires. But importantly, this does not mean that such processes stand outside of capitalism. Capital can effectively dominate production even where it doesn't immediately command the labor process—and in fact, relinquishing control over production per se can be a strategy for capital accumulation under conditions of extreme natural variability and the high risk that accompanies it. Where subsumption describes capital's absorption of production processes, suprasumption often prompts what I call its *abdication* of them. Abdication is a way for capital to offload the risk, both physical and financial, of the volatile and unpredictable patterns associated with many natural processes, while still profiting from the fruits—often quite literally—of others' labor. Whereas in industry, class power enables capital to exert direct authority over production and capture the resulting output, in nature-based sectors, it frequently allows the opposite: it permits capital to eschew direct involvement in unpromising forms of production, and to wash its hands of the problems that often attend them.

This orientation toward production and accumulation is captured by a different and infrequently discussed kind of subsumption: what Marx describes, in brief, as "hybrid" (*Zwitter*) subsumption.[66] Substantively, hybrid subsumption describes situations in which capital stands apart from the process of production altogether: it does not directly supervise and organize labor, as it does in real subsumption; it doesn't even hire wage laborers, as in formal subsumption. Capital dominates independent producers not in the hidden abode of production but in the realm of exchange, purchasing independently made products and using sheer market power to acquire them at advantageous rates. Capital, here, is personified not as the factory boss but as the merchant, middleman, or lender who offers loans at exorbitant rates and trades at exploitative prices. Rather than hiring producers and exploiting their labor, these actors, in Marx's words, simply "fee[d] on them like a parasite."[67]

The ostensibly equal relations that pertain between these buyers and sellers must be read with the kind of skepticism that Marx brings to bear on the sale of labor power. While small producers technically retain total control over production, as they become "dependent on selling to a buyer, the merchant," Marx notes, they "ultimately produce only for and through him."[68] As the historian Jairus Banaji argues, these relations of exchange therefore constitute the "domination of capital over the small producer," characterized by a "compulsion specific to capitalist relations."[69] Here, too, class rule and market rule operate in tandem—but configured differently than in the workplace.

Marx thought that hybrid subsumption, like formal subsumption, was primarily a "transitional form," one that typically occurs *prior* to either formal or real subsumption—and which is therefore often associated with a preindustrial stage of capitalism dominated by merchants, financiers, and traders: "merchant capitalism" or "commercial capitalism."[70] As I argue, however, both formal and hybrid subsumption are not only transitory modes but persistent features of capitalist production in a world of heterogeneous matter and resolutely concrete labor processes.[71] Indeed, hybrid subsumption is a misleading term: the phenomenon Marx describes is not a hybrid of real and formal subsumption, as it might initially seem, but rather a phenomenon that operates at a different level of the accumulation process altogether. It is better described as *commercial subsumption*, designating a form of domination exerted primarily through control over exchange rather than production—although this domination eventually reverberates into the production process in its own right. As we will see, commercial subsumption is particularly useful for hedging risk, managing labor, and ensuring accumulation in the face of the natural exigencies that continually afflict certain kinds of production.[72] As the sociologist Bue Rübner Hansen argues, although the Fordist factory is often treated as the teleological end point of capitalist production, formal subsumption remains central even to industrialized capitalism—and so too does commercial subsumption.[73] Rather than simply proceeding from formal to real, then, capitalism operates through a dialectic of subsumption: the real subsumption of production within the factory relies on resources obtained beyond it, which are only ever commercially or formally subsumed.

The Peculiarities of Nature-Based Production

The Natural Machine

Although all production makes use of the gifts of nature, agriculture is the domain in which its contributions are most immediately evident. This is not because agriculture is simply "more natural" than industry in some generic sense. To the contrary, the domestication of plants and animals for human use is one of the oldest forms of social production—one with a much longer human history than industrial production. *Cultivation* and *culture* share the same root; there is no less human effort and ingenuity in an ear of corn than a beam of steel. The difference in how the gifts of nature operate in industrial and agricultural production lies instead in the *qualitative* features of the natures in question, and the ways they are organized by capitalism in particular. In agriculture, nature is both instrument and raw material, subject and object of labor, producer and product. Say tellingly describes land as "a vast machine for the production of grain" and a flock of sheep as "a machine for the raising of mutton or wool"; agriculture is, in a sense, always-already automated in part.[74] Agriculture's machines are living ones; its fields *are* its factories.[75] But the differences in these kinds of machines are decisive. While agriculture can make use of inanimate machinery in certain respects, it cannot entirely replace volatile organic and atmospheric elements with inanimate energies and inorganic materials engineered to precise specifications, as industry does. Organic processes are the center around which machinery orbits, rather than the other way around.[76] And in contrast to the reliable inhuman machines of industry, agriculture's natural machines are persistently variable. No two fields are exactly the same; no two seasons are exactly the same.

The volatility and variability of these kinds of nature are vital for understanding the divergence between the industrial and agricultural sectors. Marx thought that small-scale producers would eventually be eradicated from agriculture just as they had been from industry, as capital gradually absorbed them or simply crowded them out of the market. Yet over a century after *Capital*, industrialization had not wholly triumphed in the agrarian sphere. Most obviously, peasant populations remained prevalent in the recently decolonized Third World. But even in fully industrialized countries of the capitalist West, small-scale production and family farms had persisted longer than anyone had anticipated. Although agriculture had been mechanized and productivity had increased dramatically, wage labor remained relatively circumscribed, and the likes of piecework and sharecropping unusually common.[77] If anything, the perfection of industrial production in the twentieth century made the obstacles to it in agriculture more glaring. It was with the second industrial revolution that the distinction between manufacturing and agricultural sectors took definitive shape, as manufacturing fully industrialized while agriculture lagged behind.[78]

The persistence of these seemingly anachronistic patterns of agricultural production has often been seen as an aberration to be explained. Some theorists have followed Marx in seeing them as a holdover from precapitalist modes of production, which are gradually being replaced by industrial forms. Others, like Tsing, have celebrated the resilience of small-scale agrarian production as evidence of resistance to capitalist logics—and perhaps, as resources for alternative ways of living. By contrast, I read the persistence of heterogeneous social relations in agriculture and other sectors of nature-based production not as evidence of the *absence* of capitalism, but as the result of a particular set of strategies adopted by capital in the face of intransigent natural obstacles to the total subordination of production.[79] Nature-based sectors are rife with disruptive forms of suprasumption rooted in the distinctive features of space and time, as variable as natural agents themselves. They might take the form of temporal irregularities, like sudden violent storms, or unwavering rhythms, like the implacable rotation of the Earth around the sun. Some natural agents, like the wind, are too mobile, while others, like forests, are too rooted in place. Such phenomena are not limited to agriculture, moreover. As we'll see, similar obstacles beset other kinds of nonindustrialized work—including the labor of reproducing *human* life. Although the concrete situations and strategies outlined below are necessarily specific and partial, then, they are indicative of the kinds of obstacles that the biophysical world presents to full control—and equally importantly, of the ways that capital tends to respond.

Natural Cycles and Concrete Time

The imposition of abstract time—what Postone describes as "uniform, continuous, homogeneous, 'empty' time," measured by the clock, and the measure of the wage—is often taken to be a fait accompli of capitalism.[80] Yet concrete time—time measured in relation to natural processes, from the length of a day to the cycle of the seasons or the tides—remains enormously consequential in agriculture. At the core of agricultural production are biological and chemical processes, which unfold in their own time: seeds need time to gestate, stalks to grow, fruit to ripen, livestock to mature. The free gifts of nature need time, in other words, to do their work. Whereas industrial production requires continuous inputs of human labor, agricultural production frequently entails long stretches of time in which human labor is only occasionally applied.[81] The agrarian scholars Susan Mann and James Dickinson describe this as a gap between production time and labor time: the time required to produce a good exceeds the amount of time in which labor is required.[82] This gap is a problem for capital: it means that investments made in agriculture are tied up for weeks or months—or, in the case of sectors like forestry, even years—as crops or livestock mature before a salable commodity emerges. Industries with long gaps between production time and labor time are like factories that must lie idle for long stretches. In that temporal interval, moreover, any number of things might happen to interrupt the relevant natural processes themselves, from a cold snap to an onslaught of pests. The fixed temporal order of agricultural processes, meanwhile, means that the actual sequence of labor usually can't be fully reordered for maximum efficiency, as it frequently is in industry.[83] You can concurrently produce many components of a manufactured commodity, but you can't, for example, plant and harvest simultaneously. The labor process of farming therefore cannot be fully reengineered for maximum coordination and efficiency in the way that the Fordist factory can be entirely designed to achieve continuous flow.

Much of the project of improving agricultural productivity has consisted in efforts to overcome these temporal obstacles.[84] Crop diversification and rotation are simple ways of putting both labor and equipment to work more continuously throughout the year; artificial fertilizer can replenish exhausted soil more quickly than natural regenerative processes.[85] Most flagrantly, nature itself can be reengineered to "work harder, faster, and better."[86] Nature, in other words, can be really subsumed. Thus chickens, each a tiny meat factory, are bred with giant breasts; cattle are bred to grow more quickly (a phenomenon that Marx had already observed in the mid-nineteenth century); delicate crops like tomatoes are bred to withstand mechanized harvests; "standard hogs" are bred in order to automate meatpacking.[87] What is novel in technologies like genetic modification is not the fact that humans are altering nature or even using animals instrumentally, as ethicists often claim: human societies have long bred animals and cultivated plants.[88] Rather, it is the transformation of physical processes, sometimes at the level of the protein or the cell, in pursuit of abstract value. The alteration of animals and plants is driven, like the reorganization of the factory or design of machinery, by the competitive pressure of the market. As with inanimate machines, matter reflects and mediates social relations—with the notable difference that the material entities in question are living beings. The distorted body of the meat hen, bred with gigantic breasts and tiny legs, embodies competition for market share; the body of today's hog, as anthropologist Alex Blanchette notes, is "shaped for increased rates of labor exploitation"; patented seeds express the social relation of private ownership at the level of the gene.[89]

Where production is fundamentally structured around organic, chemical, and geological processes, however, these kinds of interventions tend to hit limits. For all capital's best efforts, suprasumption persists. Crops can be engineered for drought tolerance or pest resistance—but even so, most plants will grow only within particular ranges of temperature and precipitation. Many forms of agricultural production have been significantly mechanized, but the "living machine" of the Earth can't be entirely engineered from the ground up. Certain topographies are too rugged for the use of machines; certain crops are too delicate. Perhaps most significantly, production remains tethered to the rhythms of concrete time, from gestational periods to daylight patterns to seasonal cycles. When winter comes, there is little to do but wait for the Earth to rotate once more around the sun. Thus the ecological economist Nicholas Georgescu-Roegen once declared that the dream of "factories in the open air'" would be doomed "until man conquers the cosmic power necessary for rearranging the position of the globe on the ecliptic."[90]

The extent of suprasumption is often such that although natural agents do so much gratuitous work, and in spite of sharp increases in agricultural productivity, many agricultural sectors promise relatively low rates of return with slow turnover and high risks. These elements ultimately make wide swathes of agriculture "unattractive to capitalist penetration," Mann and Dickinson argue: in light of the "peculiar nature" of certain forms of agricultural production, capital is simply uninterested in investing.[91] This, in turn, explains the anomalous and anachronistic character of the family farm: capital mitigates risks by abdicating forms of production that simply aren't worth the trouble—and small producers fill in the gaps. While Mann and Dickinson thus conclude that certain natural processes stand as "obstacles to the complete development of a capitalist agriculture," however, I reach a different conclusion: that the organization of a "capitalist agriculture" simply looks different than the organization of capitalist industry.[92]

Strategic Abdication

The absence of large-scale capital in a particular sector can be just as indicative of capitalism's overall dynamics as its presence. Abdication is a strategy by which capital relinquishes responsibility for production where risks are too high and rewards too uncertain, as they often are in nature-based sectors.[93] But if capital does not often organize agricultural production directly, it is not absent from agriculture writ large, nor from related processes of accumulation, as we can see when we take a step back to look at the cycle of production and accumulation more broadly. Where suprasumption makes production itself too irregular or risky, capitalists tend to operate at a distance, investing "upstream" or "downstream" from direct cultivation: in biotechnology or fertilizer, tools or seeds, processing or finance.

The oddities of nature-based production mean that it's often better, financially speaking, to own seed patents or a food processing plant and leave the trouble of actually growing crops or catching fish to someone else. Most agribusiness giants are really industrial producers of one kind or another: Monsanto manufactures chemicals; Bayer makes seeds; Driscoll's packs berries; Tyson packs meat.[94] These firms don't produce the berries, or the beef, or the corn: they manufacture the inputs that go into them, or process the raw harvest that comes out. Other interventions come at the point of circulation, where many of agriculture's temporal and spatial disjunctures are more easily evened out: technologies from refrigerated train cars to motorized container ships can make seasonal produce available year-round and worldwide; finance—fundamentally a tool for managing temporal disjunctures—can hedge against unpredictability through instruments like grain futures.[95] Lenders who advance funds for farmers to buy seeds or equipment can usually recoup costs regardless of how the crop turns out; merchants who offer access to consumer markets can often set the terms of exchange.

Even where agricultural production itself is not *internally* organized along capitalist lines, then, it is not plausibly understood as noncapitalist. Most agriculture, in most of the world, is still dominated by relatively small producers. They are not entirely dispossessed of the means of production, as we expect proletarians to be. They typically own tools and instruments, and sometimes even their own land and machinery. They only occasionally sell their labor and maintain nominal control over what and how they produce. Yet even small producers who own their land and use little technology do not produce autarkically or for subsistence alone, but for a vast global market. However independent their work may appear, they too are engaged in social labor, connected by the market and directed by price signals. Small farmers and peasants, just as much as wage workers, are effectively laboring for people they do not know, producing goods they will never see in their final form. And they too are dominated by capitalists—simply through a different mechanism. Here, the social power of capital is exerted through unequal relationships of exchange, even though the parties don't appear in the classical form of worker and employer who together enter the sphere of production. Domination appears instead in the form of the monopsony power of buyers, the lending power of financiers, the price-setting power of middlemen, over the producers who depend on them for access to markets and credit. Labor is exploited indirectly and at a distance, via market instruments like debt and buying power.

Although these small producers technically retain control over production, they are not really independent of capital in any meaningful sense. Their decisions are informed by both the general pressures of market rule and the direct pressures imposed by powerful commercial intermediaries. Indeed, what I've called commercial subsumption is pervasive in nature-based sectors. It describes the position of the matsutake picker who sells mushrooms to a middleman, and that of the rancher who sells calves to industrial feedlots—as well as that of many other small producers. Take, as an illustration, cocoa production. Today, most cocoa is grown by West African and South American smallholders who sell to a tiny number of global processing giants—together, three firms account for about 60 percent of the world cocoa trade—via highly financialized markets mediated by brokers. Heavy speculation on cocoa prices feeds back into cocoa production, pressuring farmers to turn over crops more quickly, resulting in lower quality cocoa and worse working conditions. The cocoa farmers don't have a boss in the way that factory workers do: no one is keeping an eye on their pace or telling them to take a shorter lunch break, let alone monitoring their behavior when they're "off the job." But they are exploited by capital nonetheless.[96]

Abdication also serves as an important strategy for managing labor in nature-based industries where natural agents fail to act as "autocrats," facilitating capital's domination of the labor process. As we've seen, the design of the machinery, the assembly line, the shop floor, and other material components of the factory all serve to discipline and order labor and enforce managerial imperatives. Where nature isn't reliable, however, it's harder to ensure that workers will be. While it's possible for workers to use natural recalcitrance to their advantage, as Malm suggests, more often it serves as an impetus to sweat labor in whatever way necessary—as suggested by Marx's example of the pottery workshop where children work late into the night. Where capital fails to "master nature" and exert total command over production, in other words, *social* strategies for deploying and controlling labor become more important. In these instances, the basic elements of capitalist domination—market rule and class rule—continue to operate, but they are aligned differently than they are in the really subsumed factory. Two configurations are particularly significant in nature-based sectors: what I call *market management* and *market subordination*.

Outsourced Domination

What I call *market management* describes instances where the force of market rule is built directly into the structure of payment, such that the market operates directly as a force for managing and disciplining labor. In the factory, capital can ensure that workers are working for every minute of their shift: it can design the production line, place managers in strategic locations, and perhaps most importantly, control the pace of production by setting the speed of the machine. In the field, however, you can't keep strawberries coming down the line. You can't, in other words, be sure that a worker paid by the hour won't mosey through the fields picking at their leisure.[97] Where capital can't control the pace of labor through the machine and the cost of human supervision is prohibitively high—perhaps because workers are mining coal deep underground, or logging timber in a distant part of a vast forest—paying wages pegged to time is a fool's errand. Instead, capital makes use of structures of payment that subject workers to market rule directly: piecework, contract labor, sharecropping. With piecework wages, for example, workers are paid by the number of goods they produce. Since workers paid by the piece will scramble to produce as much as they can, Marx observes, this form of payment usefully renders supervision of labor "superfluous."[98] Indeed, as the historian Andrew Liu notes, payment by the piece is often *more* "conducive to the intensification of labor" than payment by the wage, since it incentivizes workers to speed up of their own accord.[99] Sharecropping operates similarly, offering workers a share of profits rather than a fixed wage, and thus mobilizing labor through sheer force of market rule.[100] Small producers thus tend to be embroiled in what Mike Davis calls a "relentless micro-capitalism," subjected to vicious market competition and driven to rationalize their own labor.[101]

Relying on market management instead of directly hiring and managing labor also helps to offload the physical and financial risks that attend particularly volatile natural processes. Logging output, for example, tends to be uncertain and uneven as a result of unpredictable weather patterns and uncontrollable forest geographies. Logging is also a notoriously dangerous job, resulting in high rates of injury and death for workers—and corresponding costs to employers. Contract logging, in which mills and other forest-based producers enter into agreements with small independent logging operators, allows the former to displace responsibility for both the quantity of output and the safety of workers to the latter.[102] Sharecropping similarly operates as a form of insurance, distributing the risk of crop failure caused by bad weather or natural disaster across those who lease a plot of land.[103]

A second form of labor management operates through interpersonal and even intimate, ostensibly "extra-economic" relationships, which enable forms of discipline that aren't available within the formal labor contract, typically backed by explicit power and even violence. Indeed, outright coercion and brutality have often been common tools for managing agricultural labor. Forms of commercial agriculture have typically developed under conditions of settler capitalism in which land expropriated from Indigenous peoples is worked by unfree laborers: enslaved workers, indentured servants, convicts, debt-bonded laborers.[104] The plantation, one of the original sites of quasi-industrial agriculture, operated as a "kind of human machine," one that developed elements of Taylorism avant la lettre by closely monitoring labor productivity and enforcing labor discipline through sheer violence.[105] Overseers kept watch over the pace of labor in the fields—but the threat of physical punishment or sale served to intimidate enslaved laborers even where these managers were absent or distant. Thus in the context of capitalist slavery, Michael Gorup argues, the impersonal domination of the market exacerbated rather than undercutting the personal domination of the master: a condition he describes as "market subjection."[106] Chattel slavery is an extreme case of the interaction between market rule and direct domination. But forms of market rule exercised through often-despotic kinds of interpersonal power—a combination I describe, riffing on Gorup, as *market subordination*—are prevalent in nature-based production more broadly, and they have persisted long after chattel slavery's demise.

Market subordination is sometimes facilitated by particularly coercive market instruments, as in the forms of debt bondage and peonage historically so prevalent in nature-based industries like agriculture, fishing, and domestic service. In these cases, wages are formally exchanged for labor, but at such an extreme imbalance as to render some people subject to the virtually unchecked authority of others in near perpetuity.[107] In other cases, ostensibly noneconomic institutions like the family act as what I call *paracapitalist agents*—agents that are able to do work that capital itself cannot. By leaving the organization of production to such agents, capital tacitly enables the discipline of ambiguously free laborers by often coercive means. The family has been a particularly reliable institution for managing formally subsumed labor more generally: *Capital* is littered with examples of mothers and children working long hours in home-based production. As one of the few status-based institutions sanctioned by liberalism, moreover, the family is able to make use of forms of discipline that are unavailable within the ostensibly noncoercive employee-employer relationship.[108] Such instances, in which production for the market is internally structured by status relationships and enforced by interpersonal domination, are sometimes described as the "patriarchal regime" of production.[109] But if the family has often proved valuable in managing small-scale production more generally, it has particular advantages in agriculture. The family is a useful source of the flexible labor that the seasonal variations of agriculture require, since family members can be available to work year-round without continually being paid wages: they can be compensated with basic reproduction and commandeered into service when needed. Indeed, while the intense labor of family farming is often characterized as a form of "self-exploitation," Susan Mann notes that it is better understood as a form of patriarchal domination in which male heads of household compel women and children to work, often through uses of corporal punishment barred to formal employers.[110] As in the market subjection of chattel slavery, then, these instances of patriarchal domination are not rooted *only* in interpersonal power, but exacerbated and indeed recast by market rule.

If relationships of direct domination are particularly useful in compelling and disciplining labor on a relatively small scale—the level of the family farm or the fishing boat—on a larger scale, nature-based production tends to rely on the coercive power of the state. Migrant labor, subject to distinctively political forms of subordination, is indispensable as a form of seasonal waged labor in many nature-based sectors, including nearly all industrialized agriculture. In some cases, guestworker programs explicitly delineate a class of workers with limited rights and little political power; in others, undocumented migrants are constituted as a source of flexible and easily disciplined labor through the threat of deportation.[111] As these examples suggest, legal and political mechanisms for obtaining and disciplining labor often interact with, and reinforce, more informal patterns of racialization and social differentiation. It is telling in this respect that the term "racial capitalism" originated in a study of South African gold mining—a sector based on extraction marked by various natural peculiarities in its own right, and reliant on black workers performing "semi-slave labor" in the mines on a seasonal basis.[112]

This brief catalogue of "nonstandard" forms of discipline deployed to manage labor in the face of natural obstacles to real subsumption is hardly exhaustive. Nor are these mechanisms mutually exclusive: industrial fishing boats make use of debt-bonded migrant labor, agricultural processing behemoths buy produce from family farms that pay undocumented laborers by the piece, and so on. The key point is that while the structure of labor is often different in agriculture and other nature-based sectors than in industry, it is radically distant from the vision of independent or unalienated labor that many romanticized accounts of agrarian production suggest.

The structure of labor performed by the debt-bonded fisherman or the racially subordinated migrant farmworker is, undoubtedly, deeply coercive and often questionably legal; as such, these kinds of work have often been described in terms of "modern-day slavery." Yet the charge of slavery suggests that these forms of labor constitute archaic practices that have anachronistically persisted into the present, thus failing to register how capitalism has transformed forced labor. It threatens, in other words, to let capitalism off the hook for forms of brutality it claims to have left behind. Labor, in these cases, is typically exploited not through direct use of force, but through legal and political mechanisms: overstayed visas, contracts with hidden clauses, informal agreements that can't be adequately enforced, unpayable debt, marriage licenses. It mobilizes coercion, but also choice. That these choices are made under conditions of desperation makes them little different from the choices made by many formal wage laborers. It matters that this labor is usually *ambiguously* free rather than blatantly unfree, as in instances of chattel slavery: the difference in the freedom of these kinds of labor and "ordinary" wage labor is not so much a matter of kind as of degree.[113]

As a result, these unconventional forms of labor are sometimes characterized by theorists like Jairus Banaji as little more than "disguised wages," their true character hidden beneath other forms of appearance.[114] Yet while this frame usefully highlights the continuities between wage labor and labor deployed via other mechanisms, it threatens to overstate them: the difference between the mechanisms used to compel labor *does* matter. Sharecropping and debt bondage are *not* simply wage labor disguised by ideological mystification, but rather distinctive strategies for mobilizing labor under particular material and social conditions. Piecework is useful precisely *because* it's different from the hourly wage, and capable of addressing problems that the wage can't. So, too, does the family play a different role in managing labor than the firm, even if both are organized internally along nonmarket lines, making use of "visible hands." Although comparing these seemingly atypical forms of labor to waged labor can be politically useful—as we will see shortly—it can also unintentionally reify the wage as the only true measure of labor under capitalism. This, in turn, risks inadequate attention to the *reasons* that nonwage labor persists, the different structure of power that characterizes it, and the different kinds of strategies that workers might adopt in response.

Rethinking the Nature of Labor

The stakes of identifying certain spaces as "pericapitalist" or "noncapitalist," and more generally of identifying boundaries between capitalism and its "outside," are often not analytical so much as political. From the matsutake pickers described by Tsing to the Russian *mir* described in Marx's late writings, small-scale agrarian production has often appeared to offer an alternative to industrial capitalism and the ecological destruction left in its wake.[115] If at least *some* kinds of labor or nature have evaded capital's grasp, these analyses suggest, perhaps we can too. By contrast, the argument of this chapter might appear more sobering: that capitalism and distinctively capitalist forms of domination are omnipresent, structuring even sites and forms of production that seem to stand apart from them. It might seem to suggest that there is no escape from capitalism's logic, and hence no viable alternative to it. Yet this conclusion assumes that one must stand outside of capitalism in order to effectively challenge it.

In the classical Marxist theory of politics, by contrast, it is precisely the condition of being *internal* to capitalism that makes labor powerful. Industrialization, after all, is a double-edged sword for capital. It deprives workers of skills and exploits their labor—but it also grows their numbers and erases distinctions between them. It reveals the distance between the possibility of abundance and the reality of immiseration. It brings previously isolated workers together en masse in the factory, where they can begin to organize collectively. The socialization of labor therefore serves, paradoxically, to counteract the seriality of market rule: once atomized competitors in the market, laborers are unified by both the capitalist, whose authority interpellates them all as subordinates, and by the physical space of the factory itself, which concentrates them spatially and creates the conditions for their self-organization.[116] It is precisely because production is so tightly coordinated, moreover, that industrial workers are able to disrupt it so successfully; and because capital has invested so much in machinery that disruptions are immensely costly. Thus with the growth of industry, Marx argues, "grows the revolt of the working class, a class constantly increasing in numbers, and trained, united, and organized *by the very mechanism of the process of capitalist production.*"[117] It was precisely *because* the industrial proletariat had been made by capital, in other words, that they could unmake it. It's for this reason, too, that socialists have often looked upon peasants with suspicion, seeing them as "archaic," "sterile," or "pre-political" laggards from a bygone era who can neither hold back capitalism's tide nor transcend it toward something new.[118]

If we recognize that the likes of smallholders and independent producers are *not* plausibly thought of as standing outside of capitalism, however, the prospect of political action *immanent* to the system emerges. The petty producer has archetypically been seen as a conservative force, seeking only to protect their own private plot of land against the encroachment of the market. But recognition that the market has *already encroached*, even where people continue to own land or tools, suggests that liberation can be secured only by acting collectively with others similarly subjected to market rule and dominated by class power, whatever its particular form. From the vantage point presented here, small producers are not producing in isolation, but rather are linked by the complex interactions that compose contemporary capitalism. They might not have the same employer, but they share a common position relative to the creditors to whom they owe money, the monopolistic companies from which they buy seeds and equipment, or the industrial processors who buy their products—and have proven able to organize periodically on a massive scale to target these very institutions.[119]

The ambiguous, even contradictory class position of many producers in nature-based sectors and the dispersed and fragmented nature of production do present genuine challenges to organizing. Workers in these sectors are often isolated spatially despite being linked economically, and cooperate directly on much smaller scales. Even the largest fishing boats, for instance, are typically minuscule in size compared with on-shore processing plants. Where production is dispersed, the effect of the mass strike or shutdown is more difficult to achieve; where relatively little capital has been invested, interruptions to work are less disruptive to accumulation. Where large-scale capital operates at a distance, or through intermediaries, it may be more difficult for those subjugated by it to discern a shared enemy, or to confront one—hence the frequent appearance of agrarian politics in the form of "populist" movements rather than explicitly class struggles.[120] Where industry once socialized production and generated mass political movements, the heterogeneity of natural processes tends to generate heterogeneous forms of labor-capital relations, and in turn, heterogeneous forms of labor politics.

Yet industrial workers, too, once seemed unorganizable. If some of the tactics of classic industrial labor politics are not immediately available to those in nature-based sectors whose work is commercially rather than really subsumed, we should not thereby conclude that political organization is impossible. Both the historical conditions of political possibility and the concrete conditions of production always both enable and constrain political tactics, strategy, and action; the task of any given moment is to understand how.[121] In particular, it is vital to attend more closely not only to historical context, language, strategy, and other familiar features of political life but also to the ways that materialized social relations confront people as individuals, structure them as a group, and enable or constrain certain kinds of action; and the ways that the particularities of concrete labor processes and sites of work, from material infrastructures to temporal patterns, inform political tactics and strategies.[122] Indeed, the constraints of nonstandard labor have frequently spurred political creativity in their own right, and the temporal and material peculiarities of nature-based production present opportunities of their own. They might create physical "choke points" that are vulnerable to disruption at geographically fixed sites, like the bottlenecks exploited by British coal miners in the 1920s.[123] The rhythms of natural processes, meanwhile, create temporal choke points in their own right: strawberries or tomatoes that aren't harvested at precisely the right time will rot on the vines, giving workers outsized leverage at particular moments. While factories physically assemble workers en masse, producers in nature-based sectors are physically connected by the "natural machine" on which they work, and the complex interactions of the material world itself. The alteration of the physical world through production, even that undertaken by seemingly independent actors, is itself a means of connection and potential source of association.

Uniting the Fishery

These challenges and possibilities come into sharp relief in an example from another nature-based sector: fishing. Fishing is one of the last remaining forms of large-scale formally subsumed production, and the only form of hunting that has persisted on a commercial basis into the industrial age. Fishing resists subsumption quite simply because the ocean does. Fishers spend weeks or even months searching for autonomous, rapidly moving prey across the vast expanse of the sea amid unpredictable atmospheric and oceanic conditions. Because the reproduction of fish populations is inflected by population dynamics, climatic conditions, disease, and other factors, output often fluctuates drastically from one year to the next. Knowledge and skill are important in catching fish—but so is luck. The variability of natural conditions, from tempestuous seas to unpredictable weather, also makes fishing a particularly dangerous job. Fishers don't—and can't—own the sea itself, as farmers can own their land, but they do tend to lease or own their boats and other necessary equipment. They don't sell their labor by the hour or day. What they sell is their product: the fish.

The cannery owner, meanwhile, doesn't tell the fisher how to fish or monitor how many hours they work. They simply buy the fish at market price—effectively, by the piece. In some cases they might lease boats or offer loans to fishers without hiring them directly. For the cannery, this is a good deal. It means that fishers take the risks, both physical and financial, of the volatile and unpredictable production process and pay the costs of reproducing their lives during long stretches at sea. If they are injured or killed on the job, they alone are responsible; if they catch fewer fish than expected, they absorb the loss. Since the fishers' compensation ultimately depends on their share of the catch, they strive to maximize their output, and compete with others to sell their product. The geographical specificity of the fishery, meanwhile, and the perishability of the product mean that the cannery is often the only possible buyer, and is able to set prices accordingly. The result is that each fisher's cut of the catch, measured by the hour, often amounts to less than a standard wage.

Because fishers tend to see themselves as independent producers, their unions have been few and far between. The International Fishermen and Allied Workers of America (IFAWA), on the US West Coast in the 1940s and 1950s, is a rare exception.[124] Because they were viewed by the state as independent businessmen, their collective action was deemed illegal collusion. IFAWA instead identified as proletarians: they insisted that their primary activity was *labor*, and—as Banaji might recommend—described the price they were paid per fish as a "wage-price."[125] As Geoff Mann argues, this constituted a sophisticated way of rejecting the imperative of competition among individual fishers, instead bringing to the fore their shared domination by the canneries that loaned out equipment and purchased fish, while also organizing the traditionally waged industrial workers of the cannery.

If the cannery served as one point of connection, the fishery served as another. IFAWA organized across the oceanic span of the West Coast, bringing together smaller unions that had restricted membership to discrete fishing grounds. The union's boundaries were therefore defined by the spatial dynamics of the regional fishery—itself emergent from the interaction of fish populations, boat technology, ocean currents, weather patterns, and port locations. One of IFAWA's core concerns was the long-term health of the fishery, which it sought to manage directly. Fishing is notoriously plagued by the tragedy of the commons: each individual fisher has an incentive to catch as many fish as possible, and because the ocean can't be contained, no one can be prevented from doing so. To combat it, the union set internal standards for fishing, and sought to restrict nonmembers from the fishery. They could not directly exclude nonmembers from fishing any given span of ocean—but they could prevent them from selling any fish they caught. Because IFAWA represented both fishers and cannery workers, it could strike collective bargaining agreements with canneries to purchase only union-caught fish.

Although fishers organized around the state of the fishery, then, they did not *only* mobilize around the fishery. They did not, in other words, adopt the strategy that characterizes many agrarian and peasant movements today, of designating themselves "people of the land" (or in this case, the sea), mobilizing primarily around the direct interaction with nature.[126] The state of the ocean did serve to unify fishers around a common interest—but to actually curb the pressures of seriality driving toward tragedy, they had to confront capital directly and exert control over the means of production more broadly. By organizing across sectors—industrial and nature-based workers alike—they recognized that the cannery was, effectively, everyone's boss, and had to be confronted collectively. Capital itself, in other words, served as a potential point of connection between nature-based producers of "raw materials" and those who transformed them into finished commodities, between agriculture and industry.

The success of IFAWA shouldn't be overstated. It did not transform the fishing industry or stave off fisheries' collapse. It nevertheless offers a model of organizing across sectors, supply chains, and even ecosystems—one that has all the more salience in a world dominated by global retailing giants and planetary ecological crises. For the "peculiar" conditions of nature-based industries, beset by the phenomena of commercial subsumption and strategic abdication, today confront a massive and growing number of workers worldwide in a logistical economy in which a small number of retail behemoths set the terms. Workers in the growing "platform economy," to give just one high-profile example, are treated as independent contractors: rideshare drivers, for instance, own their own tools (a car, a phone) yet remain entirely reliant on tech intermediaries for their livelihoods.[127] Merchant capitalism has returned, the historian Nelson Lichtenstein argues, exemplified by the power of global retailers like Wal-Mart and Amazon.[128] But in some sectors, this model of organization never left. The oddities of agricultural production, then, are not so much the stubborn dregs of a bygone age as the harbingers of an uncertain future, as important for understanding the politics of capitalism as any struggle within the factory.

Conclusion

Half a century on from its celebration in *Le chant du styrène*, the industrial sublime looks rather different. The 2006 film *Manufactured Landscapes* follows the photographer Edward Burtynsky's efforts to represent the Anthropocene in image, from the kilometer-long factory in China where twenty-three thousand workers produce the majority of the world's clothes irons to the massive mines and quarries from which raw materials are extracted.[129] Where *Le chant du styrène* is tinged with the wonder and terror of the sublime but ultimately triumphant in spirit, *Manufactured Landscapes* evokes foreboding. The manufactured landscape inspires awe, but also a sense of powerlessness: although the factory is undeniably a human creation, its workings are incomprehensible. The manufactured landscape suggests, simultaneously, total human mastery of nature, and a process beyond the control of any given human being, like the sorcerer who can no longer control what he has conjured.

The half-century separating *Le chant du styrène* and *Manufactured Landscapes* is, of course, the time of the Great Acceleration. We cannot understand the astonishing transformation of our planet in this period without understanding the organization of production, and of labor—which at its heart is the process of transforming nature. At the same time, we cannot fully understand the politics of labor without attending to its concrete dimensions, and to the many forms it takes—"from the planetary mine to the global factory," as Thea Riofrancos observes.[130] It is hard today to believe that the industrial proletariat could stand in for the whole of humanity, as Lukács once suggested. In any case the era of the mass worker has passed, and with it the particular conditions of twentieth-century politics, for better and worse. Rather than bidding farewell to the working class, however—as some ecological thinkers have proposed—this conjuncture requires a more comprehensive view of the politics of production, and recognition that the politics of labor are always also the politics of nature.[131]

4

No Such Thing as a Free Gift

THE VIOLENT PARADOXES OF SOCIAL COST

IN ROBERT HEINLEIN'S science-fiction novel *The Moon Is a Harsh Mistress* (1966), an earthling walks into a bar in Luna, a penal colony on the moon, and learns a lesson: "There ain't no such thing as a free lunch." Although the bar advertises a free meal, the promise of something for nothing is a trick: the food lures in customers, but the bar inflates the prices of drinks in order to cover the cost. "Taanstafl" is the watchword on Luna, where everything has a price—even oxygen, since the lunar atmosphere is vacuum. "What you get, you pay for," a Luna resident explains.[1] The phrase would become famous as a libertarian shibboleth, particularly after Milton Friedman used it as the title for a 1975 compilation of writings.[2] For Friedman, the "free lunch myth" was epitomized by the ostensibly "free" goods and services provided by the welfare state, which in his view were paid for by the unjustified taxation of others' wealth.

But the phrase "no such thing as a free lunch" was invoked in a radically different manner by Friedman's contemporary, the left-wing ecologist Barry Commoner, who in 1971 identified it as one of the four central principles of ecology. For Commoner, the phrase neatly encapsulated the conservation principle of physics—that energy can never be created nor destroyed—in combination with the ecological tenet that everything is connected.[3] It meant, in Commoner's reading, that anything human beings took from the planetary ecosystem would eventually have to be returned to it. (It's telling, in fact, that the phrase originated in a science fiction story about life on the moon: a lunar colony is a good example of a closed ecological system.)[4] The free lunch, in Commoner's view, was the explosion of wealth in the postwar period, while the hidden "costs" were metaphorical, paid not in dollars but in starkly material terms: polluted air, deteriorating ecosystems, depleted resources, diminished health. Where on Luna even oxygen comes with a price, on Earth Commoner sought to reveal the biophysical costs lurking beneath prices measured in monetary terms.

Commoner's analysis implies a corollary: there is no such thing as a free gift. Like the free lunch, the free gift of nature is an illusion: its costs always appear elsewhere in the system. The question is not whether they are paid, but what form they take and who—or what—pays them.

———

Pollution has often been described by its defenders as the "price of progress," with the implication that it is worth paying. Those who have actually paid the costs have often disagreed. Since the advent of the industrial era, the noise, smoke, soot, dust, and other effluents generated by production have frequently generated complaints, concern, and outright conflict.[5] It is striking, then, that pollution is largely absent from Marx's work—particularly given that he wrote *Capital* in the midst of London's legendary coal-smoke fogs, which his contemporaries Charles Dickens and Herman Melville felt compelled to describe.[6] Instead it would be Marx's lifelong collaborator Friedrich Engels who described in agonizing detail the burden of pollution, waste, and disease borne by the working class in *The Condition of the Working Class in England* (1845).

In Manchester and surrounding factory towns, Engels observed, the "pall of smoke" hung in the air and coated buildings, while tannery buildings, dye works, bone mills, and gas works discharged "filth, both liquid and solid" into the River Irk and "belch[ed] forth black smoke from their chimneys."[7] Workers suffered from typhus and cholera, struggled to breathe properly, and died much younger than they ought. Those living in the poorest parts of town were twice as likely to die as those in wealthy ones. In Engels's view, this constituted "social murder": "If society places hundreds of workers in such a position that they inevitably come to premature and unnatural ends," he argued, "their death is as violent as if they had been stabbed or shot." The problem, however, was that this kind of violence was rarely recognized as such. "Everyone is responsible and yet no one is responsible," Engels wrote, "because it appears as if the victim has died from natural causes."[8] For Engels, the "disguised, malicious" nature of social murder required all the more vigilance in identifying its culprit—and the vehemence with which he condemned it was a way of bringing it to light.

Engels wrote as pollution was being politicized in industrial and urban settings, a century before it became a truly mass political issue. But the political challenges that he identified have only grown starker. The effects of pollution are today even more maldistributed than in Engels's time, and now manifest on a global scale. Its harms, too, are perhaps more disguised than ever. While the filth and smoke that choked Manchester were tangible to all, many other kinds of harmful matter, like the chemicals in pesticides, go unseen; some, like carbon dioxide, are imperceptible to human senses altogether. Efforts to politicize these conditions have tended to constitute variations on Engels's theme, calling attention to both the violence they do and to the disparity of their effects.

Politically, pollution is perhaps most widely understood as a problem of justice in the distribution of harms. For decades, environmental justice activists and scholars have drawn attention to the disproportionate siting of landfills, incinerators, chemical plants, livestock excrement, and other deleterious facilities in working-class communities and communities of color.[9] Within political theory and philosophy, too, environmental "bads" have overwhelmingly been considered through the lens of distributive justice, considered in terms of racial and global disparities, as well as in terms of the temporal distribution of risks and harms across present and future generations.[10] Critiques of unequal burdens are often paired with efforts to expose the severity of their effects, often through rhetorical means, as in Rob Nixon's influential characterization of pollution as a form of "slow violence": "a violence of delayed destruction that is dispersed across time and space."[11] Efforts to hold specific perpetrators accountable have frequently drawn on language reminiscent of that of social murder: the United Farm Workers described pesticides as "poison" in the fields; the union leader Tony Mazzocchi, of the Oil, Chemical, and Atomic Workers, charged that "murder was being committed in the workplace"; Sartre charged French mine operators with "homicide" of workers who developed silicosis.[12] Moral philosophers, meanwhile, have leveled similar charges at the level of the individual, arguing that complicity in slow violence is widespread and seeking to allocate responsibility for the harms associated with personal consumption.[13]

These diagnoses do essential work to disclose the politics lurking within seemingly amorphous miasmas, and to expose their troubling effects. There are indisputably stark and disturbing disparities in the distribution of environmental harms, which are quite plausibly understood in terms of violence: pollution really does attack people's bodily integrity, undermine their physical function, cause injury and even early death.[14] Yet while critiques of the unequal and unjust distribution of pollution rightly identify its harmful effects, they often stop short of adequately tracing its causes.[15] Efforts to more explicitly attribute blame, meanwhile, tend to oversimplify their charges in service of moral clarity. The charge of social murder is galvanizing, and illuminating in crucial respects. And yet, contra Engels, it *is* different to be killed by air pollution, or by a hurricane intensified by climate change, than to be stabbed or shot—which isn't to say that it is not as bad. The difference, moreover, isn't located *only* in the geographically and temporally diffuse character of slow violence, though these too are important. It is also rooted in the ways that these harms are produced: not by individual actors intentionally inflicting interpersonal injuries on others, but as an accidental effect of actions undertaken for different purposes altogether. The problem frequently named as social murder or slow violence is, in other words, a particularly visceral form of the unintended consequences generated by market rule. Critics of complicity are right that we are all implicated in these harms to some degree. Yet this is largely because so many of our decisions are mediated by markets in ways that constitutively exclude social costs, and divorce our actions from their effects. Although consumption is the most common culprit for pollution, moreover, its more significant origin is elsewhere: in production.

Indeed, pollution largely emerges from exactly the same production process as the commodity: the same process that generates a car, for instance, also generates smoke, ash, carbon dioxide, and other material byproducts. Unlike the commodity, however, this byproduct has no exchange value—and unlike the free gift of nature, it has no use value either.[16] Pollution, then, is an odder phenomenon than is often recognized. As the anthropologist Mary Douglas has argued, pollution cannot be understood in strictly material terms—as smoke, or dirt, or even excrement—but only as "the by-product of a systematic ordering and classification of matter."[17] Pollution is "matter out of place": matter that is not where it is supposed to be. In Douglas's view, social classifications of matter typically reflect a divide between the sacred and the profane. But this distinction can't hold in capitalism, which after all is notorious for profaning the sacred.[18] In a system where matter is ordered by prices, pollution is matter *without* a price. It is surplus matter—not simply surplus in an absolute sense, but matter in excess of what can be bought and sold. Pollution is the underside of the free gift's spontaneous and seemingly limitless bounty: the laboriously manufactured detritus that no one has agreed to buy and no one wants. Pollution is, in the words of the economist J. H. Dales, something that "no one will either pay for or accept as a gift."[19] It is the poison that lurks *within* the gift.[20]

Capital's control over production, then, is also control over what I call *byproduction*—control over what is produced unintentionally, which is not to say unknowingly. It is all too easy for capital to abdicate responsibility for the effects of byproduction: expelling surplus matter, by default, is costless. If surplus matter has no buyers, however, it nevertheless has consumers: as Commoner's "second ecological law" asserts, "Everything must go somewhere."[21] Waste does not simply disappear because it is not valued economically. The ability to impose pollution on others is another aspect of class rule—and the inability to refuse it is a form of unfreedom in its own right. The harms named as pollution or "slow violence," then, should be read as the unintentional but no less systematic consequence of a particular organization of social relations expressed in and through the material world, one that consistently compels us to treat ecological effects as costless.

This chapter, then, looks at how pollution has been represented in economic terms, via the concept of the externality. Externalities occur when economic activity causes costs for third parties that are not reflected in the costs to the producer, such that they are not taken into account in economic decisions. In retrospect, the externality is plausibly the most significant economic concept of the twentieth century: first conceptualized in 1920 to describe minor flaws in the market like the unpriced "external effects" of smoky chimneys on laundry, by the early twenty-first century it would be described as the cause of a phenomenon that threatens to end human civilization as we know it.[22] In turn, it has animated the core policy frameworks of late twentieth-century environmental politics, most obviously via carbon taxes and cap-and-trade programs, and has been taken up in many theories of just climate action. Yet the externality itself has gone largely unexamined.[23]

This chapter seeks to rectify that omission. The externality, it argues, offers a rich entry point to a political economic analysis of pollution, one that casts debates about environmental justice and moral responsibility in new light. The history of the externality is, at its heart, one of economists encountering the environment—and seeking to grapple with and contain the effects of economic activity in the material world. Although neither of its two central theorists, Arthur Pigou and Ronald Coase, was an environmental economist, the examples they used to illustrate the problem are teeming with nature: air darkened by a smoky chimney or purified by a leafy park, a field overrun with rabbits, cattle that stray from a rancher's field into a farmer's, a train whose sparking engine causes nearby woods to catch fire, a polluted stream with sickly fish, a building blocking the wind that powers a windmill.[24] While externalities are not limited to "environmental" cases, they are fundamentally concerned with the unintended consequences of action in a material world—

and so mark an iteration of the long-standing debate, outlined in chapter 2, about the relationship between intention and outcome, private and social interest, individual and collective action.

Externalities also reveal something about markets as such. In systems of logic or infrastructure, it is often the points of failure that are most revealing, and this is no less true of so-called "market failure." Most theorists of the externality assume that individuals are the basic unit of economic analysis, and markets the central institution. They treat markets, in turn, as an ideal type of allocation mechanism—a means by which goods (or bads) might be distributed via exchanges negotiated amongst individual actors—and assume markets should generally operate without intervention. But the condition of generalized market dependence, in which most people work for wages and obtain most of what they need to survive through exchange rather than through subsistence activity, is a unique and defining feature of capitalism in particular as a system of political and economic organization. It is this condition that makes the prospect of market failure so threatening—and so rich for political interrogation. Although externalities are frequently treated as an exception to the rule, they illuminate the rule of the market itself: how markets are *supposed* to work, and what happens when they become the organizing institution of collective life.[25]

A Critical History of the Externality

A Pall over Liberalism: Arthur Pigou and the Birth of the Externality

The externality was first theorized as a distinct concept in the early twentieth century by the British welfare economist Arthur C. Pigou (1877–1959). Writing, like Marx, from the vantage point of England's early and tumultuous industrialization, Pigou noted the problem that Marx had only glancingly acknowledged: that the production of commodities was often accompanied by unintentional and sometimes severe physical side effects. Pigou theorized this problem by way of novel methods in economics—namely, the recently ascendant "marginalist revolution" of the 1870s, which sought to turn economics into a modern science of markets.[26] Dispensing with the idea that value had foundations inhering in some commensurable substance, be it labor (for Ricardo) or wheat (for the physiocrats), marginalists argued that value reflected the subjective judgments of personal utility as made by consumers. Value, in other words, emerges in the course of exchange rather than production.

The early twentieth-century welfare economics to which Pigou was a contributor sought to integrate these methodological insights with those of earlier utilitarian projects aimed at maximizing social well-being, with the goal of developing a truly scientific study of social welfare.[27] Prices were crucial to this project. Money, welfare economists acknowledged, was not the only thing that mattered in life, nor even in economics—yet as the influential English marginalist Alfred Marshall observed, it was "the one convenient means of measuring human motive on a large scale."[28] Money was, he admitted, a crude measure that failed to capture all elements of economic activity—a widely recognized difficulty first discussed in systematic detail by Pigou's classic *Economics of Welfare* (1920). Following Marshall, Pigou argued that assessments of economic welfare had to use "the measuring rod of money," even if some things were beyond its scope.[29] Yet he also acknowledged that this method sometimes produced "violent paradoxes" wherein welfare and price diverged.[30] These paradoxes, stemming from disparities in use and exchange value, were often related to, though not always identical with, instances where the public welfare diverged from the interests of private investors in realizing profits. Pigou described such instances, where prices failed to reflect the effects of production on society at large, as "external economies."

The valence of the "external economy" was not always negative. Sometimes private producers accidentally generate unpriced social benefits, as when people built private parks that improved the neighborhood air.[31] (We will return to such cases in chapter 6.) Pigou's central example, however—destined to become the textbook case of the externality—was a negative one: a factory with a smoky chimney. For a British economist in the early twentieth century, smoke was an obvious example: Pigou cited the astonishing observation that in London, "owing to the smoke, there is only 12 percent as much sunlight as is astronomically possible, and that one fog in five is directly caused by smoke alone, while all the fogs are befouled and prolonged by it."[32] That smoke imposed literal costs on the community at large—"in injury to buildings and vegetables, expenses for washing clothes and cleaning rooms, expenses for the provision of extra artificial light, and in many other ways"—which were not reflected in the costs to the factory owner.[33] In such cases, Pigou argued, the pursuit of private wealth tended to diminish public welfare rather than increasing it. Externalities suggested, in other words, that private vices did not always produce public benefits. In some instances, it seemed that a market transaction could make those who were not party to it *worse* rather than better off. Fortunately, externalities seemed to be relatively rare and easily rectified. Drawing on Smith, Pigou argued that where the market failed to secure social benefits, the state was justified in intervening to address the disparity.[34] Although the precise cost of external effects was often difficult to assess, they could be estimated with reasonable accuracy and included in the price of relevant goods through a tax or similar pricing mechanism imposed by the state.[35]

For the next several decades most economists followed Pigou's view of externalities as an instance of "market failure" in which markets failed to optimally allocate resources, albeit a negligible one that could be solved with minor adjustments. Externalities remained a footnote to the canons of price theory in this period: they appeared, in the words of one mid-century welfare economist, to be "exceptional and unimportant."[36] As postwar economic growth and material throughput skyrocketed, however, pollution problems emerged or accelerated across the industrialized world. Externalities suddenly began to appear ubiquitous and significant—and a concomitant economic literature exploded. So too did public concern about the harmful effects of industrial production. It was through pollution that the environment became visible, quite literally: smog made air newly perceptible; oil spills gave water an unnatural sheen. The mainstream environmental movement developed in large part in response to this novel political object.[37]

Reciprocal Conflict: Ronald Coase and the Problem of Social Cost

As pollution grew more politically significant, the prospect that externalities constituted a potentially systematic "market failure" began to seriously concern champions of free markets, and the emerging neoliberal economists of the Chicago and Virginia Schools in particular.[38] For many liberal thinkers, as we have seen, the market has offered a way to coordinate action through freely undertaken exchange rather than direct coercion or violence; for some, even a way to achieve the common good absent universal morality. The idea that unintended consequences might be perverse—or even, in Pigou's terms, violent—fundamentally challenged this optimistic view. Pigou's account of disparities between private and public well-being seemed to cast a smoggy pall over the happy Mandevillian marriage of the individual and common good.[39]

Externalities were a problem even for those who had abandoned faith in the common good altogether—by then suspiciously totalitarian to many liberals. The prospect that many prices were missing outright cast doubt on Hayek's claim that a "spontaneous order" could be achieved through the coordinating mechanism of price. The externality was a problem, too, for the increasingly hegemonic view of markets as expressions of individual liberty. Market freedom was premised on consensual exchange—and yet externalities imposed costs on people who had *not* consented to bear them. People forced to breathe particulate matter had not agreed to do so; nor were they compensated with a share of the benefits enjoyed by those who had generated it. Why was this nonconsensual infringement on bodily autonomy acceptable where, say, forced labor was not? The externality suggested that exchange might consistently violate a liberal tenet as foundational as Mill's principle that people are free to act as they please as long as they cause no harm to others.[40]

Neoliberal and libertarian thinkers took up the challenge of the externality in different ways. Hayek's *The Road to Serfdom* (1944) had famously argued that state planning would lead to the tyrannical imposition of some people's values over others—and yet even Hayek had followed Pigou in granting the state a role in regulating the "smoke and noise of factories."[41] But if externalities were truly ubiquitous, they threatened to license a drastic extension of government and potentially severe restrictions on market freedom. Robert Nozick would struggle, in his *Anarchy, State, and Utopia* (1974), to reconcile a moral framework organized around the inviolable Kantian individual with the fact that nearly all actions have effects extending beyond parties to a contract, some of which may harm others. Nozick's entire argument for a minimal state would ultimately rely on a complicated account of compensation for "boundary crossing"—in effect, a redescription of the problem of the externality.[42] As complaints about the "smoke nuisance" intensified, Milton Friedman similarly noted that "there is no transaction between individuals that does not affect third parties to some extent, however trivial, so there is literally no governmental intervention for which a case cannot be offered along these lines."[43] The externality, he worried, could therefore be "used to justify a completely unlimited extension of government."[44]

As attention to the externality problem had grown, however, so had scrutiny of Pigou's theory. Since the 1930s, economists had chipped away at the bases of welfare economics more broadly—in particular, the idea that social welfare could be calculated in the aggregate—adopting in its place the far narrower standard of Pareto efficiency.[45] In addition, in 1960, the British economist Ronald Coase launched a major, direct critique of Pigou in his landmark article "The Problem of Social Cost."[46] Coase explicitly used the term "social cost" in place of the language of "externality," which he thought too strongly associated with Pigou's justification of government intervention.[47] Coase argued that Pigou had stated that certain private activities caused public injury

as a matter of fact: that when a factory's "smoky chimney" affected the surrounding air, for example, it constituted a clear case of social harm caused by
the factory, which should be rectified by government intervention to limit the
smoke. But Pigou's utilitarianism, he argued, had led him to import a moral
framework that informed his assessment of both the necessity and ends of
state intervention. Pigou had imbued the positive science of economics with
normative evaluation.

Coase made three key moves in response. First, he argued that economic
activities are not unidirectional but "reciprocal": their effects always go in two
directions. The smoke from the factory chimney, for example, would have
harmful effects on health only if people chose to live nearby: thus "both parties
cause the damage."[48] Conversely, to limit smoke, as Pigou proposed, would
impose a cost on the factory owner in the form of reduced production.[49] Why,
Coase asked, should the factory have to accept the costs of reducing smoke for
the benefit of the neighborhood? Why instead should nearby residents not pay
the factory to reduce the smoke, or move away from the area altogether? Economists could not answer these questions, Coase argued, without imposing moral
judgments inappropriate to a technical field. They could speak only to whether
the value of clean air, assessed in economic terms, was greater or less than the
value of the product that had generated the smoke. Second, following from this
point, Coase argued that in highlighting the disparity between public welfare
and private profit, Pigou had identified the wrong problem altogether. Only the
"total social product," computed by weighing the gains of preventing a given
activity compared with those of allowing it to continue, was relevant.[50] The goal
was not to eliminate smoke altogether: to allow *any* claim to harm to prevent a
smoky factory from operating might make everyone worse off. Rather, the goal
was to "secure the optimum amount of smoke pollution," defined as the "amount
that will maximize the value of production."[51]

Finally, the mere fact that some externalities were uncompensated was not
in itself a sufficient argument for state intervention. State action, whether in
the form of taxes or regulation, came with "transaction costs" of its own, which
might be more significant than those of either doing nothing at all or leaving
the interested parties to work it out for themselves.[52] In instances where state
action was warranted, moreover, the blunt and inefficient tools of taxation and
regulation were not the only options.[53] Instead, Coase argued that "the right
to do something which has a harmful effect (such as the creation of smoke,
noise, smells, etc.) is also a factor of production": the state should assign rights
to these activities, as it did to other factors of production, and allow private

individuals to work out the value of smokeless air for themselves.[54] Rights, in other words, could be allocated by markets, just like any other good. If a producer wanted to generate smoke, they could simply pay the person harmed for the privilege, or vice versa. Regardless of who initially owned the rights, Coase argued, they would be allocated in whatever way maximized the total value of production.[55]

The Impeccable Logic of Pollution

Coase's was hardly the final word: externalities would become a central concept in a vast literature on public and common pool goods, as well as in the emerging fields of environmental and ecological economics.[56] But his analysis was rapidly embraced as a response to the framework of "market failure," becoming one of the most cited legal papers of all time. Simplified by Chicago School economist George Stigler as the "Coase Theorem," it would become the far-reaching basis for a new approach to externalities, and a pillar of the novel "law and economics" framework, which sought to apply economics to the analysis of law.[57] It reflected the vision of markets that had become prominent in the late twentieth century, which had banished measures of social welfare except insofar as it shakes out in competitive markets ("total value production" as Pareto efficient outcome). It reflected, too, the basic principles of market freedom as articulated by Hayek: that people should be able to choose what level of pollution they are willing to tolerate. Treating the right to pollute as a commodity would simply allow people to make choices that more accurately reflected how much they valued clean air or quiet.

The Coase Theorem, and the broader law and economics project, have come under significant criticism for promoting an "economic imperialism" that treats markets as a solution to every problem.[58] Many moral and political philosophers have charged that this way of thinking wrongly seeks to apply economic analysis to "spheres" that are appropriately governed by other values and norms.[59] Pollution, it's often argued, isn't the kind of thing we should buy and sell. Michael Sandel, for example, argues that paying for the right to pollute is troubling insofar as it suggests that there is nothing morally wrong with pollution—that it is "simply the cost of doing business, like wages, benefits, and rent," while Elizabeth Anderson claims that environmental goods are "not properly regarded as commodities."[60]

Rather than simply condemning the Coasean approach, however, I am interested in what it reveals. For Coase *is* a more perceptive analyst of the externality than Pigou. He is right that Pigou's analysis relies on an unspoken and unjustified moral framework—to know that the market has failed to achieve optimal welfare, one must know what the optimal welfare is; to correct prices, a benevolent administrator (or moral philosopher) must know what they ought to be. Coase is right, too, that "social costs" are reciprocal and antagonistic—that one person's harm is another's benefit. And he is right to argue that harms like pollution are, effectively, factors of production, insofar as the transformation of some materials into new forms inevitably produces surplus matter. He is right, in other words, that Pigou and his followers take the meaning of social cost for granted and arbitrarily apply a normative standard to pollution—one that they typically do not apply to other kinds of economic goods. But the distinction between pollution and other kinds of goods just doesn't hold. Pollution, after all, is produced by the same process that produces standard commodities like cars and televisions—goods that most moral critics seem to think are legitimately bought and sold.[61] Critiques of markets that fixate on the trade in pollution or waste alone tend to miss the actual causes of most pollution: not markets in pollution per se, but markets in "ordinary" commodities; not trade in toxic waste but the more basic principles of free trade. In turn, if environmental goods and bads are continuous with other kinds, critique must focus not on *exceptions* to the rule of the market, but on the rule of the market itself.

This is illustrated by a reductio ad absurdum: Larry Summers's notorious defense, in a 1991 World Bank memo, of the "impeccable" economic logic of "dumping a load of toxic waste" in low-wage countries, especially those in Africa.[62] Summers was widely castigated for his remarks, which seemed to many to illustrate what David Naguib Pellow calls the "racist and classist culture and ideology" of Northern institutions.[63] The problem with the memo, however, is not only cultural or ideological. Repugnant though it may be, the economic logic *is* impeccable on its own terms. It is the basic logic of free trade—of market freedom. The memo itself noted as much, concluding that any objections to its argument "could be turned around and used more or less effectively against every Bank proposal for liberalization."[64] Indeed, although the memo is often discussed as if it advocated a trade in toxic waste per se, it advocated something more basic: the migration of "dirty industries" to less developed countries. It recognized, in other words, that pollution typically accompanies production. Two decades prior, Milton Friedman had made the same argument in less incendiary terms: nations could choose the pollution levels they found acceptable, he claimed, such that a higher tolerance for pollution could be a comparative advantage.[65] As Friedman asked, "If Japan chooses to subsidize the export of clean air to the United States, why should we object?"[66] Or, as Summers might have it: if African countries want to import "visibility impairing particulates" and export "pretty air" to wealthier countries, why should we object? Why, in other words, should we object if some people choose to accept the costs associated with production in order to realize the benefits? After all, this is precisely the trade that many developing countries have made in the years since.

The most obvious objection is that articulated by Debra Satz. Satz recognizes that pollution is not itself a distinctive *kind* of good, and is rightly skeptical of moral frameworks that attempt to delineate the limits of markets on the basis of the inherent meaning that goods are said to have. She objects to the trade in toxic waste on different grounds, deeming it a prime example of a "noxious market": one characterized by severe inequality between bargaining parties, as a result of which some are likely to suffer serious harms. Noxious markets, Satz charges, limit the ability of people to interact as equals.[67] We should, I think, be troubled by the noxiousness of these markets. But we should be especially troubled by how many markets turn out to be noxious ones. The severe inequality that concerns Satz is in fact the norm rather than the exception: it is the constitutive basis of class society itself.

Contra Sandel, then, pollution and social costs *are* part of the "cost of doing business," and *should* be seen as of a piece with wages and rent—which is to say, understood as expressions of capitalism's core dynamics, and as corresponding sites of political struggle. Externalities reflect precisely the disconnect between intention and consequence at the heart of market rule, and the disparity in power at the heart of class rule. They therefore open up much larger questions about the organization of political economy than is typically acknowledged.[68]

The Social Costs of Doing Business

The Violent Paradoxes of Market Rule

We can approach the role of market rule in the problem of social cost by way of a body of philosophical work focused on allocating responsibility for climate change—not because this literature attends to the market, but because it generally doesn't.[69] Within moral philosophy, climate change is often said to pose significant challenges to traditional accounts of responsibility and moral agency. It is caused by the actions of such a large and diffuse number of people that any individual's contribution seems impossible to parse: Agency is, in Stephen Gardiner's terms, "fragmented."[70] The effect of each individual's action is so small that it seems to escape responsibility—yet taken collectively, the results are catastrophic. Climate change even seems to reveal what Judith Lichtenberg describes as "new harms."[71] Once, she suggests, we could recognize the actions that caused injury and seek to avoid them—but when our most mundane activities turn out to contribute to serious problems, she observes, "not harming people turns out to be difficult and to require our undivided attention."[72] It requires reevaluation of our seemingly trivial choices: what we eat, where we live, how we get around, what we wear. Although any one person's contribution to a problem like climate change may be negligible to the point of being imperceptible, most philosophers argue that to ignore the aggregated effects of our individual actions is to make what Derek Parfit calls "mistakes in moral mathematics."[73] We each have a duty to face our contributions to the problem, and minimize actions that, when combined, add up to a serious harm.

Tellingly, in these discussions, action often amounts to consumption: iPhones, flights, steaks, SUVs. As Lichtenberg puts it bluntly, "Every bite we eat! Every purchase we make!"[74] Rather than constituting a source of "new harms," then, climate change has simply shed new light on an existing class of harms: those already embedded in our market choices, if only by exclusion from them. Yet in this literature, the market itself is almost never addressed explicitly. The link between consumption and harm, cause and effect, is framed as a direct one. While such claims aim to clarify responsibility, however, they paradoxically tend to obscure rather than illuminate the structures of action, insofar as their moral immediacy is achieved by eliminating the essential mediating social institution. It's important, in other words, that the harms that result from our purchases are *not* the same as those we enact on others directly.

Theorists of moral agency and climate change often emphasize the difficulty of knowing *how* to act rightly: avoiding complicity seems to require an immense amount of research about everything we buy. But as we've seen, epistemic problems are not exceptional but endemic to markets. By their very nature, markets systematically make the effects of our consumption opaque to us. For the most part, we have no real way of knowing what kinds of noxious matter are generated as byproducts of the commodities we buy. We may be aware of certain high-profile examples—the carbon emissions associated with flying or the deforestation associated with raising beef cattle—but there are countless others we don't take into account because we do not, cannot, and most importantly, *are not expected to* know that they occur. It is not a problem, according to the theory of market freedom, that we don't know these things—to the contrary, it is a boon. Occasionally, it may be necessary to correct missing information—though there is, as ecological economists have often pointed out, something fantastical about the prospect of internalizing *all* externalities, as if the market could provide a 1:1 model of the world in its entirety, down to the last carbon molecule. (We'll look more closely, in chapter 6, at the challenges that arise in efforts to fix the market's epistemic problems by creating novel property rights.) But the more fundamental problem, for those who seek to achieve morally correct consumption, is that market coordination is *premised* on our ignorance.

Perhaps the most significant difficulty for those concerned with moral responsibility is that market choices, particularly those made under conditions of market dependence and competition, operate within a framework that fundamentally denies it. The point of market freedom, after all, is that we *aren't* responsible for the effects of our purchases on others. Indeed, as Eric MacGilvray argues, "*market prices themselves are externalities*," insofar as *all prices* "impose costs and confer benefits on third parties in ways that no one—least of all the affected people themselves—can predict or control."[75] The externality, in other words, is not an error or absence in the market, but rather an extreme example of how markets normally function, and what they are supposed to do. This problem, of course, is the one we have examined in chapter 2: that of Hardin's tragedy and Sartre's counterfinality. It stems from choices that become problems only in the aggregate; from the way our action comes to appear as other to us—and the way that this estrangement from our action is reflected in physical form. Like Sartre's peasants, we are helplessly producing the floods that will destroy us—and also producing the floods that will destroy others, just as the peasants accidentally flood the densely inhabited plains below. Our millions of tiny, insignificant actions are channeled by market rule and unified by the atmosphere.

Although the philosophical debate has focused on the complicity of individual consumers, however, the force of market rule is most significant at the level of investment and production. Here, too, the Summers memo is illustrative: It describes how market rule drives capital to locate production wherever costs are lowest—which often means places where "social costs" can be imposed on others most cheaply and easily. So-called "less developed countries" stand in the same relation, relative to private investors, that individual laborers do relative to potential employers: they are in need of resources that others control and must compete with others to obtain them. In other words, they stand in a position of seriality relative to those with the power to invest, to employ, to generate needed goods and revenue. Market prices do contain information. But the information they contain is as much about the balance of power within a society as anything else. For what price are you willing to accept the burden of pollution, toxic waste, dirty air? The answer will depend, of course, on your circumstances, relative to those of others. An account of social cost therefore needs an account of class power and class rule.

Obscure Residues

Social costs *are* reciprocal and antagonistic, as Coase argues—but the struggle over the burden of social costs is better characterized in terms of struggle between classes with disparate power than as a market exchange between equal individuals. In turn, if pollution constitutes an unpaid factor of production, it is one that is typically appropriated by capital. These are the central insights of a less well-known twentieth-century theorist of the externality: the German economist K. W. Kapp, an institutionalist informed by the Frankfurt School of critical theory.[76] In *The Social Costs of Private Enterprise* (1950), Kapp described not the widespread affluence typically thought to characterize the postwar period, but an economy plagued by workplace injury, polluted air and water, depleted plant and animal resources, and mounting waste. All, he charged, were costs of production paid not by private industry but by "society."[77] Entire industries were profitable only because they had managed "to shift a substantial part of these costs to other persons and the community at large.[78] Kapp thought cost-shifting more pervasive even than labor exploitation, to the point that capitalism was not a font of abundance, but "an economy of unpaid costs."[79] In turn, social costs were a site of political conflict: private enterprise pushed costs onto society, and society pushed back.[80]

While Kapp framed this struggle in the Polanyian terms of the conflict between private enterprise and "society," I understand it in terms of class rule: the ability of a subset of people to remake the world by virtue of the resources they control. In the course of commodity production, raw materials are altered in composition and structure—and as we have seen, there is always an excess. While chapter 3 considered types of production that resist real subsumption altogether, suprasumption also persists in the really subsumed factory, in the form of surplus matter cast off in the course of production. As capitalism has created colossal productive forces, and even entirely novel *kinds* of matter, it has also created colossal amounts of surplus matter—and this, too, often takes unprecedented forms.

For an illustration, let's think back to *Le chant du styrène*'s documentation of the production of a plastic bowl. Strikingly, the film concludes with images of smoke billowing forth from giant vents: "Oil and coal both went up in smoke when that first chemist had the brilliant idea of turning these clouds into countless useful objects," the narrator observes. "Into new materials were these obscure residues thus transformed."[81] Yet while the film follows the conversion of hydrocarbons into plastics, it doesn't follow the "obscure residues" that emerge from the production process in its own right. Plastics are *the* material of the Great Acceleration: fully synthetic configurations of matter that had never existed before the twentieth century, which were barely used before 1941, and which now are found in nearly every crevice of the Earth. As a class of good, plastics were molded for industrial production from the start: the field of chemical engineering developed in the shadow of Taylorism, oriented in its very precepts toward achieving a continuous flow of production.[82] Plastics are economically viable only at industrial scale, moreover: because the initial molds are expensive, it's profitable to produce plastics only in vast quantities—at which point they become drastically cheaper than nearly anything else.[83] Plastics, then, appear the pinnacle of real subsumption.

Yet they also reflect the persistence of suprasumption: even these perfectly molded and moldable materials leave traces in their wake. And the residues of plastics production are no longer obscure. The petrochemical industry has for decades been the target of environmental literature and environmental justice organizing, from Carson's *Silent Spring* and Commoner's *Closing Circle* to protests in Louisiana's "Cancer Alley" and challenges by the Oil, Atomic, and Chemical Workers union.[84] Perhaps even more concerning than the "residues" produced *alongside* plastics are plastic products themselves, which have become one of the most significant contemporary sources of pollution. The plastic bowl tracked in *Le chant du styrène* is plausibly now floating in the Pacific garbage patch.[85] As this example illustrates, the line between commodities and pollution is thin—and so too is the line between the power to produce commodities and the power to generate byproducts.[86]

Class rule, then, rooted in the power to decide what to produce and how, reflects the power to decide not only which commodities to intentionally produce but also which byproducts to generate in the course of rearranging raw materials and labor processes into new forms. It is not only the power to command the labor of others within a given production process but also the power to impose costs on those who stand outside the formal production process altogether. It is not only the ability to methodically remake nonhuman beings

as factors of production—to reorder the bodies of cattle or the genetic structure of rice—but also the ability to remake, and often chaotically *dis*order, the
basic ecological conditions in which countless species live. Class rule, in other
words, consists in the power to produce the environment itself.

Expulsion and Absorption

Certain aspects of class rule as it pertains to surplus matter are illuminated by
analyses of workplace domination. When an employer purchases labor power,
they gain the power to direct the worker's bodily capacities—including in ways
that may prove damaging to them. The mine owner orders workers into the pit
thick with coal dust; the owner of the steel mill directs workers to operate the
furnace that discharges poisonous fumes. The factory owner decides, too,
whether to install a smoke filter or institute safety procedures; workers can
agree only whether to take the job they are offered.[87] Consider here G. A. Cohen's example of a chemical company that offers jobs posing serious, and
known, health risks.[88] Do the factory's workers freely choose these jobs, he
asks, or are they forced to take them? Those who argue the latter emphasize the
structural unfreedom of labor under capitalism: people need *a* job, and usually
have little choice about what it is. Those arguing the former tend to make a
version of Friedman's argument: if someone is willing to risk their health for a
better wage, why should we stop them from doing so? If someone doesn't want
to take a given job, they can look for another—they are not bound to any particular employer. The fact that they face dismal options or material hardships
does not diminish their ability to choose among them.[89] Cohen concludes that
the worker is at once freely choosing the dangerous job *and* severely restricted
in options. The worker needs a wage to survive in the near term, even at the
potential cost to life in the long run; it may very well be that their best option
is to take a health-threatening job, while others are able to "make money out of
[their] relative lack of freedom."[90] This, for Cohen, is the "structure of proletarian unfreedom."

But the structure of proletarian unfreedom extends beyond the workplace
and the work relation. Consider, here, a twist on Cohen's question: Are people
who live next to factories with smoky chimneys *forced* to live there? Coase would
answer in the negative, claiming that people are legally free to live anywhere
they can afford. Perhaps they've decided they're willing to put up with some
smoke to pay less in rent, or to have a shorter commute to work—and this is their
choice. We are not yet at the point of life on Heinlein's Luna, after all, where even

air has a cost: everyone can breathe for free. It's *clean* air that's often costly. Pollution is matter that no one wants to buy; which instead, people pay to *avoid*. Those who can't afford clean air must pay costs *in natura*. A theorist of environmental justice would rightly point out that those who live in the most polluted areas are almost always those who have the least power in society—and, we might add, in the labor market. They are those who must take the lowest paying jobs and thus the lowest cost apartments. The wealthy live in leafy neighborhoods upwind from industrial discharge; the poor, next to incinerators.[91] Often these economic constraints are reinforced by political ones, as when states issue permits for waste disposal or dumping that burden certain groups in particular; and they are nearly always exacerbated by forms of direct domination as reflected in, for example, patterns of racial segregation and legacies of colonialism.[92] The key point, however, is that this is not *only* a matter of maldistribution of harmful effects. It is also underpinned by a form of unfreedom in its own right.

The structure of unfreedom, here, lies in the inability to *refuse* costs imposed by others. It consists not in being compelled to take a job that may come with outsized risks, but being forced to passively *accept* the effects of a production process over which one has no control.[93] Labor power, after all, is simply bodily capacity: "the aggregate of those mental and physical capabilities existing in the physical form, the living personality, of a human being."[94] Marx, as we've seen, is interested in how these capacities are loaned out for periods of time, and how they're actively put to work in production. But if bodily capacities are activated to "produce use values," as Marx explores, so too are they activated when they are used as "sinks" for dis-use values.[95] Whereas the value of the commodity is realized through exchange, the negative use value of byproduction is "realized" concretely, in the bodies of those who encounter it. We can think of this exposure to surplus matter as *absorption power*: it too names the use of (human) bodily capacities in the course of production. The autonomist Marxist George Caffentzis frames this use of bodily capacity as a form of labor—what he describes as "the passive work of absorbing capital's wastes."[96]

But is precisely the *passivity* of absorption, in contrast to the activity of labor, that makes a crucial difference: it is what renders the contract unnecessary. Absorption power thus raises an issue unaddressed by labor-oriented theories of domination: namely, that it is far easier to *expel* surplus matter that affects others than it is to *compel* their labor. To use someone's labor power requires consensual exchange in some form, however constrained, because agency rests with the laborer: if you ask someone to work without pay, they can refuse. (Provided, of course, that the law and state will recognize and reinforce that refusal.) In the case of expulsion, by contrast, the agency lies with the polluter. It's easy for capital to abdicate responsibility for byproduction: the ability to pollute lies with the polluter by default, and by default it is available for free. The factory owner can dump toxins in the water or carbon in the air whether or not they have obtained consent to do so—and so they can, effectively, treat others as a sink for particulate matter or chemical waste *without* their explicit consent. Those exposed may protest, but they cannot refuse to breathe polluted air in the way that they can refuse to work. Nor can they refuse to experience a climate change-driven heat wave or flash flood. Human absorption power effectively operates as a free gift of nature. In a social order in which one group of people enjoys institutionalized structural advantage over another, the ability to expel costlessly and nonconsensually becomes a way that one group of people profits by interfering with the bodily autonomy of others.[97]

Shifting Costs Back

Coase's proposal to allocate "the right to do something which has a harmful effect," then, appears more significant than he tends to admit. It amounts to a proposal to put absorption power on par with labor power as something that has to be voluntarily exchanged rather than simply appropriated. If those subjected to capital's expulsion of surplus matter could struggle around social costs or refuse them outright, the consequences for the organization of production might be considerable. Treating the right to pollute as a factor of production that must be paid for would seem to give society a tool in the struggle to shift costs back. If, as Kapp argues, many industries are profitable *because* they shift costs onto others, forcing them to pay their full costs would presumably drive many industries to drastically reorganize production or even cease it altogether.[98] Coase, of course, has nothing of the sort in mind. It doesn't matter who initially holds the right to pollute, he claims: the relevant parties will simply negotiate an agreement that maximizes the total value of production, inclusive of any necessary compensation for harm.[99] One of them, it would seem, has to be wrong.

The key difference lies in the view of costs themselves. Kapp's claim that capitalism is objectively in deficit operates on the premise that there is a "true cost" to pay—one that can capture the various *in natura* harms to human and nonhuman life.[100] For Coase, by contrast, there are no "true" costs—there are only the prices that parties negotiate. Kapp's argument, then, is vulnerable to the same critique of moral overreach that Coase had launched at Pigou: that his conception of social costs imports a set of value judgments. Imagine, for example, that a state created a right to pollute and allocated it to residents of a neighborhood, such that an investor hoping to build a factory would have to negotiate acceptable levels of smoke exposure with everyone living in the vicinity. (Equally, we could imagine that everyone were granted an alienable right to a clean environment that they could choose to sell.)[101] If each person were paid the "true cost" of anticipated pollution, calculated in terms of lost wages, healthcare costs, shortened life-span, and so on, the sum might well be staggering, as Kapp's own estimates suggest.

But in reality, many people are likely to sell the right to pollute for far less than its "true cost." They might do so in ignorance, not understanding the likely long-term health effects; or they might be perfectly aware of the risks but need money immediately; or they might worry that the factory will move—down the road, over the border, around the world—to wherever someone will sell the right for less. When people who have nothing to sell but their labor power find that even that is not particularly valuable, they may decide that their competitive advantage lies in their willingness to accept particularly dangerous or dirty forms of production, precisely as Friedman and Summers suggest.[102] This is especially true where people are subjected to other forms of domination. As the Summers memo well illustrates, class power is typically articulated in tandem with other social relations: most notably, in these cases, those of race and nation.[103] In short, people might sell the right to pollute—the permission for someone else to impose the physical costs of production on their body—more cheaply than they "should" for precisely the same reasons that they might sell their labor cheaply: they are dependent on the market to obtain a livelihood, they own little else, and they relate to others primarily as competitors.[104] To see "social costs" as akin to wages means recognizing that, like wages, social costs will always reflect the inequalities and vulnerabilities that permeate class society.

To identify the maldistribution of externalities as reflections of class rule, conversely, might seem to miss something vital about the anomalous materiality of pollution: its amorphous quality, its diffusion, its ability to travel. Ulrich Beck, in his analysis of "risk society," acknowledges that the risks produced in the modern age are distributed unevenly—"The proletariat of the global risk society," he observes, "settles beneath the smokestacks, next to the refineries and chemical factories in the industrial centers of the Third World"—but he insists that risk is *not* fundamentally a class relation.[105] Everyone, eventually, is threatened by the risks generated by modern society: in Beck's term, "smog is democratic."[106] There is something to this. While the distribution of surplus matter is typically geographically concentrated in ways that map onto existing social inequalities, it also resists containment—by contract and private property, but also by political borders and social categories. The chemical harms visited upon exploited migrant farmworkers *do* eventually rebound upon wealthy consumers who ingest the fruits and vegetables that the former harvest. Acid rain caused by sulfur dioxide emissions does cross state and national borders. Traces of industrially produced chemicals can be found at the bottom of the ocean and the most remote points of the Earth and in the blood of nearly every person living. But Beck's claim mistakenly treats class as demography rather than social relation. To indict class rule as a significant *cause* of these effects—to locate class rule in the *power over byproduction*—is not to say that the *effects themselves* are distributed as a function of class alone.

To say that externalities must be read as the product of class rule and market rule is also not to blunt their sheer material force or reduce them to "merely" social relations. To the contrary, it is to underscore how social relations, mediated through matter, take on a life of their own. Surplus matter circulates differently than commodities; it accumulates in inverse patterns to wealth. Although it often originates at the point of production, it rarely stays there: once released into the world, it tends to travel, such that its effects may materialize far from the original site of generation. Temporally, too, physical effects of pollution often appear at a distance from their causes, such that industrial diseases tend to emerge in postindustrial times, long after factories close and jobs disappear.[107] *In natura* costs materialize in the form of smoky skies and extra brilliant sunsets, dead zones and silent springs. They appear in black lung disease among coal miners and heightened cancer rates among farmworkers exposed to pesticides, in children's asthma rates and differences in life-span; in Manchester's working class of "pale, emaciated, narrow-chested, hollow-eyed ghosts . . . weak, flabby, and lacking in all energy."[108] These too are practico-actants: human action, channeled by market rule and class rule, made manifest at the level of both the body and the biosphere.

No Outside

So far I've focused largely on social costs, understood as costs to people. But the ecological costs, those borne by nonhuman entities, are almost too vast to grasp. From an ecological perspective, the scope of the externality is almost infinite—precisely as Friedman had feared. The neoclassical assumption that a transaction *can* be contained to the parties to a contract appears delusional in a world where everything affects everything else. What is really astonishing, from this vantage point, is the idea that the revolutions in the use of nature heralded by modernity's admirers could take place without any corresponding transformations of the broader natural world—the idea, for instance, that billions of tons of organic matter, representing millions of years of concentrated life, could be extracted from the depths of the Earth and burned in a span of decades without any effect on the presently living planet.[109]

The sheer amount of surplus matter unleashed on the world in the past two centuries has transformed the ways that many kinds of creatures live in it. Some of this matter is synthetic and novel—like the microplastics that now permeate even the deep reaches of the ocean, and which do not decompose. But surplus matter has also altered energy flows and cellular structure, the molecular composition of air and chemical composition of water, such that ostensibly organic materials take on new dimensions. Algae grow naturally in many bodies of water, for instance—but algal blooms, turbocharged by fertilizer intended for crops, can suffocate aquatic fauna dependent on oxygenated water. Microbes long present in animal respiratory systems can, under abnormal weather conditions, multiply so drastically as to become deadly en masse. Indeed, the effects of surplus matter on nonhumans are much stranger—and often more ominous—than we tend to imagine. They unsettle the question of what pollution is. If, as Douglas claims, pollution is always defined in relation to particular organizations of social life, then defining pollution in relation to various forms of ecological life opens up a dizzying array of possible answers. A bright white streetlight can be pollution to a bat that hunts in the dark. The rumble of a passing freighter can be pollution to a whale that communicates through song.

If the monetary costs to human beings of surplus matter are often difficult to estimate and always imbued by social inequalities, the "costs" to nonhuman life are literally incalculable, at least in monetary terms. They appear only in natura, almost never in a form that capital can see. Just as the human economy imports "free goods" from the natural economy, the ecological economist Herman Daly argues, it also exports "bads" without having to pay for their absorption.[110] Insects can't demand compensation for the decimation of their numbers by pesticides; fish can't insist on payment for the decimation of their waters by fertilizer runoff. Even estimations of in natura costs are, necessarily, filtered through human assessments and perceptions—as we'll see in more detail in chapter 6. If it is always logical for capital to impose social costs on the poor, as Joan Martínez-Alier observes, it is more logical still to impose them on the natural world.[111]

Politicizing Byproduction

The material traces of suprasumption are often destructive. But they also have the potential to generate new forms of political collective. The classic example of the factory that spews smoke, for instance, creates a novel practico-actant in the form of air pollution—and in turn creates a novel form of connection among those exposed to it.[112] The industrial factory is already a paradigmatic example of social labor: capital brings individual workers together and coordinates their action, such that they work cooperatively even though they sell their labor individually. The surplus matter the factory generates—the smoke and effluent and chemicals and waste—also has a socializing effect outside the factory walls. As people are forced to bear the burden of private production, they are, in a sense, integrated into the production process and materially connected to others—if often against their will. The socialization of production, in other words, is also the socialization of *byproduction*. These effects are not only unifying, of course; they also expose glaring fault lines in vulnerability.[113] The burden of surplus matter, as we've seen, is not evenly distributed: it is disproportionately borne by those subjected to other forms of domination—racial oppression in particular—and can serve to reveal these social disparities.[114] Many dimensions of the latent collectives formed by novel material entities will clearly map onto existing social categories.

But other dimensions of these collectives are as heterogeneous—and potentially surprising—as the geographies and temporalities of surplus matter itself. When Sartre's peasants deforest the mountain, for instance, the flooding that results destroys their own crops and threatens the valley below. By contrast, when cattle ranchers deforest the Amazon, they don't face an immediate threat to their own production (although they might eventually, if they then overgraze the resulting pastures), but they do affect regional rainfall patterns, and increase, however imperceptibly, the prospects of significant sea level rise, which threatens coastal dwellers worldwide. A factory that emits primarily sulfur dioxide might damage the health of people living within a given radius but have no effect on those living a few miles away, while a factory that emits only carbon will have no immediate effects on nearby communities but will affect, in some small way, the entire world long into the future.[115] Often the temporalities of surplus matter are slow: the effects of materials like PCBs might generate a cancer cluster over decades; the effects of sea level rise resulting from melting ice caps will unfold over centuries. Yet they can also be frighteningly fast: industrial waste discharged into a reservoir might make people ill immediately, while algal blooms caused by fertilizer runoff can kill thousands of fish in a matter of days. The physical effects of byproduction also interact differently with the physicality of bodies themselves: their shape, size, genetic predispositions, composition—and even species.

Indeed, byproduction often reveals uncanny resonances across species boundaries. After all, it's precisely the *continuity* between humans and nonhumans that allows pollution to travel so widely, as thinkers from Rachel Carson to Winona LaDuke have emphasized. To say that social relations are materially mediated often means that they are mediated by other life forms.[116] As both Carson and LaDuke document, toxic waste often produces reproductive abnormalities and aberrations in humans and animals alike; pregnant people and animals are more likely than others to accumulate and pass on toxins.[117] The chemical agents in pesticides do not discriminate among the organisms socially categorized as "pests," which they are intended to kill, and the other organisms—from songbirds to human farmworkers—that might encounter them. Contaminated aquifers disable both humans and animals, in what Sunaura Taylor describes as an "expansive web of injury."[118] People living near the beach in Miami are threatened by sea level rise, as are those living in the lowlands of Bangladesh—and so, too, are freshwater turtles whose pools are increasingly inundated with salt water and monk seals that nest on Hawaii's low-lying beaches. Other echoes are uncannier still: The levels of chromium found in North Atlantic right whales are similar to those of factory workers engaged in metal plating processes. Because high levels of industrial contaminants accumulate in the fatty tissue of beluga whales, the blood of Inuit living in unindustrialized Greenland has levels of mercury and organochlorines on par with that of people living near mines in Latin America.[119]

These collectives initially exist in seriality, oriented toward and connected by the common threat posed by surplus matter—the smoke or the chemicals or the warming atmosphere—but organization can direct collective action toward its source. Grape and lettuce boycotts organized by the United Farm Workers, for example, drew attention to the shared vulnerability of both farm workers and consumers to the pesticides used in growing crops and sought to mobilize them in collective action against grape growers.[120] Yet as Kapp observed, and even Coase recognized, the producers of social costs tend to have the upper hand in these conflicts. Social costs are typically spread across large numbers of people, while benefits are concentrated amongst a small number of producers; benefits are realized immediately, whereas costs are often slow to emerge. These are daunting challenges. But they are not of an entirely different order than those that confront more familiar labor struggles. Movements for environmental protection are not simply new social movements entirely distinct from class-based politics, as has often been charged, nor instances of "postmaterial" politics concerned with "values" rather than "interests."[121] They are simply a different iteration of the same fundamental collective action problem, generated by the structure of market seriality. [122] What movements against the expulsion of social costs lack are the political infrastructures that can sustain collective organization in confronting concentrated power. Although unions have occasionally challenged the imposition of social costs on workers, there are no trade unions for those who bear the burden of social costs more broadly; no "pollutees' rights" for those organizing against the expulsion of surplus matter, as there are labor rights for those struggling against exploitation in the production of surplus value. But there might be. One counterintuitive place to start is with the rights of nature.

A Union of the Affected

The rights of nature are often understood as a defense of nature's intrinsic value against instrumental use, or an expression of "respect" for nature. But the legal scholar Christopher Stone's landmark "Should Trees Have Standing" (1972) originally posited the rights of nature as a legal form that might address the problem of social cost as articulated by Ronald Coase.[123] We all, Stone argued, should have to pay the "full costs that our activities are imposing on society"—yet he recognized that this ideal was rarely met with respect to the costs of pollution in particular.[124] The central problem, Stone recognized, was the mismatch between dispersed costs and concentrated benefits, and the transaction costs of collective action for those burdened by the former. [125] If, say, the dumping of toxic chemicals into a lake caused a hundred dollars' worth of damage to each person living around the lake, the total social cost might be quite high—yet it would not make sense for any individual to seek damages, and it would likely be too troublesome to organize the group to demand collective payment. As long as those affected remained atomized, the polluter would continue to reap the concentrated benefits.

Stone's ingenious solution came in the form of the personification of the environment itself. If the *lake itself* were able to bring suit for total damages to those living around it, the collective action problem would be solved. By allowing the lake itself to prove damages, he argued,

> we in effect make the natural object, through its guardian, a rural entity competent to gather up these fragmented and otherwise unrepresented

damage claims. . . . By making the lake itself the focus of these damages, and "incorporating" it so to speak, the legal system can effectively take proof upon, and confront the mill with, a larger and more representative measure of the damages its pollution causes.[126]

The lake would effectively aggregate the interests of all human beings affected by its use, potentially even including those not represented in the market or by the law, like future generations, so that their claims against their shared antagonist—the mill—could be more easily made. It would provide a vehicle for collective action among those affected by social costs.

Stone's other crucial innovation was to take seriously the costs imposed on nonhumans themselves, including those with no economic value. He sought to face up to "the death of eagles and inedible crabs, the suffering of sea lions, the loss from the face of the earth of species of commercially valueless birds."[127] There was no reason, he thought, that the environment's importance should be measured only "as lost profits to someone else."[128] Stone extended Coase's reciprocity principle to include nonhumans: in a case where someone wanted to build a mill on the river, for example, reciprocity would mean that "the mill wants to harm the river, and the river—if we assume it 'wants' to maintain its present environmental quality—wants to harm the mill."[129] A potential mill would degrade the quality of water and river life; meanwhile, the preservation of the river would harm the mill's function, or perhaps preclude it from being built altogether. There might be difficulties in determining what the river "wants" or how damages to it might be represented in terms of cost, but these could be addressed through creative estimates. The key point was that legal rights granted to the lake or river could potentially represent the interests of both humans *and* nonhumans arrayed in opposition to the mill.

Seen in this light, the rights of nature can orient attention toward the source of "harm to the river": the mill, and more pertinently, its owner. Insofar as the mill and the river are at odds, in other words, the rights of nature are effectively rights asserted against capital. Instead of reifying a given natural entity as a discrete subject of transhistorical rights, then, the rights-of-nature framework might recognize the more-than-human collectives that are brought into being by capital's transformation of the natural world.[130] Indeed, what Stone calls the "rights of nature" are better understood as *multispecies collective bargaining rights*: a legal instrument that gives members of a nascent collective constituted by surplus matter the right and ability to join forces, and that might help constitute something like a union of those subjected to byproduction.[131] The establishment of "rights of nature" in law is hardly sufficient to *generate* such a collective, of course. But it might, more modestly, provide a piece of the political infrastructure for contesting the imposition of surplus matter on humans and nonhumans alike.

Conclusion: Pollution beyond Price

As the concept of the externality discloses, human action inevitably has consequences that reverberate through the material world in unexpected ways. We will always have to decide how to measure and share in abundance and its byproducts, how to allocate necessary work and unavoidable waste. The intense difficulty of assessing responsibility in a world where our most mundane actions inevitably ripple outward, with consequences that exceed our intent or control, will remain. So too will the spatial difficulties of acting within bounded communities when the effects may have planetary repercussions, and the temporal problem of actions and effects that span generations. Any form of social organization to come will have to deal with capitalism's byproducts—*residuals*, in Andreas Folkers's term—long into the future.[132] The problem named by externalities, in other words, is genuinely challenging.

The politics of social cost, considered collectively rather than individually, can help us think about how we might approach it. Coase is right that there are no "true costs," "correct prices," or "objective values"—and so, too, in the claim that the goal is not to eliminate pollution altogether but to secure the "optimum amount." It is hard to imagine what eliminating pollution altogether would mean, or how we might act without at least some reverberations we don't intend. As Commoner reminds us, there is no such thing as a free gift: no action in the physical world that doesn't come paired with a reaction. The problem comes when the "optimum amount" of pollution and the appropriate level and distribution of social cost are decided largely as a function of value production, under conditions of class and market rule, articulated with other forms of domination; and when we organize our action in ways that resolutely sever the link between action and consequence.

But in the same way that someone might willingly do an unpleasant or even dangerous job for the benefit of a community they felt was their own, someone might willingly accept certain risks for a project to which they were committed. This is the case even now: people are often ambivalent about doing dangerous or dirty work, taking pride in their contributions to society even as they worry about the effects on their health or the world around them. Social costs, then, must be seen as sites of politics—not individualized consumer politics or Hayekian expressions of individual freedom, but collective judgments about what we value and what ends we want to achieve, refracted through conflicts across radical power imbalances. In this vein, to understand pollution in relation to unfreedom rather than sheer violence or distribution sets a demanding standard—but not a rigid one. It does not permit treating some communities as sacrifice zones or dumping grounds. At the same time, importantly, it does not prohibit any activity outright, even those with potentially harmful byproducts or effects. It instead poses a more foundational question for us to answer: what might pollution even *be* in a society ordered by something other than price?

5

Labor of Life

REPRODUCTION AND THE NATURE
OF THE HUMAN

IN 1968 the artist Mierle Laderman Ukeles had a child. Suddenly people stopped talking to her about art. She felt that she had become "a different class of human being": a mother.[1] In 1969 she wrote the "Manifesto for Maintenance Art." Challenging art's emphasis on development, innovation, novelty, creativity, and the avant-garde, the manifesto drew attention instead to the processes of preservation and care:

> Maintenance is a drag: it takes all the fucking time (lit.)
> The mind boggles and chafes at the boredom.
> The culture confers lousy status on maintenance jobs=
> minimum wages, housewives=no pay.[2]

The manifesto proposed an artwork in three parts. First, Ukeles would perform, within the space of the museum, the kinds of "maintenance every day things" that she did as a matter of daily life: sweeping, dusting, cooking, changing lightbulbs. Second, she would interview a range of workers, asking what they thought maintenance was; how they felt about doing it; how they saw the relationship between maintenance and freedom. Third, she would perform what she called Earth maintenance. Each day containers of refuse would be delivered to the museum: contents of a sanitation truck; a container of polluted air; a container of polluted Hudson River water; a container of "ravaged land." At the museum they would be rehabilitated and "depolluted."

The "Manifesto for Maintenance Art" was one of many efforts in this period, in North America and western Europe, to grapple with housework: from Betty

Friedan's *The Feminine Mystique* (1963) to Chantal Akerman's *Jeanne Dielman, 23 quai du Commerce, 1080 Bruxelles* (1975); Alice Childress's *Like One of the Family* (1956) to the Wages for Housework campaign (1972). The manifesto was informed, too, by growing environmental consciousness, marked by the publication of *Silent Spring* (1962) a few years prior and culminating in the first Earth Day the following year. In the years that followed, many others would seek to bring feminism and ecology together: in radical feminist texts like Susan Griffin's *Woman and Nature* (1978) and Mary Daly's *Gyn/Ecology* (1978); in movements like the Greenham Common women's peace camp in England, Women's Pentagon Action in the United States, Greenbelt Movement in Kenya, and Chipko movement in India.[3] But what, exactly, links these projects? What do feminism and environmentalism, housework and the earth, have to do with each other?

———

On the one hand, the connections are obvious. Ideas of the Earth as a mother are as ingrained as, and perhaps inseparable from, the idea of the Earth as a giver of gifts. Creation mythologies across a range of cultures figure the Earth as mother or goddess; even within the Christian tradition of God as Father, Pope Francis describes the Earth as mother and sister.[4] The botanist Robin Wall Kimmerer writes of the Earth as the "first among good mothers, [which] gives us the gift that we cannot provide ourselves"; Indigenous Andean movements defend Pachamama, the Earth mother; Bolivia and Ecuador have legally enshrined the "Rights of Mother Earth."[5] These associations persist in the tendency, pervasive in classical political economy, to refer to nature with feminine pronouns, describing the work "she" does for free. Even Marx cites the English economist William Petty in claiming that "labour is the father of material wealth, the earth is its mother": human labor, figured as masculine creativity, works on sheer feminine fecundity to produce wealth.[6] The French philosopher Bernard de Fontenelle declared in 1688 that "Nature is a great housewife"; three centuries later, the American ecologist Barry Commoner described ecology as "the science of planetary housekeeping."[7]

Perhaps more surprising is that similar parallels abound in feminist critiques of capitalism as well. Feminists have frequently drawn analogies between the work done, typically for free, to reproduce the human beings who comprise the laborers, citizens, and other more familiar subjects of political and economic thought, and the contributions of nonhuman nature to human life and economies. For James O'Connor and Nancy Fraser, both social reproduction and ecology are "background conditions" for production, echoing Val Plumwood's analysis of "backgrounding" as the process by which the spheres of "reproduction and subsistence" are devalued. For Maria Mies and Jason Moore, the work of both women and nature constitutes capitalism's unvalued "foundations," whose contributions are freely appropriated. For Marilyn Waring and Nancy Folbre, the contributions of both household labor and ecosystemic activity go uncounted and invisible in measurements of economic growth.[8]

And yet from a feminist perspective, these comparisons between the reproduction of human life and the gifts of nature are also vexed. Although ecological and feminist movements emerged simultaneously in the late 1960s, and have often seemed to share certain affinities, they have typically adopted radically different stances on the question of nature itself. Ecological thought frequently reminds us that human beings are part of nature, that we ourselves are animals dependent on and unavoidably connected to other kinds of life. The central impulse of contemporary feminist thought, by contrast, is to denaturalize: to reveal that women's oppression is not a biological necessity but a social convention that can be changed.[9] Feminists have often adhered to Shulamith Firestone's suggestion that "feminists have to question, not just all of Western culture, but . . . even the very organization of nature."[10]

If reproductive labor appears to be a free gift of nature, then, feminist critiques of nature pose an uncomfortable question: Why? What, exactly, unifies ecological activity and reproductive labor as "background conditions" or "maintenance work"? Why do these *particular* activities go unvalued, uncounted, unpaid? After all, ecological processes—say, an earthworm's aeration of the soil—are hardly comparable to the gestation of a human fetus, which in turn has little to do with cooking a meal or washing a floor. Why, then, do they seem to occupy the same position within capitalist societies? Does this analogy serve to reaffirm, however unintentionally, some fundamental link between earthly and womanly fertility?

Feminists are conscious of these pitfalls. Most arguments by isomorphism emphasize the social construction of both gender and nature, claiming that both women and nature have been symbolically and ideologically construed as inferior to men and culture, and economically devalued as a result. Women are said to be "defined into nature," set in opposition to the male subject; "women's work" has been "naturalized," such that it appears to emerge from women's essential character; nature itself has been defined as "everything that should be free."[11] But these answers simply raise new questions. Who exactly is defining women and nature in these terms, and how have they been so successful?

This chapter traces the widespread claim that reproductive labor is devalued because it has been ideologically "naturalized" to the ideology critique of housework advanced by the Marxist feminist Wages for Housework project, and argues that this analysis fails to offer a convincing explanation for either the low value of reproductive labor or gender oppression. What I call the "naturalization thesis" holds that ideological perceptions of reproductive labor are definitive of its status and value—while frequently losing sight of actual labor processes. This thesis also, notably, says remarkably little about nature itself. Theorists of housework insist that reproduction is *labor*, rather than *nature*—but they rarely ask why nature can be taken for free. Nor, for the most part, do they detail the *physical* aspects of reproductive labor: the concrete bodily processes involved in the "reproduction of life," or the labor activities required to sustain them. Yet as I argue, attending to the interaction of bodily and labor processes, and to their organization within capitalist societies, is vital for understanding how and why certain kinds of human labor are perpetually devalued.

Understanding the roots of these analogies has implications not only for how we understand the status of reproductive labor within capitalist societies, but for how we understand the status of nonhuman nature. Many now-canonical works of ecological thought originated in feminist analyses of the association between women and nature, from Carolyn Merchant's "death of nature" thesis to Val Plumwood's critique of Western dualism. These, in turn, have informed widespread claims in environmental studies about how nature is "seen" or "defined," including Jason Moore's influential argument that capitalism defines nature as "cheap" in order to better appropriate it. Yet many of these arguments ultimately rest on a similarly unstable account of ideology, one that no more convincingly accounts for the status of nature than it does for the status of housework. The genealogy traced in this chapter, then, illustrates the shortcomings of the "worldview approach" to the analysis of nature and capitalism outlined in chapter 1.

In its stead, this chapter offers a new account of the oft-noted parallels between human reproductive labor and the free gifts of nature. Rather than analyzing reproductive labor in terms of the "woman question" that animated earlier analyses, my account focuses on the concrete labor processes associated with these kinds of work—including the bodily processes being reproduced—and asks how they are organized by capitalism.[12] In so doing, it rematerializes labor and denaturalizes its relation to capitalism: it restores attention to labor as a material process involving living human beings, while critically assessing the social relations in which these processes take place. Just as nonhuman life processes often conflict with capitalism's drive toward abstract time and continuous production, as seen in chapter 3, so too do the temporalities of *human* life processes. The relationship between human reproductive labor and the "free gifts of nature," then, is not merely analogical or isomorphic, but continuous: both reflect a similar collision of recalcitrant biophysical processes with capitalist social forms and relations. Instead of treating reproductive labor as an inherently distinctive *type* of activity or sphere of life, one always-already informed by gender, I understand it as a formal category naming a diverse array of concrete activities unified by their structural position as a *remnant* of capitalist abstraction.[13]

This attention to the significance of life processes, embodiment, and "nature itself" in reproductive labor might seem to mark a troubling return to biologically essentialist accounts of gender. My goal is the opposite: to attend to the ways that physical and "natural" processes pertain to forms of specifically human labor without immediately gendering those forms of work.[14] My wager is that an account more narrowly focused on how the physical activities of the concrete labor process relate to capital turns out to be *less* functionalist and essentializing than one that seeks to explain gender itself in relation to either kinds of work or kinds of bodies, as socialist and radical feminisms have often tried to do.[15] While feminist analyses of the gendered division of labor have often attended to the embodiment of the *laborer*, moreover—focusing in particular on the capacity for gestation—it is the body being *labored on*, the body that is the *object* of reproductive labor, that is usually of greater significance in the organization of the relevant labor processes.

To see reproductive labor as necessarily tethered to bodily processes, finally, does not make it natural *rather than* social. The body, as Simone de Beauvoir observes, is not a thing but a situation; its physical capacities gain significance only within particular organizations of human social life. Human reproductive labor, as situated within capitalism, occupies a liminal space: it resists real subsumption *both* because it is irreducibly natural, existing in concrete time, structured by biophysical processes, unfolding according to a logic that capital cannot entirely remake or override, and therefore presenting persistent "natural barriers" to subsumption—and also because it is specifically *human*, generating a product, labor power, that is distinguished by the capacity of human beings to act in ways that other kinds of beings cannot. Reproductive labor, then, reflects the ambiguity of human labor power: at once part of and connected to the more-than-human world, while occupying a distinctive position within capitalist societies in particular. The resulting paradox—that the activities most vital to human life are often treated as free gifts—presents a particularly rich site for interrogating the relationship between labor and capitalism, and for orienting our judgments of capitalist value writ large.

Theorizing Housework

"The Monotonous Repetition of Life"

Until the late twentieth century, perhaps the most sustained consideration of household labor in political thought was to be found in Aristotle's depiction of the *oikos* as the realm of necessity, where women, slaves, and oxen perform the labor required to sustain human life, in a sphere governed by despotic norms.[16] Most modern political theorists, including political economists, gave little thought to domestic and reproductive labor, addressing it only in asides.[17] This would change radically in the twentieth century, as the emergent feminist movement put housework on the political agenda. How exactly housework should be characterized, however, has been hotly disputed.

When, in the middle of the twentieth century, Hannah Arendt described the labor of sustaining life as one of three central activities of the human condition, she echoed Aristotle in seeing it as the least human. One of the conceptual innovations of *The Human Condition* (1958)—a book which began as a meditation on and critique of Marx—is the separation of human labor into two categories, each defined by the "worldly character of the produced thing—its location, function, and length of stay in the world."[18] What Arendt calls "labor" is the activity of the *animal laborans*: the ephemeral, monotonous, and cyclical activity necessary to maintain biological processes from day to day; the thing that tethers human beings to the rest of the living world rather than the thing that sets them apart. Labor, for Arendt, produces nothing *but* life: it effectively *is* a stage of biological life, constituting a form of metabolism that does not cease until the organism dies. Although labor is a capacious category, Arendt repeatedly discusses labor in relation to biological procreation specifically, suggesting that "fertility" is labor in its purest form. It is the category of work, for Arendt, that is distinctively human: performed by the specifically human tool user, *homo faber*, who acts as "lord and master of the whole earth" to "wrench" material from nature and make durable objects capable of withstanding nature's unending cycles in order to create a stable setting for the most truly human activity of all—political action.[19] Whereas labor is unending, ceasing only when life is exhausted, work is oriented toward an end with meaning in its own right.

Arendt's description of labor finds a surprising echo in a very different text—Simone de Beauvoir's *The Second Sex* (1949), which similarly counterposes the "monotonous repetition of life" to the genuinely human activity of *homo faber*.[20] But where Arendt describes features of the human condition writ large, Beauvoir describes their allocation along gendered lines. Women, consigned to the droning repetition of reproduction and housework, are effectively *animal laborans*, "subjugated to the species" and submissive to nature; men, who transcend nature through creation, enjoy the status of *homo faber*.[21] For all the changes that modernity had brought to women's lives, Beauvoir claims, the bourgeois Western housewife remained trapped within the realm of necessity and immanence, in a liminal space between mere life and human freedom. It is housework, Beauvoir suggests, that most resembles the labor of Sisyphus, who Camus had declared the hero of existential thought: ceaseless and futile.[22] Rather than imagining the housewife happy, however, Beauvoir sought to lay her misery bare.

Beauvoir's was the opening salvo in a barrage of work addressing the figure of the housewife: the aspirational figure of (white) womanhood in the golden age of capitalism. As an emergent feminist movement challenged the gendered order of the postwar settlement, housework became a topic of intense political and economic discussion and analysis. Betty Friedan's (1963) "feminine mystique" famously dismantled the idea that women found housework fulfilling, while radical feminists critiqued "gender roles" that assigned women to domesticity.[23] Feminist thinkers were also intensely engaged with Marxist thought, both as a methodological model and an object of critique, and many sought to merge Marxist analyses of class with feminist analyses of gender. The radical feminist Shulamith Firestone argued that a material analysis of bodily difference revealed a foundational sexual division of labor, rooted in gestational capacity, that constituted women as an oppressed "sex class."[24] Socialist feminists challenged the view of the home as a "haven in a heartless world" and a refuge from a ruthless capitalism, arguing that the home, too, was a place of work.[25] Housework seemed to many to offer a new answer to Marxism's long-standing "woman question," concerning the relationship between capitalism and women's oppression—one that could root analysis of gender oppression in material conditions without suggesting, per the traditional "base-superstructure" model, that gender was "secondary" or epiphenomenal to the more foundational problem of class oppression. From these theories, a new account of reproductive labor and its relationship to nature, gender, and capitalism would emerge.

Reproducing Labor Power

Where theorists like Beauvoir and Arendt described the production of "life" endlessly and changelessly, Marxist and socialist feminists argued that under capitalism, domestic labor produces a unique commodity: labor power. In describing labor power as "the aggregate of those mental and physical capabilities existing in the physical form, the living personality, of a human being," Marx himself emphasizes the need for its constant renewal.[26] In the course of performing labor, Marx observes, "a definite quantity of human muscle, nerve, brain, etc. is expended, and those things have to be replaced."[27] Every day, the laborer sells their labor power to the capitalist; every day, they must acquire the means of subsistence—adequate food, housing, fuel, and so on—necessary to replenish their body and mind and restore their ability to return to work the next day. Marxist feminists argued that the renewal of labor power also required something Marx had not discussed: forms of unwaged labor, usually performed by the worker's wife. By cooking meals, mending clothes, cleaning house, and tending to sexual and emotional needs, (female) unwaged houseworkers readied the (male) waged worker to return to work each day; by gestating and raising children, they produced the next generation of workers. By doing this work for free, they lowered the cost of reproducing labor power, helping to keep wages down. Within this broad framework, theories of housework proliferated. Some followed Firestone's analysis of "sex class," developing an account of women's subordination rooted in gestational capacity. Others construed women's work within the household as a holdover from a precapitalist "patriarchal" or "household" mode of production that had persisted within capitalism.[28]

Perhaps the most influential strain of thought, however—both in its own time and in recent feminist revivals—was that advanced by the Wages for Housework movement.[29] Wages for Housework explicitly posed the "woman question," as articulated by Mariarosa Dalla Costa and Selma James in *The Power of Women and the Subversion of the Community* (1972), the movement's founding document—"What is the relation of women to capital and what kind of struggle can we effectively wage to destroy it?"—and offered the housewife as an answer.[30] By identifying women as an unrecognized proletariat, the housewife offered a way to reconcile feminism's "subject question" with Marxism's. Drawing on a range of influences, from Italian autonomism to dependency theory to the US welfare rights movement, Wages for Housework argued that the household was not an archaic institution persisting within capitalism, but an institution specific to capitalism itself.[31] The institution of wage labor had organized social life beyond the direct relationship of capitalist to worker, such that those who didn't earn a wage themselves had become dependent on those who did. As James argued, "Wagelessness and the resulting dependence on men is the form patriarchy takes under capitalism"; Silvia Federici would later diagnose this phenomenon as the "patriarchy of the wage."[32]

While Wages for Housework has been widely invoked, recovered, and analyzed, one of its central features has remained largely unexplored: what I describe as its *ideology critique of housework*. Wages for Housework theorists joined thinkers like Friedan in dissecting the ideology of housework, while rooting its emergence not in "society" in general, per Friedan, but in capitalism specifically. The ideology of housework, they argued, not only consigned women to the home—it also concealed their true status as workers. Their analysis of housework therefore brought the traditional project of Marxist ideology critique—identifying capitalism's distortion of reality, and demystifying false appearances in order to awaken class consciousness—to bear on neglected sphere of the household.[33] This, however, would require subtle but significant revisions to the Marxist account of ideology itself.

The Ideology Critique of Housework

The "locus classicus" of the Marxist theory of ideology is, Stuart Hall argues, the sphere of exchange, where the proletarian and capitalist appear to meet as formal equals and agree to a mutually satisfactory exchange of labor power for a wage.[34] Marx's famous descent into the hidden abode of production is itself an act of ideology critique, intended to reveal the domination and exploitation that lurk beneath the surface ideals of freedom and equality. Here, the wage itself is the vehicle of mystification: it appears to be fair payment for a given amount of work, and a deal to which both parties voluntarily agree. If the apparent freedom and fairness of this exchange purport to justify it, however, ideology does not explain *why* people work in the first place. The "doubly unfree" status of the worker does that: as Marx notes, proletarians work "in order to live."[35] This account is more challenging to apply to the household than it might initially seem. After all, the unwaged housewife doesn't enter into the ideological sphere of exchange at all. So what mystifies work if the wage does not? And how does the capitalist compel work in the *absence* of the wage? The theoretical moves of the Wages for Housework analysis are best understood as responses to these problems. Wages for Housework identified not only the wage but also *wagelessness* as tools of mystification, and looked to the ideology of gender—reinforced by the ideology of nature—to explain *why* women worked at all. All work is mystified under capitalism, Wages for Housework theorists acknowledged—but the ideological status of housework, they held, is distinctive.

While the wage seems to pay only one person, Dalla Costa and James argued, it commands the labor of two: the worker and his wife. Where the traditional Marxist critique located ideology in the wage itself, they and subsequent theorists held that the *lack* of the wage also indexed ideology at work: wagelessness "hid" housework, rendered it "invisible," "obscure[d]" the length of the working day, "mystified" the function of the family, and disguised housework's true beneficiary: not (only) men, but capital.[36] Wagelessness had made housework "*appear to be a personal service outside of capital,*" a favor provided by a woman to her husband, rather than labor exploited by capital.[37]

To explain the seemingly "voluntary servitude" of the housewife, Wages for Housework blended the Marxist critique of naturalized social relations with feminist critiques of naturalized gender relations following Beauvoir.[38] What made housework different from other kinds of work, Silvia Federici argued, was the fact that it had been treated as innate to women: "It has been transformed into a natural attribute of our female physique and personality," she wrote, "an internal need, an aspiration, supposedly coming from the depth of our female character."[39] This ideological move served an economic function, Federici charged: capitalism had "gotten a hell of a lot of work almost for free," without which it could not survive.[40] As James would observe, echoing Beauvoir's famous formulation, "Women are not born housewives, but can only become housewives because we are trained to it almost from birth."[41] This training effectively created a female role—a "servant relation" that interpellated all women, whether or not they themselves were actually married, had children, or worked outside the home. If housework was work, then, gender was its disciplinary mechanism, backstopped by the authority of nature—the most powerful ideological tool of all.

The driving project of Wages for Housework was to attack these mystifications, and its central weapon in doing so was the demand for the wage. Against critics of the movement's "economism," Federici was emphatic that the demand for the wage was not only a demand for money but, more importantly, "a political perspective" that could "demystif[y] and subver[t] the role to which women have been confined in capitalist society."[42] The wage, Federici wrote, is *the demand by which our nature ends and our struggle begins, because just to want wages for housework means to refuse that work as the expression of our nature*, and therefore to refuse precisely the female role that capital has invented for us."[43] To demand the wage was to struggle "unambiguously and directly against" the role of the housewife, against its "insidious character as femininity," and against its received status "as a biological destiny."[44] The demand for a wage identified housework as *work* rather than *nature*, and thus rendered it an appropriate object of politics.[45] It revealed that other aspects of gender relations, too, were political rather than natural: as one 1977 Wages for Housework poster declared, "WE REFUSE TO ACCEPT THAT WORKING FOR NOTHING IS 'NATURAL,' DEPENDING ON A MAN IS 'NATURAL,' HAVING OUR WOMBS AND OUR SEXUALITY CONTROLLED BY THE GOVERNMENT IS 'NATURAL.'"[46]

While the political function of the demand for the wage has been widely acknowledged and frequently embraced, its complexity remains underappreciated. The demand targeted three dimensions of ideology simultaneously. First, it sought to denaturalize *both* housework *and* the housewife. The wage, Wages for Housework theorists argued, would simultaneously make housework "visible" and "demystify" femininity, such that both housework *and* the "the female role that capital has invented" could be refused and work redistributed.[47] Wages were therefore explicitly deployed "against housework"— and implicitly, against the housewife as a figure of gendered ideology. Less often noted, however, is the difficulty of using the wage as a tool for demystification, since the wage itself also mystifies. Deployed uncritically, then, the call "wages for housework" threatens to reinforce the idea that the wage *is* a fair price for labor—precisely the idea that the Marxist ideology critique challenged, and that Wages for Housework also called into question. It seems, in other words, to fall prey to what William Clare Roberts calls "the wage fraud"—the perception that "wages express the value of labor."[48] In a crucial but largely neglected move, Wages for Housework framed the demand for the wage as also a struggle "against the wage" itself and "the capitalist relation it embodies."[49] What the demand "wages for housework" discloses, in other words, is that the wage does not reflect the value of labor at all. The demand, then, could potentially mobilize *housework against wages*: by revealing that wages do *not* actually pay for a great deal of useful labor, it could call into question the idea that the wage is an accurate measure of work's "true value"—its social or moral worth. The emancipatory function of the demand for the wage therefore entailed a tricky double move, in which the wage must be simultaneously demanded and disavowed.

As the complexity of the demand reflects, the Wages for Housework ideology critique wavered between a focus on the house*wife* (and more broadly, gender), house*work* (and more broadly, gendered labor), and the wage (and its inverse, wagelessness). This fluidity could be overlooked when these categories coincided in the figure of the unwaged female housewife. But it has proved more problematic as this analysis has circulated beyond its initial purview. So too have the problems with an ideology critique rooted in the "woman question" become more glaring as patterns of both gender and labor have changed. In particular, the explanation that reproductive labor is unwaged because it has been ideologically "naturalized" has become increasingly unstable as the theory has traveled.

Wages for Housework beyond the Housewife

Theories of housework exploded precisely as the age of the housewife was drawing to a close. The housewife had always been a historically and racially specific figure, as Angela Davis noted.[50] Many analyses of housework noted that even middle-class white women were increasingly working outside the home, especially in the emerging "service sector." By the 1980s, the analysis of housework alone seemed increasingly ill-equipped to address the complexity of both labor and gender.[51] Some feminist theorists in this period abandoned the framework of housework altogether. Others, however, made the opposite move, extending the Wages for Housework analysis beyond the housewife per se. Two traditions—"housewifization" theory and social reproduction theory—have been particularly influential in developing theories of reproductive labor since.

Theorists of "housewifization" drew most directly on the Wages for Housework ideology critique to explain the persistent "wagelessness" of a wider array of work, focusing in particular on peasant women in the Third World. "Housewifization," the sociologist Maria Mies argued, described the process of "universalizing the housewife ideology" that "define[d] women basically as housewives and sex objects."[52] Housewifization was a "strategy" for reducing labor costs: when women were defined as housewives, Mies charged, the work they did was correspondingly defined as "supplementary" rather than "breadwinning," and could be underpaid accordingly.[53] Work that had been "house-

wifized" was subject to a set of poor working conditions, ones under which
housewives had long labored: job insecurity, low wages, long hours, no labor
rights or trade unions.[54] Housewifization theorists argued, moreover, that the
housewife's conditions exemplified those under which most people worked,
such that the housewife, rather than the industrial proletariat, was the subject
with a privileged lens onto the workings of the system as a whole. The standpoint of the unwaged housewife offered a new view of capitalism altogether,
one in which waged labor was only the tip of the iceberg, beneath which lurked
a vast expanse of unwaged labor appropriated by capital—done by housewives
and the unemployed, students in the global North and subsistence farmers in
the global South.[55]

Housewifization theorists also developed the argument, already incipient
in Wages for Housework, about the association of women with nature.
"Women and colonies," Mies claimed, had been "defined into nature" so that
their work could be appropriated freely; the invocation of nature had "mystified" a gendered "relationship of dominance and exploitation."[56] According to
the "dominant logic" of Western capitalism, Claudia von Werlhof observed,
certain people were "treated as if they were nature and available gratis, like air";
their work was "pronounced to be non-labour."[57] Nature was not only a tool
of mystification but had itself been mystified: capitalism, Mies claimed, had
redefined nonhuman nature itself as a "vast reservoir of material resources to
be exploited and turned into profit."[58] Von Werlhof similarly argued that capitalism had defined nature simply as "everything that should be free (or as
cheap as possible)"—and this "brilliant ideological achievement" had facilitated the appropriation of natural resources.[59] As Mies's pithy formula concluded, the trifecta of "women, nature, and colonies" constituted the unvalued
and appropriated foundations of capitalism, its invisible but necessary "underground."[60] Federici herself would increasingly take up similar arguments in
later work, arguing that capitalism had identified women and colonized
peoples with nature in order to "justify and mystify the contradictions built
into its social relations."[61]

As these metaphors and analogies circulated, however, distinctive arguments blurred into a looser set of associations. An initially fertile exchange
among theorists of colonization, the household, and nonhuman nature gradually solidified into a series of mimetic arguments built on circular reasoning.
The unwaged status of work was said to result from the oppressive portrayal
of women, while women's subordination was conversely explained as stemming from housework's lack of a wage. Theorists of housework had drawn on

accounts of colonial and peasant economies in theorizing housework; in turn, theorists of colonialism and peasant labor drew on arguments about housework. Had the household been colonized, or had wage workers in the internal colony been housewifized?

These analogies grew still more tangled with the emergence of a parallel strain of ecofeminist work diagnosing the association between women and nature in Western thought. The historian Carolyn Merchant's study of the Scientific Revolution argued that the "image of the earth as a living organism and nurturing mother" had been replaced by a "mechanistic" image of nature as dead matter to be mastered by the male scientist.[62] In Western culture, the philosopher Val Plumwood claimed, to be "defined as 'nature' . . . is to be defined as passive, as non-agent and non-subject, as the 'environment' or invisible background conditions" against which the white male subject acts.[63] As ecofeminist perspectives were taken up more broadly, these arguments, too, looped back on themselves: on the one hand, housewives were intentionally "naturalized" because capitalism needed their work to be unwaged; on the other, housework was unpaid because it was always-already associated with women and thus with nature. The association of women with nature itself was at times presented as an ideological trick, and at others a genuine connection rooted in the direct interaction with life that supposedly characterizes women's work.[64] Had women been naturalized or nature gendered? As different arguments flattened into a catch-all explanation, "naturalization" became the force lurking behind free, cheap, or devalued work, and ideology the mechanism by which certain kinds of work, whether understood as "housework" or "reproduction," are rendered invisible and unpaid.

This expanded ideology critique would, in time, converge with an expanded account of the labor of "social reproduction," developed via a largely separate strain of socialist feminist thought. Social reproduction theory looked beyond the housewife and housework to consider a broader array of sites, processes, institutions, and people involved in the reproduction of labor power, in some instances stretching still further to describe the reproduction of "people" or "life" in general.[65] Social reproduction, in Johanna Brenner and Barbara Laslett's oft-cited definition, is an expansive category, describing "the activities and attitudes, behaviors and emotions, and responsibilities and relationships directly involved in maintaining life, on a daily basis and intergenerationally."[66] This work may be organized in various ways, as Evelyn Nakano Glenn observes: both "in and out of the household, as paid or unpaid work."[67] As such, it has come to encompass a broad but loosely defined set of activities, ranging from the biological gestation of human beings to paid service work to basic participation in social life. Notably, this definition centers on the *product* of labor: social reproduction produces labor power and/or life rather than "things," a distinction echoed in many feminist critiques of both capitalism and Marxism.[68]

As "naturalization" became a catch-all explanation for the devaluation of certain kinds of work, so too, as Lise Vogel notes, has the category of "reproductive labor" gradually become more "metaphorical than analytical."[69] Invoked to describe low-wage food service jobs alongside unwaged gestational labor, public sector education, and waged cleaning work, the category of social reproduction increasingly strains the limits of conceptual coherence. If food service work can be classified as part of "social reproduction," why not paid agricultural work? If homemaking constitutes social reproduction, why not house building? Conversely, why does the highly capitalized field of biotechnology not constitute a form of "life making"? These ambiguities reflect an imprecision about the boundaries of housework within the Wages for Housework project itself. As one Wages for Housework flyer proclaimed, "We are teachers and nurses and secretaries and prostitutes and actresses and childcare workers and hostesses and waitresses.... [W]e have chopped billions of tons of cotton, washed billions of dishes, scrubbed billions of floors, typed billions of words, wired billions of radio sets, washed billions of nappies, by hand and in machines."[70] This (partial) list of "housework" is remarkably broad: the activities it names are waged and unwaged, domestic and industrial, intimate and public.

What ultimately holds them together is the residual mark of the "woman question" under which they were originally analyzed. Reproductive labor is usually defined according to some combination of three criteria, which typically remain implicit: first, the *social identity or classification* of those performing labor (women; Black women); second, labor's *status under capitalism* (unwaged; value-producing); and third, the *material activity or kind of product* generated by labor (labor power, life). While social reproduction is technically a gender-neutral category defined by the *product* of labor (labor power; life), for example, it often remains implicitly defined in terms of the *subject* tasked with this kind of labor (women). Similarly, while "housewifization" ostensibly describes a way of reducing labor costs, it rests on the perception and treatment of people in keeping with certain social categories (women, housewives). The imperative to link the analysis of "reproductive labor" to the "woman question" has encouraged the conflation of these distinct categories of analysis—even as historical changes have rendered the relationship between these categories more tenuous than ever.

Although the intellectual traditions of social reproduction theory and housewifization theory largely developed on separate tracks, their insights are often combined in contemporary feminist analyses, which employ expansive definitions of reproductive labor and feature the ideology critique of naturalization as the central mechanism by which these kinds of work are rendered invisible and un(der)paid. This increasingly axiomatic argument explicitly contrasts reproductive labor with other kinds of labor, which are presumably recognized and valued rightly, and attributes its mistaken valuation to a distinctive kind of ideological mystification. It reifies a separate sphere of "reproduction" and its ostensible relationship to both capitalism and gender, casting a wide array of activities in terms of unpaid "women's work"—regardless of who actually does them or under what conditions. It is precisely in treating reproductive labor as an exception to the rule, however, that this critique tends to obscure the reasons for its persistently low value.

Against the "Naturalization Thesis"

The widening of the theoretical aperture described above rightly seeks to capture major changes to work and gender in the past several decades, from changing family structures to global migration to deindustrialization. One of the most significant is in the location and organization of "housework" itself: much of the work once done in the private household, from childcare to laundry to food preparation, is now performed for wages in the commercial service sector. Despite a different relationship to the wage, family, and workplace, it's often noted that these kinds of waged labor share many of the characteristics of unwaged housework: namely, that they are poorly paid and socially underrecognized.[71] This raises a new question: Why do these kinds of work remain poorly remunerated even where they are waged, and even when they are no longer done only or even primarily by women? Or, as Federici asks, "Why is producing cars more valuable than producing children?"[72]

What I call the "naturalization thesis" offers an explanation in two parts: certain activities are "naturalized" as women's work, such that women are expected to do them for little or no pay, while at the same time, certain activities are seen as less valuable because women do them. In other words, it makes two claims simultaneously—one about why *women* tend to do certain kinds of work, and one about why certain *kinds* of work are not valued. But the ideology critique developed by Wages for Housework doesn't function in the same way when (re)applied to waged work. An account of ideology developed ex-

pressly to extend the critique of waged labor to *unwaged* work becomes inco-
herent when applied to categories like "social reproduction" or "reproductive
labor," in which waged and unwaged work intermingle.

On the one hand, the naturalization thesis relies on a functionalist understanding of gender: capitalism needs reproductive labor to be free, and thus it
is made so by the naturalized ideology of gender. "Housework was transformed into a natural attribute, rather than being recognized as work, because
it was destined to be unwaged," Federici declared, explicitly analogizing capital
to God: "In the same way as god created Eve to give pleasure to Adam, so did
capital create the housewife to service the male worker."[73] In such formula-
tions, a personified capital seems to act intentionally with the explicit goal of
rendering reproduction free.[74] Other analyses of reproductive labor make telling use of the passive voice: women *are defined* into nature or *are naturalized*
by an unnamed entity; women and nature *are declared* unproductive.[75] But
how, exactly, does capitalism do all of this? How does it so successfully deceive
us, to the extent that we willingly live in the family orders it requires or express
ourselves in the gender presentations it finds useful? This is a familiar problem:
feminists have often argued that accounts of gender rooted entirely in capitalism are unsatisfactory, insofar as they grant capitalism extraordinary power to
make human social relationships and identities.[76] A claim this strong—that
capital is remaking people's most intimate sense of themselves, on a global
scale—demands at least some account of the mechanisms by which ideology
operates. It demands, too, an account of what distinguishes capital's treatment
of reproductive labor: if capitalism relentlessly commodifies human activity,
why *hasn't* it commodified housework in particular? If capital has the power
to make labor free or cheap through ideological mystification, why would it
not simply "naturalize," and thereby appropriate, *more* forms of work? Instead,
many accounts of reproductive labor simply gesture to a capital that operates
as Federici describes it—as an omnipotent, quasi-divine power.

The naturalization thesis, however, is also unsatisfactory as an account of
labor. It fails to offer a convincing explanation for why certain kinds of labor
tend to be poorly paid even when they are waged. Significantly, the naturalization thesis transforms the justificatory role of ideology into a causal force.
Most theorists of ideology acknowledge the former, claiming that ideology
disguises domination or makes it palatable. Some, however, argue that the
beliefs of the dominant also have causal effects on the constitution of reality.[77] Deployed to explain the low value of *waged* reproductive work, the naturalization thesis does the latter. It suggests that capital *itself* is hoodwinked by

ideology, such that it employs and pays people on the basis of attitudes rather than costs—a claim that implies a substantial, and considerably idealist, revision of our understanding of capitalism.[78] If ideology can have such strong causal effects in the realm of "reproductive labor," after all, it can have nearly *any* effects, and we should expect them to extend much further.[79] There is an important difference between the claim that, because domestic labor or care work is poorly waged and often unpleasant work, it tends to be done by those with the least power in the labor market—frequently subjects of gendered and racial oppression—and the claim that domestic labor is poorly waged *because* it is done by those who suffer gendered and racial oppression. Similarly, there is a difference between the argument that some *people* are seen as more suited to certain kinds of poorly paid labor, perhaps because they have indeed been socially "trained" in certain skills (e.g., women are often socialized to be nurturing), and the argument that those kinds of *work* are poorly paid because the people who typically do them have been "defined into nature." In the former, ideology is justificatory; in the latter, it is causal. Where attitudes are afforded causal significance, ideology critique threatens to become a set of just-so stories that claim to explain everything, and end up explaining little.[80]

Tellingly, the causal account of ideology is also directly at odds with the functionalist tendency described above. To see gender as functional for capital implies that gender is a "merely cultural" phenomenon generated by the more foundational economic base, while claims that beliefs about gender drive the valuation of labor suggest that ideology has primacy *over* the economic.[81] The naturalization thesis, then, is not only unpersuasive as a theory of either labor or gender, but internally contradictory as a theory of both.

Naturalization without Nature

The naturalization thesis, finally, rests on an unsatisfactory account of *nature itself*. Perhaps more accurately, it is unsatisfactory by omission: most feminist analyses of "naturalization" leave the problem of nature itself altogether unexamined. In seeking to denaturalize "women's work," they take for granted that defining people or activities "into nature" means that they can be freely appropriated, while rarely asking why nature itself is treated this way. These analyses therefore leave intact the underlying division between the free gifts of nature and value-producing human labor, and leave the status of nature within capitalism unchallenged. At the same time, the distinctively *physical* elements of reproducing human life tend to receive short shrift in accounts of "social reproduction." Although theories of reproductive labor often invoke "life-making," and loosely describe associated tasks, they rarely address the particularities of life processes themselves.[82]

Where nature is addressed directly in feminist theories of labor, it is nearly always in discursive terms, which analyze how nature is portrayed via images or represented in culture, how nature is "seen" or "defined." The naturalization thesis thus reflects a broader discursive turn in political and social theory that conceives of nature not as a material force in its own right, but as an idea, concept, or construct deployed in service of social projects.[83] This turn has dominated the study of nature even within environmental studies—and the ideology critique of naturalized housework has directly informed analyses of the relationship between nature and capitalism in particular.

The influence of the naturalization thesis on environmental thought is illustrated most clearly by Jason Moore's influential theory of "Cheap Nature," which is exemplary of what I have called the worldview approach to diagnosing capitalism's relationship to nature. While Moore frames his account as a theory of real abstraction, it is better understood as an extension of the ideology critique of naturalization to nature itself, one which develops housewifization theory's tentative moves in this direction to underpin a sweeping critique of capitalism.[84] Moore charges capitalism with not only *appropriating* the unpaid work of both human beings and extra-human natures but also *constituting* them as such: the "unpaid work of 'women, nature, and colonies,'" he claims, echoing Mies, "are not merely plundered but *actively created*" through processes of scientific knowledge-making.[85] Efforts to make nature legible through epistemic practices like quantification, Moore argues, should be understood as a "strategy" undertaken with a "goal" of securing access to natural resources at low cost.[86] A central tool of this strategy is the ideological power of the "Cartesian binary," which privileges society over nature and helps capitalism to "code" both nature and certain kinds of labor as nonvaluable.[87] Moore's account, while illuminating in many respects, suffers from the same problems that plague theories of reproductive labor grounded in the naturalization thesis. To argue that capitalism intentionally "defines" nature as a free gift, that it actively *renders* nature cheap, and that it has done so successfully for hundreds of years, attributes to capital remarkable powers of ideological mystification—even "genius"—spanning both continents and centuries.[88]

More broadly, the embrace by feminists of a fully socially constructed view of reproduction and even nature itself is born out of an admirable desire to avoid biological essentialism or natural determinism. Yet it betrays a striking anxiety about the status of physical nature within social theory. As Lena Gunnarsson notes, "Although denying biology any significance for social matters seems to be aimed at putting a final nail in the coffin of biological determinism, the move actually depends on a deterministic notion of the biological."[89] Only if physical phenomena really *are* decisive, after all, would acknowledging their force constitute determinism. Attending to how bodily processes and capacities operate within particular social orders, by contrast, means attending not only to their sheer physical capacity or to how they are *perceived* but also to how they are ordered and organized—in this instance, by capital. To paraphrase Beauvoir, the situation of the body, within capitalism, is to be at once life and potential labor power—and to be both subject and object of labor.[90] My wager is that looking more closely at the interaction of life processes with labor processes, while *detaching* the analysis of reproductive labor from the "woman question" altogether, ultimately allows for sharper and more nuanced analyses of *both* labor and gender.

Reproductive labor is difficult to make valuable, I argue, not because it has been ideologically naturalized, but because the physical activities it entails—which are inextricably linked to bodily processes and functions—are difficult to make efficient within a capitalist organization of production. My epistemic provocation, here, is that understanding reproductive labor requires theorists to take not the standpoint of the housewife, à la housewifization theory, but that of capital—to consider how and why capital organizes labor as it does.[91] The goal of capital is to reproduce *itself* by generating profit, not to reproduce a particular set of gender relations. The former may entail the latter—but it may equally entail what Angela Davis describes as the "supersession" of a gendered division of labor.[92] Capital, moreover, is neither intentional nor omnipotent in its ability to coordinate social activity in service of accumulation. Indeed, as attention to the service sector shows, certain kinds of labor have proven remarkably difficult to make valuable despite capital's best attempts. Capitalism's failure to pay for reproductive labor, in my account, is incidental rather than intentional, stemming from the disinterested processes of capital investment rather than a plot to keep reproductive labor in particular unwaged or a patriarchal commitment to the super-exploitation of women. The unwaged status of certain kinds of work reflects capital's *abdication* of responsibility for them rather than the active construction of their cultural and social meaning.

Housework beyond the Household

The Domestic Labor Debates

How else might we approach the problem of housework? An older set of debates among Marxists and Marxist feminists concerning the relationship of housework to capital—the "domestic labor debates"—offers clarifying resources.[93] While the domestic labor debates are often dismissed as a "wrong turn" for Marxist feminism, they are more illuminating than their reputation for technical pedantry might suggest.[94] Rather than orienting analysis around the relationship between gender and capitalism, as thinkers of the "woman question" do, they consider how concrete labor processes are situated within capitalist social relations; and rather than reifying "reproduction" as a distinct sphere, they interrogate the meaning of productive labor.

In colloquial use, the terms *productive* and *unproductive* are often taken to hold both a metaphysical and moral valence: productive labor is often understood as that which creates a physical object in the world, as well as activity deemed socially useful or desirable. "Unproductive" labor, by contrast, seems to connote labor that creates nothing and does little; labor that no one really needs, and which perhaps isn't really labor at all. Adam Smith, for example, differentiated between productive and unproductive labor on the basis of the physical product it generated: the labor of the productive manufacturer, he argued, "realizes itself in some particular subject or vendible commodity, which lasts for some time a least after that labor is past." The labor of the unproductive "menial servant," by contrast, did not: "his services generally perish in the very instant of their performance, and seldom leave any trace or value behind them."[95]

But this is not how Marx uses these terms. The difference between productive and unproductive labor has nothing to do with either the kind of labor in question or its product. To call labor *productive*, for Marx, describes *only* the relationship of labor to capital: productive labor is labor that produces surplus value for capital; unproductive labor is that which does not.[96] Any kind of activity, resulting in any kind of product, can be productive or unproductive depending on its context. Nor does this distinction reflect whether work is waged. A waged cook working in restaurant owned by someone else undertakes productive labor, since they prepare food which is sold for a profit, but both a chef who is paid to cook for a private household and a person cooking their own dinner are unproductive, since the food they prepare is consumed directly.[97] Against the idea that "productive" labor is virtuous, moreover, Marx argues that "to be a productive laborer is ... not a piece of luck, but a misfortune": it means that one is being exploited.[98] To call labor productive, that is, is not to assign it moral worth or significance.

The traditional Marxist account of domestic labor holds that it is unproductive: it is useful for members of the household, but it is not employed by capital to produce commodities for sale. Wages for Housework took issue with this characterization, arguing that housework *was* directly productive of surplus value, or at least, an essential condition of its production.[99] These claims were often motivated by the desire to articulate feminist projects in terms of the struggle against capitalism: as Federici and Cox argued, "If our kitchens are outside of capital, then our struggle to destroy them will never succeed in causing capital to fall."[100] For more orthodox Marxists, by contrast, the question was not whether domestic work was "really work": it clearly produced use values for members of the household, like meals and clean clothes. But most Marxists argued that domestic labor simply did not produce surplus value for capital and therefore did not constitute productive labor in a Marxian sense, regardless of how useful it was or how onerous.[101] Those working in the household are not employed by capital directly or co-ordinated with other laborers through the market. Instead, they are isolated in their homes, producing at their own pace and on their own schedule; the goods and services they produce are consumed by family members but not exchanged. Most reached the conclusion that housework is useful and necessary to human life in general, and often to processes of capital accumulation, but not *itself* productive of value.

The debate sought to impose rigor on the broad and wide-ranging set of claims made by theorists of housework, and usefully redirects attention to the social relation between labor and capital. The problem, however, is that it takes "housework" too literally. As a result it borders on tautology: it analyzes work already classified as "domestic," that which takes place in the sphere of the private home or family, and concludes that this work is not directly productive for capital in part *because* it is done at home. Nothing about the *labor itself*, however, understood as a set of activities, precludes it from being classified as productive in the Marxian sense. What happens, then, when this labor is performed outside the home? Examining the waged work of the service sector in its own right, rather than simply extending the naturalization thesis to explain it, can help us move beyond the focus on "wage-lessness" or "unpaid labor" and turn attention instead to the question of why some kinds of work, *even when waged*, resist organization along the lines of capitalist rationality.

The Service Sector Debates

The notoriously capacious "service sector" is often discussed in Smithian terms: as comprising activities that do not leave behind an object that can be stored or circulated, and that must be consumed as soon as they are produced.[102] But the defining characteristic of services in modern economics, as most prominently discussed by the economist William J. Baumol, is that they tend to resist the kinds of productivity gains that characterize manufacturing.[103] Manufacturing, in Baumol's account, is "technologically progressive": improvements in machinery make it possible to make goods more efficiently, such that the same output can be achieved with fewer workers. Services, by contrast, are "technologically stagnant": they are hard to mechanize, industrialize, or speed up, which means it is difficult to reduce the amount of labor they require. (To illustrate this point, Baumol famously used the example of a string quartet: four people were needed to play the same piece of music in both 1850 and 1950.) Not *all* services are technologically stagnant: some, like telecommunications, do realize productivity gains. The problem is concentrated in what Baumol describes as *"personal* services"—those that entail "direct, face-to-face interaction between those who provide the service and those who consume it," which rely on a "a human element not readily replaceable by machines."[104]

Whereas wage increases in technologically productive sectors can be offset by growing productivity, in labor-intensive service sectors, wage increases have an outsized effect on production costs. Keeping costs down typically entails either wage suppression or a sheer reduction of labor time per "unit" produced, which is usually correlated to decreases in quality. Higher patient-to-nurse ratios are strongly correlated with worse health outcomes, for example; similarly, larger class sizes correspond to worse educational outcomes. Over time, the disparity between productivity in "technologically progressive" and "stagnant" sectors tends to rise, as efficiencies continue to develop in the former, while productivity in the stagnant sector remains low. The costs of technologically progressive goods continually decline, while those of labor-intensive services stay even or increase. Even if the costs of labor-intensive goods remain stable on their own terms, they tend to rise *relative* to the persistently falling costs of goods in high-productivity sectors. The result is that even as manufactured goods become increasingly affordable, including once-luxury items like cars and computers, services like health care become increasingly unaffordable—even as workers in the latter sectors are paid relatively low wages. Baumol names this phenomenon the "cost disease."

From a Marxian vantage point, Aaron Benanav and John Clegg note, Baumol's distinction between "progressive" and "stagnant" sectors reflects Marx's distinction between formal subsumption and real subsumption. Services are simply the class of processes that resist real subsumption—those activities that are not easily mechanized, industrialized, scaled, or substituted with manufactured goods. As Benanav and Clegg conclude, "*those activities that remain services tend to be precisely the ones for which it has so far proven impossible to find a replacement in the world of goods.*"[105] Yet while critical theories of service work have addressed the cost disease, its significance for the analysis of "reproductive labor" has gone largely unrecognized.

The cost disease suggests that the low value of reproductive labor stems not from the ideological trick of "naturalization," but rather from the fact that the physical *qualities* of certain activities resist industrialization, economies of scale, and automation. The failure to automate reproductive labor is not for lack of imagination. In 1920, W.E.B. Du Bois had argued that the work done by domestic servants was an "anachronism" overdue for mechanization; half a century later, Shulamith Firestone proposed automating gestation and Angela Davis proposed industrializing housework.[106] Yet a great deal of housework has remained in the category of technologically stagnant personal services. The language of the remainder, in fact, is precisely how the Marxist feminist Jean Gardiner described housework in 1975; as she observes, "Many of the services *which have remained domestic tasks* are actually not subject to major savings in labor time."[107] As Maya Gonzalez and Jeanne Neton have more recently argued in their discussion of reproductive labor, "There is always a remainder[:] . . . what cannot be subsumed or is not worth subsuming."[108] The repeated language of the *remainder* points to a phenomenon that will by now be familiar: despite capitalism's tendency to pull everything into its orbit, to formally and then really subsume all activity, it does not always succeed. From this perspective, "services" and "housework" share core characteristics despite their different locations—the domestic setting of housework versus the private, market-mediated service sector. They are the labor processes that resist real subsumption; they are what is left over once capital has absorbed and reorganized the activities that it can make productive. But this leaves one more question unanswered: What activities *are* these, and why do they, in particular, resist subsumption? Why are they so difficult for capital to absorb?

The Labor Process and Life Process

To answer these questions, we have to look more closely at the labor processes in question—which requires recognizing how closely they are bound up with the life processes of human beings. While the distinctive nature of life processes in reproductive labor has largely vanished from recent analyses, it is prominent in many older accounts of "housework." Suzanne Gail describes household tasks as "concerned with simply keeping level with natural processes . . . which once done are not done for good, and will have to be done all over again."[109] Housework battles perpetually against entropy, against the tendency toward disorder and decay, as in Beauvoir's memorable description of the housewife's struggle: "She attacks life itself. . . . [S]he would like to stop everyone from breathing. . . . Seeing life as a promise of decomposition demanding more endless work, she loses her *joie de vivre.*"[110] Or consider the poem in which the housewife dreams of the housework-free afterlife: "where they don't eat there's no washing of dishes."[111] Gestation and childcare, in particular, are frequently identified as processes that cannot be shared, redistributed, or mechanized. Beauvoir describes gestation as a process that "no machine can rush" or "slow down," one that "the most ingenious machines fail to divide or multiply."[112] James and Dalla Costa note that while technological innovation had reduced the amount of necessary work in industry, "the same cannot be said of housework. . . . [The housewife] is always on duty, for the machine doesn't exist that makes and minds children."[113]

Indeed, it is striking, upon surveying the range of twentieth-century thought about reproductive labor, how consistently accounts that emphasize the significance of life processes accord with those that describe labor's formal qualities. Arendt's division between labor, as the ceaseless production of life, and work, as the production of durable objects, maps almost perfectly onto the definition of social reproduction as "life-making activities," set in opposition to "thing-making or profit-making"—and so too onto the distinction between services and manufacturing, Baumol's technologically stagnant and progressive sectors, and even Marx's unproductive and productive labor. From a Marxist perspective, this is perplexing, because the material content of the labor process is supposedly irrelevant to whether labor is productive of value for capital. Why, then, does the specifically capitalist division of labor so closely resemble the transhistorical concept of the labor of *life* articulated by Arendt and even Beauvoir? Why does the distinction between "things" and "life" so closely track that between real and formal subsumption? Why, in other words, does producing life seem *not* to produce value?

The answer here will be familiar from chapter 3. Reproductive labor, as much as agriculture, is a nature-based sector—which is not to say that it is *natural*—and the disparities between biophysical processes and patterns of capital accumulation that present obstacles to the capitalization of agriculture are present, too, in the reproduction of *human* life. Where in agriculture the land is both instrument and object of labor, in reproductive work it is the human body that is at once subject and object of labor. Where agriculture works on a natural machine, the work of reproduction attends to bodily cycles and processes that operate on their own time. The capacities that are the hardest for capital to replace and automate are the ones that are most fundamentally linked to specifically human life processes—the processes that continually reproduce the human body itself.

Attention to life processes, and biological reproduction in particular, might seem to suggest a troublesome return to the idea that reproduction is a distinctively natural activity, threatening to "renaturalize" housework, and in turn to redraw the much-disavowed link between women and nature. "Are not women admitting," Merchant asks in her own study analogizing women to nature, "that by virtue of their own reproductive biology . . . they are in fact closer to nature than men and that indeed their social role is that of caretaker?"[114] But to attend to how human life processes are organized by capital emphatically does *not* require that we identify the womb in particular as a point of connection to the Earth. To do so is to collapse the enormous diversity of life-forms into a single temporality of "nature" aligned with a subset of human bodily processes—paradoxically, one associated with the unearthly moon—while at the same time treating certain human bodily processes (gestation, menstruation) as uniquely connected to life cycles, while ignoring those common to all human beings (digestion, sleep, death). More generally, feminist analyses of the sexual division of labor have typically focused on body of the *laborer*—as in Firestone's account of "sex class" rooted in the capacity for gestation. But all labor is embodied: the worker in the automobile plant has to sleep, eat, and defecate as regularly as the worker in the daycare center. The more significant difference between the auto worker and the care worker is in the nature of the *product*. What is most significant in organization of most reproductive labor, in other words, is not the body of the *laborer*, but the body *being reproduced*. The problem of caring for children is simply an acute illustration of the problem of care for living beings more generally, and the challenges that arise in attending to the life processes of others. From this angle, elements like age and ability are typically more significant in the organization of labor processes than the traits associated with sex.[115]

As Gabriel Winant notes, Marx's description of the need to reproduce labor power—his observation that a "definite quantity of human muscle, nerve, brain, etc." is expended in labor each day and must be replaced—is far too neat. "The quantity of human muscle, nerve, brain, etc., can hardly be definite: its expenditure will necessarily vary worker to worker, day to day, according to an infinity of contingencies that are partly opaque to all involved."[116] We can't measure the "quantity of brain" that needs replenishing at the end of an exhausting day in the way we can measure the number of widgets that a factory has committed to producing. Nor do we know what, exactly, is required to replenish that quantity: how many hours of sleep or what kinds of food. It is the very indeterminacy and unpredictability of human needs, born out of the resolutely qualitative processes of bodily function and the subjective elements of human consciousness, that make the act of tending to these needs nearly impossible to standardize or mechanize—and that render the labor processes built around them especially difficult for capital to make productive.

Thus health care is an exemplary case of the cost disease for reasons long noted by feminist theorists: care fundamentally requires attention and responsiveness to the needs of others, as Joan Tronto observes.[117] To restore someone's health (and, incidentally, their ability to work) requires assessing their condition, monitoring their symptoms, administering medication or physical intervention as necessary, being available if they take a turn for the worse. Care also typically requires concrete time in which natural processes unfold within the human body itself—what Mary Mellor calls "biological time."[118] The reproduction of human bodies requires time for the regeneration of cells, digestion of food, and other sorts of biophysical processes operating beyond direct human control. While these processes are undoubtedly human, they are rarely consciously controlled in the way that Marx suggests that truly human labor is. As Sophie Lewis argues, "There is clearly a case for considering pregnancy a kind of ecosystem service or *animal* labor."[119] A fetus must gestate within a human body, and a higher wage will not make it come to term sooner. But if pregnancy is perhaps the most obvious example, it is far from the only one. A growing child needs human care, but more caretakers will not make a child grow faster. Every night when we sleep, we restore some unspecified quantity of brain function. Someone who is fighting an illness may need human attention, but they also need time for their body to produce antibodies. The actions of human viscera, we might say, help produce labor power in the same way Say notes that the sheep's viscera help produce wool. These elements are not *like* gifts of nature; they are not simply *naturalized*—they *are* gifts of nature.

Many human life processes are regular and repetitive, as Arendt and Beauvoir suggest—but they are also beset by unpredictable interruptions. The needs of embodied humans emerge on their own terms, not those of the timesheet or billing cycle. To provide care therefore requires a considerable amount of idle time, in which carers are available in case they are needed without knowing exactly when how they will be called upon. In care work, in other words, the disjuncture between the concrete time of the body and the abstract time of the hourly wage is particularly acute, and the gap between production and labor time is particularly large. Caring patterns might be altered in response to the cycle of a parent's work schedule or a paid caregiver's working hours, and the quality of care may be compromised in order to economize on labor costs. But they cannot be scheduled for maximum efficiency in the way that the tasks of industrial production can.

If this gap is most acute with respect to care, however, it is apparent in some form in most household tasks.[120] Activities like cooking typically require intermittent attention over long stretches of time, during which natural processes unfold absent inputs from human labor: when baking a loaf of bread, for instance, one has to wait for the yeast to act and the dough to rise. As this illustration suggests, the reproduction of human life is fundamentally a more-than-human undertaking.[121] The food we eat is composed of nonhuman biomass digested with the help of microbes and converted into human cells. The air we breathe is produced by plants that absorb carbon dioxide and generate oxygen, which in turn rely on countless organisms to make soil—as we will examine more closely in the next chapter. Time spent "in nature" can be mentally and physically restorative; conversely, the intake of pollutants and toxins can be disabling and exhausting. The basic activities of the household reflect our necessary engagement with the more-than human world: cooking is the quintessential moment of transition between nature and culture, the raw and the cooked; cleaning removes unwanted matter, from mud to insects to smoke from the nearby factory chimney.[122]

The reproduction of human beings is not *only* natural, of course. Theorists of social reproduction are right to emphasize that reproduction isn't just a matter of sustaining life but of making people, developing human capacities, and recreating a broader set of social relations.[123] The standard of reproduction is set not by a biological minimum, but in accordance with social expectations, legal requirements, and cultural norms. What counts as good care, for instance, is subjective, and is itself often the site of negotiation and struggle.[124] As ever, the distinction between social and natural is itself difficult to parse: children who haven't eaten breakfast will struggle to focus on lessons; language difficulties can interrupt medical care. Providing care and other personal services therefore requires not only attention to physical needs but affective and emotional aptitude, interpersonal responsiveness, and other social skills. Yet these elements only exacerbate the cost disease, insofar as they tend to make human labor harder to replace, and render the work required to reproduce human beings still more "indeterminate." The production of human life, then, is *simultaneously* labor-intensive and nature-intensive: it requires a great deal of distinctively human labor time, which is difficult to make more efficient, and it requires time in which natural processes unfold, which similarly resist efficiency and acceleration.

The work of reproducing human beings would be both labor- and nature-intensive under any social order. But this quality takes on distinctive features in a system where production is oriented toward profit. It is because capital allocates investment according to the prospects of profitability that labor-intensive services are costly and underprovided, while manufactured goods are cheap and prevalent. The cost disease describes a fundamental tendency of capitalist economies, one that pertains to all sectors where productivity gains fail to keep pace with those of industry—and one that is incurable as long as productivity gains diverge. As Baumol argues, the cost disease is the result of "economic forces so powerful that they constantly break through all barriers erected for their suppression."[125] It is the unintended consequence of the way that particular labor processes develop within broader trajectories of production; a perverse outcome of a system where power over investment is private and driven by market rule; an instance of counterfinality in its own right.

The Abdication of Reproduction

We tend to envision a fully capitalist mode of reproduction as fully industrialized—like "a baby farm with paid employment and no sentiment," as Sheila Rowbotham once imagined, or the automatic feeding machine of Chaplin's *Modern Times*.[126] As we've seen, capital often *is* intensely involved in life making: it is extremely intentional in producing the lives of the animals and plants that generate commodities like milk and wheat. The reproduction of pigs, for example, is tightly managed, from the selection of genetic traits to the insemination of the sow to the scheduled delivery of piglets.[127] Visions of the dystopian "baby farm" thus recognize the continuity between human and animal lives in their own right, suggesting that eventually we too will be treated like livestock. And indeed, where human beings have been held as property—as chattel, a term itself derived from cattle—human reproduction has often been brutally controlled, as feminist scholars of slavery have detailed.[128] But for the most part, what is distinctive about human reproductive labor under capitalism is its product: at once human life and labor power. It is not the human being who is bought or sold as a commodity, but their time. Rather than organizing reproduction on an industrial model, then, capital usually leaves the reproduction of labor power up to workers themselves, on the assumption that they will find some way of staying alive between shifts; it doesn't care how, exactly, they do.[129] The result is that the reproduction of human beings is typically much *less* tightly organized than the reproduction of nonhuman nature.

Capital will provide whatever aspects of "housework" it can make profitable, and the sectors of "industrialized housework" that have been the most capitalized are those that are most amenable to productivity gains. Fast food restaurants, for example, rely on frozen, precut, and otherwise prepared food, produced industrially, that can be made to order quickly on an assembly-line model with a high degree of mechanization. In care, by contrast, there are few such productivity gains to be had. Institutional care achieves some modicum of efficiency by grouping those in need of care in a physical space, enabling cooperation among workers. Many medical technologies automate the work of attention, monitoring a patient's condition and sounding an alert when human labor becomes necessary. Communication technologies can improve coordination among different care providers. But these are a far cry from the productivity gains of the industrial factory, where efficiencies of scale are such that each additional widget is essentially costless. Providing additional people with care, by contrast, generally just requires more labor. It has, as Emma Dowling puts it, an "infinite marginal cost."[130] The only way to reduce labor costs in these sectors, as Winant shows, is to reduce labor time, typically with significant consequences for quality, or to suppress wages—and often both. Thus sectors like care are, by and large, "unattractive" to capitalist investment, to echo Mann and Dickinson on agriculture.[131] Some attract no capital investment at all.

The upshot is that capital does not "create" the family, or "invent" the housewife, at least not directly or intentionally. Instead, capital abdicates responsibility for reproducing labor power—and other agents fill the gap. From this vantage point, the household is not an institution carrying over from a precapitalist era, comprising a stable set of functions, nor a last bastion of noncommodified interpersonal relations protected by moral virtue, as it has often been imagined. It is, rather, a *remnant* of capitalism's reorganization of production; a space *abdicated by capital but fully internal to capitalism*.[132] It is the catchall for activities that, because they are not amenable to productivity gains, have not been really subsumed, and likely never will be. It is also the repository for services that the cost disease has made too expensive. While it is often observed that housework has migrated out of the household and into the private sector, other work has migrated in: as the cost of services skyrockets and public budgets decrease, households increasingly pick up the slack.

The family, of course, is the paradigmatic paracapitalist agent for the provision of care. It exemplifies the phenomenon of market subordination, in which intimate and interpersonal forms of domination interact with market rule. Because household labor doesn't produce an immediate commodity for sale, market pressures are less immediate for households than they are for firms—but they are present nonetheless. When the market starts to pinch, the burden of household work often grows heavier. When paid childcare becomes unaffordable, households may make the decision for one adult to stay home with the children—thus creating a situation of asymmetric dependence. Significantly, although this dependence, and the exposure to domination that comes with it, is typically strongly gendered, it is not necessarily rooted in sheer patriarchal power or ideological mystification. It may well result from a mutual agreement rooted in a rational calculation about the comparative earning power of the relevant parties, which will very often map onto patterns of racial and gender oppression. Intimate dependence and direct domination, in other words, are in this instance downstream from market rule rather than counterposed to it.

The family, however, is not the only such agent. As in other nature-based sectors, the organization of reproduction is heterogeneous; it takes, as Winant notes, a "vast diversity of forms," organized by an array of institutions.[133] As in other nature-based sectors, this general heterogeneity is nonetheless marked by familiar patterns of exploitation, in which aspects of market rule and class rule interact with more direct and interpersonal forms of domination. Workers in these sectors are typically paid extremely low wages for long hours, echoing patterns of "sweated labor" more broadly. Management is often displaced, either onto interpersonal relationships or the market itself, as personified by consumers who interact directly with service providers: tipping makes the customer the boss, home health aides are often employed by an agency but directed by a patient's family members, and so on. Here, too, political subordination is a tool in the struggle to keep labor costs down: global "care chains" bring migrant women from the global South to the global North, often under dubious legal conditions that subject them to the domination of employers unchecked by legal protections.[134] The key mechanism here is not ideology but power;

waged reproductive workers are motivated not by an internalized sense of gendered duty but by the familiar power of employer over employee: the power of the sack, given force by the double freedom of the worker.

For the most part, then, reproduction within capitalist societies is a far cry from the visions of industrial human production that populate dystopian imaginaries. It tends, instead, to be a cobbled together patchwork of public and private, household and market; childcare provided by family members and babysitting by electronics, meals from fast food restaurants and an undocumented nanny paid under the table. Feminists have frequently criticized Hobbes's view of human beings springing up spontaneously like mushrooms from the Earth, pointing to the forms of active labor and care that go into the formation of human beings as social and political selves—and rightly so.[135] But understood *in relation to capital*, the production of human labor power *is* much more like the production of fungi than the production of pigs or cattle. A loosely organized network of social and natural relationships produces, through indirectly organized and largely unsubsumed processes, an embodied human being whose labor power is eventually purchased by capital—or not.

Conclusion: Reorganizing Reproduction

The shared position of social and ecological reproduction, human and Earth maintenance, is not the result of ideological mystification, as is often charged. It reflects, instead, the anomalies that result when labor processes centered around recalcitrant physical elements exist in a world that is generally organized by capital. It's this recalcitrance that underpins the cost disease in sectors where human life processes are the object of labor, and that leads to the abdication by capital of many aspects of human reproduction altogether.

The cost disease also has environmental consequences in its own right. It explains, for one thing, the devaluation of maintenance that Ukeles's "Manifesto" decries. Because services become ever more expensive relative to ever-cheapening manufactured goods, both spending and investment trend toward the latter. Thus consumer goods are plentiful—often too plentiful—even as the things most necessary for life are scarce. As labor-intensive services grow more costly, meanwhile, repairing and maintaining things becomes more expensive than simply buying new ones. So too do public services like sanitation work—another form of maintenance, and a major focus of Ukeles's later oeuvre—become increasingly costly.[136] The kinds of work that sustain and improve both human and nonhuman life without increasing resource use or generating dangerous byproducts, in other words, are precisely those that capital is least likely to provide.[137]

The cost disease points to deep-seated structural tendencies of capitalism. It will not be countered, as even Baumol notes, by the "invisible hand of the market" alone.[138] Yet it need not be fatal. To balance out the growing disparity between productivity of different sectors, Baumol observes, requires taking action at the level of society writ large and considering "how we order our priorities."[139] The kinds of socially valuable, labor-intensive work that capital will not provide can be supported through public investment—which means that genuinely valuing the labor of supporting life will require collective decisions about social aims and active efforts to counteract the force of market rule. Struggles about reproduction, then, are never *only* about reproduction: they are about how societies choose to organize labor and allocate resources more broadly; about what kinds of work we think are valuable and important, regardless of whether they are productive of value for capital. To see human reproduction as continuous with both other forms of human labor and more-than-human forms of life, in turn, requires thinking more expansively about how ways of living, both human and nonhuman, might be organized; about how else we might live together and make a shared world on our only planet.[140]

In these projects, feminist theories of labor remain an invaluable aid. As the widespread resonance and uptake of Marxist feminist analyses in contemporary life reveals, reproductive labor is particularly generative of critiques of capitalist valuation—perhaps more so than any other kind of work.[141] Because reproductive labor bears so directly on nearly everyone's lives, it is frequently where the gap between capitalist value and other kinds of valuation is most immediately visible—and often most personally painful. Feminist theories have done vital work to politicize these kinds of labor, and to challenge capitalism's failure to recognize their value. But they have also, too often, served to reify reproductive labor as something that really *does* stand apart from other kinds of work—thereby reinforcing capitalism's categories rather than unsettling them. Analyses of reproductive labor frequently confuse the things that capitalism *tends not* to commodify for things that it *should not*—and in turn, tend to valorize those things as good in themselves. Because reproductive labor is often unpaid, moral philosophers have often lauded it as the commodity's opposite—the gift—suggesting that it stands fundamentally apart from the logic of exchange.[142] Celebrations of "life making" or "care," even when offered by Marxist and socialist feminists, tend to imbue these kinds of labor with moral virtue in their own right—and can suggest that they

are more inherently worthy than other kinds of work. Even calls to pay reproductive labor its "true value" suggest that wages generally *do* reflect labor's
social worth. In so doing, they can accidentally reinforce the idea that other
forms of work *are* rightly valued by capital; that other kinds of work *are* waged
as they ought to be.

The great legacy of Wages for Housework, then, is to remind us that capitalism will never pay what reproductive labor "is worth," because that is simply
not what the wage does. The cost disease, too, undermines the idea that the
wage paid for labor reflects its value to society—and as such, might help to
politicize the way that labor of all kinds is valued. In observing that many kinds
of human labor that we recognize as worthwhile are not valuable on capitalism's terms, we might begin to question those terms in their own right. Instead
of simply asking why reproductive labor in particular is devalued, in other
words, we might begin to ask: What kind of system is it that evaluates the work
of generating and sustaining human life as worthless—and why should we
trust it to evaluate anything else as we think it should?

6

Planetmaking

NATURE AS CAPITAL

ON SEPTEMBER 26, 1991, outside Tucson, Arizona, eight people dressed in bright red jumpsuits locked themselves inside a three-acre steel-and-glass dome filled with over three thousand species of animals and plants, not to emerge for two full years. They planned to show that the structure—known as Biosphere 2—was capable of sustaining life while completely sealed off from Biosphere 1—the Earth. A successful project would act as a prototype for sustaining life on other planets, or on the Earth itself in the event of a nuclear winter. Amid Biosphere 2's seven biomes—desert, rainforest, savannah, marsh, ocean, city, farm—the Biospherians would grow their own food and conduct research. As on Biosphere 1, they would rely on plants and animals to produce oxygen and absorb carbon dioxide, fertilize the soil and consume waste. But whereas on Biosphere 1 atmospheric and oceanic processes circulated carbon, water, waste, and nutrients, within Biosphere 2 that work was mechanized. Beneath the rainforest and desert landscape was a massive technosphere comprising three acres of electrical, mechanical, and plumbing systems intended, as one Biospherian put it, "to replicate many of Earth's free services." Machines powered by diesel generators desalinated water and treated wastewater, created breezes and ocean waves, heated and cooled the air. Biosphere 2 was, as one inhabitant called it, "the garden of Eden on top of an aircraft carrier."[1]

Life in Biosphere 2, however, was not Edenic. Soon after the dome was sealed, as many as 30 percent of species died off, including all pollinators, leading to an explosion of ants and cockroaches. Oxygen levels dropped precipitously, while carbon dioxide and nitrous oxide rose to dangerous levels. It later turned out that microbes in the soil produced carbon dioxide faster than plants could absorb it, while the structure's concrete foundations absorbed more oxygen than expected. Biosphere 2 most obviously demonstrated a core principle of ecology: that human survival depends on many other forms of life. Biosphere 1 was clearly much more complicated than anyone had imagined.[2] But the true lesson of Biosphere 2, the biologist John Avise argued, was an economic one: it had made it possible to construct "a more explicit ledger" of the Earth's free services. It had cost over $150 million to keep eight humans alive for two years in Biosphere 2. As Avise pointed out, "These services are provided to the rest of us more-or-less cost-free by natural processes, but if we were being charged, the total invoice for all Earthospherians would come to an astronomical three quintillion dollars for the current generation alone!"[3] A few years later, a group of scientists would look to Biosphere 2 in producing a more precise estimate. The services provided by Earth's biosphere, they calculated, were worth approximately $33 trillion—about twice world GDP at the time. Relative to the cost of Biosphere 2, they concluded, "Biosphere 1 (the Earth) is a very efficient, least-cost provider of human life-support services."[4]

———

In classical political economy, natural agents appear as contributors to production, conventionally understood: sheep's viscera help produce wool; wind drives the sails of merchant ships; fertile soil helps crops grow. But each of these is dependent on countless others that go unmentioned. Soil is "produced" by countless worms, fungi, mites, and other insects, which decompose organic debris and transfer nutrients between plants. Bacteria in the sheep's gut help the sheep digest grass; bees pollinate the plants the sheep eat; plants capture solar energy and convert it to a form the sheep can process—which brings us back to the soil. Even the wind wouldn't blow in the same way without temperature patterns linked to global climate regulation, itself maintained by a complex array of living systems. These natural agents don't go directly into commodity production—but they regenerate the ones that do. More than that, they constitute Earth's "life support systems"— the carbon cycle, water purification, soil fertility, and other elements which make the planet habitable. Thus, Anna Tsing argues, "making worlds is not limited to humans." Rather, "all organisms make ecological living places, altering earth, air, and water."[5] These multispecies activities are more than world-making: they are *planet*making. The actions and interactions of various life forms, from amoebas to sequoia, have over millions of years shaped Earth's

very geology and atmosphere so significantly as to make it a qualitatively different kind of planet than Mars or Venus.[6]

These planetmaking abilities, however, are currently in serious decline. "We
are currently damaging [the natural world] so profoundly that many of its
natural systems are now on the verge of breakdown," David Attenborough
warns.[7] Warning signs have long been on the horizon. In 1973, amid debates
about resource scarcity and the limits to growth, the economist William Nordhaus noted—in a piece otherwise refuting ecological doomsaying—that "if
the price system malfunctions, as is currently the case for free but scarce public
environmental resources—then perverse outcomes are possible."[8] Five
decades later, this "malfunction" persists, and perverse outcomes have materialized. "The value of natural entities such as mangroves, wetlands, and coral
reefs," the economist Partha Dasgupta observes, lies in their contributions to
human well-being, which "don't appear in the marketplace."[9] As the ecologist
Gretchen Daily argues, "The disparity between actual and perceived value is
probably nowhere greater than in the case of ecosystem services."[10] Two common strategies for rectifying this disparity have emerged.

The first strategy proposes to price nature, often described in terms of
"natural capital" or "ecosystem services," in recognition of ecosystems' economic contributions. It is exemplified by a statement by Henry Paulson, former secretary of the US Treasury, and now a staunch advocate for natural
capital valuation: "People assume that natural capital is a free good, and if you
don't put a value on it, they will value it as zero."[11] Like it or not, this position
holds, goods are assessed in terms of their monetary value. If nature is to be
protected, it must have a price: its use and exchange value must be brought
more closely into alignment, whether by requiring "payment for ecosystem
services," accounting for natural capital, or creating markets in "natural assets."[12] The goal, in the words of the biologist Edward O. Wilson, is "to give
the invisible hand of free-market economics a green thumb."[13]

The second strategy, a moral critique that insists on nature's pricelessness,
has developed in vehement opposition to the first. Critics argue that price is
an inappropriate metric for the more-than-human world, one that degrades or
diminishes precisely what it seeks to capture. Some things should not be for
sale, they argue—and nature is one of them. "Dear neoliberal economists,"
André Gorz asked scornfully in 1983, "how much is a ray of sunlight worth?
Fresh air without lead or sulphur fumes?"[14] Instead of trying to translate the
intrinsic, ethical, or aesthetic value of nature into monetary terms, Gorz and
others insist, we must learn to value nature in ways that can't be costed.

Advocates of pricing nature correctly identify the problem: that in a world of generalized commodity exchange, things without exchange value are treated as worthless. Critics, meanwhile, rightly identify the gap between exchange value and other kinds, indexing a critique of capitalism's form of value even where capitalism is not invoked directly. Yet while these strategies—to value nature in terms of price, or to protect nature *from* price—point in opposite directions, neither has been successful. Efforts to price nature have repeatedly *failed* to make certain kinds of nature valuable in economic terms, however impoverished those terms may be. Efforts to render nature priceless, meanwhile, have failed to protect it from the market—even as many of nature's gifts remain free.

Nature, as we've seen, is a free gift by default. It can't appear in the marketplace in its own right, and it can't demand a wage for its services, however valuable they might be. To have a price, it needs a human representative—which is to say it needs an owner. And if Western thought has often conceived of nature as a gift from God to all of humanity in common, it has just as often defended its appropriation as private property. Nature's gifts, for many, are meant to be alienated and owned, worked and improved. Most obviously, Locke's foundational account of property describes the process of enclosing nature's gifts: the observation that God had given the Earth to "men" in common is for Locke simply a prelude to explaining how an individual might justifiably claim it as his own. The role of labor in making land productive is key to this argument: land "left wholly to Nature," Locke argues, is merely "waste."[15]

Locke's account of ownership conveniently justified the expropriation of land from Indigenous peoples of the New World.[16] It also, Marx charged, concealed the violent appropriation of commons used by English peasants—the process of "so-called primitive accumulation," capitalism's original sin.[17] Many of capitalism's other critics have tracked its advancement via the continued process of enclosure—not least, of ever more gifts of nature. Already in the sixteenth century, Thomas Müntzer, the radical theologian and leader of the German Peasant Wars, lamented that "all creatures have been turned into property, the fishes in the water, the birds in the air, the plants on the earth," declaring that "the creatures, too, must become free."[18] Four centuries later, the political scientist James Scott would ruefully describe "the inexorable incorporation of what were once thought of as free gifts of nature: forests, game, wasteland, prairies, subsurface minerals, water and watercourses, air rights . . . breathable air, and even genetic sequences, into a property regime."[19] We should not be surprised, in other words, to find capital enclosing the gifts of nature. This, after all, is where capital begins. What *is* surprising, however—and what requires attention—is the fact that some gifts *remain* free; that even today, some—indeed, many—creatures have *not* yet been turned into property. If capitalism relentlessly commodifies, why are ecosystem services still "valued as zero"? Why *have* some gifts of nature remained free?

Capital's failure to enclose these gifts is not for lack of trying. The uncultivated land that Locke dismissed as mere waste is now figured as the site of potentially valuable ecosystem services. The past few decades have seen the proliferation of programs in "natural capital accounting" and companies purporting to trade in "natural assets," proclaiming ecological nature to be a source of untapped value—and a corresponding rash of critiques decrying the commodification of life itself. But the gifts of nature described in terms of natural capital and ecosystem services have proved remarkably difficult to make into property. Critics of commodification have misidentified the problem afflicting the biosphere: not that capital has absorbed all of life, but that it has abdicated responsibility for so much of it. As this chapter shows, ecosystems are ultimately better thought of as infrastructures rather than commodities: as systems that support a range of other activities rather than as discrete goods or services to be exchanged directly.[20] This perspective on ecosystems reorients attention away from moral debates about commodification, and towards political questions: What kinds of work do ecosystems do, and for whom? What kinds of ecosystem *public* services do we need to make our planet a livable one for humans and nonhumans alike?

To Price or Not to Price?

Nature's Economy

Those who study the nonhuman world have long trumpeted its usefulness for human life—often drawing on the language of economics to illustrate the point. The nineteenth-century naturalist Ernst Haeckel famously coined the term "ecology" with the word *oikos* in mind, proposing that "the living organisms of the earth constitute a single economic unit resembling a household or family."[21] The nineteenth-century ecologist George Perkins Marsh had observed the "services" rendered to human beings by various minuscule organisms; Charles Darwin described the "offices" that different creatures occupied; Rachel Carson wrote of bacteria, fungi, algae, and flies "working in sun and rain, during the hours of darkness."[22]

When the term "ecosystem services" per se was first deployed, however, in the 1970 report *Man's Impact on the Global Environment*, it was to report their alarming decline. Ecosystems, long thought of as sources of "renewable resources," were being exhausted: depleted through overuse, overburdened by pollution, damaged by extraction, harvested outright. Their destruction, the report warned, threatened to "annihilat[e] natural life on the planet" altogether.[23] Suitably alarmed by this possibility, many ecologists sought to describe ecosystems' contributions to human life in hopes of bringing them to public attention. Economics seemed to many like an effective—if controversial—idiom for conveying nature's usefulness to an "ecologically disconnected" population.[24] As the ecological economist Herman Daly wrote in his 1968 "Economics as a Life Science":

> The entire physical environment is capital, since it is only through the agency of air, soil, and water that plant life is able to capture the solar energy upon which the whole hierarchy of life (and value) depends. Should not these elements receive the same care we bestow upon our other machines? And is not any theory of value that leaves them out rather like a theory of icebergs that fails to consider the submerged 90 per cent?[25]

Daly's was one of a flurry of metaphors comparing nature to capital in this period. The economist E. F. Schumacher argued that "the capital provided by nature and not by man" was being used up rapidly; the agrarianist Wendell Berry described soil fertility as "the major capital of any farm"; the ecologist Barry Commoner wrote of the "biological capital" of the "ecosphere."[26]

Although initially figurative, efforts to represent nature economically became increasingly literal. In the United States, the environmental legislation of the early 1970s required assessment of the costs of regulation on industry, driving an early round of efforts to quantify the value of ecosystems. These often generated surprisingly high numbers.[27] They also generated considerable debate. As natural capital moved from metaphor to estimate, disputes raged over how the functions of ecosystems should be defined and assessed. What kind of a thing *are* ecosystem services? And what, for that matter, is "value"? In enumerating nature's benefits, ecologists have typically focused on anthropocentric use values, detailing the rich variety of ways, both material and immaterial, in which ecosystems contribute to human life, health, and happiness. Rendering these in monetary terms, however, is rarely straightforward. Some services performed by ecosystems can be measured in biophysical terms—it is possible to assess, roughly, how much carbon a forest stores or how many carcasses a vulture decomposes—but it's not always clear how physical assessments should translate into prices. Even if the value of a single ecosystem service—carcass decomposition, say—can be roughly estimated, the value of the entire ecosystem is much harder to assess, since the loss of any one function typically affects others. Still more difficult to quantify are subjective elements like "immaterial" benefits, aesthetic value, and ethical commitments. What is the beauty of a pristine lake worth? How much does someone value living in a world where a rainforest exists, even if they never visit it? How much would someone pay to prevent the extinction of a species they don't know exists? Can spiritual relationships really be calculated in monetary terms? Are these appropriate ways of assessing moral value at all?[28]

To illustrate these questions, consider the whale. Whales have historically provided many materials useful for commodity production, from blubber rendered into oil to baleen made into corset stays. In some parts of the world, they are a source of food. To some people they are relations; to others, they are inspiring and beautiful, offering meaning or entertainment. Even those who never see a whale in person may want to know that they are out there somewhere. Still other contributions come in the course of whales' daily lives, during which they do not interact with human beings at all. Whales circulate nutrients throughout the ocean as they migrate, as well as when they dive to feed and rise to the surface to breathe, contributing to the growth of carbon-storing phytoplankton. Throughout their lives, their bodies accumulate and store carbon, removing it from the atmosphere. Even upon their death, their carcasses provide a food source for many other kinds of marine life.[29]

Economists have painstakingly developed methods for calculating the monetary value of each of these gifts. The value of whales' beauty might be estimated via whale-watching revenues; the value of their existence, by how much people are willing to pay for lobster caught with whale-safe traps. The value of whale meat eaten by subsistence hunters can be compared to the cost of purchasing beef; the value of carbon absorption can be calculated in relation to the price of carbon credits. The value of the whale within the ecosystem is trickier, since these services are valuable only in relationship to the whale's broader ecosystem—the phytoplankton it eats, the fish that clean parasites from its skin, the bacteria that help it digest. Calculating any one benefit alone, meanwhile, neglects all the others. In 2020 the International Monetary Fund nevertheless estimated the value of a single whale at about $2 million, amounting to $1 trillion for the entire living stock—about a third of the present market capitalization of Apple.[30]

Hostile Worlds

To many people, to put a price on a whale seems like a mistake that only the IMF could make. At every point in the development of methods for calculating nature's economic value, beginning with the very earliest cost-benefit assessments, critics have emphasized their limits.[31] Those opposed to ecosystem pricing tend to argue that nature and the economy belong not only to separate spheres but to what the sociologist Viviana Zelizer calls "hostile worlds"—modes of existence so contradictory that any contact is liable to lead to "moral contamination."[32] From this vantage point, to put a dollar sign on "priceless" aspects of nature is not only a category error but worse—a misrecognition that threatens nature's very integrity.[33] To describe invaluable things in terms of price, Robin Wall Kimmerer argues, has the paradoxical effect of cheapening them—of demoting them from the sacred to the mundane, converting the infinite to the payable.[34] Monetary value, moral critics insist, cannot possibly capture the intrinsic worth of whales as living, sentient beings; the beauty of seeing a whale breach; the status of whales as relations; or even the totality of whales' contributions to biospheric function. For many biocentric and eco-centric thinkers, economic valuation is only the most egregious form of a more foundational error: the entire ecosystem services framework is ethically compromised insofar as it treats nonhuman beings as instrumental means to human ends.[35] Critiques of instrumental value are frequently paired with critiques of rationalization and commensurability echoing Adorno and Hork-heimer's *Dialectic of Enlightenment*. As the geographer Sian Sullivan claims, something is lost "in the world-making mission to fashion and fabricate the entire planet as an abstracted plane of (ac)countable, monetizable and potentially substitutable natural capital."[36] Anxieties about the valuation of nature also frequently echo anxieties about the effects more broadly on human political and moral subjectivity of the permeation of market logics and economic rationality into all aspects of life. Michael Sandel argues that market value "crowds out" other kinds of norms and valuations, diminishing other motivations for care.[37] Cost-benefit analyses, John O'Neill argues, degrade politics, treating it as a "surrogate market" rather than a site of deliberation or contestation.[38]

These critiques are compelling—and advocates for ecosystem services will grant many of them. Ecosystem services are recognized to be a simplifying device with well-known shortcomings: "Just as it would be absurd to calculate the full value of a human being on the basis of his or her wage-earning power, or the economic value of his or her constituent materials," Gretchen Daily acknowledges, "there exists no absolute value of ecosystem services waiting to be discovered and revealed to the world by a member of the intellectual community."[39] Many see their work as a necessary evil—a last resort when appeals to nature's intrinsic value have failed. Donella Meadows, a coauthor of the *Limits to Growth*, has argued that pricing nature is an act of "ignorance and arrogance"—but holds that it should be done anyway.[40] Pavan Sukhdev, the director of a major nature-valuation project, describes the economic valuation of nature as "humanity's greatest failure," reflecting the lack of an "'ethic of care' for nonhumans."[41] Advocates for pricing ecosystem services, however, are relentlessly pragmatic. Perhaps it is unpleasant or unwieldy to contemplate nature in terms of costs—but people already *are* assessing nature's value and making decisions accordingly. They simply assess its value at zero. Even rough estimates, they insist, are better than continuing to let nature count for nothing.

Advocates of pricing ecosystems aren't wrong to note that nature is valued at zero by default. Contained in this statement is the recognition that the free gift of nature really does have the force of a real abstraction, in that it organizes our activity even when we are not conscious of it—and even when we are Indeed, many critics of commodification make the mistake of identifying capitalism by the presence, rather than absence, of price; by the form of the commodity rather than that of the free gift. But the free gift is a form fully internal to capitalism.[42] Absent a wider critique of capitalist valuation, then, the insistence that nature should remain priceless amounts to an argument that capitalism should continue treating nature *as it already does*. But both critics and advocates of valuing ecosystems in monetary terms have often mistaken the project of calculating values for that of assigning prices. They have tended to collapse the difference between various ways of assessing nature's economic value, treating accounting, estimation, and even quantification as akin to commodification.

Take, for example, the study estimating the value of the Earth's biosphere at $33 trillion. The number reflects a monumental effort to assess ecological values of all sorts, taking an ecumenical approach to two decades of work developing methodologies for measuring ecosystem services and compiling a wide array of valuation studies, using methods ranging from assessments of people's willingness to pay to preserve beautiful landscapes to biophysical assessments of the role of various ecosystemic functions to estimated costs of technological substitution.[43] It quickly became notorious as a reductio ad absurdum of the logic of ecosystem accounting: Who could possibly put a price on the whole Earth?

But the point of calculating the value of the biosphere, its authors insisted in a subsequent paper—which also revised its estimated worth to $125 trillion—was not that ecosystem services should *actually* be commodified. Rather, it was an "awareness raising exercise" meant to "reframe the relationship between humans and the rest of nature."[44] It was, in other words, equivalent to Silvia Federici's insistence that the demand "wages for housework" was intended as a "perspective" on women's position under capitalism. Of course it was absurd to imagine buying the entire Earth; of course no one was actually expected to pay $33 trillion. To the contrary, the point of the spectacular price tag was precisely that preserving free ecosystem services would cost much *less* than replacing them. The estimate, in other words, was not really a demand for payment, but an act of disclosure intended to draw attention to the importance of ecosystem services to human welfare—and to their remarkably low cost. Relative to the alternatives, preserving nature's gifts is an incredible bargain.

The difference between calculation and commodification is illustrated even more clearly by projects that seek to turn natural capital accounting to more explicitly radical ends. Natural capital accounting underpins estimates of the ecological debt incurred by the global North, which diagnose the long-standing appropriation of unvalued ecological resources from the South, and critiques of "ecologically unequal exchange," which charge that the long-noted disparity in the terms of trade between producers of "primary" commodities (copper, iron ore) and "value-added" commodities (computers, microwaves) is exacerbated by the failure of prices to take the depletion of natural capital into account.[45] Natural capital accounting, in other words, has been used as a way to disclose unequal relationships between the global North and South, and to animate demands for ecological reparations. As Democratic Republic of Congo president Félix Tshisekedi has argued, "Africa's ecosystems provide free crucial services to the world. African forests and oceans serve as natural carbon sinks. It is time for Africa to be compensated—for the good of the continent and the planet."[46] This is a demand, effectively, of wages for *oikos*-work.[47] As with the demand of "wages for housework," however, the act of disclosure alone has been largely ineffectual. Ecosystem services remain, for the most part, as free as ever—and as threatened. While tools for natural capital accounting have proliferated, they have remained largely at the level of measurement and assessment performed by multilateral institutions and nongovernmental organizations: they provide advisory content, but do not actually factor into market decisions or corporate balance books. If ecological debt is increasingly acknowledged in rhetoric, it is as far as ever from being paid.

Accounting for natural capital is simply not the same thing as commodifying it. Describing a watershed as a source of valuable water filtration services or estimating the cost of replacing it does not actually render it an exchangeable commodity; it does not force anyone to pay for the services that the watershed provides. Indeed, where estimations of nature's value are often seen as the first step on a steep and slippery slope to commodification, those actually *trying* to commodify nature have found it an uphill battle. As the *Financial Times* observes, "Setting up whales as a carbon-based asset entails several tricky steps."[48] Estimating the value of a whale, however complicated, is the easy part. Actually attaching a price to a whale is much harder.

Owning Nature to Save It

It is not natural capital accounting but the creation of property rights in ecosystem services that is the holy grail for many market environmentalists. The theory is that doing so will give their owners a claim to any revenues that ecosystem services generate, and hence a stake in the preservation of the ecosystem in question. In this vision, debates about the correct way to assess nature's value are beside the point. Once property rights are assigned, nature's value doesn't need to be calculated at all: markets will "discover" the right price through the regular process of exchange.

To understand the basic idea, we can return to the Pigou-Coase debate canvassed in chapter 4. Although the smoky chimney has since become the paradigmatic illustration of the "negative externality," Pigou had also mentioned a positive variation: the "uncompensated services" of air improved by parks and forests.[49] In 1952, the economist James Meade developed this strand of Pigou's theory by considering the example of an apple farm whose trees provided a "free lunch" of nectar to the bee colony next door.[50] Because the apple grower was uncompensated for the services their trees provided, Meade posited, they might not produce enough blossoms to keep the bees fed, resulting in suboptimal levels of honey. Thus the "unpaid benefits" the apple trees provided to the bees should be calculated, Meade suggested, and the "capitalists in apple-farming" subsidized for the lunch they provided.[51]

The Coaesian counter would later come from the Chicago School economist Steven Cheung. In fact, Cheung observed, bees provided pollination services to apple farmers rather than the other way around—but not for free.[52] There was already a fully functioning market in pollination services: beekeepers had been renting out beehives to farmers ever since industrially organized orchards had eradicated the "nonproductive" weeds that attracted wild pollinators in the early twentieth century. Whereas Pigouvians relied on a fable of bees, Cheung concluded, the facts offered evidence in support of the Coase Theorem: given adequate property rights and incentives, private actors could come to mutually beneficial agreements without government interference in prices. There was no reason to believe that similar contracts could not be created to govern other natural resources.

The past three decades have seen numerous efforts to realize Cheung's vision, whether seeking to establish companies that traffic in nature conservation; create markets in ecosystem services, biodiversity offsets, and carbon credits; or, most recently, to establish nature as an "asset class." The Intrinsic Exchange Group, one self-proclaimed "natural asset company," declares that "Nature's economy is larger than our current industrial economy and we can tap this store of wealth." An investment report predicts that "protecting nature" could generate as much as $10 trillion in business.[53] Nature, another proclaims, is "the world's most undervalued asset class."[54]

These projects have been met with challenges in their own right. Where moral philosophers have rued the imposition of economic and instrumental value on intrinsically valuable entities, Marxists have typically charged that the creation of markets in nature marks a new round of enclosure. Critiques in this vein frequently draw on David Harvey's concept of "accumulation by dispossession," itself an update of Marx's analysis of "so-called primitive accumulation."[55] Where Marx saw primitive accumulation as the origin of capital itself through the conversion of commonly owned assets to privately held property, Harvey argues, following Rosa Luxemburg, that this kind of accumulation is not limited to an original moment, but constitutes a continual process. Capital repeatedly uses extra-economic force to privatize resources and expel those reliant on them, thereby creating the conditions for new rounds of accumulation and staving off its own tendencies toward stagnation. "The wholesale commodification of nature in all its forms," Harvey argues, is an exemplary instance of accumulation by dispossession.[56]

Following Harvey, natural capital and ecosystem service programs have frequently been described in terms of "nature as accumulation strategy," "accumulation by decarbonization," "accumulation by conservation," "neoliberal conservation," and a "great expropriation of the global commons and the dispossession of humanity on a scale exceeding all previous human history."[57] The geographer Neil Smith asserts that capitalism is undertaking "a major strategy for ecological commodification, marketization and financialization which radically intensifies and deepens the penetration of nature by capital."[58] The commodification of ecosystem services, the geographer Morgan Robertson has argued, is nothing less than a step toward the "monetization and financialization of the conditions of life" on par with the commodification of human labor power.[59] In the twenty-first century, Nancy Fraser warns, the "commodification of nature has proceeded far beyond anything Polanyi imagined," extending to the likes of carbon emissions and environmental derivatives.[60] Markets in ecosystem services, many critics claim, will unleash a new wave of "green grabs" as capitalists buy land to speculate in newly financialized natures, in the process displacing those reliant on those ecosystems for survival. The result, these accounts suggest, will be a world fully owned by capital, down to the last organism and even carbon molecule.

What is most striking today, however, is not the extent to which ecosystemic natures have been commodified, but the fact that they largely have *not* been. True markets in ecosystem services have failed to materialize on a large scale—not because society has moved to counter the market, but because capital has shown little interest. Far from a sector worth twice global GDP, natural capital has attracted, Jessica Dempsey and Daniel Chiu Suarez observe, only "slivers of slivers of slivers" of private investment, on the order of a few billion dollars rather than the trillions imagined.[61] Private funding accounts for only one-sixth of global funding for biodiversity conservation projects, and much of that is philanthropic.[62] The proliferation of accounting standards and even new financial instruments has not translated into actual investment. Voluntary carbon markets issue only about $2 billion in credits annually; the New York Stock Exchange recently withdrew its proposal to list natural asset companies.[63] Rather than being overwhelmed with a flood of speculative investment, conservationists rue the "biodiversity finance gap." The Convention on Biodiversity has stated that private finance alone "will never be sufficient" for achieving biodiversity goals.[64] Even the Paulson Institute acknowledges that "we cannot rely on economic models, market forces, or the private sector alone to solve the problem of unprecedented global biodiversity loss."[65] Nature, in other words, has not appeared to be a very good accumulation strategy at all.

———

Moral and Marxist critics of commodification, for all their differences, share a conviction: that the market always moves to encompass more of the world. Capitalism relentlessly prices and commodifies, buys and sells. "In search of profit, capital stalks the whole earth," Neil Smith declares. "It attaches a price tag to everything it sees and from then on it is this price tag which determines the fate of nature."[66] Michael Sandel similarly frets that "we are moving toward a society in which everything is up for sale."[67] Pricing nature, in other words, is the default. It is what will happen if we *fail* to push back against the market, if we fail to actively assert that nature is valuable beyond price. But as we've seen, capital does not just advance and absorb: it also withdraws and expels, abdicates and neglects. Rather than accumulation by dispossession, ecosystem services are another instance of a different phenomenon: *abdication through disinterest.*

A twist on the economists' fable of the bees explains why. Today, the honeybees that animated Cheung's triumphant defense of property rights hardly seem like the poster child for sustainable resource management. If anything, they seem the opposite: honeybees have, in recent years, become a high-profile example of ecological collapse. Honeybee populations have declined sharply over the past several decades as a result of pesticide use, habitat loss, and climate change, which have eliminated their sources of food and made them more susceptible to diseases and parasites.[68] And yet while honeybees continue to die in large numbers each year, they are not actually at risk of *total* population collapse. Beekeepers *have* learned to manage the new age of habitat disruption, stress, and disease, at least enough to maintain baseline populations. Honeybees, however, are an unusual kind of bee. They have long been domesticated, meaning that they can be physically controlled, and there are clear institutional frameworks in place designating them as property. From the perspective of political economy, they are essentially tiny livestock: more like cattle, pigs, and horses than wild bumblebees, wasps, or butterflies.[69] They are not, in other words, representative of most ecosystem services.

It is wild bees—addressed by neither Meade nor Cheung—that are in more serious trouble. Wild bees are among an estimated 1,200 vertebrate and 100,000 invertebrate species worldwide—including moths, butterflies, bats, and birds—that pollinate both agricultural and nonagricultural plants.[70] The Coaseian solution of property rights simply doesn't work here: whether or not you *should* be able to buy the services of a wild pollinator, the fact is that you simply *can't.* There is no one whom you can pay to command their services and ensure that they show up on schedule. In turn, there is no one to make sure they are fed if apple blossoms disappear, nurse them back to health when mites strike, or split the hive to help them breed. Wild hives may contribute to public benefits, but their well-being isn't directly linked to the private benefit of any individual. Even though many people have some small interest in preserving wild pollinators and the ecosystems they replenish, no one has an immediate financial interest in caring for wild pollinators themselves. (Although some people might still do so out of personal proclivity—as in the phenomenon of "pollinator gardens.") This is a problem, because however repugnant one finds the prospect of owning a wild bee or a whale, Cheung, like Coase, isn't entirely wrong. Nature can appear in the market only where it's represented in terms of price—and hence where it is alienated as property held by a human owner.

Natural Communia

This kind of price—the "price paid to the owner of natural forces or mere products of nature for the right of using those forces"—is what Marx calls rent. Rent includes the payment for things generated *entirely* by nature; it's paid, Marx notes, "only because he is the 'owner,' *the owner of land*, whether this consists of soil, forest, fish pond, waterfall, building land, or anything else."[71] Rent, in other words, reflects not the application of labor or investment, but sheer control of assets. It is not a mode of accumulation, but one of distribution: a transfer of surplus value produced by one capitalist to another, the extraction of payment for gifts that once were free.[72] Rent does not, then, signify a new regime of accumulation rooted in the commodification of everything. It has nevertheless seemed like a feasible way to attach prices to ecosystem services. The problem, for would-be biospheric rentiers, is that the physical qualities of ecosystems tend to elude the level of control that commanding rent requires. The key difference between natural resources and ecosystem services—between the figuratively priceless diamond and the literally priceless atmosphere, the honeybee and wild wasp—is that natural resources can be monopolized, alienated, and sold, while ecosystem services, by and large, cannot.[73]

Many features of ecosystems and the contributions they make to our lives and economies are not easily captured by private property. Some are too mobile to enclose: air circulates, birds migrate. Others are not mobile enough: you can pick an apple from a tree and ship it around the world, but you can't harvest and transport the shade its leaves provide. Nor can you store it up to use later: like human services, ecosystem services last only as long as they are actively being produced; and most are produced only as long as they exist in relation to one another. Natural resources are discrete objects and entities that can be extracted or closed off from broader ecological and social relations; ecosystem services, by contrast, exist only in a web of relationships from which they can't be isolated or extricated. The useful services they provide emerge from their very life processes and their interactions with one another. If you put a whale in an aquarium tank, it may provide human entertainment and even existence value—but it won't feed ocean dwellers or stimulate phytoplankton growth.[74]

Physical obstacles to ownership are not necessarily insuperable. This, after all, is what property rights are for: asserting a claim to things that can't be secured through physical control alone. Financialization, in particular, has been seen as one way to make ecosystems salable—a way to abstract away from entities that remain stubbornly concrete. Elements of ecosystems can be represented as buyable units in the abstract, whether or not those representations adequately represent the underlying ecosystems. Perhaps you can't buy the tree's carbon sequestration services directly, but you can buy a carbon credit.[75] In contrast to gifts of nature that are easily appropriated, however—like the apple that Locke's laborer plucks from a common orchard—the process of making ecosystem services into commodities is elaborate. Ecosystems must be mapped, their services identified, their contributions measured. A gigantic apparatus must be constructed to assess and verify whether these abstractions are really representing the physical activities they claim to be.

Perhaps the biggest problem, however, comes in creating *demand* for gifts of nature that give too freely. While an instrument might be designed to *represent* a unit of carbon, it can't become a *commodity* unless those who don't pay can be excluded from using it.[76] That some natural entities preclude such exclusion has long been noted. In the sixth century, the Roman emperor Justinian had declared that "by the natural law itself the following are common to all: air, running water and the sea, and with it the shores of the sea."[77] A millennium later, the Dutch jurist Hugo Grotius concluded of the "free sea" that "nature . . . commandeth it should be common"; four centuries after Grotius, the economist J. H. Dales noted, "About the only things in this world that are not owned in any meaningful sense are the high seas and their animal inhabitants," which were "owned in common because there is no alternative."[78] In 1932, the legal scholar Samuel Wiel named air, running water (and by extension, oil and gas), sea, and seashores to be elements wherein communal ownership was "compelled by natural necessity," describing them in terms of "natural communism."[79]

As the lineage dating to Justinian suggests, the physical properties of these natural agents, and the obstacles they present to certain forms of human use, have not themselves changed. They have taken on significance with the emergence of capitalism, however. By now, nearly everything that can be enclosed has been— and those that cannot stand out all the more starkly. Not only air and sea but most ecosystem services are best characterized by Jean-Baptiste Say's observation that "the wind turns our mills, and even the heat of the sun co-operates with human industry; but happily no man has yet been able to say, the 'wind and the sun's rays are mine, and I will be paid for their productive services.'"[80] The term *capital* itself was originally used to describe heads of cattle. But cattle, like honeybees, are ownable, alienable, exchangeable—precisely what ecosystem services are not. Natural capital, then, is a misnomer. Ecosystem services are better described as *natural communia*—the Latin term for property held by all.

In neoclassical economics, these kinds of entities are typically known as public goods: one person can use them without preventing anyone else from doing so, and no one can be stopped from using them. While pure public goods can't be depleted, many other ecosystem services fall into the related category of "common pool goods"—goods that can eventually be exhausted, but that it is difficult to prevent others from using. In fact, it is only recently that the atmosphere *itself* has come to appear more like soil fertility than like sunlight—as something that human use could substantially alter or diminish. From the perspective of an economist, the Anthropocene might be thought of as the shift of many goods from the status of public goods to common pool goods: the realization that human activity and use *can* change and consume goods once thought immutable and indestructible.

While the generosity of the unowned wind and sun was for Say a happy fact, for economists it is a problem. It is precisely because of the abundant generosity of these public goods that they are often "underprovided": no one has a financial incentive to provide these goods if they cannot charge others to use them or prevent nonpayers from benefiting.[81] Ecosystems, of course, provide themselves. But no one will bear the opportunity costs of ecosystems' conservation—the costs of, say, preserving a wetland instead of turning it into a housing development—if they can't prevent others from paying for them in turn. To put it simply: Why buy the ecosystem when you can get the service for free? As the natural capital economist Dieter Helm has bluntly observed, "No private company is going to get into this business."[82]

Are ecosystems thereby safe from the "annihilating" force of the market? Hardly. In a world where most things are commodities, natural communia are under threat—not from enclosure, but from erosion. This is, of course, the basic insight of Hardin's tragedy of the commons, which claims that things that aren't owned will be destroyed. Hardin, as we've seen, treats the commons as a timeless phenomenon rooted in the simple fact of material scarcity. Contra Hardin, however, this tragedy arises not from the sheer fact of common property, but from the fact that commons today exist as patches of recalcitrant matter within a largely commodified world. This tragedy, in other words, is one generated by market rule.[83] And yet the state of natural communia within capitalism stands a challenge, too, for Hardin's critics, from Elinor Ostrom to Peter Linebaugh, who counter that commons are typically governed according to internal rules and norms.[84] While these scholars have tended to address the commons as an institutional form that can be studied in isolation, or as alternatives to the market altogether, the fact is that market rule will weigh on any commons, however well governed internally, that isn't entirely self-sufficient. There are no historical precedents, moreover, for the management of planetary commons like the atmosphere and oceans—and no way for smaller-scale commons to escape their planetmaking force. In other words, the commons cannot really be understood apart from state and market, as Ostrom suggests—let alone in opposition to them, as Linebaugh claims. Against the view that capitalism is equivalent to privatization, capitalism's social relations fundamentally structure even the commons.

Surplus and Abjection

Today, capitalism increasingly orders the world—not only within spaces of overt production but also many natural elements that have not been subsumed, commodified, or forced into production at all.[85] In fact, capitalism organizes very few of the *kinds* of beings on Earth directly. It's hard to say that those it does are being cared for, exactly. Honeybees may not be at threat of extinction, but they still die in large numbers each year. Chickens are the most numerous animals on the planet, but most live miserable lives, confined to tiny cages or overcrowded barns. Milk cows are artificially inseminated over and over, only to have their calves taken away as soon as they're born. Still, the usefulness of these beings to capital means that vast resources are poured into their reproduction. By contrast, capital is largely indifferent to the fate of species that are not themselves "cash crops" (corn, palm oil, wheat) nor livestock (cattle, pigs, chickens) nor immediately essential to core aspects of production (honeybees).

Even today, contra Müntzer, the vast number of creatures remain free, in that they are unowned. But they are not *themselves* free, in the sense of liberated. They are, we might say, doubly free: free from ownership, and free from the care—however violent—that attends it. For if capitalism has remade much of the physical world through intentional absorption, it has remade it even more powerfully through neglectful omission. The intensive cultivation and use of even a tiny subset of the nonhuman world ripples through the biosphere writ large, as capital reorients ecosystems around a few profitable species. Agriculture diverts the material resources of a given region—from the centuries of energy stored in the soil to the glacial melt flowing through rivers—into the cultivation of a few kinds of profitable life: corn, wheat, cotton.[86] Useful organisms are extracted from ecosystems, as Troy Vettese notes, leaving holes in the tightly woven web of life, while surplus matter is dumped into them, disrupting chemical flows and food chains.[87] The effects on the species that capital ignores are wide-ranging: their habitats are fragmented, their food sources diminished, their migration patterns interrupted, their water sources fouled. Today 60 percent of land mammals are livestock, and another 36 percent are human beings; only a meager 4 percent are wildlife.[88] As Alexis Pauline Gumbs notes, the endangerment of marine mammals, like the near-extinction of the vaquita porpoise and Atlantic right whale, is "what capitalism means on an interspecies scale."[89]

Many forms of life therefore constitute what we might call "surplus species": the species, organisms, and ecosystems whose capacities are essentially irrelevant to capital, and which are therefore left to fend for themselves. They are structurally comparable to those human beings whom Marx described as "surplus populations": the masses of people whose labor is superfluous to capital's needs, who need a job but cannot find one, and who have to find some other way to reproduce their lives. People in this position are subjected to a distinctive form of domination in their own right. Adam Smith counterposes the self-interested mutual cooperation of the butcher, baker, and brewer to the servile position of those entirely dependent on others: "Nobody but the beggar," he claims, "chooses to depend chiefly upon the benevolence of his fellow-citizens."[90] However unequal the exchange of labor power for a wage may be, it nonetheless contains an element of reciprocity. The seller of labor power, however desperate, has something that capital needs—and thus something of value to withhold. Those who can't sell their labor, by contrast, lack access to the wage, and thus to everything the wage can buy—even as they remain dependent on markets to access necessary goods. "Wageless life" therefore tends to be precarious; Tania Murray Li argues that people in this position are effectively "let die."[91] They must depend on the benevolence of their "fellow-citizens" for survival—and hence they become vulnerable to the arbitrary power of others. This combination of radical market dependence and asymmetric personal dependence constitutes what I call *market abjection*.

Many of the nonhumans that capital doesn't need are in a similar position: precarious, dependent, abject. To be of no interest to capital can be a blessing: bowhead whale populations rebounded in the Arctic, for example, when commercial whalers finally left them alone.[92] But for many others—perhaps most—capital's disinterest is a death sentence. They are neither raw material nor potential commodity, valuable neither in exchange nor as sources of rent. This does not mean that they are useless to human beings: an estimated 70 percent of the global poor depend directly on wild species for subsistence, at least in part, meaning that they suffer most directly the loss of ecosystem services. Nearly everyone derives pleasure from unowned and unmanaged beings in some form or another. We all, as the very idea of ecosystem services makes clear, rely on them for basic survival. But however valuable these entities may be as means of subsistence, or aesthetic pleasure, or simply in their own right, they struggle to attract interest from the relevant parties: the private investors who can ensure their survival. They are exploited and even annihilated not by virtue of being incorporated into the market, as in the phenomenon that Keeanga-Yamhatta Taylor describes as "predatory inclusion," but by being excluded from it.[93] While this resembles the phenomenon that Ruth Wilson Gilmore describes as "organized abandonment," wherein both capital and states disavow responsibility for land and labor, for the most part it is not actively organized or planned.[94] It is a form of neglect stemming from *disinterested exclusion*, resulting in *disorganized abandonment*—another dimension of nonresponsibility under capitalism.

The problem, then, isn't what it's typically said to be: that capital is commodifying life itself or enclosing the last remaining commons. Most forms of life on Earth almost certainly won't be commodified; some seemingly can't be. What is most damning, in this situation, is not the condition of being subjected to instrumental use, or even lacking use value—but that of being useless to capital in particular. The results are often violent, even brutal. But this violence is of a distinctive kind: it is not the overt destruction associated with processes like whaling or logging, but rather the accidental byproduct of ostensibly bloodless economic processes.

States of Nature

If capital won't provide ecosystems and their services, who will? At least since Adam Smith, the answer to the problem of underprovided public goods has been the state. The role of the state, Smith argues, is to provide goods and services that are socially valuable but not privately profitable.[95] The state's role, in other words, is to solve capital's collective action problem—to coordinate what capital proves unable to, on a scale beyond what any individual firm or household could manage. If this constitutes a frank acknowledgment that capital is parasitic, or at least reliant, on other institutions and agents, it is also fairly run of the mill. Even Friedrich Hayek, in his notoriously antistate polemic *The Road to Serfdom*, acknowledges that the state has a legitimate role in providing what the market cannot—including, notably, a "substitute for the regulation by the price mechanism" to address "certain harmful effects of deforestation, or of some methods of farming."[96]

Indeed, for all the critical attention devoted to the rapacious energies of capital and markets, it is the state that has been the driving force behind efforts to constitute nature as capital. It is the state that initially undertook assessments of ecological value, for use in cost-benefit analyses of public programs, and that has devised strategies for incorporating the estimated value of nature into national accounts.[97] It is the state that has funded most ecosystem service conservation outright, paid people to steward ecosystems, and administered funds supplied by multilateral institutions. It is the state, too, that has engineered and administered the banner examples of ecosystem services in action, from the preservation of the New York City watershed as a water filtration device to Costa Rica's conservation of wide swathes of forest.[98] For that matter, most so-called "markets" in ecosystem services are really just misleadingly labeled regulations or subsidies, in which states set targets or offer incentives to producers who adopt ecologically sustainable practices.[99] Where actual markets in ecosystem services do exist, states play an outsized role in them: they not only create, recognize, and enforce property rights, as all markets require, but create demand itself through regulations that require the purchase of the likes of carbon credits. Because payments for ecosystem services are, essentially, rents, as Romain Felli notes, they are contingent on control over resources—and ultimately on the state's power over territory.[100]

Smith's classic examples of the goods that states should provide are infrastructural elements like bridges and roads. Many ecosystems, too, are better understood as infrastructures than commodities—as the foundations *beneath* value-generating activity rather than sources of value in themselves.[101] Infrastructure is a formal category, defined in relation to the activities it supports. As the trajectory from Smith to Hayek makes clear, state provision of infrastructure does not necessarily constitute a challenge to capitalism, and is indeed often undertaken to facilitate capital investment.[102] Indeed, in capitalist societies, the category of infrastructure tends to signify areas where the market fails to provide goods that are widely recognized as useful and even necessary; it designates unproductive expenditures that capital is unlikely to provide. The state often operates as a paracapitalist agent, doing things capital needs but can't do for itself. Yet if ecosystemic infrastructures, like built ones, are often oriented toward facilitating production and accumulation—toward protecting what James O'Connor calls the "conditions of production"—they might also be oriented toward sustaining human and nonhuman life regardless of their contributions to accumulation—toward supporting what O'Connor describes as "means of life," and Winona LaDuke and Deborah Cowen describe as "alimentary infrastructures."[103] A wetland, for example, might be preserved in order to provide a "waste management" facility for a nearby industrial plant, or to provide habitat for local waterfowl and flood protection to nearby towns. A watershed might be preserved as part of the water filtration infrastructure for a multinational beverage corporation, or as a source of fresh water for nearby residents. A prairie might be managed for cattle ranching, with wolves eliminated and wild horses culled, or rewilded to support a wider range of species.[104]

If the role of the state in providing ecosystem services does not signify a break with capital, then, it does signal productive tensions. Capital's reliance on the state to provide at least some of the things it needs opens a political door—one that might lead to more overt battles over control of investment.[105] Although the state is often inclined to provide what capital needs, its actions are never driven *only* by value in the way that capital's are. A key question, then, is whether and under what conditions the state will secure "means of life" that are *not* also conditions of production. To understand ecosystem services as *public* services, in other words, is to open them up to public and political contestation. It raises the question: Who benefits from nature's gifts, and to what purposes are they put?

Perhaps most significantly, the state's role in making natural capital marks an acknowledgment that some things simply *will not* be valued on capital's terms, and must be assessed in other ways. We are used to evaluating the worth of commodities in exchange. But because the free gifts of nature don't appear in the market, they can only be evaluated politically.

The free gift of nature, as I have argued, is a real abstraction: it is the way we tend to treat and value nature by default. It reflects not a conscious decision to value nature at zero, or an active process of reasoning, but an outcome of our actions and relationships, something we do unwittingly.[106] Natural capital, by contrast—understood as an effort to assert the economic value of ecological nature—is an *artificial abstraction*. It is a category that does *not* have self-sustaining force in the world, one that cuts *against* the real abstractions generated by exchange under conditions of market rule, and which therefore must be constantly asserted and enforced.[107]

Artificial abstractions are not *false* or imaginary any more than real abstractions are true or natural. They can have real force in the world. But their construction and deployment are laborious in a way that the real abstraction's are not, and more prone to failure. These forms of valuation must be consciously undertaken and constantly reinforced—nearly always by the artificial man of the state.[108] As such, artificial abstractions often seem like an intrusion into voluntary social practices or distortions of spontaneous order. In my view, this is their great virtue. Artificial abstractions reveal the political questions lurking within prices, the many kinds of value that the value form neglects. They force the question of value from the realm of unthinking action to that of conscious reflection. Although decades of efforts to make nature into capital have failed to make prices stick, then, they have successfully brought to light the questions that are nearly always disguised beneath prices.

The extremity of the disjuncture between what nature's value "should" be and what it is thus presents a particularly acute portrait of capitalism's general mismeasurement of wealth. It poses a similar question to that raised by the devaluation of reproductive labor: if the planetary processes that constitute the bases of life on Earth itself are not valued *at all*, why would we expect capitalism to value anything else as we think it should? The recognition that decisions about nature's value must be made politically rather than in the market thus allows us to revisit the core question of the ecological ethics debates— What *is* an ecosystem worth?—in a different register.

Conclusion: Conscious Planetmaking

Planetary ecosystems are presently in a dire state. For decades, capitalism has proposed to hold the solutions: in new forms of property rights, new kinds of markets, new representations of concrete natures in abstract terms. Public, private, and nonprofit sectors have constructed an elaborate labyrinth of social and economic institutions—in the words of the geographer Eric Swyngedouw, "a truly Stalinist-bureaucratic institutional structure"—in service of making nature into credits, capital, or assets; buying and selling ecosystem services; pricing nature to save it.[109] Recent speculations about markets in "natural assets" are only the most recent iteration of a dream, now over three decades old, of unlocking the wealth that nature's free gifts seem to hold.[110] So far, however, its realization remains elusive. Making ecosystems into revenue-generating property—let alone growth-stimulating assets—is, as we have seen, enormously complicated, and rarely successful.

Actually protecting ecosystem services, however, is much simpler.[111] For the most part it just means preserving swathes of land large enough to keep ecological relations intact—and then leaving them alone. Ecosystems are, in a sense, already socialized, insofar as their physical qualities resist the relations of private ownership; they are already automated, in that they largely work on their own, with a bit of maintenance here and there. Why work so hard to make them monopolizable by private interests instead of embracing them as a public good? Why, put simply, should the state go to so much trouble to privatize and capitalize nature instead of socializing it?

The socialization of nature, Jacob Blumenfeld argues, would "take ecosystems seriously as sites of political contest and coordinated planning, so that non-monetary questions about the value of nature can even be asked in the first place, and proactively planned for in accordance with multiple criteria of human and non-human flourishing."[112] It would be what we might think of as a form of conscious planetmaking. Conscious planetmaking does not mean indulging in the fantasy that we can engineer the Earth to precise specifications or bring it under total control—neither of which, I think, is either possible or desirable. It simply means taking collective responsibility for maintaining, remaking, and cultivating the multispecies worlds upon which human beings rely not only for mere survival but for lives that are pleasurable, fulfilling, and meaningful.[113]

Worldmaking has often been conceived as a distinctively human practice. For Hannah Arendt, the world is a *human* world of durable artifacts, which can withstand the perpetual cycles of nature. When we make the world, we make a lasting place for human beings to act and appear. The "durable human world" itself, however, is constituted not only by the exclusively human action of *homo faber* but by the activities of the more-than-human world, which Arendt classifies as the ostensibly ephemeral cycles of labor. "Natural" entities like old growth forests or wetlands may be durable, worldly things, potentially lasting thousands of years—and they too are the subjects of human cultivation, meaning making, and care. They exist not only in "cyclical" patterns but have their own histories of change and disruption as well as ongoingness, which are intertwined with and perhaps now inseparable from human histories. Conscious planetmaking means we must recognize that these activities cannot be somehow cordoned off from human politics, as Arendt suggests, but must be fully integrated into political life.

To socialize nature would, then, bring political forms of decision-making and planning to bear on ecosystems rather than leaving them to the whims of the market. The particular dimensions of what this might entail will vary with the needs of people, production, and of course, ecosystems themselves— which are always defined relationally. Ecosystems, we might say, are not *things*; they are *situations*.[114] In some cases, conscious planetmaking might mean setting aside vast expanses of forest or plains to regenerate—not by barring human interaction altogether, as colonial conservationists often have, but simply by preventing their conversion to sites of commodity production. It might mean creating green spaces in urban areas, where people can cool off in summer heat and migrating birds can pause amid hemisphere-spanning flights. It will frequently mean restoring Indigenous land tenure.[115] While often planetmaking will simply mean leaving nature to do its work, in some instances it may require more active forms of care and intervention, as envisioned by Indigenous thinkers like Nick Estes and ecofeminists like Ariel Salleh.[116] Ecosystem maintenance could be structured as public works programs—as indeed many payment-for-ecosystem-services programs already are.[117] Rather than "crowding out" spontaneous and unalienated care for nature, as the hostile worlds thesis suggests, compensating these kinds of work might help *generate* care for ecosystems by encouraging new forms of interaction and attention.[118] A new class of ecological laborers, in turn—what geographers have described as a growing "eco-proletariat" of those laboring in the ecosystem service economy—might develop new forms of labor politics and new modalities of struggle, in which the interests of humans and ecosystems are more closely aligned.[119]

Debates about the value of nature, in other words, are never simply about ethics or "the environment." They are also, always, debates about what we produce and why; about who decides, and toward what ends. Thus as with reproduction, decisions about ecosystem services can never be contained to ecosystems themselves: they will inevitably address other aspects of social life. Easing pressure on wild lands might require building dense social housing and transit to arrest the drive toward sprawling settlements. Making use of the free gifts of sun and wind might require the construction of publicly owned energy infrastructures; supplementing natural carbon sequestration might require publicly owned carbon capture.[120] Perhaps most significantly, struggles to constitute ecosystems as public services and alimentary infrastructures will inevitably pose challenges to economies as presently construed. Mainstream economics tends to conceive of public goods merely as supplements to private provision. But here, as with negative externalities, the scope of the free gift threatens to explode the category altogether. For to provide ecosystem public services at the necessary scale will entail massive reorientation of private as well as public goods. Preserving ecosystems as natural communia will mean *not* using them for oil, or timber, or cattle. It will, in some cases, require unmaking infrastructures built by and for capital: filling in coal mines or dismantling pipelines, expropriating privately held land and restoring it to common ownership. It might mean curbing forms of production that encroach on wild lands or expel destructive byproducts into atmospheric and oceanic commons.[121] It will require, in other words, confronting capital's rule over our shared planet.

The frameworks of infrastructure and socialization will seem, to some, too instrumentalizing, too oriented toward human needs. But "use value" doesn't have to mean anthropocentric instrumentality. It can mean use to other kinds of beings, usefulness within the web of life. The very idea of an ecosystem, after all, reflects the fact that organisms are constantly making *use* of one another— often violently. To see ecosystems as infrastructure, then, might simply mean recognizing the ways they support the very beings that compose them. Just as human standards of living are rooted not only in sheer biophysical need but social and cultural expectation, moreover, so too should our assessment of the standard of planetary living encompass more than sheer planetary boundaries. A truly good standard of living would almost certainly, as Sharon Krause argues, aim at the flourishing and freedom of humans and nonhumans alike—as reflected in the Amerindian idea of *buen vivir/sumac kawsay*.[122] The essential point is that "use" is an entirely different metric than "exchange."

Nor does socializing nature necessarily mean social *ownership* of nature in perpetuity. Marx himself is surprisingly visionary on this front. After capitalism had been transcended, he thought, "private ownership of the globe by single individuals will appear quite as absurd as private ownership of one man by another." Collective ownership is not the necessary alternative to private property; ultimately, "even a whole society, a nation, or even all simultaneously existing societies taken together, are not the owners of the globe . . . like *boni patres familias*, they must hand it down to succeeding generations in an improved condition."[123] Natural communia might be used by all—and owned by none.

Socialized natures will not, on their own, undo either the value-form itself or the disciplinary pressures it puts on the state. They might nevertheless constitute a ground, often quite literally, upon which broader collectives might be built, and from which capitalism's planetmaking power might be challenged. What the framework of socialized natures as a means to conscious planetmaking recognizes is that we are responsible for the shape of the planet going forward, whether we like it or not. This doesn't mean we have total control over the world, or that human power is—let alone should be—unlimited. It does mean that we can't expect ecosystems to keep regenerating themselves in a world that treats them as worthless. It recognizes relationships to nature as capitalism has made them in order to confront the drivers of environmental destruction head-on. It dispels the fantasy of an authentic nature whose intrinsic value we can simply affirm, and recognizes that we cannot avoid making decisions about which natures to use in which ways. It can nevertheless encompass the idea that nature has value beyond its use value to us—while also recognizing that we are ultimately responsible for the natures we choose to protect and restore, transform and remake, cultivate and leave be.

In this project, Donna Haraway's vision of earthly survival remains indispensable:

> For salamanders, regeneration after injury, such as the loss of a limb, involves regrowth of structure and restoration of function with the constant possibility of twinning or other odd topographical productions at the site of former injury. The regrown limb can be monstrous, duplicated, potent. We have all been injured, profoundly. We require regeneration, not rebirth, and the possibilities for our reconstitution include the utopian dream of the hope for a monstrous world without gender.[124]

We live in a world that has been injured, profoundly. But we cannot respond by imagining a return to a bygone world made whole again or rebirth in a fresh new one. As we attempt to restore some degree of structure and function to this world, we can—and must—learn about and from the more-than-human world on which we depend, and assess the needs of nonhuman beings in making judgments about what we ought to do. But in a world that has been so radically remade, we cannot simply *return* to "natural cycles" or patterns, or reproduce the old; rather, we must ourselves take responsibility for composing them, while never imagining we can make them entirely as we please.

Proposals to "repair" or "restore" the planet therefore must answer the questions: Which ecosystems—and whose—will we repair and restore? Which—and whose—flourishings will we enable? What planet are we making, and for whom? Rather than seeking to restore an imagined natural harmony, in other words, a project of more-than-human repair must be what the philosopher Olúfẹ́mi Táíwò describes as a "constructive" one—informed by the harms of the past, but oriented toward the needs of the future.[125] A constructive view of ecological reparations cannot be rooted in the appeals to an originary nature that lurk beneath many calls for the restoration of natural balance—or even for reconciling humanity and nature by suturing the "metabolic rift." The planet we make going forward will not be like the one that has existed at any previous point in history. If this is daunting, it is also unavoidable. There is no other planet on which we can make a world; no Biosphere 2 to which we can escape.

7

Freedom beyond the Free Gift

"MECHANIZATION," the architect and futurist Buckminster Fuller wrote in *Fortune* in 1940, "the harnessing of energy, is man's answer to slavery."[1] Fuller estimated that the world population—then approximately 2.1 billion—relied on an energy output equivalent to that expended by 37 billion human beings working forty hours per week. The United States alone accounted for over half of this energy use. To denote the annual energy output of an average human man working forty hours per week, Fuller introduced a new term: the *energy slave*. Fuller intended energy slaves to stand as the human equivalent of terms like *horsepower*. But his choice of terminology also evokes a social theory. Fossil fuels, it implies, have liberated human beings from forms of drudgery to which all previous societies were subjected. It intones, too, a warning about modern decadence: we all have servants silently toiling on our behalf, without whom we could not survive. Fossil fuels, Fuller intimates, have allowed modern society to ignore an ancient problem: that life is a lot of work.

Six decades later, the journalist Andrew Nikiforuk would update Fuller's argument while making its underlying thesis more explicit in his book *The Energy of Slaves*.[2] The energy use of the average North American, Nikiforuk argues, is equivalent to the labor of eighty-nine human beings.[3] For Nikiforuk, this means that we all live like the slaveholders we now condemn, whether Roman patricians or Southern plantation owners—and for Nikiforuk, this is not a celebration of modern abundance but a condemnation of modern life. The use of oil, he charges, has licensed frivolous consumption and thoughtless behavior. We are now so wholly dependent on an increasingly scarce resource that even if we could somehow muster the will to resume the burden of manual labor, we could not possibly substitute human energies for the work oil now performs. This is not only a matter of scale; the density and portability of oil are simply irreplaceable. Human laborers could not power a plane, for example, or even an automobile. When the "gift of coal and oil" is depleted, he warns, modern societies will be in trouble.[4]

The objection to the terminology of energy slaves is obvious: that it utterly fails to capture the meaning of slavery. It simply doesn't make sense to refer to inanimate energy as a "slave": oil may be composed of biological material, but it matters that it isn't alive, and it matters that it isn't human. To be enslaved is to exist in a social relationship of domination, forced to labor and even simply to live at someone else's command. By contrast, while we might be troubled by the way oil is obtained or the effects of its use, it's not clear what, if anything, is morally wrong with using this particular form of inanimate energy in itself. To compare the use of oil to the forced labor of human beings, then, seems not only offensive but oblivious.

Yet if few today use the language of energy slaves, many contemporary anxieties about freedom are underpinned by an analysis that echoes Fuller's and Nikiforuk's. "The mansion of modern freedoms," the historian Dipesh Chakrabarty argues in an influential essay, "stands on an ever-expanding base of fossil fuel use."[5] It is these cheap, intensive sources of energy that have made it possible for human beings to produce more food with less labor, move more widely and rapidly, and develop intellectual and artistic capacities that demand time and resources.[6] For Chakrabarty, the expansion of freedom in the twentieth century in particular—the enfranchisement of women worldwide, decolonization and declarations of self-determination by newly independent nations, the expansion of human capacities and extension of human lives—stands in troubling juxtaposition with the deterioration of our earthly home. The Anthropocene seems to many to definitively settle the debate on the side of the view that, as philosopher Pierre Charbonnier claims, "Nothing is more material than freedom."[7] In a materially finite world, however, this appears a serious liability. The reliance of modern human life on such vast inputs from the nonhuman world, and the revelation that those ostensibly free gifts come with serious material costs, prompts an unsettling question: What happens if we *stop* treating nature as a free gift? As Chakrabarty asks, "Is the Anthropocene a critique of the narratives of freedom?"[8]

The archetypal modern narrative of freedom is a progressive one: a story of greater human freedom and flourishing enabled by the steady pace of human reason, which has gradually subjugated nature to our command and liberated human beings from its capricious and uncaring grip. Although within critical scholarship this is more often encountered as a foil than a genuinely held article of faith, it is probably still the dominant ideology of modern freedom in the West, and in much of the rest of the world too.[9] What is striking, then, is its reappearance even in critical theory at a moment of apparent danger. To believe that modern freedoms are threatened, after all, one must believe that they have, to at least some degree, been achieved. There is, then, something ironic in Chakrabarty's troubled question. Freedom, which on the left has often appeared so elusive and unachievable, has been, in Chakrabarty's reckoning, *too* successful, *too* pervasive, *too* widely achieved. We *were* free, Chakrabarty suggests—at least some of us, those of us in the industrialized capitalist West; or at least some of those, the white, the male, the owners of automobiles and suburban single-family homes equipped with washing machines. So maybe not that many of us after all, and not for very long.

And yet it is too easy to simply wave away the concerns raised by Chakrabarty and others. They index a widely held fear—that an ecologically sustainable society will be more austere, and hence less free; that the freedom many of us enjoy is, as Elisabeth Anker suggests, an "ugly" one.[10] Even those convinced that capitalism bears the lion's share of responsibility for the profligate use of nature's gifts might wonder whether the freedoms that have been advanced under capitalist modernity, however inadequate or partially realized, are possible without it. In this chapter, then, I want to face more directly the question that has shadowed the claims of this book: How might we live differently? What else might freedom mean?

———

Capitalist unfreedom, I've argued, consists in the structural force of class rule, as realized through domination in the workplace and the imposition of social costs, the offloading of reproductive labor and the neglect of entire species. It consists, too, in the mute compulsion of value, the ways that our individual actions are channeled and directed by impersonal social structures, our alienation from our capacity for self-determination—what I have described as market rule. Capitalist unfreedom consists in the ways that our judgments of the world, and the decisions we are able to make about it, are funneled through a narrow set of evaluations that constrain the possibilities available to us. By compelling us to treat nature as a free gift, capitalism limits our ability to act on our judgments about what would constitute appropriate, respectful, or reciprocal relationships to nonhuman nature; about how we ought to value other kinds of beings, and how we might live differently as a result.

To resist bad faith, I've argued, is to recognize that the way that capitalism compels us to treat the more-than-human world is not the only way that we could—and so too, that freedom itself is not *inherently* tragic, as some ecological thinkers imply. To the contrary, there is good reason to think, as Sharon Krause argues, that an ecologically sustainable world would be a more emancipated one.[11] But freedom doesn't come with guarantees. Freedom is not, as Linda Zerilli reminds us, a means to an end—even the end of ecological sustainability.[12] To close with an appeal to freedom, then, isn't to offer a solution to ecological dilemmas or a balm to ecological anxiety. A noncapitalist world would not automatically remedy the problems this book has identified, or resolve the dilemmas of making a living on a damaged planet. What it could do, simply, is to face these problems more directly. The recognition that human lives are fundamentally bound up not only with those of billions of other human beings but also with those of countless nonhumans, both living and not, means that our decisions about how to organize ourselves as human beings will inevitably also be decisions about how to organize the nonhuman world. They will always, in other words, be potentially political matters, concerned with the organization of collective life, and therefore perpetually open to contestation rather than permanently settled. This concluding chapter, then, doesn't offer a vision of what a postcapitalist world might look like so much as a set of questions it might face. It considers how critics of capitalism have imagined freedom beyond it, and what we might take from these visions past as we attempt to chart our way in an uncertain future.

Historically, two visions of freedom have been particularly powerful for capitalism's critics: one, a view of freedom as material, realized by transcending the realm of necessity; the other, a view of freedom as social, consisting in freedom from domination by others. The first is associated with classical Marxism from Karl Kautsky to G.A. Cohen, and more recently with visions of "fully automated luxury communism"; the second, with critical theory and, more recently, radical republicanism. Each speaks to vital human aspirations—yet neither is fully adequate to our present. The material view makes freedom dependent on transcending nature, in most cases—and more occasionally, in submitting to it. The social view, by contrast, says little about nature at all, locating freedom in formal relationships between human beings who seem to float free of earthly concerns.

A core argument of this book is that the material and the social must be understood in relation to each other, as mutually mediated. This is what Simone de Beauvoir's concept of ambiguity recognizes: that social and material, form and content, can't be prized apart. Ambiguity, in turn, is a vital resource for thinking about the possibilities of social life in a rapidly changing material world. I draw on Beauvoir's account of ambiguous freedom to chart a different path through the dilemma of necessity and freedom, and to foreground the ongoing task of socialist politics: not to offer a definitive answer to the question of what nature is worth or how we should live together, but to continually reevaluate these questions in relation to one another.[13]

Material Freedom, Tragic Freedom

The claim that "nothing is more material than freedom" has typically been made by the left. It is socialists who have argued that they will finally realize the universal freedom in practice that liberalism can guarantee only formally, and achieve the freedom from labor that capitalism promises but can never actually deliver. Within the Marxist and socialist tradition, this aspiration has often been expressed in terms of Marx's famous distinction, outlined ever so briefly in volume 3 of *Capital*, between the realm of freedom and the realm of necessity:

> The realm of freedom actually begins only where labor which is determined by necessity and mundane considerations ceases; thus in the very nature of things it lies beyond the sphere of actual material production. . . . Freedom in this field can only consist in socialized man, the associated producers, rationally regulating their interchange with Nature, bringing it under their common control, instead of being ruled by it as by the blind forces of Nature; and achieving this with the least expenditure of energy and under conditions most favorable to, and worthy of, their human nature. But it nonetheless still remains a realm of necessity. Beyond it begins that development of human energy which is an end in itself, the true realm of freedom, which, however, can blossom forth only with this realm of necessity as its basis. The shortening of the working day is its basic prerequisite.[14]

This passage is one of the most famous in all of Marx's oeuvre. It has been widely embraced, even as its meaning is hotly disputed. Although it has seeming significance for ecological debates, as suggested by its references to the "metabolic interaction with nature" and "expenditure of energy," its precise valence is as contested as any other aspect of Marx's corpus.[15] More instructive than parsing Marx's own meaning, then, is to consider how freedom and necessity have been taken up with respect to questions of nature, material abundance, and scarcity.

Freedom beyond Necessity

One interpretation—perhaps the most common—focuses on freedom from necessary labor. Marx is clear that *working less* is the aim of a socialist society, and on this most socialists will agree. The view of freedom from the difficulty of toil, from the struggle to wrest a living from nature, echoes an ancient one. "If each tool could perform its task on command," Aristotle had argued, if "shuttles wove cloth by themselves . . . a master craftsman would not need assistants, and masters would not need slaves."[16] Put bluntly, slavery would be inevitable as long as tools could not do their own work. Marx had castigated Aristotle for justifying slavery, but other socialist thinkers accepted his reasoning. The Czech-Austrian socialist Karl Kautsky, leading theorist of the Second International and perhaps the most influential interpreter of Marx in the late nineteenth and early twentieth centuries, saw ancient Athens as the epitome of freedom beyond necessity—the "only society of thinkers and artists devoted to science and art for their own sakes"—and also as evidence that only modern industry could realize freedom for all. Until the era of machinery, he agreed, activity for its own sake "was possible only by throwing upon others the burden of labor, by exploiting them."[17] Capitalism made clear that machinery alone was insufficient for liberation: the advent of self-operating tools, where privately owned, had not freed most people from the need to work, but, rather, had emptied labor of its intellectual content and made the worker an appendage to the machine. But the socialist use of machinery, Kautsky thought, could enable "freedom from labor" for all, and make time for the "freedom of life, freedom for artistic and intellectual activity, freedom for the noblest enjoyment."[18] It could, in other words, universalize the freedom that in Athens had been limited to the few—while avoiding the evil of slavery that had poisoned it. Much of twentieth-century Western Marxist and socialist thought would follow suit, proclaiming that socialism would master nature in order to achieve freedom and justice among human beings.

As the twentieth century progressed and the era of mass consumption arose, however, this view of freedom from *necessary labor* has often blurred into a view of freedom from *necessity as scarcity*. Freedom, on this view, is not *only* an abundance of free time—it is not, in other words, the condition of preindustrial leisure that Marshall Sahlins famously described as "stone age economics"—but also an abundance of material goods.[19] The philosopher G. A. Cohen agreed with Kautsky that socialism would be able to reduce labor hours in a way that capitalism could not—while claiming that a "radically reduced working day" would require "astronomically high levels of productive power."[20] This is not because productive power is, strictly speaking, necessary to reduce work, but rather because, in Cohen's view, class society itself is "derivative" from the struggle to wrest a living from nature. In Cohen's reading, a Marxist theory of history holds that as long as scarcity persists, some people will force others to perform unpleasant but necessary labor in their stead: "Men would relate in connections of mastery and servitude until they were masters of the physical world."[21] Capitalism's "dominion over nature" not only makes possible an abundance of goods or time in their own right, enabling hedonistic enjoyment or the expansion of human capacities; rather, material abundance is the basic condition for ending the domination of one person by another. As Cohen would come to argue in his later work, "It was because he was so uncompromisingly pessimistic about the social consequences of anything less than limitless abundance that Marx needed to be so optimistic about the possibility of that abundance."[22] The obvious problem with this view is that any limits to abundance will necessitate limits to freedom.

Already in the late 1970s, Cohen had worried that the looming "resource crisis" cast doubt on the possibility that human labor could be replaced entirely and the realm of freedom expanded universally.[23] By the 1990s, his concern about the material limits to abundance would animate his embrace of egalitarian philosophy. Whereas it had previously been possible to believe that equality was both "historically inevitable and morally right," enabled by an eventual superabundance he thought guaranteed by the Marxist philosophy of history, the prospect of perpetual scarcity required more explicit arguments for equality.[24] The anxiety that resource constraints will make freedom beyond necessity impossible has only intensified in the decades since. The geographer Matt Huber has more recently argued that Marx's view of freedom beyond necessity is a view of freedom based on "material abundance" and relief from the "toil of labor"—a freedom that has thus far been achieved through use of fossil fuels.[25] Rather than retreating from the aspiration to freedom beyond necessity, Huber argues that a solar-powered eco-socialism could use the renewable energy of the sun to power collectively owned productive forces and achieve abundance for all.[26] Yet even this positive vision is motivated by precisely the same pessimistic, even fatalist view that Cohen sees in Marx. Without abundant sources of nonhuman energy, Huber warns, making possible other forms of material abundance, forms of unfree labor are doomed to return.[27] The writer Leigh Phillips puts it even more bluntly: "Energy is freedom. Growth is freedom."[28]

The most extreme version of freedom as total abundance comes in Aaron Bastani's vision of "fully automated luxury communism," in which all necessary labor is performed by robots and everyone enjoys the kinds of luxurious consumption presently restricted to the megawealthy.[29] Necessity is here characterized not only by the persistence of necessary labor, nor even the scarcity of necessary goods, but by the persistence of scarcity in *any* form. Freedom, similarly, consists not only in free time but in the expansion of luxury consumption in particular. While previous attempts to realize communism were thwarted by inadequate technological development, Bastani argues, the advent of information technologies means that the end of scarcity is finally possible. Yet the prospect of limited resources tinges even this utopian futurism with an undercurrent of desperation: persistent scarcity, Bastani worries, will lead to persistent conflict. It is imperative that a socialist society find new sources of nature's gifts— gleaned from mineral-rich asteroids, perhaps—or else full automation of labor will be impossible, and the realm of freedom will remain forever "out of reach."[30] Bastani's seemingly extravagant optimism, in other words, is necessitated by a fundamentally pessimistic view of the prospects for freedom in a world of anything less than truly limitless material abundance.

As these examples illustrate, the idea that freedom is material is not necessarily an ecologically sanguine one. To the contrary, it has often seemed to position freedom as zero sum: achieved only at someone, or something, else's expense. The ecosocialist Mary Mellor calls freedom beyond necessity a "parasitical transcendence," premised on shifting the burden of necessity onto others.[31] The implication is that a society that no longer avails itself of nature's free gifts will be doomed to more time-consuming and arduous labor and the development of fewer capacities by fewer people. Perhaps worst of all, it predicts that such a society will revert to forms of hierarchy and overt unfreedom, in which the many labor so that the few can contemplate. This is precisely the fear underpinning many ecological anxieties about freedom. As Chakrabarty states outright, "We do not need massive slave or forced labor to build the monuments of modern societies . . . because energy is cheap."[32] (Indeed, the "liberation of women" is so often attributed to washing machines and refrigerators, conceived as a side effect of industrialization, that it can come to seem a threat.)[33] These accounts suggest that the universalist aspirations of modernity, however disingenuous, partial, or exclusionary, amount to little more than fossil-fueled fantasies. The past two centuries have constituted an extraordinary exception from the norm of human life, but we will eventually revert to the violent and unfree norm: a Hobbesian world of conflict or an Aristotelian world of hierarchy, where the freedom of some comes at the expense of that of others.[34]

A third view is more pessimistic still, insisting that even total abundance would, in the words of the Italian Marxist Sebastian Timpanaro, fail to "free man from his biological limits."[35] Here, necessity is not the persistence of necessary labor, nor even scarcity, but *is equated with nature itself*—what Timpanaro calls the "autonomous and invincible reality" of the material world that inevitably exceeds human or social control.[36] For Timpanaro, recognizing this physical reality—a materialism he claims Marxists have typically neglected—gives rise to a "materialist pessimism," insofar as the realm of freedom can never truly be free of the necessity of illness, decay, and ultimately death.[37] Timpanaro's view is strikingly echoed by that of the radical feminist Shulamith Firestone, his contemporary, whose *Dialectic of Sex* similarly challenged Marxism's neglect of the physicality of the body—for Firestone, too, the most material base of all.[38] The sexual division of labor, Firestone argued, made women the "slave class that maintained the species in order to free the other half"— Aristotle's argument, applied to gender.[39] While Firestone is associated with the revolutionary optimism of her proclamation that scientific advances had made possible the transcendence of nature and abolition of sex class, it too is underpinned by a materialist pessimism rooted in her conviction that only technology could end women's oppression. Firestone must be a technological liberationist, in other words, *because* she is a biological determinist, one who believes that freedom is impossible as long as sexual difference persists. Nature itself sets the limits of freedom, and so nature itself must be mastered; if ectogenesis isn't around the corner, then neither is liberation.

What is striking is the remarkable lack of faith in freedom that these views betray. They rest on a view of human beings as not only constrained but determined by nature, responding to material scarcity in predictable, even mechanical ways: enslaving or coercing others in order to escape harsh labor, struggling to maximize their share of social surplus whatever the cost to others. Freedom, here, is an elusive prize, possible only under a strict set of material conditions— and perhaps not even then. It is contingent on total control of nature and vulnerable to chance events: a change in the climate that reduces agricultural productivity or a paucity of mineral-bearing asteroids. Freedom, paradoxically, appears largely out of our hands. If this determinism paints a grim picture of human life in the face of material finitude, it also lets human societies off the hook by suggesting that under certain conditions domination is simply unavoidable. This view is, it seems to me, crucial to resist, not least because it suggests that a future on a hotter and more volatile planet not only might but *must* be a bleak one. Because necessity is persistent, it claims, freedom must be tragic.

Freedom within Necessity

If freedom can be curtailed by the basic fact of ongoing contingency—by the fact that human beings are mortal with unceasing material needs, living in a finite world—then perhaps this kind of freedom is simply not possible at all. Perhaps, feminist and ecological thinkers in particular have argued, there is something wrong with this vision of freedom altogether. Against it, many have offered an alternative: the realization of freedom *within* necessity.[40] As eco-feminists Maria Mies and Vandana Shiva argue, "To find freedom does not involve subjugating or transcending the 'realm of necessity' but rather focusing on developing a vision of freedom, happiness, the 'good life' within the limits of necessity, of nature." While freedom from necessity can only ever be partial, "freedom *within* the realm of necessity can be universalized to all."[41]

This is, at first glance, an appealing prospect. The critique of "freedom beyond necessity" has obvious force. The idea of transcending the material world altogether is fantastical, and the idea that freedom requires total material abundance seems to render its pursuit futile. Yet upon closer look, accounts of freedom within necessity too often amount to endorsements of unmediated relationships to a romanticized nature, often achieved only through certain kinds of labor. The limitation of this view is most evident in Mies's account of a "feminist concept of labor" as one that rejects "the Marxist view that self-realization, human happiness, freedom, autonomy—the realm of freedom—can be achieved only *outside* the sphere of necessity and of necessary labour."[42] Labor engaged in the "*direct production of life* or of use values," Mies argues—in particular, the work of mothers and peasants and subsistence producers—is "always both" necessary and free.[43] More broadly, she claims, a feminist concept of labor entails "*a direct and sensual interaction with nature, with organic matter and living organisms.*"[44]

This celebration of a "direct" interaction with nature, already present in Mies's early housewifization theory, would become increasingly significant as she developed a more explicitly ecofeminist position. So too would a critique of technology as inherently alienating, reflecting a hubristic attempt to escape from nature instead of demonstrating humility and "respect" for "nature's limits."[45] Reproductive technology in particular, in Mies's view, is a force for domination rather than liberation—a form of "vivisection by the techno-patriarchs."[46] Against it, she celebrates a vision of organic holism: to conceive and gestate a child without reproductive technology, she claims, is to experience the "natural creativity" of the body and the wild within oneself; to restore the "living power" destroyed by modern science.[47]

Rather than freedom realized *within* necessity, then, this is a view of necessity *as* freedom. Instead of seeing the body as an inevitable limit on freedom, as Timpanaro and Firestone do, Mies insists that it is freedom's source—but only if its given constraints are accepted as necessary limits. She similarly collapses the distinction between the content of labor and its form of organization, equating labor that "directly produces life" with labor performed with some measure of autonomy. It is not a coincidence, as Mies herself notes, that the forms of "sensuous" labor that she identifies as both necessary and free are those that have largely escaped real subsumption, even within capitalist societies: they may be exhausting, boring, or unpleasant, but they *are* mostly organized by workers themselves, even if not entirely under conditions of their choosing. It is this, rather than the fact of their connection to "life" per se, that makes it possible for them to be both burden and pleasure, that allows a degree of freedom within necessity. This view is not, in fact, so far from Marx's own, insofar as it recognizes that the labor required to sustain life can be organized more or less freely—and closer still to Marx's embrace, in earlier work, of unalienated labor as a means to human development. Yet Mies's antipathy to any form of mediation or transformation threatens to equate the given with the necessary. Doing so evinces a remarkable disinterest in necessity itself—in understanding the material conditions of the world as they actually are, while also considering how they *might* be; and thus in contemplating what we might become other than what we are.[48]

When necessity is equated with nature, however, freedom within necessity becomes a truism. It isn't actually possible to defy the necessity of the physical world, after all, or to overcome genuine natural limits. Rather than *transcending* "nature as necessity," the forms of scientific knowledge that Mies decries as domination simply alter our view of what necessity *is* and how we might act differently within it. Rather than seeing efforts to alter the physical world as efforts to *transcend* nature, then, they might better be understood in terms of what David James calls a removal of "surplus practical necessity"—the elimination of constraints which turn out not to be truly necessary after all—or what John Bellamy Foster calls "freedom *as* necessity," in which the realm of human possibilities are expanded through knowledge of nature.[49]

Those who champion freedom beyond necessity suggest that human freedom is possible only under narrow circumstances of superabundance—perhaps only when we can mine asteroids. This view of freedom quickly becomes absurd. But so too does the declaration that freedom can be realized only within a thin band of relationships and activities deemed *truly* natural; that freedom means accepting the world as it's given rather than asking how it might be made. In both accounts, it is ultimately nature that determines the possibilities and meaning of freedom: on the one hand a nature we must escape, and on the other a nature we must embrace.

Social Domination and Nature Neutrality

If one irony can be found in the fact that the freedom the left has long declared unrealized is now charged with the destruction of the Earth as we know it, another lies in the fact that the revival of left thinking about freedom in recent years has turned away from material questions altogether. Whereas the traditional Marxist view of freedom counterposes freedom and necessity, and sometimes freedom and nature, its most robust contemporary alternative says little about necessity or nature at all. Critiques of social domination, whether rooted in the tradition of crtical theory or neorepublicanism, focus on unfree social relations rather than the material conditions required for emancipation.

This orientation toward the social is perhaps most explicit in the republican tradition. Nondomination is simply freedom from the arbitrary power of one person over another, its foremost theorist Philip Pettit argues. While freedom understood in a more general sense might take into account material factors, from physical disability to climatic conditions, they are not relevant to freedom as nondomination.[50] Natural constraints may shape the conditions in which nondomination is exercised—but they neither grant this form of freedom nor take it away. Similarly, although access to material resources may increase a person's "extent of undominated choice," and an unequal distribution of resources may facilitate domination, a lack of resources is not *itself* a source of domination.[51] While nondomination has been much debated since, this aspect of Pettit's view has remained largely intact, even among those who have taken republican thought in otherwise novel directions. Radical republicans have argued that republicanism cuts against the domination of workers by bosses and of labor by capital, that it requires strong checks on business by the state, even that nondomination requires a fully socialist government—but for the most part, they have accepted and even affirmed Pettit's purely social view of domination.[52] Against Cohen's argument that socialism requires massive productivity, for instance, William Clare Roberts argues that the conditions for socialism are not objective or material at all. Marx, he claims, "says nothing about the natural world; he is focused squarely on social relations."[53]

There is, perhaps counterintuitively, a sense in which republicanism's "nature neutrality" might be comforting to the ecologically anxious. If freedom is not defined by the escape from necessary labor, then the imperative to substitute nonhuman energy for human labor is less acute; if freedom does not require any particular level of material wealth, then the prospect of "limits to growth" appears less threatening. As Daniel Luban notes, it is precisely nondomination's "indifference" to historical and material conditions that "allows the theory to 'travel' easily across history," from ancient Rome to modern times.[54] Perhaps freedom as nondomination can similarly "travel" across ecological conditions—say, from the preindustrial era when the atmospheric carbon concentration measured approximately 280 parts per million to the contemporary 422 ppm (and rising).[55] While modern political thought lies in the shadow of the Anthropocene, republicanism's roots in the ancient past offer a view of freedom before fossil fuels. At the same time, as long as the principle of nondomination is met, republicanism appears equally plausible on a dying Earth or lifeless Mars. Nondomination thus appears worrisomely indifferent to the material situations and constraints within which human beings make their lives. A vision of freedom so agnostic about the conditions of earthly life seems an ill fit for a world so beset by material challenges.

If accounts of nondomination are rarely explicit about their material underpinnings, however, they have more significant implications for the question of what societies produce and how than they typically acknowledge. Some contemporary republicans are explicit that the challenge to workplace domination does *not* bear on the organization of production itself: while Elizabeth Anderson criticizes the "private government" of the workplace, for example, she accepts that the firm itself is justifiably characterized by "hierarchies of authority" oriented toward the technical goals of efficiency and productivity, questioning only whether that hierarchy can legitimately be extended beyond the workplace.[56] Although many radical republicans propose more drastic changes in the social organization of production, meanwhile, they have had surprisingly little to say about how this might bear on productivity itself.[57] It's possible to imagine a drastically expanded version of the republican "association of producers," encompassing the full span of production addressed here, attending to the reproduction of human life and ecosystems alongside industrial and agricultural goods, while also taking into account "disuse" values like pollution: a "cooperative commonwealth" that includes miners, farmers, "meta-industrial" laborers, carers, and others—and perhaps even, in some way, nonhuman beings. But production in this kind of genuinely cooperative commonwealth would surely look radically different than it does now—and different too than the kind of industrial commonwealth imagined by the likes of the Knights of Labor.[58] It would presumably generate different levels of material surplus and throughput, and hence make possible—or preclude—different patterns of consumption, distribution, and social life. These implications, however, are almost never confronted directly by contemporary republican theorists.

They are more apparent within the critical theory tradition, which addresses the organization of production more explicitly. As we've seen in chapter 3, critics of social domination like Harry Braverman and Moishe Postone argue that capitalism has remade not only the social organization of production but also the technologies of production themselves. This constitutes a significant departure from classical Marxism's more technically neutral view of technology, which holds that a socialist society could simply use the machines developed by capitalism for different purposes. If we see the productive forces as *themselves* shaped by the imperatives of capitalism, however, it's harder to see how they could be put to alternative ends.[59] On this view, the ends are encoded at the level of means: industrial production interpellates human beings as sources of wage labor and nonhuman nature as free gifts, imposes abstract time and space on concrete processes and places, and reduces labor itself to repetitive drudgery. Rather than simply redistributing the same kinds of wealth produced in the same ways, then, genuinely transcending capitalism would "entai[l] a fundamental transformation of production, of the way people work."[60] In a noncapitalist world, Postone argues, "not only the goal of machine production but the machines themselves will be different."[61]

This imperative, already daunting, is all the more so when we consider the biospheric transformations canvassed here. Animals and plants have been made into machines, ecosystems converted to factories and sliced through with roads, the very atmosphere altered. If the machines would need to be different, then it follows that nearly everything else would need to be different too. At a point when the technosphere (factories, roads, buildings, cropland) outweighs all earthly biomass, this is not a heartening prospect.[62] In any case it is not actually clear we know how to live otherwise. Industrialization has transformed production qualitatively as well as quantitatively. Stainless steel, for example, is produced at a size, strength, and smoothness that no preindustrial forge has ever achieved, making possible in turn the construction of buses, skyscrapers, railways.[63] Conversely, industrial production has eroded the skills and capacities once used to produce differently: it has diminished countless kinds of human skill and cooperation, as theorists from Marx to Braverman have long observed; but so, too, have a vast number of nonhuman capacities been lost, suppressed, and eradicated altogether. The disappearance from our world of a huge number of beings and their long-evolved abilities, their strange and often astounding ways of surviving on our shared planet, has ominous implications for the future of noncapitalist life on earth. In emphasizing the extreme *difficulty* of breaking with capitalism's organization of production, then, this analysis seems to jump from frying pan into the wildfire.

To say that the modern world is largely—perhaps even entirely—of capitalism's making, in other words, tells us very little about how we might make a different one. Postone suggests only that a socialist society could continue to enjoy the productivity gains and abundance that he claims capitalism specifically has produced. He grants that capitalism's productivity *has*, at least in part, freed humanity "from its overwhelming dependence on the vagaries of its natural environment," but gestures only vaguely to a reorganization of labor that would retain high levels of productivity while also allowing for "a more consciously controlled relationship with the natural environment."[64] Others working in this vein tend to follow suit, where they address such questions at all. They imply that large-scale industrial production can simply be achieved differently: that an emancipatory form of social labor will nevertheless deliver the high levels of productivity on which those in capitalist society have come to depend, without the high levels of social cost that we have come to deplore. When we see abundance as a social relation, Aaron Benanav argues, we will recognize the full human capacity of each individual and organize both work and distribution accordingly; necessary labors can be made satisfying and done willingly, without either explicit coercion or the hidden coercion of the wage; goods can be made plentiful enough that they can be distributed without any medium of exchange, even as some assessment of ecological harms is incorporated into their production.[65] Where theorists of tragic necessity are often optimistic about the prospects of achieving material abundance but pessimistic about social relations, then, critics of social domination tend to be silent on the question of material abundance but optimistic about the capacity for social reorganization.

These tensions are perhaps best illustrated by Martin Hägglund's vision of "spiritual freedom."[66] Hägglund explicitly challenges readings of Marx that envision freedom as "superabundance," instead grounding freedom in the necessary finitude of our embodied lives, which are necessarily dependent on others and which will inevitably end. Capitalism's measure of value—socially necessary labor time—is perverse, he argues, insofar as it treats the realm of necessity as the end of existence; while capitalism's compulsion to generate ever more value means that it can never deliver on the promise of free time. The measure of value in a democratic socialist society, Hägglund argues, would be the inverse of capitalism's socially necessary labor time: "socially available free time" in which we can commit ourselves to the projects we find meaningful, such that a democratic socialist society would be committed to reducing labor time "through technological innovation."[67] Yet Hägglund, too, avoids the question of how technology itself will be developed and organized, the materials with which it will be made, and the energy that will power it. Although he explicitly connects the finitude of human life to earthly finitude, meanwhile, the singular measure of value he recommends threatens to bring them into conflict. As Hägglund argues, "Labor time is intelligible as a cost only because we value our finite lifetime *as our own free time.*"[68] Nature, in this inverted measure of value, remains something like a free gift when set against human labor: a costless replacement for our precious and finite time, one that we might be tempted to overuse.

A democratic socialist society *could*, as these theorists argue, make more intentional decisions about resource use and ecological protection. It isn't a priori impossible that such a society could develop an entirely novel yet highly productive set of technologies. Yet a critique that names industrialization as specifically capitalist, as these analyses do, must at least accept the *potential* loss of the kinds of abundance that this form of production has generated. To charge that modern life as we know it is a distinctively *capitalist* form of life, as many of these thinkers do, grants a claim often made by capitalism's defenders: that capitalism is primarily responsible for modernity's wonders as well as its horrors. Capitalism may produce material wealth only as a side effect of pursuing value—but it produces material wealth nonetheless. The *kinds* of material wealth it produces might not be those we would choose for ourselves; and as we have seen, the imperatives of market rule frequently mar the quality of the things capitalism makes.[69] Yet it is evidently true that the changing material basis of human societies makes possible different kinds of lives, and that the appeal of (capitalist) modernity must be taken seriously. This, after all, is why Cohen's political argument rests on separating the material-technical and the social-political: it allows capitalism's achievements to be separated from its failings. Postone's insistence on their imbrication offers no such consolation. But if we see the material and social as intertwined rather than modular, we have to see the goods and evils that result in the same way.

As Roberts argues, for Marx, "the goods promised and delivered by capitalism are *inseparable* from the evils that follow in their train." The good isn't just an illusion to be dispelled; rather, "the good and the evil are *really both there*."[70] Capitalism promises to increase material wealth, which is produced only via the "despotism" of the factory; it promises to increase wages, which occurs only with rising exploitation; it promises abundance and equality, while also producing an abundance of suffering.[71] To these, we might add two more: capitalism promises to use resources more efficiently, but tears through them at an ever-greater pace; it promises material prosperity, while undermining forms of earthly abundance. Capitalism *does* produce enormous quantities of wealth—and it *also* produces vast quantities of waste, junk, detritus, surplus matter. It transforms nonhuman nature in ways that sustain human life, and in ways that threaten the future of life on Earth. It is *genuinely* both.

Political theory does not need to—and I think cannot—resolve these questions. We might, however, confront them more directly: the challenges of social freedom in a material world are not ones that contemporary theorists of freedom can avoid.[72] More generally, a purely social theory of (non)domination simply doesn't speak to the most pressing anxieties of freedom today: that an ecologically sustainable society will be less free, and that a free society will be ecologically catastrophic. To bracket the question of nature altogether is simply to bracket too much.

Ambiguous Freedom: Beauvoir's Situated Existentialism

The material conditions of life are surely relevant to freedom; and yet where they determine the very possibility of freedom, freedom becomes a contradiction. The social relations within which we exist are fundamental to freedom; and yet without an account of how we might meaningfully realize freedom in the sensuous world, freedom becomes empty. We need to move beyond these poles—necessity and freedom, pessimism and optimism—toward something more ambiguous: a view of politics and human possibility cognizant of both human purpose and material constraints, acceptance of finitude paired with skepticism of the given. This is what Simone de Beauvoir's philosophy of ambiguity can help us do.[73]

Freedom, for Beauvoir as for Sartre, consists in the ability to be other than what one is: to reflect on and choose how to act within the world as it is given, to assert our values by committing our lives to them. And yet freedom is also, always, situated: *both* social *and* material, both enabled and constrained by the material world and by other people. Ambiguity, for Beauvoir, stems from the fundamental human condition of being an embodied consciousness: at once a subject and an object, rational and sensuous. We are at once an inner life and "a thing crushed by the dark weight of other things," a "thinking reed" that is part of the natural world and yet also stands apart from it.[74] Instead of trying to resolve this ambiguity, Beauvoir embraces it: "Let us try to assume our fundamental ambiguity."[75] Ambiguity suggests a way of navigating between a materialist pessimism, which posits the contingency of the world as a strict limit to freedom, and a social optimism, which holds that freedom is *only* a matter of social relations.[76]

Indeed although existential freedom is associated with values, it is more material than often acknowledged. Insofar as we must seek not only to hold but to *realize* our values, freedom consists in the effort to pursue our projects in a world that is mostly made of other things.[77] Without a body or a physical world, there would be nothing to distinguish fantasy from its realization—and hence no way to act at all. We could simply imagine climbing a rock that stands in our path, and it would be done. Instead, we come to know the world and its constraints by trying to act in it. It's only when we try to scramble up the rock and slide back down that we realize that it can't be climbed after all—at least, not by us, not now. In the process we learn something about the material world itself. Freedom and necessity, here, are not spatially distinct "realms" that can be clearly distinguished and bounded, such that one is always "in" one or another. We are always, in all realms and aspects of our lives, embodied beings whose ability to act at all is *both* enabled and constrained by a world we do not control. The degree to which the given world enables or constrains us, moreover, can't be determined a priori, but only in relation to our projects: if I want to cross a path, a boulder will be an obstacle, but if I want to practice rock climbing, it will be a boon. This is what the existentialist concept of the situation captures: the encounter between a free consciousness and the world as it is given, not only by nature but by the unchangeable effects of past human action.[78] When we imagine that our situation determines our possibilities, we treat ourselves as pure objects: we are in bad faith, attributing our actions to nature rather than taking responsibility for them. But we also delude ourselves when we imagine that we can make our fate alone—that we are pure subjects unencumbered by either the material world or the existence of others.

Many of Beauvoir's own meditations on freedom concern the way that the relation between freedom and constraint plays out within the space of the human body. The body, for Beauvoir, is vitally important as the physical form through which we encounter the world. Yet although we exist only and always in a body, Beauvoir insists, "the body itself is not a brute fact": the body is not, in itself, *necessity*.[79] "The body is not a thing, it is a situation," she argues. "It is our grasp on the world and the outline for our projects."[80] Some of its aspects are universal: all human beings must grapple with our bodily needs, which both enable and constrain our projects; we all depend on others at points in our lives; and we all eventually die.[81] Others are more specific: other people perceive us in terms of gender, race, size, age, as we do them. The particular dimensions of our bodies set constraints on what we can do, as do the natural and built environments, and the social categories through which we are interpellated. While women's oppression is often attributed to biological features, Beauvoir observes that everyone has a body; what requires explanation is why men's bodies are seen to constitute a "direct and normal link with the world" while women's are thought to constitute "a prison, burdened by everything that particularizes" them.[82] Physical traits—muscular strength or gestational capacity—are important, but their significance can only be defined socially. *The Second Sex* (1949) is Beauvoir's attempt to grapple with this problem— with the ways that we are unequally situated *socially*, and with the way that institutional structures can freeze us as objects rather than permitting us to act as subjects, informing the way we live in our very bodies.[83]

Yet Beauvoir's analysis of the relationship between physical embodiment and social situation has invited a contradictory set of criticisms within feminist thought. On the one hand, Beauvoir has been criticized for inadequately recognizing the force of nature; on the other, for attempting to conquer nature entirely.[84] But her view is simply that the social and natural must always be thought together. Women are not wombs, she insists, oppressed only by virtue of biology—and so technology cannot be the sole source of their liberation, as Firestone proposes. But it also follows that technology cannot be the source of their oppression, as Mies suggests. Technologically enabled changes in physical capacities do change women's situation and the possibilities available to them; they do not, in themselves, make women free or unfree.

Beauvoir's perspective on the relationship of freedom to technology has implications beyond gender or even embodiment. It suggests a third way between determinist views of technology—like the idea that freedom relies on fossil fuels—and the purely social view that neglects material conditions entirely. The automobile, for example, is often held up as an emblem of modern freedom threatened by limits on fossil fuel use. But from a Beauvoirian vantage point, it's not so clear that automobiles are vehicles of freedom at all.[85] Cars genuinely have opened up certain concrete possibilities: they have made it possible for us to rapidly move when and where we please. Freedom isn't in the car itself, however, but in the capabilities it affords and the projects it enables—the ability to get someplace we want to go, while exercising some autonomy over our time.

In the situation of a society where cars are *necessary*, moreover, they may appear as a constraint on freedom rather than an enabling condition for it. Are you free if you have to own a car to get to work; if you have to spend two hours a day in traffic; if to buy the car you must take out a loan at an usurious interest rate; if you are liable, by virtue of your race, to be stopped by the police while driving; if you run a high risk of a disabling or deadly accident?[86] Resource-intensive ways of living are not always expressions of freedom even for consumers; often they are responses to terms set by a society over which one has very little control. A collectively taken decision to forgo internal combustion engines in favor of improved public transit would not be a constraint on freedom, but an act *of* freedom—a decision to live differently in the world—far more so than accepting the necessity of sitting in traffic every day simply because the highway is already there. As Beauvoir notes, "To be free is not to have the power to do anything you like; it is to be able to surpass the given toward an open future."[87]

The ambiguity of the human body also opens up questions of embodied life on an earthly planet. Beauvoir, like Hägglund, recognizes that the finitude of human life makes choices about how to spend our time precious. But where Hägglund focuses on the *quantitative* amount of time available to us, Beauvoir is also concerned with the *qualitative* dimensions of finitude—with the way our finite bodies might aid or check our ability to realize certain aims—without thereby suggesting, as Timpanaro does, that this finitude itself *precludes* genuine freedom. In her discussion of aging, for example, she argues that we become old *both* because of how we are perceived by others *and* because we recognize the physical limits placed on our projects by the changing capacities of own bodies.[88]

Recognizing that our physical existence is shaped by the more-than-human world, in turn, suggests that the condition of the biosphere can constrain our projects as much as the condition of our bodies. To riff on Beauvoir: the Earth is the grounds for our consciousness and our being, the outline of our projects, the world that we attempt to grasp and in which our action necessarily unfolds. It is both the condition of and constraint upon our freedom. Ecological conditions do not *define* freedom, any more than having ovaries makes one free or unfree. And yet many projects become impossible when the temperature is consistently 40°C, or when the water is running brown from the tap.[89] It's difficult to train for a marathon when the air is with thick with smog, or to learn to read when the schoolhouse is flooded. When islands disappear beneath the waves, so too do many of the projects of the people who have long called them home; when other species disappear from the places where humans live, or from the planet altogether, we lose a whole range of possibilities for acting in relation to other forms of life—and even for interacting with one another. You can't fish in the afternoon without any fish or birdwatch without any birds.[90]

This is why the defense of freedom today cannot simply bracket the planetary conditions in which free projects unfold. Whether average world temperatures rise 1.5°C or 3°C or even higher has immense consequences for the range of options open to billions of human beings—let alone for the natural freedom of countless nonhumans. But to suggest, as David Wallace-Wells does, that a warmer world will necessarily be one in which the "horizon of human possibility [is] dramatically dimmed" altogether is to cede too much.[91] Instead we must pose the questions: What are the institutions and infrastructures, both social and physical, that can enable a substantive freedom for ambiguous beings even in the face of tumultuous planetary conditions? What must we do to make freedom possible on a damaged planet?

Indeed, decisions about how to live together on our shared planet are often where—to use a quintessential metaphor of the Great Acceleration—the rubber hits the road. It is here that choices start to cut, that values become concrete. "This elusive body is precisely the necessity of there being a choice," Sartre notes, "i.e. the necessity of my not being everything all at once."[92] So too with land: the Chilean Salar de Atacama can be protected as a home for wildlife and source of freshwater for nearby communities or mined for lithium; it cannot be both simultaneously.[93] Scarcity is indeed a social relation, but a materially finite world will pose many such choices. Should we build solar panels in a desert habitat to replace electricity generated by coal? How much land or sea should we set aside for other species to enjoy their own natural freedom? What should we do with the world we've already made: with the highways, nuclear waste, parking lots? At present these decisions are largely made under conditions of market and class rule, funneled through a single and narrow standard of value. But some version of these choices will appear in any society, if not necessarily in precisely the same form. The freedom to genuinely make them would give many of the debates canvassed in this book real stakes.[94]

Such debates will inevitably be conflictual. There are, Beauvoir recognizes, no guarantees that our freely willed projects will coincide with those of others; and when they conflict, there are no absolute values that can resolve them. Against the view of existentialism as moral nihilism, however, Beauvoir argues that we need other free subjects to assess, recognize, and support our own projects: "Our freedoms support each other like the stones in an arch, but in an arch that no pillars support."[95] Ambiguous freedom, in other words, is a resolutely *interdependent freedom*, one that both fundamentally relies on others and is vulnerable to them.[96] While Beauvoir's ambiguous freedom echoes aspects of Hegelian social freedom, then, it does not promise an eventual resolution. "I remember having experienced a great feeling of calm on reading Hegel in the impersonal framework of the Bibliothèque Nationale in August 1940," she recounts late in the *Ethics*. "But once I got into the street again, into my life, out of the system, beneath a real sky, the system was no longer of any use to me: what it had offered me, under the show of the infinite, was the consolations of death, and I again wanted to live in the midst of living men."[97] To imagine the resolution of all contradictions is to imagine a world where people are no longer acting freely. The goal of the "revaluation of values" is not to settle on a *single* value to organize social life, à la Hägglund's socially available free time. The point, rather, is that the *evaluation of values* is precisely the task of a free society—one that can never be definitively concluded.

Because freedom is a project that can have no final resolution, we must continuously reevaluate our projects and commitments in light of what they disclose about the world. Climate change has genuinely revealed something novel about how the world works: it has demonstrated what happens when large quantities of fossil fuels are burned, under any social conditions; and made clear that materials and technologies once evaluated as liberatory have had effects and meanings we did not intend or anticipate. This realization is often disorienting, even unmooring. But it need not be tragic. In fact, it is vital *not* to frame these ongoing judgments in terms of tragedy, as so many efforts to grapple with the transformation of our planet do. Tragedy, David Scott observes, is particularly adept at representing "ambiguous moments of historical transformation, moments when possible futures seem less certain than they once did."[98] We are in one such ambiguous and uncertain moment, and many have responded by reading the past anew. The optimism of "futures past" stands chastened, in many analyses, by the tragic freedom of the Anthropocene. But why must ambiguous moments flip into tragic ones upon reevaluation? Why not *stay* with the trouble of ambiguity? Perhaps, pace Chakrabarty, we don't need "narratives of freedom" at all. For to continually reevaluate the way we live in the world isn't a tragedy, but the very expression of freedom itself.

Beauvoir's account of ambiguous freedom is not so much an objective as a method: a process rather than a set of principles, something that must be perpetually pursued with others and that will never be fully achieved. Freedom for Beauvoir is distinctly nonutopian—or perhaps it is an ambiguous utopia in the manner of Ursula LeGuin's Anarres, a free but imperfect world that must be persistently reassessed or risk sclerosis.[99] It is a perspective suited to what Stuart Hall calls a "Marxism without guarantees"—a method appropriate for a world of radical uncertainty.[100] As Beauvoir notes, "Freedom is not decided with a view to a salvation that would be granted in advance. It signs no pact with the future. If it could be defined by the final point for which it aims, it would no longer be freedom."[101] The past is given and unchangeable, but its meaning must always be reevaluated; the future is permanently open, never to be resolved.[102] Climate change is sometimes said to put an end to the modern idea of the future, insofar as the future now appears as a limit rather than an open horizon. But from an existentialist perspective this is nonsensical: the future is always open, whether we like it or not.

Conclusion: Toward an Existentialist Crisis

If a material existentialism can help us imagine freedom in a postcapitalist future, it also offers resources for navigating the challenges we will face in the interim. Beauvoir was deeply attuned to the perversities of modern unfreedom: "The more widespread their mastery of the world," she notes, "the more they find themselves crushed by uncontrollable forces. . . . [E]ach one has the incomparable taste in his mouth of his own life, and yet each feels himself more insignificant than an insect within the immense collectivity whose limits are one with the earth's."[103] Human beings, at the start of the Great Acceleration, seemed to have conquered the forces of nature, and yet generated only more destruction; each person was acutely aware of their own individual existence, and yet equally conscious of their inability to act meaningfully in an interconnected world of billions that seemed to be spiraling out of control. As Daniela Dover and Jonathan Gingerich observe, Beauvoir saw existentialism as the only philosophy that could motivate "responsible collective action in the face of the simultaneous horrors of fascism, capitalism, and imperialism."[104] So, too, might it serve to guide collective action in the face of the unnatural disasters we face today—and that we will continue to face long into the future. For climate change is not the kind of problem that can be "solved"; it is a feature of our world from here on out. Even if carbon is removed from the atmosphere and temperatures stabilized, the disruption that warming has wrought on the planet and its beings is irreversible. In this sense, capitalism's material traces will undoubtedly last longer than capitalism itself.[105]

Existentialism is sometimes dismissed as an "emergency" notion of freedom, oriented toward the extreme choices faced by those in occupied France: collaborate or join the Resistance. These are hardly the choices of everyday life, critics charge; to extrapolate from such circumstances is to project an impossibly heroic view of human existence. And yet surely we are in an emergency. The declaration that climate change is an "existential crisis" has become a platitude, and yet genuinely existentialist responses—ones that seriously reevaluate our projects and commitments in light of what our actions have disclosed about the world—are exceedingly rare. Scientific evidence warns that we are exiting the period of the Holocene, and with it leaving behind the geological conditions that have sustained the development of human societies as we have known them thus far. The future will be hotter, more tempestuous, less predictable. It will also, some argue, be more violent and more desperate, plagued by scarcity rather than abundance. Life, some conclude, will be nasty, brutish, and short. But to simply accept these conclusions is to succumb to a form of bad faith, one that attributes our action to nature. Another comes in the conclusion that it is "too late" to act, because certain amounts of warming are "baked in" or certain tipping points have been reached. There are indeed points of irreversible change—we have already crossed many of them—but there is no point at which it is "too late," not least because it can always get worse.

This is not to deny the real force of the given; the real constraints that earthly situations will pose. Deteriorating material conditions undoubtedly make choices harder, and options worse. But they do not force us to harden borders against climate refugees, hoard resources, or throw others off the "lifeboat." They do not force us to take the path of "climate barbarism."[106] The choices before us may be stark; they may come at great personal cost; they may be between very bad options—but they remain choices for which we must take responsibility, which we must justify, and which we must accept as our own rather than attributing them to the necessities imposed by temperature rise. In the vision of true freedom as existing only beyond the realm of necessity, our choices are only between different things we see as good in themselves. Should we contemplate or paint, criticize or fish? If these choices strike us as relatively trivial, it is for good reason. If we are really free only when our choices are good ones—when we live in conditions of total abundance and plenty—freedom doesn't mean much. Surely the freedom that really matters is the freedom we exercise in challenging circumstances.

At this existential juncture in our collective history, this distinctly nonutopian politics is indispensable. "To come down to earth," Beauvoir observes, "means accepting defilement, failure, horror; it means admitting that it is impossible to save everything; and what is lost is lost forever."[107] Rather than encouraging quietism or fatalism, however, the possibility and perhaps even the certainty of failure are the foundation of free action: "It is because there are real dangers, real failures and real earthly damnation that words like victory, wisdom, or joy have meaning."[108] There are real dangers ahead. There will undoubtedly be failures. We will not save everything, and we can only hope to avoid earthly damnation. It is all the more important, then, that we do not relinquish the aspiration to freedom in advance. Freedom in a climate-changed world will undoubtedly be demanding—but this is what it means to be free.

Epilogue

AFTER THE GIFT

THE CHILDREN'S book *The Giving Tree* (1964) tells the story of a tree and a human boy. As a child, the boy swings from "her" branches, eats her apples, sleeps in her shade, and loves the tree in return.[1] As he grows older, however, the relationship grows lopsided. "I want to buy things and have fun," the boy says. "I want some money. Can you give me some money?" The tree responds: "I have no money. I have only leaves and apples." The tree gives the boy her leaves and apples to sell in the city. When he returns, he asks for more. He takes her branches to build a house, and her trunk to build a boat, leaving her alone and unhappy. As an old man, he returns to her stump to rest—making the tree happy at last. The story strikes many readers as disturbing in its portrayal of a deeply one-sided relationship—which has seemed to many a barely veiled allegory of motherhood. From an ecological perspective, it appears a parable about the callous depletion of resources by a society that treats nature as the source of inexhaustible gifts—food, shade, company, building material—until nothing is left but a tired stump.

For all that *The Giving Tree* appears a generic allegory of human selfishness, however, it illustrates precisely the peculiar kind of gift this book has described: the free gift of nature. The story depicts only the relationship between the tree and the boy. But their relationship is implicitly structured by others. The things the tree has to offer the boy in kind—entertainment, food, shade, company—clearly don't count for much in the world beyond. In that other world, the boy needs money—and to get it, he has to take the tree's apples and sell them. Silverstein stacks the moral deck by telling us he wants to buy things and have fun—these, it's implied, are frivolous desires. But even leaving aside this condemnation, most of the people who cut down trees to sell them in the city do so to buy basic necessities. They convert branches to charcoal, to sell to urban workers who need to cook their food; or ferry logs down the river, to sell to lumber wholesalers. They don't do so because they are ungrateful or spoiled, as the boy is implied to be—or at least, no more so than anyone else. Nor is it because they don't understand the possible environmental consequences. They do so because in a world where most things are for sale, they can't live off the gifts of the trees alone. *The Giving Tree*, in other words, shouldn't be read as an allegory about the selfishness of human nature in general but as an illustration of how capitalism frequently compels us to treat even the nonhuman beings that we genuinely care about, even those we love.

———

Many have drawn the conclusion that it is time to start giving back. Instead of only asking what the Earth will give us, Robin Wall Kimmerer argues, we must ask, "What can I give in return for the gifts of the Earth?"[2] Kimmerer, too, writes of giving trees—but hers are particular rather than allegorical, and so too are their gifts. The black ash gives bark that can be woven into beautiful baskets. The maples of the northeastern United States give warmth in the winter and sugary sap in the spring; their leafy branches provide cool shade in the summer and return nutrients to the soil in the fall. The cedars of the Pacific Northwest give wood and bark from which the region's Indigenous peoples once made canoes and paddles, nets and ropes, arrows and harpoons. Those who take these gifts without returning them, Kimmerer argues, violate the very meaning of the gift. A free gift isn't really a gift at all.[3] Kimmerer's is one of many contemporary calls for a less unidirectional relationship to nature, often informed by Indigenous perspectives and echoing a long lineage of thought that posits the gift against the commodity.[4] They dovetail with desires to rethink relationships to the more-than-human world more broadly, as political theorists and moral philosophers call upon us to treat animals with justice and nature with respect.[5]

Some even suggest that to treat nature as a free gift violates ecological principles themselves. Reciprocity, Kimmerer argues, is "how the biophysical world works."[6] Trees, Rob Nixon argues, exhibit "forest altruism," communicating with and nurturing one another in an interspecies community.[7] Appeals to the symbiotic entanglements of the altruistic forest or the networked fungi are only the most recent of recurrent efforts to locate in nature a model of the gift values of reciprocity, echoing Pyotr Kropotkin's identification of mutualist principles in flocks of birds.[8] And yet here, as ever, choices of examples betray as much about a given thinker's commitments as they do about the principles of nature itself. Consider, by comparison, Georges Bataille's theorization of the gift as an inherently *nonreciprocal* form capable of subverting bourgeois exchange, inspired by the abundance of energy bestowed by the sun upon the Earth.[9] These two radically opposed visions of the gift—one describing a condition of deep reciprocity; the other, the sheer impossibility of *any* return—both rest on appeals to natural phenomena As such, they illustrate the historian of science Lorraine Daston's observation that the sheer "plenitude of orders" found in nature undercuts the claim of any single one to authority: "Which nature?"[10]

We can't, as I've argued, derive political principles from nature, and it's equally doubtful that any single principle—even reciprocity—can suffice as a principle for how we ought to treat nature in general. The more-than-human world is simply too multitudinous, too complex, for a single standard to apply—justice or flourishing or nondomination or even reciprocity, however asymmetrical.[11] Whereas the framework of the "free gift" treats all of nature as equivalent, abandoning it will require attention to the specificity of different elements of the more-than-human world. A forest and the sun are alike only insofar as neither is human; they give drastically different kinds of gifts, and surely demand different kinds of response. This perspective, in turn, requires us to take seriously what other organisms and species need to live and flourish, and to take those needs into account in our own decisions about collective life. We can, and must, judge the state of the planet we are making by assessing whether it works for beings other than ourselves. As we navigate an increasingly unfamiliar future, we will need to learn much more about and from the world around us—not in order to command it, but in order to be more responsive to and responsible for it, in all its extraordinary capacities. While nature shouldn't be our model, the more-than-human world can be our guide—a resource for finding our way along the challenging path ahead.[12]

Many more questions will undoubtedly occur along the way. Should we privilege the needs of individual organisms or the aggregate category of species; the functioning of ecosystems qua infrastructures or the particular relationships we, whether as individuals or groups, have to specific nonhuman beings? Can we attribute "ends" to an ecosystem or species in the way that we can to an individual animal—and can we do so without reimporting an implicit view of divine purpose? Should we cull members of one species to protect endangered members of another? Where cosmologies conflict or priorities diverge, how do we decide between them? Should we err on the side of noninterference with other beings or recognize our obligations to care for those species whose ways of life we have already fundamentally altered? Is true reciprocity possible across species, or is the language of "the gift" only ever a euphemism for ongoing human appropriation?

These are the kinds of challenging, rich, exciting, frightening questions that will open up when we can think beyond the free gift. They cannot be settled by always-ideological appeals to "natural" order, harmony, or balance; and we can't avoid importing our own expectations, desires, visions, projections, and understandings of the nonhuman world. What we can do is to recognize this. We can be forthright about *which* natures we are looking to for guidance and why, about which natures we are calling to protect and respect. At the end of the day, they are decisions that only we can make, and for which we must take responsibility. We must let go, in other words, of the fantasy that we can step outside of human perspectives or human concepts of value. If this is anthropocentric, I think it is also honest. Many nonhuman beings have capacities for thought, creativity, and expression; they have complex social structures and interactions; they have their own kinds of freedom, which an ecological existentialism could, and I think should, take seriously.[13] But this would not alter the *particular* responsibility we have as free human beings. Regardless of the capacities of other kinds of life, what we do know for sure is that we are material, embodied beings who can engage in normative reflection and undertake actions that we affirm as being, in some way, our own.[14]

Nor should the reality of ecological interdependence disguise the fact that some degree of asymmetrical dependence between humans and nonhumans is unavoidable. The difficult fact is that nonhuman beings are systematically vulnerable to human power, subjected to the decisions that we make about how to act. There's no going back from what we know now: that we can, should we choose, destroy not only ourselves but the conditions of habitability for much of life as we know it. This doesn't mean we have total control over the shape of the world, or that our power is—let alone should be—unlimited. It's not to say that human beings are superior to other kinds, or that we deserve to decide their fate. It simply means that they can't stop us, so any limits are ones we'll have to set for ourselves.

To insist that the value of nature must be what we make of it doesn't mean that we can't declare elements of nature precious, sacred, worth protecting at any cost. As Steven Vogel notes, "to assert that *value can be determined only by humans* is not to assert that *only humans have value.*"[15] If anything, it simply puts the charge on us to realize our stated values in our lived commitments. Rather than a call to abandon the project of asserting the value of nature, in other words, this is an injunction to attend to it much more closely than we have done.

Instead of gesturing to possible answers to the questions raised above, then, I simply want to emphasize that these vital debates are largely arguments about the dimensions of a postcapitalist world—one in which capitalism's law of value doesn't reign supreme. Questions about how we might weigh qualities like beauty, cultural meaning, anthropocentric use, and ecocentric significance register a desire to value nature on other terms.[16] Conversations about how we ought to relate to the nonhuman others with whom we share a world are vitally important for developing these judgments and visions of alternatives. So too are proposals for how we might begin to actively cultivate alternative relationships to the more-than-human world, and for institutions that might genuinely incorporate considerations of nonhuman wellbeing.[17] Yet visions of alternatives, however compelling, must ultimately contend with capitalism's persistent worldmaking power.

Doing so will require more than the ethical reawakening that many recommend. Thinkers of multispecies relations tend to suggest that we might develop gratitude for nature's gifts through either intimate knowledge of other beings or awe at their very otherness. We should cultivate the "arts of noticing," Anna Tsing suggests, and look more closely at "assemblages of entangled ways of life."[18] Martha Nussbaum urges us to remain open to the kind of wonder that can "awake[n] a nascent ethical concern."[19] More generally, writing on ecology tends to dwell on the positive affects spurred by experiences of nature—beauty and wonder, love and care. Many ways of describing idealized relationships to nature—"home," "nurturer," "mother"—are quite literally domesticating. But these, too, are ways of limiting what nature can be. When other beings truly flourish in their own forms of life, we (or at least some of us) may sometimes find them (or at least some of them) disgusting, frightening, threatening, or simply boring. When we know nonhumans better, we may be more afraid of them, more bent on their domination or destruction.[20] These, too, are the kinds of challenges that a more emancipated world would have to face.

I want to close, then, with two stories of my own: the first, a wondrous encounter with nature, which reveals the limits of affect in the face of real abstraction; the second, a distinctly unpleasurable and disquieting experience of nature, which reveals the kaleidoscopic possibilities that lie beyond capitalism's social forms.

———

The first is taken from Herman Melville's *Moby-Dick*, a novel famously concerned with the conflict between man and nature—and also with the conflict between the passions and the interests.[21] Ahab, the mad hunter of the white whale, is explicitly motivated by his passion for vengeance, to which he appears "ready to sacrifice all mortal interests."[22] He explicitly scorns economic motivations: it may well be that "money's to be the measurer," he observes, that "the accountants have computed their great counting-house the globe, by girdling it with guineas, one to every three parts of an inch."[23] But for Ahab, these calculations are meaningless beside his obsession. Ahab's passion isn't *for* nature: he rejects the money-measure not in order to save the whales but to destroy one in particular. But if Ahab is out for revenge, the rest of the crew are on the *Pequod* to make money. They are a global cast of proletarians who must sell their labor to survive, in many cases because they have been brutally dispossessed from their native lands, and who—like many other workers in nature-based industries—will earn only a share of what they catch.[24] They are not thereby immune to passionate action; they are exhorted by Ahab to join his "romantic" crusade, and often react viscerally to the violence and beauty that characterize life at sea. But vengeance, the first mate Starbuck points out, "will not fetch thee much in our Nantucket market."[25]

One scene in particular dramatizes this conflict—in this case, one between an experience of passionate wonder in an encounter with whales and the economic interests that drive the crew to hunt them. The *Pequod* is sailing through the Strait of Sunda, near Indonesia, when a "spectacle of singular magnificence" appears on the horizon: a "continuous chain of whale-jets" sparkling, signifying a huge number of whales beneath the waves. The *Pequod* gives chase and approaches the herd, which has created a circular perimeter within which mothers and calves can be protected. The harpooner Queequeg spears a whale on the outskirts of this barricade, and it drags the small whaling boat into the circle's midst. The boat suddenly enters a magical space: an "enchanted calm," a "wondrous world," an "enchanted pond."[26] The whales are so unafraid that they swim right up to the boats, Ishmael marvels: "It almost seemed that some spell had suddenly domesticated them."[27] The whalers, too, are "entranced" as they watch the whales and their strange world beneath the waves; in them, Ishmael seems to see "the subtlest secrets of the seas."[28] The whalers pat the whales on the forehead and scratch their backs with their harpoons. It is a scene of peace, calm, delight—and above all, wonder. But the charmed circle lasts only a few moments before another harpooned whale, frenzied with pain and fear, upsets the defensive formation and destroys its inner calm. The wondrous encounter is over. Both humans and whales return to their roles: the humans are once again whalers; and the whales, their prey. When it comes to the Nantucket market, wonder is worthless; only "blubber was money."[29]

Most of us do not enact violence towards the nonhuman world as immediately as the crew of the *Pequod*. But it is no less embedded in our daily lives, hidden by time and space, but most of all the market itself—by the bloodless prices that tell us what nature is worth. Melville himself makes this point bluntly: the lamps and candles of cozy domesticity, he observes, are bought at the price of brutality towards man and beast alike.[30] So too are ours today. In some instances that brutality is hidden by space—by the distance, say, between the destruction of the Amazon and the burger we eat half a world away; in others, by time, as in the "slow violence" that characterizes the gradual effects of surplus matter. It is nearly always hidden by price. We may wonder at whales—but regardless of what calculations the IMF makes, living whales are worth little more today than they were in Melville's time.[31] We might incorporate some "social costs" into prices via the likes of Pigovian taxes, or exercise some degree of care through consumer practices—voluntarily paying a little extra for cage-free eggs or recycled toilet paper, at least if we can afford to do so. But even the most conscientious consumer cannot avoid the fact that most of our actions are mediated by price, in ways that render most of nature's gifts invisible by default, and that make a mockery of our good intentions. As we've seen, the free gift is the default form in which nature appears in a system structured by wage labor, commodity exchange, and the pursuit of abstract wealth.

Here I want to turn to my second story: the narrator Roquentin's famously unsettling encounter with a chestnut tree in Sartre's *Nausea* (1938). Walking through the French town of Bouville, Roquentin questions nature's seemingly wondrous appearance: the people admiring the loveliness of the green sea, the priest who sees in its beauty the divine, he claims, have been deceived. For Roquentin "the *true* sea is cold and black, full of animals; it crawls under this thin green film made to deceive human beings."[32] When he arrives at a park, "suddenly, the veil is torn away. I have understood, *I have seen*."[33] Familiar things—the gates, the bench, the grass and, especially, the chestnut tree—are no longer perceptible according to their familiar roles. Roquentin's chestnut tree isn't the tender giver of Silverstein's fable, or the nurturing "mother tree" of the altruistic forest. It isn't a carbon sequestration service provider or a source of lumber, either. Rather, the chestnut tree makes Roquentin nauseous because it exceeds his grasp; because it is *there* beyond his own ability to comprehend it.[34]

Roquentin describes this with horror: an oak is "half-rotten," life an expression of "weakness," the garden an "ignoble mess."[35] It is, in other words, hardly
the kind of wondrous attitude toward nature that contemporary ecological
writing seeks to inculcate. It might seem to simply reflect the modern, urban
European's tragic alienation from nature—compounded by the aftereffects of
a bad trip—and perhaps it does.[36] The point isn't that Roquentin's perception
is superior or his affect correct. We might wonder, with Iris Murdoch, why he
finds "the contingent overabundance of the world nauseating rather than glori-
ous."[37] But if his response to the tree is one of horror, it is also a "horrible ec-
stasy."[38] The vertiginous realization that we live in a world that we do not fully
understand, a world that does *not* necessarily care about us, bestow its gifts, or
reciprocate our gaze, can be its own kind of awe—an awe at the genuine strange-
ness of other beings, their profusion, their existence in *excess* of our needs or
desires; their existence whether we like it or not. Roquentin's nausea serves as
a reminder that encounters with the otherness of the nonhuman given do not
automatically inculcate wonder or gratitude; and indeed, that we need not *only*
be grateful for what is given—an attitude that can slip into acceptance of the
given as the necessary.[39] Instead, what Roquentin concludes from his encounter with the tree is that "the essential thing is contingency": it is not necessary
that things be as they are. For him it is this contingency that is "the perfect free
gift."[40] Contingency serves as a reminder that the free gift of nature as capitalist
social form is only *one* way of perceiving and relating to our multitudinous
world—all the more so when we take into account the abundance of ways that
nonhumans might perceive it—and more than that, that all ways of relating to
the world are partial rather than necessary.[41]

Ending the form of unfreedom that compels most of us to treat most of
nature as a free gift most of the time would not tell us how we ought to relate
to, value, or treat different kinds of nonhuman beings. It would not necessarily
usher in a new age of harmony between humanity and nature; it would not
automatically repair the damage done. It would simply allow us to make different kinds of decisions than the ones that capitalism offers. It would broaden the
range of values we can assert and the projects we can choose, both individually
and collectively. Perhaps we would choose to act little differently than we presently do—although, as I have suggested, it is hard to see how the freedom of all
human beings is compatible with our present treatment of the more-than-
human world on which we universally but unevenly depend. But we would, at
least, be more responsible for our actions, for perpetually evaluating, revising,
and enacting our commitments.

Simone de Beauvoir concludes *The Second Sex* not with a description of what the truly "independent woman" would be like, but rather with the hope that, released from the obligation to adhere to gender roles, human beings could relate to one another freely, in many more ways than a society structured around binary sex allows. This is what I think we might hope for: a world in which, freed from the roles we are assigned, human beings might be able to interact with and relate to the vast array of nonhuman beings in ways that reflect a fuller spectrum of existence—with curiosity and pleasure, disgust and respect, wonder and fear, awe and delight. The sea around us is *at once* a green film of beauty and a dark, cold expanse full of animals. It is Ishmael's enchanted pond and the *Pequod's* killing ground. What Rachel Carson calls the "fierce uncompromise of sea life" itself might spur *both* wonder and dread, inspiration and horror, love and perhaps even eros.[42] The point is not that we should be disgusted by or afraid of other forms of life—only that we should remain open to what Sophie Lewis describes as "the possibility of something genuinely weird, perhaps epistemically dangerous."[43] The Earth is what it appears to us—and also so much more. It is the agents we do not know are there, as well as those that reveal themselves to us in time. It is reciprocal and also parasitical, harmonious and also ruthless. It is what is given to us but also what we make of it. The question before us is what we will make of it, and with it, in the time to come.

ACKNOWLEDGMENTS

THERE ARE no free gifts—and yet I have received many more in the writing of this book than I can adequately reciprocate.

This project began many years ago as a dissertation—and even before that as a paper written for Karen Hébert, who had the foresight to suggest that it might develop into something more. It was subsequently guided by a wonderfully eclectic committee that often understood it better than I did. Jim Scott's keen interest in the world and irreverent spirit of inquiry invariably pushed me to think more creatively; I wish he could have seen the fruit of our conversations. David Grewal has been a steady guide through the often-treacherous terrain of political economy, a continual source of encouragement, and a generous host from coast to coast. First as a mentor, now as a colleague, and always as a friend, Karuna Mantena's wisdom, generosity, and warmth have been invaluable as I've meandered down the path of an academic career. When I needed it most, Joanna Radin gave me hope that intellectual life could be both brilliant and humane—and still does. Michael Denning, whose oceanic knowledge is matched only by his unwavering commitment to a democratic life of the mind, has been a model of intellectual integrity and academic solidarity. I wouldn't have made it to grad school at all without Rob Reich and Josh Cohen, who taught me how to think like a political theorist and suggested I might have a future in it.

In both organized and ambient ways I learned a great deal from friends and peers in graduate school, including Carmen Dege, Eta Demby, Stefan Eich, Ted Fertik, Adom Getachew, Lisa Gilson, Mie Inouye, Max Krahé, Tim Kreiner, Lizzie Krontiris, Erin Pineda, Hari Ramesh, Nica Siegel, Anurag Sinha, Hillary Taylor, and Gabriel Winant. Aaron Greenberg taught me—both overtly and through example—how to do political thought while also living a political life. Late-night conversations with Jonny Bunning got me through the first few years and have changed my thinking ever since. I was also fortunate to be part of a number of working groups which provided camaraderie and genuine intellectual community. The Political Theory Women's Writing Group was a remarkable space of solidarity and support, with particular thanks to our fearless leader Anna Jurkevics. I loved spending two years as an active member of the inimitable Working Group on Globalization and Culture, and I'm grateful to the many people who have passed through the Marxism and Cultural Theory reading group over the years.

Much of what I know about politics I learned from comrades in GESO/Local 33—UNITE HERE, who taught me that freedom is a collective project and an endless meeting. Solidarity forever to the many generations of GESO, and especially to Charles Decker, Ian Dunn, Lena Eckert-Erdheim, Sarah Eidelson, Andrew Epstein, Ted Fertik, Adom Getachew, Kelly Goodman, Aaron Greenberg, Leana Hirschfield-Kroen, Mie Inouye, Chris McGowan, Lukas Moe, Erin Pineda, Julia Powers, Hari Ramesh, Emily Sessions, Anita Seth, Tif Shen, Nica Siegel, Josh Stanley, Simon Torracinta, Gabe Winant, and Lindsay Zafir.

Two years as a postdoctoral fellow at the Harvard University Center for the Environment gave me the time and space to rip up my dissertation and rewrite it more or less from scratch, and offered a welcome, diverse intellectual community even after campus shut down in March 2020. Thanks especially to Jim Clem, Katrina Forrester, Michael Sandel, Dan Schrag, and my fellow fellows. The Somerville Soviet—Tim Barker, Adom Getachew, Aaron Kerner, Sam Payne, Charles Petersen, Quinn Slobodian, Ben Tarnoff, Moira Weigel, Kirsten Weld, and Gabe Winant—was a reliable source of camaraderie and support through the highs and lows of that strange time, and the head-spinning turn from canvassing to quarantining.

Barnard College has been a wonderful place to finish this book. I'm grateful to my colleagues in political science for their warmth and support, and to colleagues across the street at Columbia for welcoming me into a vibrant political theory community. I'm especially grateful for the wisdom of Ayten Gündoğdu and Karuna Mantena, and for Séverine Autesserre's work to support me as chair. I'm thankful, too, for my amazing students, who constantly stimulate my thinking and keep me on my toes, and whose remarkable courage has served as political inspiration in dark times.

Many people have offered comments, discussion, and suggestions on pieces of the manuscript over the years, which have shaped it in ways large and small: thanks to Kye Barker, Pierre Charbonnier, Daniel Aldana Cohen, Chiara Cordelli, Kevin Duong, Paulina Ochoa Espejo, Jeffrey Flynn, Max Foley-Keene, Alex Gourevitch, John Hultgren, Alex Kirshner, Hélène Landemore, Melissa Lane, Ainsley LeSure, Geoff Mann, Robyn Marasco, Lida Maxwell, Erin Pineda, Tully Rector, Corey Robin, Melvin Rogers, Helen Galvin Ross, Annie Stilz, Joel Wainwright, and Milo Ward. I also presented pieces of the book at many institutions over the years, and received crucial feedback along the way. I'm grateful to those who invited me to share my work, and to audiences, discussants, and organizers at Aarhus, Bennington College, Brown, Chicago, CUNY Graduate Center, Duke, Fordham, Goethe University Frankfurt, Harvard, Humboldt, London's Institute of Historical Research, the New School, NYU, the Pioneer Valley Political Theory Workshop, Princeton, Sciences Po, UC Santa Barbara, the University of Minnesota, University of Virginia, the University of Washington, and Utrecht, as well as at ASPLP, APSA, WPSA, and APT. Thanks especially to Norman Wirzba and the Kenan Institute for Ethics at Duke, which welcomed me into the Anthropocene Working Group at a late date and generously supported my subsequent research. I'm also grateful to be connected to many brilliant colleagues at the Brooklyn Institute for Social Research, and for the model of public intellectual life it offers; thanks especially to Ajay Singh Chaudhary for enriching conversations on shared interests over the years.

I loved spending a year at the Institute for Advanced Study, where I finally finished a draft of the book manuscript between walks in the woods and climate cinema screenings. I feel incredibly fortunate to have been a part of the Climate Crisis Politics group—an exceptional group of scholars, and remarkable source of both camaraderie and intellectual stimulation. Thank you to Hillary Angelo, David Bond, Wendy Brown, Heather Davis, Julia Dehm, Christina Dunbar-Hester, Stefan Eich, Andreas Folkers, Kian Goh, Maira Hayat, Lynne Huffer, Philippe Le Billon, Nayanika Mathur, and Tim Mitchell. Andreas Folkers, in particular, was a true kindred thinker whose ideas often uncannily mirrored my own and reliably provoked them. Wendy Brown's acute observations cut to the heart of the book's trouble spots, and her encouragement helped me to work through them. Tim Mitchell's questions always helped me to turn problems around and see them in new light.

A manuscript workshop at Barnard in the fall of 2022 featured a true dream team—Nancy Fraser, Ayten Gündoğdu, Sharon Krause, Karuna Mantena, Fred Neuhouser, Will Roberts, and Carl Wennerlind—whose generous and perceptive comments made a sprawling manuscript immeasurably sharper, as I've only come to appreciate more each day. Jed Britton-Purdy's bracingly accurate comments spurred a ruthless edit and a new chapter. A manuscript swap with Lida Maxwell yielded both insight and inspiration. Gautham Shiralagi's characteristically incisive comments at a crucial stage of revision helped me work through a long-standing impasse, and our ongoing conversations have unfailingly helped me to both interrogate and hone my ideas. Daniela Dover's late-stage read was instrumental in sharpening the book's final form, and indispensable in boosting morale. Since the dissertation stage, Adom Getachew has offered comments and advice on everything from the framing of arguments to the publishing process; so far she has yet to be wrong. Katrina Forrester has supported me in countless ways and read more drafts of some chapters than I can remember; I'm not sure I ever would have figured out what I wanted to say about Marxist feminism—and much else—without our conversations. I couldn't ask for a better companion in book-writing than Thea Riofrancos, who discussed ideas and read drafts, commiserated and celebrated over years of parallel progress. For over half my life, Gabe Winant has been such a constant intellectual and political companion that I can hardly disentangle our thoughts; I can't imagine where or who I'd be without our friendship. Sophie Lewis, my surrogate cyborg sibling, has been a comrade across continents and projects, and is a regular interlocutor in my inner dialogue even across distance. One of the unexpected pleasures of this project was developing an enthusiasm for existentialism, and finding others who would not only tolerate but share it: thanks to Daniela Dover, Ted Fertik, Jonathan Gingerich, and Ben Kunkel for both indulging me in going down this particular rabbit hole and helping me figure out what I might find there—and, especially, to Gautham Shiralagi.

A great deal of intellectual life happens outside of formal academic settings—not to mention most of life. Over the many (many) years I've been working through the arguments of this book, many friends and colleagues have talked through ideas, read related work, or shared in political projects. Thanks to Amna Akbar, Grey Anderson, Leah Aronowsky, Tim Barker, Aaron Benanav, Keith Brower Brown, Marius Bickhardt, Jacob Blumenfeld, Quentin Bruneau, Will Callison, Daniela Cammack, Danielle Carr, Charmaine Chua, Dan Denvir, Rafael Khachaturian, Adam Leeds, Dan Luban, Jamie Martin, Ben McKean, Sophie Smith, Amia Srinivasan, Astra Taylor, Zoe VanGelder, Natasha Wheatley, Troy Vettese, and Lindsay Zafir. Getaways with Ava Kofman and Giles Harvey have periodically provided welcome interruptions to the writing grind. Ben Kunkel and Hermione Hoby have been unparalleled hosts in the mountain West and incomparable companions in hiking and conversation. The Charente Political Theory Workshop provided an extraordinarily delightful blend of writing and distraction: thanks to Sophie, Amia, Gabe, Adom, and Goose for alternately aiding and derailing writing progress.

Many comrades have helped me stay tethered to the political questions animating this work. Kate Aronoff, Daniel Aldana Cohen, and Thea Riofrancos—

Comrade Planet—have been indispensable to my thinking about climate for nearly a decade; I still can't quite believe we wrote a whole other book along the way to this one. The Climate and Community Institute has been a steadying and inspiring source of political and intellectual collaboration for many years; thanks especially to Batul Hassan and Patrick Bigger for many illuminating conversations. I'm grateful, too, to editors who have helped me work through some of these ideas in other formats, and who have made me a much better writer over the years. Thanks to editors at *Jacobin, Dissent, Logic, n+1, New Left Review, Boston Review*, and *Verso*, especially Natasha Lewis, Matt Lord, David Marcus, Nikil Saval, Nick Serpe, Ben Tarnoff, Micah Uetricht, and Susan Watkins. Certain arguments and ideas have appeared previously in journals and magazines, including the *American Political Science Review, Nomos, Logic*, and *Jacobin*; I'm grateful for permission to use this material.

At Princeton, Rob Tempio has expertly stewarded the project from early conversations to the final manuscript. I'm grateful to him for believing in the project from the start and for his equanimous guidance through the process. Chloe Coy provided top-notch editorial support, and Maia Vaswani was both wonderfully meticulous and graciously patient as a copyeditor. Two reviewers provided exceptionally helpful comments, at once supportive of the project and keen in their suggestions for how it could be made stronger; the book has changed significantly for the better as a result.

My family has patiently supported this project for many years, even when I suspect they feared I'd never finish. My grandparents, John and Barbara Battistoni and Dorothy and Carl Ritz, were unwaveringly encouraging; I've thought often of how proud they would have been to see this book in print. Marielle and Jim Fortune provided a welcome haven from the manuscript during many restorative visits—often made gloriously chaotic by Rita, Joseph, Michael, and John Paul, all of whom joined the family in the time it took me to revise. Katie Battistoni has been an unwavering companion in the highs and lows of finishing a long-gestating project, and having her and Andy Cush around the corner in Brooklyn is a source of great solace and pleasure. Paul Harris and Pascale Torracinta have offered sustenance both physical and psychic while patiently listening to me proclaim the book "almost done" over many meals, visits and vacations. It's impossible to count the ways that my parents, Rick Battistoni and Betsy Ritz, have contributed to this book, from reading drafts to scouting artwork. But beyond any concrete measure, the things they've taught me are at its heart, as I realize more each day.

It's especially hard to know how to thank Simon Torracinta, and especially hard to imagine what this book would be without him. For years he has read everything I've written and improved it all, this manuscript in particular. He has contributed to this book at every possible level: he's talked through endless iterations of arguments and read a truly astonishing number of drafts, conjured up cover ideas and fixed citations. When my muscle, nerve, brain, and so on were expended, he helped replenish them; and at the end of the working day he makes life a joy. I fear I can't reciprocate the gifts he's given, but I'll spend my life trying.

NOTES

Introduction

1. Bruno Latour and Peter Weibel, eds., *Critical Zones: The Science and Politics of Landing on Earth* (MIT Press, 2020).

2. Yinon M. Bar-On, Rob Phillips, and Ron Milo, "The Biomass Distribution on Earth," *Proceedings of the National Academy of Sciences of the USA* 115, no. 25 (2018): 6506–11.

3. Jared Farmer, *Elderflora: A Modern History of Ancient Trees* (Basic Books, 2022); Adam Welz, *The End of Eden: Wild Nature in the Age of Climate Breakdown* (Bloomsbury, 2023); Ed Yong, *An Immense World: How Animal Senses Reveal the Hidden Realms around Us* (Random House, 2022).

4. Intergovernmental Panel on Climate Change, "Summary for Policymakers," in: *Climate Change 2023: Synthesis Report. Contribution of Working Groups I, II and III to the Sixth Assessment Report of the Intergovernmental Panel on Climate Change*, ed. Hoesung Lee and José Romero (IPCC, 2023): 1–34.

5. David Wallace-Wells, *The Uninhabitable Earth: Life after Warming* (Tim Duggan Books, 2019).

6. Intergovernmental Science-Policy Platform on Biodiversity and Ecosystem Services, *Summary for Policymakers of the Global Assessment Report on Biodiversity and Ecosystem Services of the Intergovernmental Science-Policy Platform on Biodiversity and Ecosystem Services* (IPBES, 2019).

7. For a few key works in the now-massive literature on the Anthropocene: Paul J. Crutzen, "The Geology of Mankind," *Nature* 415 (2002): 23; Will Steffen, Paul Crutzen, and J. R. McNeill, "The Anthropocene: Are Humans Now Overwhelming the Great Forces of Nature?," *Ambio* 36 (2007): 614–21; Christophe Bonneuil and Jean-Baptiste Fressoz, *The Shock of the Anthropocene: The Earth, History and Us*, trans. David Fernbach (Verso, 2016); Andreas Malm and Alf Hornborg, "The Geology of Mankind? A Critique of the Anthropocene Narrative," *Anthropocene Review* 1, no. 1 (2014): 62–69; Heather Davis and Zoe Todd, "On the Importance of a Date, or Decolonizing the Anthropocene," *Acme: An International Journal for Critical Geographies* 16, no. 4 (2017): 761–80.

8. Nicholas Stern, "The Economics of Climate Change," *American Economic Review* 98, no. 2 (2008).

9. Pavan Sukhdev, "Put a Value on Nature!," *TedGlobal*, July 2011, transcript, https://www.ted.com/talks/pavan_sukhdev_put_a_value_on_nature/transcript?subtitle=en.

10. Jonathan Guthrie, "Our £135bn Debt to the Humble Bee," *Financial Times*, August 5, 2022.

11. Wallace-Wells, *Uninhabitable Earth*, 161; Dipesh Chakrabarty, "The Climate of History: Four Theses," *Critical Inquiry* 35, no. 2 (2009): 212, 221; William Connolly, *Climate Machines, Fascist Drives, and Truth* (Duke University Press, 2019), 62; John Gray, "This Changes Everything: Capitalism vs the Climate Review," *Guardian*, September 22, 2014, https://www.theguardian.com/books/2014/sep/22/this-changes-everything-review-naomi-klein-john-gray.

12. For historical and genealogical analyses of nature and politics: Katrina Forrester and Sophie Smith, eds., *Nature, Action and the Future: Political Thought and the Environment* (Cambridge University Press, 2018); Duncan Kelly, *Politics and the Anthropocene* (Polity, 2019); Cara New Daggett, *The Birth of Energy: Fossil Fuels, Thermodynamics, and the Politics of Work* (Duke University Press, 2019); Pierre Charbonnier, *Affluence and Freedom: An Environmental History of Political Ideas*, trans. Andrew Brown (Polity, 2021); Crina Archer, Laura Ephraim, and Lida Maxwell, "Introduction: Politics on the Terrain of Second Nature," in *Second Nature: Rethinking the Natural through Politics*, ed. Archer, Ephraim, and Maxwell (Fordham University Press, 2014), 1–25.

13. The injunction against committing the "naturalistic fallacy," often traced to David Hume's argument against deriving moral judgments from factual conditions, is one of modern philosophy's most foundational (albeit one that has itself been challenged in recent years). See Hume, *A Treatise of Human Nature* (1738–40; Clarendon, 1975); Lorraine Daston, *Against Nature* (MIT Press, 2019).

14. G. A. Cohen, *Karl Marx's Theory of History: A Defence* (1978; Princeton University Press, 2000), 107. See also Alex Callinicos, "G. A. Cohen and the Critique of Political Economy," *Science & Society* 70, no. 2 (2006): 252–74.

15. Bill McKibben, "The End of Nature," *New Yorker*, September 3, 1989.

16. For a smattering of the massive literature on nature: Raymond Williams, "Ideas of Nature," in *Problems in Materialism and Culture* (Verso, 1980), 69–85; William Cronon, ed., *Uncommon Ground: Rethinking the Human Place in Nature* (W. W. Norton, 1996); Donna Jeanne Haraway, *Simians, Cyborgs, and Women: The Reinvention of Nature* (Routledge, 1991); Bruno Latour, *The Politics of Nature: How to Bring the Sciences into Democracy*, trans. Catherine Porter (Harvard University Press, 2004); Bill McKibben, *The End of Nature* (Random House, 1989); Steven Vogel, *Against Nature: The Concept of Nature in Critical Theory* (State University of New York Press, 1996); Noel Castree, *Making Sense of Nature* (Routledge, 2014); Jedediah Purdy, *After Nature: A Politics for the Anthropocene* (Harvard University Press, 2015); Jane Bennett and William Chaloupka, eds., *In the Nature of Things: Language, Politics, and the Environment* (University of Minnesota Press, 1993); Daston, *Against Nature*. For a critique of the critique of nature: Andreas Malm, *The Progress of This Storm: Nature and Society in a Warming World* (Verso, 2018).

17. William Cronon, "Introduction: In Search of Nature," in Cronon, *Uncommon Ground*, 23–56.

18. Dipesh Chakrabarty, "Climate and Capital: On Conjoined Histories," *Critical Inquiry* 41 no. 1 (2014): 1–23; see also Dipesh Chakrabarty, *The Climate of History in a Planetary Age* (University of Chicago Press, 2021); Nigel Clark, *Inhuman Nature: Sociable Life on a Dynamic Planet* (SAGE, 2011).

19. Bruno Latour, *The Pasteurization of France*, trans. Alan Sheridan and John Law (Harvard University Press, 1988); Latour, *Facing Gaia: Eight Lectures on the New Climatic Regime*, trans. Catherine Porter (Polity, 2017); Latour, *Down to Earth: Politics in the New Climatic Regime* (Polity, 2018).

20. Charbonnier, *Affluence and Freedom*.

21. Chakrabarty, *Climate of History*; Latour, *Down to Earth*; William E. Connolly, *Facing the Planetary: Entangled Humanism and the Politics of Swarming* (Duke University Press, 2017); Jane Bennett, *Vibrant Matter: A Political Ecology of Things* (Duke University Press, 2010).

22. Simon L. Lewis and Mark A. Maslin, *The Human Planet: How We Created the Anthropocene* (Yale University Press, 2018).

23. Connolly, *Climate Machines*, 64; see similar arguments in his *Facing the Planetary*; Daggett, *Birth of Energy*, 188.

24. Charbonnier, *Affluence and Freedom*, 261.

25. For reflections on this challenge: Wendy Brown, *Nihilistic Times: Thinking with Max Weber* (Harvard University Press, 2023), 5.

26. For environmental political theory: Robyn Eckersley, *Environmentalism and Political Theory: Toward an Ecocentric Approach* (State University of New York Press, 1992); Robert Goodin, *Green Political Theory* (Polity, 1992); John Barry, *Rethinking Green Politics: Nature, Virtue, and Progress* (SAGE, 1999); John M. Meyer, *Political Nature: Environmentalism and the Interpretation of Western Thought* (MIT Press, 2001); John Dryzek, *Rational Ecology: Environment and Political Economy* (Basil Blackwell, 1987); Eckersley, *The Green State: Rethinking Democracy and Sovereignty* (MIT Press, 2004); Andrew Dobson, *Green Political Thought*, 2nd ed. (Routledge, 1995); Dobson, *Justice and the Environment: Conceptions of Environmental Sustainability and Theories of Distributive Justice* (Oxford University Press, 1998); John S. Dryzek and David Schlosberg, eds., *Debating the Earth: The Environmental Politics Reader* (Oxford University Press, 1998); Timothy W. Luke, *Ecocritique: Contesting the Politics of Nature, Economy, and Culture* (University of Minnesota Press, 1997); Luke, *Capitalism, Democracy, and Ecology: Departing from Marx* (University of Illinois Press, 1999); William Ophuls, *Ecology and the Politics of Scarcity: Prologue to a Political Theory of the Steady State* (W. H. Freeman, 1977).

27. If science does the work of what Bruno Latour calls "purification," then "the economy" is where mediation occurs and hybrids are generated: Bruno Latour, *We Have Never Been Modern*, trans Catherine Porter (Harvard University Press, 1993).

28. Although for a work that subtly links environmental questions to economic ones, see Duncan Kelly's *Politics and the Anthropocene*.

29. See Branko Milanovic, *Capitalism, Alone: The Future of the Economic System That Rules the World* (Harvard University Press, 2019); see also John Dryzek, *The Politics of the Earth: Environmental Discourses* (Oxford University Press, 1997).

30. Per Nancy Fraser, *Cannibal Capitalism: How Our System Is Devouring Democracy, Care, and the Planet—and What We Can Do about It* (Verso, 2022).

31. Jason Moore, *Capitalism in the Web of Life: Ecology and the Accumulation of Capital* (Verso, 2015).

32. I draw here on Adom Getachew's analysis of *worldmaking* as an anticolonial project— yet whereas Getachew highlights a liberatory project *contesting* the dominant, and dominating, world order, I focus on the forces making the dominant order itself. See Adom Getachew, *Worldmaking after Empire: The Rise and Fall of Self-Determination* (Princeton University Press 2019), 2.

33. Anne Robert Jacques Turgot, *Reflections on the Formation and the Distribution of Riches*, trans. William J. Ashley (1770; Macmillan, 1898); cited in Margaret Schabas, *The Natural Origins of Economics* (University of Chicago Press, 2005), 54.

34. Jean-Baptiste Say, *A Treatise on Political Economy, or The Production, Distribution and Consumption of Wealth* (1803; 4th ed., 1819), trans. C. R. Prinsep (Claxton, Remsen and Haffelfinger, 1880; repr. Augustus M. Kelley, 1971), 63. All references are to the 1971 edition.

35. Adam Smith, *An Inquiry into the Nature and Causes of the Wealth of Nations*, ed. R. H. Campbell and A. S. Skinner (Cambridge University Press, 1976); David Ricardo, *On the Principles of Political Economy, and Taxation*, in *The Works and Correspondence of David Ricardo*, vol. 1., ed. Piero Sraffa (Cambridge University Press, 1951; Liberty Fund, 2004), 286–87.

36. Jean-Jacques Rousseau, *Discourse on the Origin and Foundations of Inequality among Men, or Second Discourse*, in *The Discourses and Other Early Political Writings*, trans. Victor Gourevitch (Cambridge University Press, 1997), 161; John Locke, *Two Treatises of Government*, ed. Peter Laslett (Cambridge University Press, 1988), 286.

37. Locke, *Two Treatises*, 287.

38. Immanuel Kant, "Conjectures on the Beginning of Human History," in *Kant: Political Writings*, trans. H. B. Nisbet, ed. Hans Reiss, 2nd ed. (Cambridge University Press, 1991), 225; see Christine Korsgaard, *Fellow Creatures: Our Obligations to the Other Animals* (Oxford University Press, 2018).

39. Wendell Berry, *The Gift of Good Land: Further Essays Cultural and Agricultural* (North Point, 1981); Francis, *Laudato Si': On Care for Our Common Home* (Libreria Editrice Vaticana, 2015), 49.

40. On the gift in Western philosophy: Georges Bataille, *The Accursed Share: An Essay on General Economy*, vol. 1, trans. Robert Hurley (Zone Books, 1991); Jacques Derrida, *Given Time: I. Counterfeit Money*, trans. Peggy Kamuf (University of Chicago Press, 1992); Marcel Hénaff, *The Philosopher's Gift: Reexamining Reciprocity*, trans. Jean-Louis Morhange (Fordham University Press, 2019).

41. Winona LaDuke, *All Our Relations: Native Struggles for Land and Life* (South End, 1999), 115; Robin Wall Kimmerer, *Braiding Sweetgrass: Indigenous Wisdom, Scientific Knowledge, and the Teachings of Plants* (Milkweed Editions, 2013), 24.

42. Kimmerer, *Braiding Sweetgrass*, 28.

43. For the classic anthropological account: Marcel Mauss, *The Gift: Forms and Functions of Exchange in Archaic Societies*, trans. W. D. Halls (1966; Routledge, 1990); for its translation to social theory: Karl Polanyi, *Primitive, Archaic, and Modern Economies: Essays of Karl Polanyi*, ed. George Dalton (Anchor Books, 1968); Polanyi, *The Great Transformation: The Political and Economic Origins of Our Time* (1944; Beacon, 2001); for an influential popular account: Lewis Hyde, *The Gift: Imagination and the Erotic Life of Property* (Vintage, 1983). These traditions, moreover, are not as separate as they might seem: Western anthropologists often projected their own perspectives onto non-Western gift cultures; Western philosophers like Bataille and Derrida, meanwhile, directly engaged the work of anthropologists like Mauss in their own theorizations. On this history: Grégoire Mallard, *Gift Exchange: The Transnational History of a Political Idea* (Cambridge University Press, 2019); Edward LiPuma and Moishe Postone, "Gifts, Commodities, and the Encompassment of Others," *Critical Historical Studies* 7, no. 1 (2020): 167–200.

44. For visions of alternative economies rooted in the gift: J. K. Gibson-Graham, *The End of Capitalism (as We Knew It): A Feminist Critique of Political Economy* (University of Minnesota Press, 2006); David Graeber, *Debt: The First 5,000 Years* (Melville House, 2011).

45. Theodor Adorno, *Negative Dialectics*, trans. E. B. Ashton (Continuum, 1973), 5; Max Horkheimer and Theodor W. Adorno, *Dialectic of Enlightenment*, ed. Gunzelin Schmid Noerr, trans. Edmund Jephcott (1944; Stanford University Press, 2002). See also Vogel, *Against Nature*, 71–73.

46. Thanks to Katrina Forrester for this observation.

47. On residuals: Andreas Folkers, "Fossil Modernity: The Materiality of Acceleration, Slow Violence, and Ecological Futures," *Time & Society* 30, no. 2 (2021): 223–46.

48. For recent works: Andreas Malm, *Fossil Capital: The Rise of Steam Power and the Roots of Global Warming* (Verso, 2016); Moore, *Capitalism in the Web of Life*; Jason Moore, ed., *Anthropocene or Capitalocene? Nature, History, and the Crisis of Capitalism* (PM, 2016); Raj Patel and Jason Moore, *A History of the World in Seven Cheap Things: A Guide to Capitalism, Nature, and the Future of the Planet* (University of California Press, 2017); Fraser, *Cannibal Capitalism*; Naomi Klein, *This Changes Everything: Capitalism vs. the Climate* (Simon and Schuster, 2014); Johanna Oksala, *Feminism, Capitalism, and Ecology* (Northwestern University Press, 2023); Kate Aronoff, *Overheated: How Capitalism Broke the Planet—and How We Fight Back* (Bold Type Books, 2021); Ian Angus, *Facing the Anthropocene: Fossil Capitalism and the Crisis of the Earth System* (Monthly Review, 2016); Joel Kovel, *The Enemy of Nature: The End of Capitalism or the End of the World?*, 2nd ed. (Zed Books, 2007); Jason Hickel, *Less Is More: How Degrowth Will Save the World* (Penguin Random House, 2020); Kohei Saito, *Slow Down: The Degrowth Manifesto* (Astra House, 2024); Matthias Schmelzer, Aaron Vansintjan, Andrea Vetter, *The Future Is Degrowth: A Guide to a World beyond Capitalism* (Verso Books, 2022); Giorgos Kallis, Susan Paulson, Giacomo D'Alisa, and Federico Demaria, *The Case for Degrowth* (Polity, 2020).

49. For critiques of Marx's anthropocentrism: Ted Benton, *Natural Relations: Ecology, Animal Rights and Social Justice* (Verso, 1993); Eckersley, *Environmentalism and Political*

Theory. For the ecological Marx: John Bellamy Foster, *Marx's Ecology: Materialism and Nature* (Monthly Review, 2000); Foster and Paul Burkett, *Marx and the Earth: An Anti-Critique* (Haymarket, 2016); Foster, Richard York, and Brett Clark, *The Ecological Rift: Capitalism's War on the Earth* (Monthly Review, 2010); Kohei Saito, *Karl Marx's Ecosocialism: Capital, Nature, and the Unfinished Critique of Political Economy* (Monthly Review, 2017); Saito, *Marx in the Anthropocene: Towards the Idea of Degrowth Communism* (Cambridge University Press, 2023).

50. This question is arguably the best one-sentence summary of Marx's method. See Karl Marx, *Capital: A Critique of Political Economy*, trans. Ben Fowkes, vol. 1 (Penguin Books, 1976), 174. See also Louis Althusser, "The Object of *Capital*," pt. 4 in *Reading Capital: The Complete Edition*, by Althusser, Étienne Balibar, Roger Establet, Pierre Macherey, and Jacques Rancière (1965; Verso, 2016).

51. See Diane Elson, *Value: The Representation of Labour in Capitalism* (1979; Verso Books, 2015); Michael Denning, "Representing Global Labor," *Social Text* 25 no. 3 (92) (2007): 128.

52. On the critique of political economy: Moishe Postone, *Time, Labor, and Social Domination: A Reinterpretation of Marx's Critical Theory* (Cambridge University Press, 1993); Michael Heinrich, *An Introduction to the Three Volumes of Karl Marx's Capital*, trans. Alex Locascio (Monthly Review, 2012); Werner Bonefeld, *Critical Theory and the Critique of Political Economy: On Subversion and Negative Reason* (Bloomsbury, 2014).

53. Onur Ulas Ince has recently proposed to rematerialize political thought, in the sense of restoring questions of political economy—but here, I mean it in a double sense, at once returning attention to political economy while restoring *materiality* to political economy itself. See Ince, *Colonial Capitalism and the Dilemmas of Liberalism* (Oxford University Press, 2018), 3.

54. Donna Haraway describes these as "naturecultures": Haraway, *The Companion Species Manifesto: Dogs, People, and Significant Otherness* (Prickly Paradigm, 2003).

55. William Clare Roberts describes this mode as "purely immanent critique"; Søren Mau, as "absolute historicism." See Roberts, "Under Capitalism, We're All Dominated by the Invisible Threads of the Market," *Jacobin*, March 3, 2023, https://jacobin.com/2023/03/mute -compulsion-soren-mau-book-review; Søren Mau, *Mute Compulsion: A Marxist Theory of the Economic Power of Capital* (Verso, 2023), 72.

56. Bennett and Chaloupka, introduction to *In the Nature of Things*, xi. Marx's Aristotelian underpinnings sometimes lead him in this direction: see William Clare Roberts, *Marx's Inferno: A Political Theory of Capital* (Princeton University Press, 2017), 136. For a critical reading of Marx's Aristotelian naturalism: Melinda Cooper, "The Living and the Dead: Variations on de Anima," *Angelaki* 7, no. 3 (2002): 81–104.

57. A few landmark works, reflecting a range of approaches, include: Aldo Leopold, *Sand County Almanac; and Sketches Here and There* (Oxford University Press, 1949); Paul W. Taylor, *Respect for Nature: A Theory of Environmental Ethics* (1986; Princeton University Press, 2011); Peter Singer, *Animal Liberation: A New Ethics for Our Treatment of Animals* (New York Review, 1975); J. Baird Callicott, *In Defense of the Land Ethic: Essays in Environmental Philosophy* (State University of New York Press, 1989); Bill Devall and George Sessions, *Deep Ecology: Living as if Nature Mattered* (Peregrine Smith, 1985).

58. Purdy, *After Nature*, 21.

59. Jean-Paul Sartre, *Being and Nothingness: An Essay in Phenomenological Ontology*, trans. Sarah Richmond (1943; Washington Square, 2018); Sartre, *Existentialism Is a Humanism*, trans. Carolyn Macomber (1946; Yale University Press, 2007); Sartre, *Critique of Dialectical Reason*, ed. Jonathan Rée, trans. Alan Sheridan-Smith, vol. 1 (Verso, 2004); Simone de Beauvoir, *Philosophical Writings*, ed. Margaret A. Simons (University of Illinois Press, 2004).

60. Sianne Ngai, *Theory of the Gimmick: Aesthetic Judgment and Capitalist Form* (Harvard University Press, 2020), 51. On the mismeasure of wealth: Patrick Murray, *The Mismeasure of Wealth: Essays on Marx and Social Form* (Brill, 2016).

61. Ngai, *Theory of the Gimmick*, 1, 51.

62. Ngai, *Theory of the Gimmick*, 225.

63. On the "inside/outside" distinction: Nancy Fraser, "Behind Marx's Hidden Abode: For an Expanded Conception of Capitalism," *New Left Review*, no. 86 (2014): 55–72; Nancy Fraser and Rahel Jaeggi, *Capitalism: A Conversation in Critical Theory* (Polity, 2018). For a persuasive critique of "two-level" approaches: Chris O'Kane, "Critical Theory and the Critique of Capitalism: An Immanent Critique of Nancy Fraser's 'Systematic' 'Crisis-Critique' of Capitalism as an 'Institutionalized Social Order,'" *Science & Society* 85, no. 2 (2021): 207–35. For an instructive methodological critique of Karl Polanyi on related grounds: Melinda Cooper, *Family Values: Between Neoliberalism and the New Social Conservatism* (Zone Books, 2019).

64. Will Steffen, Wendy Broadgate, Lisa Deutsch, Owen Gaffney, and Cornelia Ludwig, "The Trajectory of the Anthropocene: The Great Acceleration," *Anthropocene Review* 2, no. 1 (2015): 81–98. On periodization: Lewis and Maslin, *Human Planet*.

65. Horkheimer and Adorno, *Dialectic of Enlightenment*, 12; Hannah Arendt, *The Human Condition*, 2nd ed. (1958; University of Chicago Press, 1998), 97.

66. J. R. McNeill and Peter Engelke, *The Great Acceleration: An Environmental History of the Anthropocene Since 1945* (Harvard University Press, 2014), 8–9, 137–38.

67. McNeill and Engelke, *Great Acceleration*, 5.

68. Echoing Geoff Mann in *Our Daily Bread: Wages, Workers, and the Political Economy of the American West* (University of North Carolina Press, 2012), 30.

69. Taking methodological cues from Karl Marx, *Grundrisse*, trans. Martin Nicolaus (1939; Penguin 1973); Stuart Hall's "Rethinking the Base and Superstructure," lecture 4 in *Cultural Studies 1983: A Theoretical History*, ed. Jennifer Daryl Slack and Lawrence Grossberg (Duke University Press 2016).

70. C.f. Fraser, "Behind Marx's Hidden Abode."

Chapter 1

1. While the emphasis on "ideas of nature" is widespread, key texts include Val Plumwood, *Feminism and the Mastery of Nature* (Routledge, 1993); Carolyn Merchant, *The Death of Nature: Women, Ecology, and the Scientific Revolution* (Harper Row, 1980): 2–3; Max Horkheimer and Theodor W. Adorno, *Dialectic of Enlightenment*, ed. Gunzelin Schmid Noerr, trans. Edmund Jephcott (1944; Stanford University Press, 2002). For discussion: William Leiss, *The Domination of Nature* (George Braziller, 1972).

2. Merchant, *Death of Nature*, 2–3. For a more skeptical view of Merchant's account: Paul Warde, *The Invention of Sustainability: Nature and Destiny c. 1500–1870* (Cambridge University Press, 2018).

3. Jason Moore, *Capitalism in the Web of Life: Ecology and the Accumulation of Capital* (Verso, 2015), 18.

4. Moore, *Capitalism in the Web of Life*, 4. For discussion: Sara Nelson, "Review: *Capitalism in the Web of Life*," *Antipode Online*, March 9, 2016, https://antipodeonline.org/2016/03/09/capitalism-in-the-web-of-life/; Out of the Woods Collective, *Hope against Hope: Writings on Ecological Crisis* (Common Notions, 2020).

5. Karl Marx, *Capital: A Critique of Political Economy*, vol. 1, trans. Ben Fowkes (Penguin Books, 1976), 874 (subsequent citations are to this edition); Onur Ulas Ince, "Primitive Accumulation, New Enclosures, and Global Land Grabs: A Theoretical Intervention," *Rural Sociology* 79, no. 1 (2014): 104–31; Robert Nichols, *Theft Is Property! Dispossession and Critical Theory* (Duke University Press, 2020); William Clare Roberts, "What Was Primitive Accumulation? Reconstructing the Origin of a Critical Concept," *European Journal of Political Theory* 19, no. 4 (2020): 532–52.

6. Karl Marx, *Grundrisse*, trans. Martin Nicolaus (1939; Penguin Books 1993), 489; John Bellamy Foster, *Marx's Ecology: Materialism and Nature* (Monthly Review, 2000); Foster and Brett Clark, *The Robbery of Nature: Capitalism and the Ecological Rift* (Monthly Review, 2020). For commentary on alienation from nature: Steven Vogel, "Marx and Alienation from Nature," *Social Theory and Practice* 14, no. 3 (1988): 367–87; Vogel, "On Nature and Alienation," in *Critical Ecologies: The Frankfurt School and Contemporary Environmental Crises*, ed. Andrew Biro (University of Toronto Press, 2011), 187–205.

7. On the change in the status of land: Nichols, *Theft Is Property!*; Glen Sean Coulthard, *Red Skin, White Masks: Rejecting the Colonial Politics of Recognition* (University of Minnesota Press, 2014). On "ongoing" primitive accumulation: Rosa Luxemburg, *The Accumulation of Capital: A Contribution to the Economic Theory of Imperialism*, ed. Peter Hudis and Paul Le Blanc, trans. Nicholas Gray and George Shriver, vol. 2 of *The Complete Works of Rosa Luxemburg* (1913; Verso, 2016); David Harvey, *The New Imperialism* (Oxford University Press, 2003).

8. Søren Mau, *Mute Compulsion: A Marxist Theory of the Economic Power of Capital* (Verso 2023).

9. As we'll see, while many elements gleaned from nature are bought and sold, there is a vital distinction between wage labor as a relation between human beings, in which one person pays for the use of another person's time, and the property relation of ownership that governs the use of nature's gifts.

10. Alfred Sohn-Rethel, *Intellectual and Manual Labour: A Critique of Epistemology*, trans. Martin Sohn-Rethel (1970; Haymarket Books, 2020), 17.

11. Sohn-Rethel, *Intellectual and Manual Labour*, 14–24; Alberto Toscano, "The Open Secret of Real Abstraction," *Rethinking Marxism* 20, no. 2 (2008): 273–87; cf. Michael Heinrich, *An Introduction to the Three Volumes of Karl Marx's "Capital,"* trans. Alex Locascio (Monthly Review, 2012), 49; Aboo Aumeeruddy and Ramon Tortajada, "Reading Marx on Value: A Note on Basic Texts," in *Value: The Representation of Labour in Capitalist Economy*, ed. Diane Elson (CSE Books, 1979), 1–13; Sianne Ngai, *Theory of the Gimmick: Aesthetic Judgment and Capitalist Form* (Harvard University Press, 2020).

12. For an insightful analysis of how these terms have been deployed in Marxist thought: Neil Smith, *Uneven Development: Nature, Capital, and the Production of Space*, 3rd ed. (University of Georgia Press, 2008). For an early account of "nature" in Marx's thought: Alfred Schmidt, *The Concept of Nature in Marx*, trans. Ben Fowkes (1962; Verso, 2014).

13. Although it has important precursors, particularly in the work of Soviet economist Isaak Rubin, the theoretical core of the post-1960 German *Neue Marx-Lektüre*, and its associated "value-form" (*Wertform*) approach, was initially pioneered by Hans-Georg Backhaus and Helmut Reichelt—students of Theodor Adorno clustered around the Frankfurt Institute of Social Research. A (hardly exhaustive) selection of significant texts in this tradition includes: Helmut Reichelt, *Zur logischen Struktur des Kapitalbegriffs bei Karl Marx* (Europäische Verlagsanstalt, 1970); Michael Heinrich, *Die Wissenschaft vom Wert: Die Marxsche Kritik der politischen Ökonomie zwischen wissenschaftlicher Revolution und klassischer Tradition* (VSA-Verlag, 1991); Hans-Georg Backhaus, *Dialektik der Wertform: Untersuchungen zur Marxschen Ökonomiekritik* (Ça ira, 1997). Notable allied works include: Isaak Illich Rubin, *Essays on Marx's Theory of Value*, trans. Miloš Samardžija and Fredy Perlman (1928; Black Rose Books, 1973); Moishe Postone, *Time, Labor, and Social Domination: A Reinterpretation of Marx's Critical Theory* (Cambridge University Press, 1993). For useful overviews, see especially: Riccardo Bellofiore and Tommaso Redolfi Riva, "The *Neue Marx-Lektüre*," *Radical Philosophy*, no. 189 (2015): 24–36; Heinrich, *Introduction* Elson, Value.

14. I make no claim to offer a definitive ontology. For a survey of other understandings of the nature-society relation: Philippe Descola, *Beyond Nature and Culture*, trans. Janet Lloyd (University of Chicago Press, 2014).

15. Kate Soper, *What Is Nature? Culture, Politics, and the Non-Human* (Blackwell, 1995), 132–33.

16. Andreas Malm, *The Progress of This Storm: Nature and Society in a Warming World* (Verso, 2018), 55. Sartre makes a similar claim in his argument that Marxism is "both monist and dualist": Jean-Paul Sartre, *Critique of Dialectical Reason*, ed. Jonathan Rée, trans. Alan Sheridan-Smith, vol. 1 (Verso, 2004), 25.

17. Soper, *What Is Nature?*, 126, 139.

18. See Alfred Crosby, *Ecological Imperialism: The Biological Expansion of Europe, 900–1900* (Cambridge University Press, 1993); Joachim Radkau, *Nature and Power: A Global History of the Environment* (Cambridge University Press, 2008); Fredrik Albritton Jonsson, *Enlightenment's Frontier: The Scottish Highlands and the Origins of Environmentalism* (Yale University Press, 2013); Warde, *Invention of Sustainability*; Fredrik Albritton Jonsson and Carl Wennerlind, *Scarcity: Economy and Nature in the Age of Capitalism* (Harvard University Press, 2023); Charbonnier, *Affluence and Freedom*.

19. Anne Robert Jacques Turgot, *Reflections on the Formation and the Distribution of Riches*, trans. William J. Ashley (1770; Macmillan, 1898), 46; cited in Margaret Schabas, *The Natural Origins of Economics* (University of Chicago Press, 2005), 54. On the physiocrats: Elizabeth Fox-Genovese, *The Origins of Physiocracy* (Cornell University Press, 1976); Istvan Hont, *Jealousy of Trade: International Competition and the Nation State in Historical Perspective* (Harvard University Press, 2005); Jonsson and Wennerlind, *Scarcity*; David Singh Grewal, *The Invention of the Economy: A History of Economic Thought* (Harvard University Press, forthcoming). For a comparison of this logic to the Linnaean system of natural order: Donald Worster, *Nature's Economy: A History of Ecological Ideas*, 2nd ed. (Cambridge University Press, 1994).

20. Turgot, *Reflections*, 9; cited in Schabas, *Natural Origins*, 54.

21. As the rival Italian economist Pietro Verri would point out, the land does not actually produce new matter any more than the watchmaker: Verri, *Meditazioni sulla economia politica* (1773), cited in Paul Christensen, "Historical Roots for Ecological Economics—Biophysical versus Allocative Approaches," *Ecological Economics* 1 (1989): 17–36. See also Cosimo Perrotta, *Unproductive Labour in Political Economy: The History of an Idea* (Routledge, 2018); François Quesnay, *Analyse du tableau économique*, in *Physiocrates*, ed. Eugène Daire, vol. 1 (Librarie de Guillaumin, 1846), 57–78.

22. Jean-Baptiste Say, *A Treatise on Political Economy, or The Production, Distribution and Consumption of Wealth* (1803; 4th ed., 1819), trans. C. R. Prinsep (Claxton, Remsen and Haffelfinger, 1880; repr. Augustus M. Kelley, 1971).

23. Bruno Latour, *Reassembling the Social: An Introduction to Actor-Network Theory* (Oxford University Press, 2005).

24. Say, *Treatise on Political Economy*, 74.

25. Say, *Treatise on Political Economy*, 64.

26. Say, *Treatise on Political Economy*, 76.

27. Say, *Treatise on Political Economy*, 75.

28. Say, *Treatise on Political Economy*, 126.

29. Say, *Treatise on Political Economy*, 66.

30. Say, *Treatise on Political Economy*, 74.

31. John Locke, *Two Treatises of Government*, ed. Peter Laslett (Cambridge University Press, 1988), 288, 298.

32. Adam Smith would repeat a similar charge, replacing the Native ruler with the "African king." Even Marx suggests at times that natural abundance inhibits the development of productive forces and hence precludes historical progress. On Locke's theory of improvement and its role in justifying dispossession: James Tully, *An Approach to Political Philosophy: Locke in Context* (Cambridge University Press, 1993). See also Onur Ulas Ince, *Colonial Capitalism and the Dilemmas of Liberalism* (Oxford University Press, 2018).

33. Adam Smith, *An Inquiry Into the Nature and Causes of the Wealth of Nations*, ed. R. H. Campbell and A. S. Skinner (Cambridge University Press, 1976), 1: 363. For Smith's specific view of the physiocrats: Smith, *Wealth of Nations*, 2: 674–79. For a critique of Smith's reading: Philip Mirowski, *More Heat than Light: Economics as Social Physics, Physics as Nature's Economics* (Cambridge University Press, 1989), 165–171. For the significance of nature in Smith's thought: Jonsson, *Enlightenment's Frontier*; Schabas, *Natural Origins*, 79–101.

34. Smith, *Wealth of Nations*, 364.

35. David Ricardo, *On the Principles of Political Economy and Taxation*, in *The Works and Correspondence of David Ricardo*, vol. 1, ed. Piero Sraffa (Cambridge University Press, 1951; Liberty Fund, 2004), 287.

36. R. D. Collison Black, Alfred William Coats, and Craufurd Goodwin, eds., *The Marginal Revolution in Economics: Interpretation and Evaluation* (Duke University Press, 1973).

37. Advocates for restoring nature to economics include: E. F. Schumacher, *Small Is Beautiful: Economics as if People Mattered* (Harper and Row, 1973); Herman E. Daly, *Steady-State Economics: The Economics of Biophysical Equilibrium and Moral Growth*, 2nd ed. (1977; Island, 1991); Daly, "On Economics as a Life Science," *Journal of Political Economy* 76, no. 3 (1968): 392–406.

38. William Cronon, *Nature's Metropolis: Chicago and the Great West* (W. W. Norton, 1991), 149–50.

39. Richard White, *The Organic Machine: The Remaking of the Columbia River* (Hill and Wang, 1995); Bathsheba Demuth, *Floating Coast: An Environmental History of the Bering Strait* (W. W. Norton, 2019), 16–17.

40. Karl Marx, "Critique of the Gotha Program," in *Later Political Writings*, ed. Terrell Carver (Cambridge University Press, 1996), 208. For critiques of Marx's ostensible neglect of nature: Daly, *Steady-State Economics*, 196; Nicholas Georgescu-Roegen, *The Entropy Law and the Economic Process* (Harvard University Press, 1971), 2. For a thorough response: Paul Burkett, *Marxism and Ecological Economics: Toward a Red and Green Political Economy* (Brill, 2006). For illuminating and comprehensive exegeses of Marx's writings on nature: Burkett, *Marx and Nature: A Red and Green Perspective* (St. Martin's, 1999); Foster, *Marx's Ecology*; John Bellamy Foster and Paul Burkett, *Marx and the Earth: An Anti-critique* (Haymarket, 2016); Kohei Saito, *Karl Marx's Ecosocialism: Capital, Nature, and the Unfinished Critique of Political Economy* (Monthly Review, 2017); Saito, *Marx in the Anthropocene: Towards the Idea of Degrowth Communism* (Cambridge University Press, 2023).

41. Karl Marx, *Economic Manuscript of 1861–63*, notebook 6, trans. Emile Burns, in *Marx & Engels Collected Works*, vol. 30 (Lawrence and Wishart, 1988), 352–53. To some degree the category of surplus is always social, insofar as even the minimum required for basic reproduction is socially specific.

42. Marx, *Economic Manuscript*, 353.

43. Karl Marx, *Capital: A Critique of Political Economy*, vol. 3, trans. Ernest Untermann, in *Marx & Engels Collected Works*, vol. 37 (1894; Lawrence and Wishart 1998), 732–33; italics mine.

44. Say, *Treatise on Political Economy*, 90.

45. Marx, *Economic Manuscript*, 353.

46. The exception is the invaluable analysis offered by Burkett in *Marxism and Ecological Economics* and *Marx and Nature*. Marx's own term is *Gratisnaturkraft*. Although "free gift of nature" is Ernest Untermann's 1909 translation, the phrase doesn't appear in David Fernbach's 1981 translation. More important than the precise language is the concept, which is well captured by the odd term.

47. Marx, *Capital*, 1: 932.

48. Marx, *Capital*, 1: 174; italics mine. For discussion: David Harvey, *The Limits to Capital* (Verso, 2018): 37; Elson, *Value*.

49. For a discussion that emphasizes the dimension of "doubling": Paul North, "Editor's Introduction," in Karl Marx, *Capital: Critique of Political Economy*, vol. 1, trans. Paul Reitter, ed.

North and Reitter (Princeton University Press, 2024): xlvi–xlviii. Reitter's excellent translation appeared in fall 2024, too late to be a significant reference point for this manuscript.

50. Marx, *Capital*, 1: 131, 126, 138. To have a dual character is not in itself capitalist, just as there are social forms that are not capitalist. Use and exchange value are familiar concepts within classical political economy, but Marx's point is that while many societies have some kind of exchange, it is only in capitalism that exchange becomes the dominant mode of acquiring goods, including human labor power.

51. Marx, *Capital*, 1: 139.

52. Marx, *Capital*, 1: 138.

53. Marx, *Capital*, 1: 163.

54. Marx, *Capital*, 1: 163.

55. Marx, *Capital*, 1: 165.

56. Marx, *Capital*, 1: 284–85. Again, this should not be taken to suggest that the labor process is ever *entirely* general; labor processes are always socially determined in some way.

57. Marx, *Capital*, 1: 129.

58. Marx, *Capital*, 1: 131; 283–306. On abstract labor see also: Postone, *Time, Labor, and Social Domination*; Werner Bonefeld, "Abstract Labour: Against Its Nature and on Its Time," *Capital & Class* 34, no. 2 (2010): 257–76; Heinrich, *Introduction*.

59. Marx, *Capital*, 1: 131.

60. Marx, *Capital*, 1: 176.

61. Karl Marx, *A Contribution to the Critique of Political Economy*, in *Marx & Engels Collected Works*, vol. 29 (1859; Lawrence and Wishart, 1987), 270.

62. See also Saito, *Karl Marx's Ecosocialism*, 118; Sebastiano Timpanaro, *On Materialism*, trans. Lawrence Garner (New Left Books, 1975); Schmidt, *Concept of Nature in Marx*. On use value: Bolívar Echeverría, "'Use-Value': Ontology and Semiotics," *Radical Philosophy*, no. 188 (2014): 24–38. For a non-Marxist critique along these lines: Jane Bennett, *Vibrant Matter: A Political Ecology of Things* (Duke University Press, 2010).

63. Marx, *Capital*, 1: 165; italics mine.

64. Moore, *Capitalism in the Web of Life*; Andreas Malm, *Fossil Capital: The Rise of Steam Power and the Roots of Global Warming* (Verso, 2016).

65. On humanism, see Louis Althusser, *For Marx*, trans. Ben Brewster (1965; Verso, 2005). On anthropocentrism: Ted Benton, "Humanism = Speciesism: Marx on Humans and Animals," *Radical Philosophy*, no. 50 (1988): 4–18. See also Judith Butler, "The Inorganic Body in the Early Marx: A Limit-Concept of Anthropocentrism," *Radical Philosophy*, no. 206 (2019): 3–17.

66. Marx, *Capital*, 1: 284.

67. Marx, *Capital*, 1: 284.

68. On the objectifying will: G.W.F. Hegel, *Elements of the Philosophy of Right*, trans. H. B. Nisbet (1820; Cambridge University Press, 1991), §41–64. For Marx's account of labor and "species being": Karl Marx, *Economic and Philosophic Manuscripts of 1844*, "Estranged Labour," in *Marx & Engels Collected Works*, trans. Martin Milligan and Dirk J. Struik, vol. 3 (Lawrence and Wishart, 1975), 270–282. For commentary: Nichols, *Theft Is Property!*, 75.

69. Louis Althusser would dismiss this attention to the qualities of human beings as idealist mysticism irrelevant to the "scientific" analysis of capitalism: Althusser, *For Marx*; Althusser, *The Humanist Controversy and Other Writings*, trans. G. M. Goshgarian, ed. François Matheron (Verso, 2003). For critiques of Marx's anthropocentrism: Timothy Ingold, "The Architect and the Bee: Reflections on the Work of Animals and Men," *Man* 18, no. 1 (1983): 1–20; Maan Barua, "Animating Capital: Work, Commodities, Circulation," *Progress in Human Geography* 43, no. 4 (2019): 650–69; Benton, "Humanism = Speciesism." See also Butler, "Inorganic Body." For the critique of Marx's Eurocentric view of "production": Descola, *Beyond Nature and Culture*.

70. See Benton, "Humanism = Speciesism." On nonhuman consciousness: Peter Godfrey-Smith, *Other Minds: The Octopus, the Sea, and the Deep Origins of Consciousness* (Farrar, Straus

and Giroux, 2016); Robert Lurz, ed., *The Philosophy of Animal Minds* (Cambridge University Press, 2012); Frans de Waal, *Are We Smart Enough to Know How Smart Animals Are?* (W. W. Norton, 2016).

71. See, e.g., Matt Huber, "Value, Nature, and Labor: A Defense of Marx," *Capitalism, Nature, Socialism* 28, no. 1 (2017): 39–52.

72. Postone, *Time, Labor, and Social Domination*, 312; see also Harry Braverman, *Labor and Monopoly Capital: The Degradation of Work in the Twentieth Century* (1974: Monthly Review, 1998).

73. Notably: Braverman, *Labor and Monopoly Capital*; Sohn-Rethel, *Intellectual and Manual Labour*.

74. Marx, *Capital*, 1: 292.

75. Marx, *Capital*, 1: 134.

76. Marx, *Capital*, 1: 135; italics mine.

77. For the physiological interpretation: Axel Kicillof and Guido Starosta, "On Materiality and Social Form: A Political Critique of Rubin's Value-Form Theory," *Historical Materialism* 15, no. 3 (2007): 9–43. For a critique and broader discussion of the concept of abstract labor: Bonefeld, "Abstract Labour"; see also Rubin, *Marx's Theory of Value*.

78. Marx, *Capital*, 1: 128; italics mine. On the term Marx uses to describe congealed labor in German—*Gallerte*, denoting a blob of gelatin—see Paul Reitter's note on translation in Princeton edition of *Capital* (796n.ix).

79. For a rich discussion of Marx's use of physiological language: Ngai, *Theory of the Gimmick*, 174–95.

80. On an "energy theory of value": e.g., Robert Costanza, "Embodied Energy and Economic Valuation," *Science* 210, no. 4475 (1980): 1219–24. See also Herman Daly and Alvaro Umaña, eds., *Energy, Economics, and the Environment* (Westview, 1981); Philip Mirowski, "Energy and Energetics in Economic Theory: A Review Essay," *Journal of Economic Issues* 22, no. 3 (1988): 811–30. On nonhuman value more generally: Giorgos Kallis and Erik Swyngedouw, "Do Bees Produce Value? A Conversation between an Ecological Economist and a Marxist Geographer," *Capitalism Nature Socialism* 29, no. 3 (2018): 36–50.

81. Braverman, *Labor and Monopoly Capital*, 50–51.

82. Mau, *Mute Compulsion*, 93–7. See also Joseph Fracchia, "Beyond the Human-Nature Debate: Human Corporeal Organization as the First Fact of Historical Materialism," *Historical Materialism* 13, no. 1 (2005), 39.

83. Mau, *Mute Compulsion*, 95, 114–19. For a similar argument: Malm, *Progress of This Storm*.

84. Marx, *Capital*, 1: 273.

85. Braverman, *Labor and Monopoly Capital*, 37.

86. Soper, *What Is Nature?*, 126.

87. Diane Elson similarly emphasizes the "indeterminateness of human labor": Elson, *Value*, 128.

88. Andrés Saenz de Sicilia, "Subsumption," in *SAGE Handbook of Marxism*, vol. 1, ed. Beverley Skeggs, Sara R. Farris, Alberto Toscano, and Svenja Bromberg (SAGE, 2021), 617.

89. Braverman, *Labor and Monopoly Capital*, 39.

90. See Benton, "Humanism = Speciesism."

91. Marx, *Capital*, 1: 270. I examine the reproduction of labor power, which Marx argues sets its value, in chapter 5 in particular.

92. It is common to encounter circuitous statements to the effect that human labor is special because it is human: as, for example, Harry Braverman's statement that labor power is "a special category, separate and inexchangeable with any other, simply because it is human" (*Labor and Monopoly Capital*, 51).

93. Marx, *Capital*, 1: 270.

94. The recognition that capitalism has sometimes coexisted with slavery, and even possible *necessity* of slavery for early accumulation, does not undermine the fact that capitalism generally and primarily relies on wage labor; it certainly does not undermine the key point that enslaved human beings *could* have been paid a wage, whereas the nonhuman animals to which enslaved humans were often compared could not. In other words, this argument does not depend on the resolution of the ongoing debate about the relationship of capitalism to slavery. For key works in this substantial literature: Eric Williams, *Capitalism & Slavery* (1944; University of North Carolina Press, 2021); Walter Johnson, *Soul by Soul: Life Inside the Antebellum Slave Market* (Harvard University Press, 1999); Stephanie E. Smallwood, *Saltwater Slavery: A Middle Passage from Africa to American Diaspora* (Harvard University Press, 2007); John Clegg, "A Theory of Capitalist Slavery," *Journal of Historical Sociology* 33, no. 1 (2020): 74–98. On the figure of "the human" in colonialism and slavery: Sylvia Wynter, "Unsettling the Coloniality of Being/Power/Truth/Freedom: Towards the Human, after Man, Its Overrepresentation—an Argument," *CR: The New Centennial Review* 3, no. 3 (2003): 257–337.

95. Thanks to Andreas Folkers for emphasizing this point.

96. Cf. Elson, *Value*. There are, of course, exceptions, most of them politically constituted: welfare programs, cash transfers, gifts and bequests, and so on.

97. E. P. Thompson, "Time, Work-Discipline, and Industrial Capitalism," *Past & Present* 38, no. 1 (1967): 61.

98. "If a lion could talk, we wouldn't be able to understand it": Ludwig Wittgenstein, *Philosophical Investigations*, trans. G.E.M. Anscombe, P.M.S. Hacker, and Joachim Schulte (1953; Wiley Blackwell, 2010), 235. For a discussion: Cary Wolfe, *Animal Rites: American Culture, the Discourse of Species, and Posthumanist Theory* (University of Chicago Press, 2003), 44–95.

99. I don't mean that general human capacities for abstract thought, symbolic exchange, etc., render those who do not have such capacities—whether as a result of age, ability, or other factors—*not* human, nor that societies or cultures that do not primarily utilize the social form of the wage are "less human." The claim that certain qualities are *distinctively* human does not entail that they are *universally* human.

100. Silvia Federici, *The Patriarchy of the Wage: Notes on Marx, Gender, and Feminism* (PM, 2021). For a similar argument: Angela Davis, "Women and Capitalism: Dialectics of Oppression and Liberation," in *Marxism, Revolution, and Peace*, ed. Howard L. Parsons and John Somerville (B. R. Grülner, 1977), 146–82.

101. See John Dryzek, *Rational Ecology: Environment and Political Economy* (Basil Blackwell, 1987).

102. Thanks to Will Roberts for suggesting this language.

103. Malm, *Fossil Capital*.

104. Elson, *Value*, 174.

105. Karl Marx, *Economic Manuscript of 1861–63*, trans. Emile Burns, in *Marx & Engels Collected Works*, vol. 31 (1863; Lawrence and Wishart, 1989), 467–68.

106. Paul Burkett, "Value, Capital and Nature: Some Ecological Implications of Marx's Critique of Political Economy," *Science & Society* 60, no. 3 (1996): 332–59. For other recent analyses of rent: Romain Felli, "On Climate Rent," *Historical Materialism* 22, no. 3–4 (2014): 251–80; Brett Christophers, *Rentier Capitalism: Who Owns the Economy, and Who Pays for It?* (Verso, 2020); Kallis and Swyngedouw, "Do Bees Produce Value?"; Diego Andreucci, Melissa García-Lamarca, Jonah Wedekind, and Erik Swyngedouw, "'Value Grabbing': A Political Ecology of Rent," *Capitalism Nature Socialism* 28, no. 3 (2017): 28–47.

107. Donna J. Haraway, *Simians, Cyborgs, and Women: The Reinvention of Nature* (Routledge, 1991).

108. See Marx, *Capital*, 1: 932. See also for discussions of reification: Georg Lukács, *History and Class Consciousness: Studies in Marxist Dialectics*, trans. Rodney Livingston (MIT Press,

1967); Andreas Folkers, "Staying with the Rubble: Residual Reification and Reparative Critique" (unpublished manuscript, 2024).

109. Sartre, *Critique of Dialectical Reason*, 71.

110. Sartre, *Critique of Dialectical Reason*, 122–252.

111. On the nonidentity of nature: Theodor Adorno, *Negative Dialectics*, trans. E. B. Ashton (Continuum, 1973).

112. Fredric Jameson, foreword to Sartre, *Critique of Dialectical Reason*, xxiii.

113. Bennett, *Vibrant Matter*; Bruno Latour, *We Have Never Been Modern*, trans. Catherine Porter (Harvard University Press, 1993).

114. Cf. the discussion of "actants" in Bruno Latour's *Reassembling the Social*.

115. For a bravura analysis of this phenomenon: Folkers, "Staying with the Rubble."

116. Cf. Malm, *Fossil Capital*, 197; Carolyn Merchant, *Autonomous Nature: Problems of Prediction and Control from Ancient Times to the Scientific Revolution* (Routledge, 2016), 161; Silvia Federici, *Re-enchanting the World: Feminism and the Politics of the Commons* (PM, 2018), 190; Federici, *Beyond the Periphery of the Skin: Rethinking, Remaking, and Reclaiming the Body in Contemporary Capitalism* (PM, 2019). For an important critique of these tendencies in feminist thought: Lena Gunarsson, "The Naturalistic Turn in Feminist Theory: A Marxist-Realist Contribution," *Feminist Theory* 14, no. 1 (2013): 3–19.

117. Cf. Dryzek, *Rational Ecology*.

118. Moore, *Capitalism in the Web of Life*, 205; Anna Lowenhaupt Tsing, *The Mushroom at the End of the World: On the Possibility of Life in Capitalist Ruins* (Princeton University Press, 2015).

119. Nigel Clark, *Inhuman Nature: Sociable Life on a Dynamic Planet* (SAGE, 2011).

120. For an account of such aporia as constituting alternatives to capitalism: J. K. Gibson-Graham, *The End of Capitalism (as We Knew It): A Feminist Critique of Political Economy* (University of Minnesota Press, 2006).

121. Cf. Simone de Beauvoir, *The Ethics of Ambiguity*, trans. Bernard Frechtman (1947; Open Road, 2018). For related thoughts on the politics of ecology and meaning: Geoff Mann, "Should Political Ecology Be Marxist? A Case for Gramsci's Historical Materialism," *Geoforum* 40 (2009): 335–44.

Chapter 2

1. Rahel Jaeggi, "What (if Anything) Is Wrong with Capitalism? Dysfunctionality, Exploitation and Alienation: Three Approaches to the Critique of Capitalism," *Southern Journal of Philosophy* 54, no. S1 (2016): 44–65; Norman Geras, "The Controversy about Marx and Justice," *New Left Review* I/150 (1985): 47–85; Vanessa Christina Wills, *Marx's Ethical Vision* (Oxford University Press, 2024); G. A. Cohen, *On the Currency of Egalitarian Justice, and Other Essays in Political Philosophy*, ed. Michael Otsuka (Princeton University Press, 2011).

2. John Bellamy Foster, *Marx's Ecology: Materialism and Nature* (Monthly Review, 2000); Foster, Richard York, and Brett Clark, *The Ecological Rift: Capitalism's War on the Earth* (Monthly Review, 2010); Kohei Saito, *Karl Marx's Ecosocialism: Capital, Nature, and the Unfinished Critique of Political Economy* (Monthly Review, 2017); Kohei Saito, *Marx in the Anthropocene: Towards the Idea of Degrowth Communism* (Cambridge University Press, 2023).

3. Max Horkheimer and Theodor W. Adorno, *Dialectic of Enlightenment*, ed. Gunzelin Schmid Noerr, trans. Edmund Jephcott (Stanford University Press, 2002); Herbert Marcuse, "Ecology and Revolution," in *Collected Papers of Herbert Marcuse*, vol. 3, *The New Left and the 1960s*, ed. Douglas Kellner (1972; Routledge, 2005), 173–76; Alfred Schmidt, *The Concept of Nature in Marx*, trans. Ben Fowkes (1962; Verso Books, 2014); Marcuse, *One-Dimensional Man: Studies in the Ideology of Advanced Industrial Society* (Routledge and Kegan Paul, 1964); William Leiss, *The Domination of Nature* (George Braziller, 1972).

4. Rob Nixon, *Slow Violence and the Environmentalism of the Poor* (Harvard University Press, 2011); Steve Vanderheiden, *Atmospheric Justice: A Political Theory of Climate Change* (Oxford University Press, 2008); Stephen M. Gardiner, *A Perfect Moral Storm: The Ethical Tragedy of Climate Change* (Oxford University Press, 2011); Henry Shue, *Climate Justice: Vulnerability and Protection* (Oxford University Press, 2014); David N. Pellow and Robert J. Brulle, *Power, Justice, and the Environment: A Critical Appraisal of the Environmental Justice Movement* (MIT Press, 2005).

5. Karl Polanyi, *The Great Transformation: The Political and Economic Origins of Our Time* (1944; Beacon, 2001); James O'Connor, "Capitalism, Nature, Socialism: A Theoretical Introduction," *Capitalism, Nature, Socialism*, 1, no. 1 (1988): 11–38; see also Nancy Fraser, *Cannibal Capitalism: How our System is Devouring Democracy, Care, and the Planet—and What We Can Do about It* (Verso, 2022); Jason Moore, *Capitalism in the Web of Life: Ecology and the Accumulation of Capital* (Verso, 2015).

6. For the classic discussion of capitalism as "progress in the art, not only of robbing the worker, but of robbing the soil": Karl Marx, *Capital: A Critique of Political Economy*, vol. 1, trans. Ben Fowkes (Penguin Books, 1976), 638. See also John Bellamy Foster and Brett Clark, *The Robbery of Nature: Capitalism and the Ecological Rift* (Monthly Review, 2020).

7. For versions of these questions: Crina Archer, Laura Ephraim, and Lida Maxwell, eds., "Introduction: Politics on the Terrain of Second Nature," in *Second Nature: Rethinking the Natural through Politics*, ed. Archer, Ephraim, and Maxwell (Fordham University Press, 2014), 1–25; Jane Bennett and William Chaloupka, eds., "Introduction: TV Dinners and the Organic Brunch," in *In the Nature of Things: Language, Politics, and the Environment*, ed. Bennett and Chaloupka (University of Minnesota Press, 1993), vii–xvi; Kate Soper, *What Is Nature? Culture, Politics, and the Non-human* (Blackwell, 1995); Steven Vogel, *Against Nature: The Concept of Nature in Critical Theory* (State University of New York Press, 1996); Vogel, *Thinking like a Mall: Environmental Philosophy after the End of Nature* (MIT Press, 2015).

8. On the "silence of nature" and the authoritarianism lurking in the claim to "speak for nature": Vogel, *Thinking like a Mall*; Bruno Latour, *The Politics of Nature: How to Bring the Sciences into Democracy*, trans. Catherine Porter (Harvard University Press, 2004).

9. For an important existentialist critique of capitalist unfreedom rooted in a synthesis of Marx, Hegel, and Kierkegaard (although curiously not addressing Sartre or Beauvoir), see Martin Hägglund's *This Life: Secular Faith and Spiritual Freedom* (Pantheon, 2019).

10. Jean-Paul Sartre, *Being and Nothingness: An Essay in Phenomenological Ontology*, trans. Sarah Richmond (1943; Washington Square, 2018), 78; Sartre, *Existentialism Is a Humanism*, trans. Carolyn Macomber (1946; Yale University Press, 2007); Simone de Beauvoir, *The Ethics of Ambiguity*, trans. Bernard Frechtman (1947; Open Road, 2018); Beauvoir, *Philosophical Writings*, ed. Margaret A. Simons (University of Illinois Press, 2004). See also Fredric Jameson, foreword to *Critique of Dialectical Reason* by Sartre, ed. Jonathan Rée, trans. Alan Sheridan-Smith, vol. 1 (Verso, 2004), xiii–xxxiii; Jameson, *Marxism and Form: Twentieth-Century Dialectical Theories of Literature* (Princeton, 1971); David Detmer, *Freedom as a Value: A Critique of the Ethical Theory of Jean-Paul Sartre* (Open Court, 1986); István Mészáros, *The Work of Sartre: Search for Freedom and the Challenge of History* (Monthly Review, 2012); Sonia Kruks, *Simone de Beauvoir and the Politics of Ambiguity* (Oxford University Press, 2012); Mark Poster, *Existential Marxism in Postwar France: From Sartre to Althusser* (Princeton University Press, 1975).

11. Elisabeth Anker, *Ugly Freedoms* (Duke University Press, 2022).

12. For discussion: Debra Satz, *Why Some Things Should Not Be for Sale: The Moral Limits of Markets* (Oxford University Press, 2010); Amartya Sen, *Development as Freedom* (Oxford University Press, 1999).

13. Robert Dahl, *Who Governs? Democracy and Power in an American City* (Yale University Press, 1961). For cogent analyses of rule see also: Melissa Lane, *Of Rule and Office: Plato's Ideas*

of the Political (Princeton University Press, 2023); Patchen Markell, "The Rule of the People: Arendt, Archê, and Democracy," *American Political Science Review* 100, no. 1 (2006): 1–14.

14. For a few works in a rapidly growing field: Alex Gourevitch, *From Slavery to the Cooperative Commonwealth: Labor and Republican Liberty in the Nineteenth Century* (Cambridge University Press, 2014); Gourevitch, "Labor Republicanism and the Transformation of Work," *Political Theory* 41, no. 4 (2013): 591–617; Bruno Leipold, Karma Nabulsi, and Stuart White, eds., *Radical Republicanism: Recovering the Tradition's Popular Heritage* (Oxford University Press, 2020); Bruno Leipold, *Citizen Marx: Republicanism and the Formation of Karl Marx's Social and Political Thought* (Princeton University Press, 2024); Gourevitch and Corey Robin, "Freedom Now," *Polity* 52, no. 3 (2020): 384–98; Tom O'Shea, "Socialist Republicanism," *Political Theory* 48, no. 5 (2020): 548–72; O'Shea, "Radical Republicanism and the Future of Work," *Theory & Event* 24 no. 4 (2021): 1050–67; Nicholas Vrousalis, *Exploitation as Domination: What Makes Capitalism Unjust* (Oxford University Press, 2023); Elizabeth Anderson, *Private Government: How Employers Rule Our Lives (and Why We Don't Talk about It)* (Princeton University Press, 2017); Lillian Cicerchia, "Structural Domination in the Labor Market," *European Journal of Political Theory* 21, no 1 (2022): 4–24. For a review and critique of the limits of this literature that accords with my own in key respects: Chiara Cordelli, "What Is the Wrong of Capitalism?" *American Political Science Review* (2025): 1–16. https://doi.org/10.1017/S000305542500005X.

15. For a useful synthesis of "market virtues": Satz, *Why Some Things*. Relatedly: Anderson, *Private Government*; Albert O. Hirschman, *The Passions and the Interests: Arguments for Capitalism before Its Triumph* (Princeton University Press, 1977).

16. Marx, *Capital*, 1: 280.

17. See Göran Therborn, *What Does the Ruling Class Do When It Rules? State Apparatuses and State Power under Feudalism, Capitalism, and Socialism*, 2nd ed. (Verso, 2008).

18. Nicholas Vrousalis, "Freedom and Republicanism in Roberts' Marx," *Capital & Class* 41, no. 2 (2017): 378–83.

19. Søren Mau, *Mute Compulsion: A Marxist Theory of the Economic Power of Capital* (Verso, 2023); William Clare Roberts, "Class in Theory, Class in Practice," *Crisis and Critique* 10, no. 1 (2023): 249–62. Ellen Meiksins Wood describes the location of authority in investment decisions in terms of the separation between the economic and political: Wood, *Democracy against Capitalism: Renewing Historical Materialism* (Cambridge University Press, 1995).

20. Vrousalis, *Exploitation as Domination*, 1.

21. G. A. Cohen, "The Structure of Proletarian Unfreedom," *Philosophy and Public Affairs* 12, no. 1 (1983): 3–33.

22. Tom O'Shea, "Are Workers Dominated?," *Journal of Ethics and Social Philosophy* 16, no. 1 (2019): 1–24; Anderson, *Private Government*; Michael Burawoy, *The Politics of Production: Factory Regimes under Capitalism and Socialism* (Verso, 1985); R. H. Coase, "The Nature of the Firm," *Economica* 4, no. 16 (1937): 386–405; Benjamin McKean, *Disorienting Neoliberalism: Global Justice and the Outer Limit of Freedom* (Oxford University Press, 2020); Alfred Chandler, *The Visible Hand: The Managerial Revolution in American Business* (Harvard University Press, 1993).

23. For a recent effort to address the power of investment from the vantage point of political theory: Cordelli, "What Is the Wrong of Capitalism?"; Chiara Cordelli, "Socialism as Reconciliation" (unpublished manuscript, 2024).

24. Anderson, *Private Government*.

25. Brett Christophers, *The Price Is Wrong: Why Capitalism Won't Save the Planet* (Verso, 2024).

26. On race, capitalism, and racial capitalism: Stuart Hall, "Race, Articulation, and Societies Structured in Dominance [1980]," in *Essential Essays*, vol. 1, ed. David Morley (Duke University Press, 2018), 195–245; Barbara Jeanne Fields, "Slavery, Race and Ideology in the United States of America," *New Left Review* I/181 (1990): 95–118; Cedric Robinson, *Black Marxism* (University

of North Carolina Press, 1999); W. E. Burghardt Du Bois, *Black Reconstruction in America, 1860–1880* (1935; Free Press, 1998); Destin Jenkins and Justin Leroy, eds., *Histories of Racial Capitalism* (Columbia University Press, 2021). On gender and capitalism: Shulamith Firestone, *The Dialectic of Sex: The Case for Feminist Revolution* (1980; Farrar, Straus, and Giroux, 2003); Zillah R. Eisenstein, ed., *Capitalist Patriarchy and the Case for Socialist Feminism* (Monthly Review, 1979); Michèle Barrett, *Women's Oppression Today* (Verso, 1980); Lise Vogel, *Marxism and the Oppression of Women: Toward a Unitary Theory* (983; Haymarket 2013); Angela Y. Davis, *Women, Race, & Class* (Random House, 1981); Cinzia Arruzza, "Remarks on Gender." *Viewpoint Magazine*, September 2, 2014, https://viewpointmag.com/2014/09/02/remarks-on-gender/.

27. See, e.g., David Wallace-Wells, *The Uninhabitable Earth: Life after Warming* (Tim Duggan Books, 2019), 30.

28. Anker, *Ugly Freedoms*, 151, 159.

29. Tad Skotnicki, *The Sympathetic Consumer: Moral Critique in Capitalist Culture* (Stanford University Press, 2021); Leif Wenar, *Blood Oil: Tyrants, Violence, and the Rules That Run the World* (Oxford University Press, 2017).

30. Wenar, *Blood Oil*.

31. David Estlund, "What's Unjust about Structural Injustice?," *Ethics* 134, no. 3 (2024): 333–59.

32. Louis Althusser, *Lenin and Philosophy and Other Essays*, trans. Ben Brewster (Monthly Review, 2001), 81.

33. Niko Kolodny, "Rule over None I: What Justifies Democracy?" *Philosophy and Public Affairs* 42, no. 3 (2014): 195–229; Niko Kolodny, "Rule over None II: Social Equality and the Justification of Democracy," *Philosophy and Public Affairs* 42, no. 4 (2014): 287–336.

34. Marx, *Capital*, 1: 1051.

35. Drawing on the ancient Greek *"axía"* (αξία), for value.

36. Eric MacGilvray, *Liberal Freedom: Pluralism, Polarization, and Politics* (Cambridge University Press, 2022), 118.

37. Bernard Mandeville, *The Fable of The Bees; or, Private Vices, Publick Benefits* (1714 Liberty Fund, 1988); Adam Smith, *An Inquiry into the Nature and Causes of the Wealth of Nations*, ed. R. H. Campbell and A. S. Skinner (Oxford University Press, 1976). On the "invisible hand": Emma Rothschild, *Economic Sentiments: Adam Smith, Condorcet, and the Enlightenment* (Harvard University Press, 2002); Hirschman, *Passions and the Interests*; Daniel Luban, "What Is Spontaneous Order?," *American Political Science Review* 114, no. 1 (2020): 68–80; Steven G. Medema, *The Hesitant Hand: Taming Self-Interest in the History of Economic Ideas* (Princeton University Press, 2009).

38. See Friedrich A. Hayek, *The Road to Serfdom* (1944; Routledge Classics, 2001); Hayek, *The Constitution of Liberty* (University of Chicago Press, 1960); Milton Friedman, *Capitalism and Freedom* (University of Chicago Press, 1960); Milton Friedman and Rose Friedman, *Free to Choose: A Personal Statement* (1980; Mariner Books, 1990).

39. Hayek, *Road to Serfdom*, 63.

40. Robert Nozick, *Anarchy, State, and Utopia* (Basic Books, 1974).

41. Luban, "What Is Spontaneous Order?"

42. As most clearly outlined by Friedrich A. Hayek in "The Use of Knowledge in Society" *American Economic Review* 35, no. 4 (1945): 519–30.

43. Hayek, *Constitution of Liberty*, 143.

44. Hayek, *Constitution of Liberty*, 139. As MacGilvray observes, this contradicts Hayek's argument that we *can't* know what the market will do: when we spend money on education, we can't know what jobs will exist in ten years, whether someone will invent a machine that makes us redundant, etc.

45. On "willingness to pay": Marion Fourcade, "Price and Prejudice: On Economics and the Enchantment (and Disenchantment) of Nature," in *The Worth of Goods*, ed. Jens Beckert and Patrik Aspers (Oxford University Press, 2011), 41–62. On "revealed preferences": D. Wade Hands, "Paul Samuelson and Revealed Preference Theory," *History of Political Economy* 46 (2014): 85–116.

46. Eric MacGilvray, *The Invention of Market Freedom* (Cambridge University Press, 2011).

47. Strikingly, Pettit frequently uses the analogy of "weather" and the "weather eye" to illustrate the effects of domination on interpersonal relations wherein the dominated is constantly attentive to the whims of the dominator—even though he denies that the weather itself can be a source of domination: Philip Pettit, *Republicanism: A Theory of Freedom and Government* (Oxford University Press, 1997); Pettit, "Freedom in the Market," *Politics, Philosophy & Economics* 5, no. 2 (2006): 131–49. For critiques of Pettit's read of the market: Steven Klein, "Fictitious Freedom: A Polanyian Critique of the Republican Revival," *American Journal of Political Science* 61, no. 4 (2017): 852–63; Jan Kandiyali, "Should Socialists be Republicans?," *Critical Review of International Social and Political Philosophy* 27, no. 7 (2024): 1032–49.

48. William Clare Roberts, *Marx's Inferno: A Political Theory of Capital* (Princeton University Press, 2017), 58; William Clare Roberts, "Reading Capital as Political Theory: On the Political Theory of the Value-Form," in *Marx's Capital after 150 Years: Critique and Alternative to Capitalism*, ed. Marcello Musto (Routledge, 2019), 228.

49. Roberts, *Marx's Inferno*, 85.

50. Sean Irving, *Hayek's Market Republicanism: The Limits of Liberty* (Routledge, 2020).

51. Hayek, *Road to Serfdom*, 210. For another defense of liberty in notably republican terms: Hayek, *Constitution of Liberty*, 57–72.

52. See Daniel Luban, "In Marx's Republic," *Nation*, April 4, 2018, https://www.thenation.com/article/archive/in-marxs-republic/.

53. Moishe Postone, *Time, Labor, and Social Domination: A Reinterpretation of Marx's Critical Theory* (Cambridge University Press, 1993), 30. For related accounts of domination: Michael Heinrich, *An Introduction to the Three Volumes of Karl Marx's Capital*, trans. Alex Locascio (Monthly Review, 2012); Mau, *Mute Compulsion*; Hägglund, *This Life*.

54. C.f. Postone, *Time, Labor, and Social Domination*, 182.

55. Hayek, *Road to Serfdom*, 217.

56. Hayek, *Constitution of Liberty*, 134; echoed in Hayek, *Road to Serfdom*. See discussion by MacGilvray in *Invention of Market Freedom* and by Gourevitch and Robin in "Freedom Now."

57. Sartre, *Being and Nothingness*, 78; see also Sartre, *Existentialism Is a Humanism*.

58. Gourevitch and Robin, "Freedom Now," 393. Indeed, Gourevitch and Robin's critique of the market echoes mine in certain respects—but rather than staying with market unfreedom and articulating its basis, they pivot to labor domination.

59. Gourevitch and Robin, "Freedom Now," 393, 394.

60. Although Hayek was happy to appeal to traditions to stabilize the social order, justifying these as "grown" or "evolved" social institutions to which people have "voluntarily" conformed: Hayek, *Constitution of Liberty*, 122–23. For a critique of potentially conservative moralism: Nancy Fraser, "A Triple Movement?," *New Left Review*, no. 81 (2013): 119–32; Fraser and Rahel Jaeggi, *Capitalism: A Conversation in Critical Theory* (Polity, 2018); Daniela Dover and Jonathan Gingerich, "Towards an Existentialist Metaethics," in *Analytic Existentialism*, ed. Berislav Marušić and Mark Schroeder (Oxford University Press, 2024), 180–205.

61. Tully Rector, "Market Socialism as a Form of Life," *Review of Social Economy* 79, no. 3 (2021): 581–606.

62. See Jameson, *Marxism and Form*.

63. On the *Critique*: Terry Pinkard, *Practice, Power, and Forms of Life: Sartre's Appropriation of Hegel and Marx* (University of Chicago Press, 2022); Joseph A. Catalano, *A Commentary on Jean-Paul Sartre's "Critique of Dialectical Reason": Volume 1, "Theory of Practical Ensembles"* (University of Chicago, 1986); Jairus Banaji, "Dialectic and History: Work, Alienation, Classes and the State in Sartre's *Critique of Dialectical Reason*" (1978), *Historical Materialism* (blog), July 17, 2021, https://www.historicalmaterialism.org/dialectic-and-history-work-alienation-classes-and-the-state-in-sartres-critique-of-dialectical-reason-1978/; Ronald Aronson, "Revisiting Exis-

tential Marxism," *Sartre Studies International* 25, no. 2 (2019): 92–98. On the structure-agency dilemma in Marxism more generally: Alex Callinicos, *Making History: Agency, Structure, and Change in Social Theory* (Brill, 2004); William Clare Roberts, "The Red Pill: Breaking Out of the Class Matrix," *Radical Philosophy*, no. 213 (2022): 57–65. On the "conferral" of roles: Vrousalis, "Freedom and Republicanism."

64. As Young discusses with respect to gender: Iris Marion Young, "Gender as Seriality: Thinking about Women as a Social Collective," *Signs* 19, no. 3 (1994): 713–38. Seriality is also a significant concept in Young's important account of structural responsibility. Indeed, although Young's analysis has become a touchstone for contemporary work on structural responsibility, including responsibility for climate change, its Sartrean roots—and hence its significance for theorizing not only justice but *freedom*—are rarely acknowledged. Iris Marion Young, *Responsibility for Justice* (Oxford University Press, 2011).

65. Sartre, *Critique of Dialectical Reason*, 281.

66. Sartre, *Critique of Dialectical Reason*, 282.

67. See Roberts, *Marx's Inferno*, 90.

68. Sartre, *Critique of Dialectical Reason*, 288. See also Søren Mau's claim that the market transmits "not information but compulsory commands": Mau, *Mute Compulsion*, 186.

69. Young, "Gender as Seriality," 726.

70. Thanks to Max Foley-Keene for suggesting this framing. Indeed, although Sartre characterizes seriality as a fundamental tendency of human action in a world of inevitable scarcity, his analysis is better understood as a projection of the conditions of capitalist sociality into those of human life writ large. Michel Foucault's famous dismissal of Sartre's *Critique*—as "the magnificent and pathetic effort of a man of the nineteenth century to think the twentieth"—is remarkably off the mark: to the contrary, the *Critique* is deeply concerned with the forms of collective action at the heart of twentieth-century social thought and practice. Michel Foucault, "L'homme est-il mort? [1966]" in *Dits et écrits*, vol. 1, ed. Daniel Defert, François Ewald, and Jacques Lagrange (Gallimard, 1994), 540–44. For a discussion of Sartre's concept of scarcity: Mészáros, *Work of Sartre*, 298–306; Jameson, *Marxism and Form*.

71. Stuart White, "The Republican Critique of Capitalism," *Critical Review of International Social and Political Philosophy* 14, no. 5 (2011): 561–79.

72. See David Naguib Pellow, *Resisting Global Toxics: Transnational Movements for Environmental Justice* (MIT Press, 2007); Laura Pulido, "Geographies of Race and Ethnicity II: Environmental Racism, Racial Capitalism and State-Sanctioned Violence," *Progress in Human Geography* 41, no. 4 (2017): 524–33. On the "race to the bottom": McKean, *Disorienting Neoliberalism*.

73. Roberts, *Marx's Inferno*, 85.

74. Allan Schnaiberg, *The Environment: From Surplus to Scarcity* (Oxford University Press, 1980); see also Kenneth A. Gould, David N. Pellow, and Allan Schnaiberg, *Treadmill of Production: Injustice and Unsustainability in the Global Economy* (Paradigm, 2008), 7; Barry Commoner, *The Poverty of Power: Energy and the Economic Crisis* (Knopf, 1976); Stephen G. Bunker, "Raw Material and the Global Economy: Oversights and Distortions in Industrial Ecology," *Society & Natural Resources: An International Journal* 9, no. 4 (1996): 419–29; Postone, *Time, Labor, and Social Domination*; Moore, *Capitalism in the Web of Life*.

75. See Young, *Responsibility for Justice*.

76. Jon Elster, *Logic and Society: Contradictions and Possible Worlds* (John Wiley and Sons, 1978), 108; Elster, *Making Sense of Marx* (Cambridge University Press, 1985), 24–26. On unintended consequences more generally: Luban, "What Is Spontaneous Order?"; Richard Vernon, "Unintended Consequences," *Political Theory* 7, no. 1 (1979): 57–73.

77. Sartre, *Critique of Dialectical Reason*; Garrett Hardin, "The Tragedy of the Commons," *Science* 162, no. 3859 (1968): 1243–48; Mancur Olson, *The Logic of Collective Action* (Harvard University Press, 1965); Ulrich Beck, *Risk Society: Towards a New Modernity*, trans. Mark Ritter (SAGE, 1992). See also Richard Tuck, *Free Riding* (Harvard University Press, 2008).

78. Hardin, "Tragedy of the Commons," 1244.

79. Cf. the accounts of tragedy in Martha Nussbaum's *The Fragility of Goodness: Luck and Ethics in Greek Tragedy and Philosophy* (Cambridge University Press, 2001) and David Scott's *Conscripts of Modernity: The Tragedy of Colonial Enlightenment* (Duke University Press, 2004. For historical context, see Rob Nixon, "Neoliberalism, Genre, and 'The Tragedy of the Commons,'" *PMLA* 127, no. 3 (2012): 593–99; Matto Mildenberger, "The Tragedy of the 'Tragedy of the Commons,'" *Scientific American Blog*, April 23, 2019, https://www.scientificamerican.com /blog/voices/the-tragedy-of-the-tragedy-of-the-commons/.

80. Richard Posner and David Weisbach, *Climate Change Justice* (Princeton University Press, 2010). For counterargument: Michaël Aklin and Matto Mildenberger, "Prisoners of the Wrong Dilemma: Why Distributive Conflict, Not Collective Action, Characterizes the Politics of Climate Change," *Global Environmental Politics* 20, no. 4 (2020): 4–27.

81. Elinor Ostrom, *Governing the Commons: The Evolution of Institutions for Collective Action* (Cambridge University Press, 1990); Silvia Federici, *Re-enchanting the World: Feminism and the Politics of the Commons* (PM, 2018).

82. Hardin, "Tragedy of the Commons," 1244.

83. S. Vogel, *Thinking like a Mall*, 202.

84. Jameson, foreword to Sartre, *Critique of Dialectical Reason*; Elster, *Logic and Society*. As Terry Pinkard argues in *Practice, Power, and Forms of Life*, it is not only an *unintended* consequence but also a result brought about by *intentional* action.

85. Sartre, *Critique of Dialectical Reason*, 687, 734; see Jairus Banaji, "Sartre and His *Critique of Dialectical Reason*," *Historical Materialism* (blog), accessed October 20, 2024, https://www .historicalmaterialism.org/figure/sartre-and-his-critique-of-dialectical-reason/.

86. Sartre, *Critique of Dialectical Reason*, 124.

87. Sartre, *Critique of Dialectical Reason*, 163. For the classic empirical study of land use, erosion, and peasantries: Piers Blaikie, *The Political Economy of Soil Erosion in Developing Countries* (Routledge, 1985). Thanks to Geoff Mann for this suggestion.

88. Sartre, *Critique of Dialectical Reason*, 164.

89. Sartre, *Critique of Dialectical Reason*, 163.

90. Sartre, *Critique of Dialectical Reason*, 164.

91. Alberto Toscano, "Antiphysis/Antipraxis: Universal Exhaustion and the Tragedy of Materiality," in *Materialism and the Critique of Energy*, ed. Brent Ryan Bellamy and Jeff Diamanti (MCM', 2018), 488. For a counter-reading: Christopher Turner, "The Return of Stolen Praxis: Counter-Finality in Sartre's *Critique of Dialectical Reason*," *Sartre Studies International* 20, no. 1 (2014): 36–44; see also Robert Boncardo, "Sixty Years of Sartre's Critique: Revisiting *The Critique of Dialectical Reason* Today," *Thesis Eleven* 161, no. 1 (2020): 108–23; Pinkard, *Practice, Power, and Forms of Life*, 33.

92. Judith N. Shklar, *The Faces of Injustice* (Yale University Press, 1990); Pettit, *Republicanism*; Rahel Jaeggi, *Critique of Forms of Life*, trans. Ciaran Cronin (Belknap Press of Harvard University Press, 2018).

93. S. Vogel, *Against Nature*.

94. Cf. S. Vogel, *Thinking like a Mall*; Andreas Folkers, "Fossil Modernity: The Materiality of Acceleration, Slow Violence, and Ecological Futures," *Time & Society* 30, no. 2 (2021): 223–46.

95. After all, the bus is often not just a generic experience of seriality but an expression of class often articulated through race: over 90 percent of Los Angeles bus riders, for example, are people of color.

96. See McKean, *Disorienting Neoliberalism*; Skotnicki, *Sympathetic Consumer*.

97. See Young, *Responsibility for Justice*; McKean, *Disorienting Neoliberalism*.

98. Sartre, *Critique of Dialectical Reason*, 164. See also Young's discussion in *Responsibility for Justice*.

99. Sartre, *Being and Nothingness*, 103.

100. Sartre, *Being and Nothingness*, 104.

101. See D. W. Phillips, "Bad Faith and Sartre's Waiter," *Philosophy* 56, no. 215 (1981): 23–31; Anthony Manser, "Unfair to Waiters?" *Philosophy* 58, no. 223 (1983): 102–6.

102. Sartre, *Critique of Dialectical Reason*, 231.

103. Sartre, *Critique of Dialectical Reason*, 325; see also Jairus Banaji, *Theory as History: Essays on Modes of Production and Exploitation* (Brill, 2010), 152.

104. For an illustration: Barbara Ehrenreich, "Nickel-and-Dimed," *Harper's*, January 1999. On Ehrenreich's "tacit working existentialism": Gabriel Winant, "You Don't Want to Know This? On Barbara Ehrenreich," *n+1* 44 (2022), https://www.nplusonemag.com/issue-44/dead-people-rule/you-dont-want-to-know-this/.

105. Young, *Responsibility for Justice*, 40.

106. Jade Schiff, *Burdens of Political Responsibility: Narrative and the Cultivation of Responsiveness* (Cambridge University Press, 2014); cf. "response-ability" in Donna J. Haraway, *When Species Meet* (University of Minnesota Press, 2007), 86–93.

107. S. Vogel, *Against Nature*.

108. Hägglund, *This Life*.

109. Cf. Hägglund, *This Life*, 22; Sharon Krause, "Bodies in Action: Corporeal Agency and Democratic Politics," *Political Theory* 39, no. 3 (2011): 299–324.

110. S. Vogel, *Against Nature*, 164.

Chapter 3

1. Alain Resnais, *Le chant du styrène*, 35mm (Les Films de la Pléiade, 1958).

2. Victor Hugo, "Ce siècle est grand et fort. Un noble instinct le mène," in *Œuvres complètes de Victor Hugo: Les voix intérieures*, vol. 6 (Eugène Renduel, 1837), 5–6. Author's translation.

3. Pap A. Ndiaye, *Nylon and Bombs: DuPont and the March of Modern America* (Johns Hopkins University Press, 2007), 123.

4. Ernst Friedrich Schumacher, *Small Is Beautiful: Economics as if People Mattered* (Harper and Row, 1973).

5. Classic texts on the labor-environment tension include: Richard White, "'Are You an Environmentalist or Do You Work for a Living?': Work and Nature," in *Uncommon Ground: Rethinking the Human Place in Nature*, ed. William Cronon (W. W. Norton, 1995), 171–85; André Gorz, *Farewell to the Working-Class: An Essay on Post-Industrial Socialism* (Pluto, 1982); Rudolf Bahro, *Socialism and Survival* (Heretic Books, 1982). For more recent reviews of these debates: Matt Huber, *Climate Change as Class War: Building Socialism on a Warming Planet* (Verso, 2022); Stefania Barca, "Labour and the Ecological Crisis: The Eco-modernist Dilemma in Western Marxism(s) (1970s–2000s)," *Geoforum* 98 (2019): 226–35; Barca, *Workers of the Earth: Labour, Ecology and Reproduction in the Age of Climate Change* (Pluto, 2024); Chad Montrie, *Making a Living: Work and Environment in the United States* (University of North Carolina Press, 2008).

6. For discussion of "new social movements": Ernesto Laclau and Chantal Mouffe, *Hegemony and Socialist Strategy: Towards a Radical Democratic Politics*, trans. Paul Cammack and Winston Moore (Verso, 1985); Jürgen Habermas, "The Movement in Germany: A Critical Analysis," chap. 3 in *Toward a Rational Society: Student Protest, Science, and Politics* (Beacon, 1970); Steven M. Buechler, *Social Movements in Advanced Capitalism: The Political Economy and Cultural Construction of Social Activism* (Oxford University Press, 1999); Nancy Fraser, "From Redistribution to Recognition? Dilemmas of Justice in a 'Post-Socialist' Age," *New Left Review* I/212 (1995): 68–93. For a review of the literature: Nelson A. Pichardo, "New Social Movements: A Critical Review," *Annual Review of Sociology* 23 (1997): 411–30.

7. Nicholas Vrousalis, *Exploitation as Domination: What Makes Capitalism Unjust* (Oxford University Press, 2023), 129.

8. On the bracketing of production: Nancy Fraser and Rahel Jaeggi, *Capitalism: A Conversation in Critical Theory* (Polity, 2018), 4–9. On the distributive justice tradition: Katrina Forrester, *In the Shadow of Justice: Postwar Liberalism and the Remaking of Political Philosophy* (Princeton University Press, 2019).

9. On "socio-neutral: G. A. Cohen, *Karl Marx's Theory of History: A Defence* (1978; Princeton University Press, 2000), 94. John Rawls, too, famously proclaimed agnosticism between capitalism and socialism: Rawls, *A Theory of Justice*, rev. ed. (1971; Harvard University Press, 1999).

10. For an older tradition theorizing democracy and work: Carole Pateman, *Participation and Democratic Theory* (Cambridge University Press, 1970); Joshua Cohen, "The Economic Basis of Deliberative Democracy," *Social Philosophy and Policy* 6, no. 2 (1989): 25–50. For a Rawlsian approach to "justice in production": Nien-Hê Hsieh, "Survey Article: Justice in Production," *Journal of Political Philosophy* 16, no. 1 (2008): 72–100. For neorepublican accounts: Alex Gourevitch, "Labor Republicanism and the Transformation of Work," *Political Theory* 41, no. 4 (2013): 591–617; Gourevitch and Corey Robin, "Freedom Now," *Polity* 52, no. 3 (2020): 384–98. For recent liberal-democratic critiques of the workplace: Elizabeth Anderson, *Private Government: How Employers Rule Our Lives (and Why We Don't Talk about It)* (Princeton University Press, 2017); Hélène Landemore and Isabelle Ferreras, "In Defense of Workplace Democracy: Towards a Justification of the Firm–State Analogy," *Political Theory* 44, no. 1 (2016): 53–81. For an overview of recent theories of work: Steven Klein, "Life beyond Work: On the Political Theory of Capitalism," *Political Theory* 51, no. 1 (2023): 271–78.

11. E. P. Thompson, "Time, Work-Discipline, and Industrial Capitalism," *Past & Present* 38, no. 1 (1967): 56–97; Harry Braverman, *Labor and Monopoly Capital: The Degradation of Work in the Twentieth Century* (1974: Monthly Review, 1998); Moishe Postone, *Time, Labor, and Social Domination: A Reinterpretation of Marx's Critical Theory* (Cambridge University Press, 1993); see also David F. Noble, *Forces of Production: A Social History of Industrial Automation* (Knopf, 1984); Donald MacKenzie, "Marx and the Machine," *Technology and Culture* 25, no. 3 (1984): 473–502.

12. For important work on subsumption: Massimiliano Tomba, *Marx's Temporalities* (Brill, 2012); Andrés Saenz de Sicilia, "Subsumption," in *SAGE Handbook of Marxism*, ed. Beverley Skeggs, Sara R. Farris, Alberto Toscano, and Svenja Bromberg (SAGE, 2021); Raju J. Das, "Reconceptualizing Capitalism: Forms of Subsumption of Labor, Class Struggle, and Uneven Development," *Review of Radical Political Economics* 44, no. 2 (2012): 178–200.

13. For "nature-based" industries: William Boyd, W. Scott Prudham, and Rachel A. Schurman, "Industrial Dynamics and the Problem of Nature," *Society & Natural Resources* 14, no. 7 (2001): 555–70.

14. Walt Whitman Rostow, *The Stages of Economic Growth: A Non-communist Manifesto* (Cambridge University Press, 1960); Theodore W. Schultz, *Transforming Traditional Agriculture* (Yale University Press, 1964); James C. Scott, *The Moral Economy of the Peasant: Rebellion and Subsistence in Southeast Asia* (Yale University Press, 1976); Samuel L. Popkin, *The Rational Peasant: The Political Economy of Rural Society in Vietnam* (University of California Press, 1979); Eric R. Wolf, *Peasant Wars of the Twentieth Century* (Harper and Row 1969); Wolf, *Peasants* (Prentice-Hall, 1966); Clifford Geertz, "Studies in Peasant Life: Community and Society," *Biennial Review of Anthropology* 2 (1961): 1–41; W. E. Burghardt Du Bois, *Black Reconstruction in America, 1860–1880* (1935; Free Press, 1998).

15. Anna Lowenhaupt Tsing, *The Mushroom at the End of the World: On the Possibility of Life in Capitalist Ruins* (Princeton University Press, 2015); Tsing, "Sorting Out Commodities: How Capitalist Value Is Made Through Gifts," *HAU: Journal of Ethnographic Theory* 3, no. 1 (2013): 21–43.

16. Tsing, *Mushroom*, 65; see also J. K. Gibson-Graham, *The End of Capitalism (as We Knew It): A Feminist Critique of Political Economy* (University of Minnesota Press, 2006).

17. John M. Brewster, "The Machine Process in Agriculture and Industry," *Journal of Farm Economics* 32, no. 1 (1950): 80–81. The farmer is particularly significant in the work of the Chicago

School economist Theodore Schultz: Theodore W. Schultz, *Agriculture in an Unstable Economy* (McGraw-Hill, 1945); Schultz, "Investment in Human Capital," *American Economic Review* 51, no. 1 (1961): 1–17. On the figure of rural producers in the Sagebrush Rebellion: John Hultgren, *The Smoke and the Spoils: Anti-Environmentalism and Class Struggle in the United States* (MIT Press, 2025); Jedediah Purdy, *After Nature: A Politics for the Anthropocene* (Harvard University Press, 2016). Thanks to Gautham Shiralagi for suggesting this angle.

18. Cf. Thomas Jefferson, *Notes on the State of Virginia* (John Stockdale, 1787). On yeomen: Barbara Jeanne Fields, "Slavery, Race, and Ideology in the United States of America," *New Left Review* I/181 (1990): 95–118.

19. Cowboys, meanwhile, were rural proletarians: exploited and underpaid seasonal workers. Mark Lause, *The Great Cowboy Strike: Bullets, Ballots & Class Conflicts in the American West* (Verso, 2018).

20. Echoing Andrew Liu's reorientation of the study of Chinese and Indian tea production: Andrew B. Liu, *Tea War: A History of Capitalism in China and India* (Yale University Press, 2020), 275; see also W. Scott Prudham, *Knock on Wood: Nature as Commodity in Douglas-Fir Country* (Routledge, 2012).

21. Within legal scholarship, such phenomena are primarily considered as a matter of neo-Brandeisian antimonopoly; as I show here, these relationships must be situated within broader patterns of capitalist power and domination. For relevant legal scholarship: Lina M. Khan, "Amazon's Antitrust Paradox," *Yale Law Journal* 126 (2017): 710–805; Sanjukta Paul, "Methodological and Normative Elements of the New Antitrust," *Journal of Antitrust Enforcement*, 11, no. 2 (2023): 253–58.

22. David S. Landes, *The Unbound Prometheus: Technological Change and Industrial Development in Western Europe from 1750 to the Present*, 2nd ed. (1969; Cambridge University Press, 2003), 21.

23. Emmanuel-Joseph Sieyès, "What Is the Third Estate?," in *Political Writings*, ed. Michael Sonenscher (1789; Hackett, 2003), 94.

24. Jean-Baptiste Say, *A Treatise on Political Economy, or The Production, Distribution and Consumption of Wealth* (1803; 4th ed., 1819), trans. C. R. Prinsep (Claxton, Remsen and Haffelfinger, 1880; repr. Augustus M. Kelley, 1971), 86.

25. David Ricardo, *On the Principles of Political Economy and Taxation*, in *The Works and Correspondence of David Ricardo*, vol. 1, ed. Piero Sraffa (Cambridge University Press, 1951; Liberty Fund, 2004), 76n; emphasis added.

26. Carolyn Merchant, *The Death of Nature: Women, Ecology, and the Scientific Revolution* (1980; HarperOne, 2020); Vandana Shiva, "Reductionism and Regeneration: A Crisis in Science," in *Ecofeminism*, by Maria Mies and Shiva, 2nd ed. (Zed Books, 2014), 22–25.

27. For critiques of Marx as a Promethean: Troy Vettese and Drew Pendergrass, *Half-Earth Socialism: A Plan to Save the Future from Extinction, Climate Change and Pandemics* (Verso, 2022), 34; Ted Benton, "Marxism and Natural Limits: An Ecological Critique and Reconstruction," *New Left Review* I/178 (1989): 51–86. For a clarifying account of this discourse: Kate Soper, "Greening Prometheus: Marxism and Ecology," in *The Greening of Marxism*, ed. Benton (Guilford, 1996), 81–102.

28. Karl Marx and Friedrich Engels, "Manifesto of the Communist Party [1848]," in *Marx & Engels Collected Works*, vol. 6 (Lawrence and Wishart, 1976): 489.

29. Karl Marx, *Capital: A Critique of Political Economy*, vol. 1, trans. Ben Fowkes (Penguin Books, 1976), 508.

30. Marx, *Capital*, 1: 510 mine.

31. Marx, *Capital*, 1: 443. Thanks to Will Roberts for pushing me to develop this argument more clearly.

32. Marx, *Capital*, 1: 508.

33. Marx, *Capital*, 1: 447; see also Postone, *Time, Labor, and Social Domination*, 327–28.

34. Marx, *Capital*, 1: 451.

35. Marx, *Capital*, 1: 549–50.

36. Marx, *Capital*, 1: 477.

37. Michael Burawoy, *The Politics of Production: Factory Regimes under Capitalism and Socialism* (Verso, 1985).

38. Saenz de Sicilia, "Subsumption," 618.

39. Tomba, *Marx's Temporalities*; Andrés Saenz de Silicia, "Being, Becoming, Subsumption: The Kantian Roots of a Marxist Problematic," *Radical Philosophy*, no. 212 (2022): 35–47.

40. Marx, *Capital*, 1: 1021.

41. Marx, *Capital*, 1: 1021.

42. See Braverman, *Labor and Monopoly Capital*, 134; MacKenzie, "Marx and the Machine," 487.

43. Marx, *Capital*, 1: 1021.

44. This is also the moment of a crucial shift from absolute to relative surplus value: Marx, *Capital*, 1: 605.

45. Marx, *Capital*, 1: 605.

46. Marx, *Capital*, 1: 605; more broadly, chaps. 13 and 15(e).

47. Postone, *Time, Labor, and Social Domination*, 16. Relatedly: Braverman, *Labor and Monopoly Capital*. For a recent account of the factory as characterized by practices aimed at control: Lucas Pinheiro, "Protocols of Production: The Absent Factories of Digital Capitalism," *American Political Science Review* (2024), 1–14, https://doi.org/10.1017/S0003055424000911.

48. This, in turn, accords with dominant analyses in science and technology studies; indeed, many critical analyses of technology originated, in some sense, with Braverman's analysis. See, e.g., Donna J. Haraway, "Monkey Business: Monkeys and Monopoly Capital," *Radical Science Journal* 10 (1980): 107–14. I owe this insight to Simon Torracinta.

49. Anderson, *Private Government*; Burawoy, *Politics of Production*; Gourevitch and Robin, "Freedom Now"; Alex Gourevitch, "Labor and Republican Liberty," *Constellations* 18, no. 3 (2011): 431–54; Iñigo González-Ricoy, "The Republican Case for Workplace Democracy," *Social Theory and Practice* 40, no. 2 (2014): 232–54.

50. Braverman, *Labor and Monopoly Capital*, 134. Relatedly: Jean-Paul Sartre, *Critique of Dialectical Reason*, ed. Jonathan Rée, trans. Alan Sheridan-Smith, vol. 1 (Verso, 2004), 187, 207. On the automation of managerial labor: Jason E. Smith, *Smart Machines and Service Work: Automation in an Age of Stagnation* (Reaktion, 2020); see also Gavin Mueller, *Breaking Things at Work: The Luddites Are Right about Why You Hate Your Job* (Verso, 2021).

51. Sartre, *Critique of Dialectical Reason*, 789; MacKenzie, "Marx and the Machine," 596. On "machine fetishism": Andreas Malm, *Fossil Capital: The Rise of Steam Power and the Roots of Global Warming* (Verso 2016), 200–202; Alf Hornborg, *The Power of the Machine: Global Inequalities of Economy, Technology, and Environment* (AltaMira, 2001).

52. Paramount Plus, "*I Love Lucy*/ Lucy and Ethel at the Chocolate Factory (S2, E1)" (1952), YouTube, August 30, 2022, https://www.youtube.com/watch?v=AnHiAWlrYQc.

53. Marx, *Capital*, 1: 545.

54. William Stanley Jevons, *The Coal Question: An Inquiry concerning the Progress of the Nation, and the Probable Exhaustion of Our Coal-Mines* (Macmillan, 1865), 122. Marx almost perfectly echoes Jevons on this point: "The most essential condition for the production of machines by machines was a prime mover capable of exerting any amount of force, while retaining perfect control" (*Capital*, 1: 506).

55. Jevons, *Coal Question*, 150–151.

56. Jevons, *Coal Question*, 143–144.

57. Malm, *Fossil Capital*, 313.

58. Malm, *Fossil Capital*, 312; see an echo in Marx: *Capital*, 1: 498.

59. Malm, *Fossil Capital*, 312–313.

60. For a critique of Malm's exclusive focus on energy: Bue Rübner Hansen, "The Kaleido-scope of Catastrophe: On the Clarities and Blind Spots of Andreas Malm," *Viewpoint Magazine*, April 2021, https://viewpointmag.com/2021/04/14/the-kaleidoscope-of-catastrophe-on-the-clarities-and-blind-spots-of-andreas-malm/.

61. Saenz de Sicilia, "Subsumption," 617.

62. Vaclav Smil, *Energy and Civilization: A History* (MIT Press, 2018); Lewis Mumford, *Technics and Civilization* (Harcourt, 1934).

63. Postone, *Time, Labor, and Social Domination*, 186–225; Thompson, "Time," 56–60.

64. Max Horkheimer and Theodor W. Adorno, *Dialectic of Enlightenment*, ed. Gunzelin Schmid Noerr, trans. Edmund Jephcott (1944; Stanford University Press, 2002); Christopher J. Arthur, "The Possessive Spirit of Capital: Subsumption/Inversion/Contradiction," in *Rereading Marx: New Perspectives after the Critical Edition*, ed. Riccardo Bellofiore and Roberto Fineschi (Palgrave Macmillan, 2009), 148–62.

65. Burawoy, *Politics of Production*, 14.

66. Marx, *Capital*, 1: 645. On hybrid subsumption: Das, "Reconceptualizing Capitalism"; Saenz de Sicilia, "Subsumption."

67. Marx, *Capital*, 1: 645.

68. Karl Marx, *Grundrisse*, trans. Martin Nicolaus (1939; Penguin 1973), 510; Jairus Banaji, Theory as History: Essays on Modes of Production and Exploitation (Brill, 2010), 275.

69. Banaji, Theory as History, 308–9; see also Banaji, *A Brief History of Commercial Capitalism* (Haymarket Books, 2020); Vrousalis, *Exploitation as Domination*; Nicholas Vrousalis, "Capital without Wage-Labour: Marx's Modes of Subsumption Revisited," *Economics & Philosophy* 34, no. 3 (2018): 411–38.

70. Marx, *Capital*, 1: 645; see also Tomba, *Marx's Temporalities*, 149; Saenz de Sicilia, "Subsumption," 622.

71. Das, "Reconceptualizing Capitalism"; Neil Smith, *Uneven Development: Nature, Capital, and the Production of Space*, 3rd ed. (University of Georgia Press, 2008); Nelson Lichtenstein, "The Return of Merchant Capitalism," *International Labor and Working-Class History* 81 (2012): 8–27.

72. Henry Bernstein, *Class Dynamics of Agrarian Change* (Kumarian, 2010), 89–100.

73. Hansen, "Kaleidoscope of Catastrophe."

74. Say, *Treatise on Political Economy*, 86n. The term *automatic* itself originally described the animate processes of living things, like the pumping of blood. See J. Smith, *Smart Machines and Service Work*, 21.

75. See, e.g., Erich W. Zimmermann, *World Resources and Industries* (Harper, 1951), 116; Deborah Kay Fitzgerald, *Every Farm a Factory: The Industrial Ideal in American Agriculture* (Yale University Press, 2003), 109; Gabriel Winant, "'Green Pastures of Plenty from Dry Desert Ground': Nature, Labor, and the Growth and Structure of a California Grape Company," *Enterprise & Society* 16, no. 1 (2015): 109–40.

76. David Goodman, Bernardo Sorj, and John Wilkinson, *From Farming to Biotechnology: A Theory of Agro-industrial Development* (Basil Blackwell, 1987), 21; Susan Archer Mann, *Agrarian Capitalism in Theory and Practice* (University of North Carolina Press, 2017), 38.

77. Susan A. Mann and James M. Dickinson, "Obstacles to the Development of a Capitalist Agriculture," *Journal of Peasant Studies* 5, no. 4 (1978): 466–81; Geoff Mann, *Our Daily Bread: Wages, Workers, and the Political Economy of the American West* (University of North Carolina Press, 2012).

78. Henry Bernstein, "Agriculture/Industry, Rural/Urban, Peasants/Workers: Some Reflections on Poverty, Persistence, and Change," in *Peasant Persistence and Poverty in the Twenty-First Century*, ed. Julio Boltvinik and Susan Archer Mann (Zed Books, 2016), 171–205.

79. Cf. Stephen Bunker, "Staples, Links, and Poles in the Construction of Regional Development Theory," *Sociological Forum* 4, no. 4 (1989): 589–610.

80. Postone, *Time, Labor, and Social Domination*, 202.

81. Karl Marx, *Capital: A Critique of Political Economy*, vol. 2, trans. David Fernbach (1885; Penguin Books, 1993).

82. S. Mann and Dickinson, "Obstacles." Building on Marx's comment: "The nonidentity of production time with labour time can be due generally only to natural conditions" (*Grundrisse*, 668); Marx, *Capital*, 2, chaps. 5 and 13. See also discussions of "eco-regulatory" labor in Ted Benton's "Marxism and Natural Limits"; and response in Paul Burkett's *Marx and Nature: A Red and Green Perspective* (St. Martin's, 1999), 33–48.

83. Brewster, "Machine Process in Agriculture and Industry."

84. S. Mann and Dickinson, "Obstacles," 472.

85. Jasper Bernes, "The Belly of the Revolution: Agriculture, Energy, and the Future of Communism," in *Materialism and the Critique of Energy*, ed. Brent Ryan Bellamy and Jeff Diamanti (MCM', 2018), 331–75.

86. Boyd, Prudham, and Schurman, "Industrial Dynamics," 564.

87. Marx describes Robert Bakewell's experiments in breeding cattle: Marx, *Capital*, 2: 314–15; for more on Bakewell: Harriet Ritvo, "Possessing Mother Nature. Genetic Capital in Eighteenth Century Britain," in *Early Modern Conceptions of Property*, ed. John Brewer and Susan Staves (Routledge, 1995), 413–26. On engineering crops: Jack Kloppenburg, *First the Seed: The Political Economy of Plant Biotechnology, 1492–2000* (Cambridge University Press, 1988); Jim Hightower and Agribusiness Accountability Project Task Force on the Land Grant College Complex, *Hard Tomatoes, Hard Times: A Report of the Agribusiness Accountability Project on the Failure of America's Land Grant College Complex* (Schenkman, 1973). On the "standard hog": Alex Blanchette, *Porkopolis: American Animality, Standardized Life, and the Factory Farm* (Duke University Press, 2020). For other studies of capitalism and biotechnology: Donna J. Haraway, *Modest_Witness@Second_Millennium.FemaleMan©_Meets_OncoMouse™: Feminism and Technoscience* (Routledge, 1997); Kenneth Fish, *Living Factories: Biotechnology and the Unique Nature of Capitalism* (McGill-Queen's University Press, 2013).

88. Martha Nussbaum, *Justice for Animals: Our Collective Responsibility* (Simon and Schuster, 2023).

89. Blanchette, *Porkopolis*, 191; Kloppenburg, *First the Seed*.

90. Nicholas Georgescu-Roegen, "Process Analysis and the Neoclassical Theory of Production," *American Journal of Agricultural Economics* 54, no. 2 (1972): 285; see also Zimmermann, *World Resources and Industries*, 113.

91. S. Mann and Dickinson, "Obstacles," 471.

92. S. Mann and Dickinson, "Obstacles," 478. Fully industrialized forms of agriculture, reflecting high levels of productivity, investment of fixed capital, and extensive use of wage labor, have generally taken hold only under specific conditions, most often in settler colonies in which expropriated land, often acquired via the extirpation of Indigenous residents, is paired with a quasi-democratic state empowering (white) settlers. Capitalist transitions in agrarian sectors have also been driven by the planning states of the twentieth century. Even where such transitions have occurred, however, agriculture has retained a distinctive character relative to industry; as Don Mitchell observes of Californian agriculture, "Fordism never quite dawned": Mitchell, "Taylorism Comes to the Fields: Labor Control, Labor Supply, Labor Process, and the Twilight of Fordism in California Agribusiness," *Economic Geography* 99, no. 4 (2023): 359. See also Margaret FitzSimmons, "The New Industrial Agriculture: The Regional Integration of Specialty Crop Production," *Economic Geography* 62, no. 4 (1986): 334–53. On capitalist agriculture and settler societies: Philip McMichael, *Settlers and the Agrarian Question: Capitalism in Colonial Australia* (Cambridge University Press, 1984); Christopher Isett and Stephen Miller, *The Social*

History of Agriculture: From the Origins to the Current Crisis (Rowman and Littlefield, 2016); Aziz Rana, *The Two Faces of American Freedom* (Harvard University Press, 2010). Thanks to Gautham Shiralagi for pressing me on this point.

93. On capitalist strategies for the "deployment of labor": Jairus Banaji, "Illusions about the Peasantry: Karl Kautsky and the Agrarian Question," *Journal of Peasant Studies* 17, no. 2 (1990): 288–307; Prudham, *Knock on Wood*; Miriam J. Wells, "What Is a Worker? The Role of Sharecroppers in Contemporary Class Structure," *Politics & Society* 13, no. 3 (1984): 295–320; George L. Henderson, *California and the Fictions of Capital* (Temple University Press, 2003); A. Haroon Akram-Lohdi and Cristóbal Kay, "Surveying the Agrarian Question (Part 1): Unearthing Foundations, Exploring Diversity," *Journal of Peasant Studies* 37, no. 1 (2010): 177–202. See also the discussion of subsumption and agriculture in Luis Arizmendi's "Baroque Modernity and Peasant Poverty in the Twenty-First Century," in *Peasant Poverty and Persistence in the 21st Century*, edited by Julio Boltvinik and Susan Archer Mann (Zed Books, 2016), 141–67.

94. Bernstein, "Agriculture/Industry," 175; Henry Bernstein, "Is There an Agrarian Question in the 21st Century?," *Canadian Journal of Development Studies/Revue canadienne d'études du développement* 27, no. 4 (2006): 449–60; Bernstein, "Notes on Capital and Peasantry," *Review of African Political Economy* 10 (1977): 60–73.

95. Not coincidentally, modern finance initially developed largely as a tool to manage risk in nature-based industries like farming and whaling: William Cronon, *Nature's Metropolis: Chicago and the Great West* (W. W. Norton, 1991); Jonathan Levy, *Freaks of Fortune: The Emerging World of Capitalism and Risk in America* (Harvard University Press, 2012); Barbara Adam, *Timescapes of Modernity: The Environment and Invisible Hazards* (Routledge, 1998).

96. Thomas F. Purcell, "'Hot Chocolate': Financialized Global Value Chains and Cocoa Production in Ecuador," *Journal of Peasant Studies* 45, no. 5–6 (2018): 904–26.

97. Winant, "Green Pastures"; Walter Johnson, *River of Dark Dreams: Slavery and Empire in the Cotton Kingdom* (Harvard University Press, 2013).

98. Marx, *Capital*, 1: 695.

99. Liu, *Tea War*, 71.

100. Nonwaged forms of work may also have the political benefit of disorganizing labor: sharecropping, for instance, can drive farmworkers to identify with capital rather than labor. Wells, "What Is a Worker?"; Wells, "Resurgence of Sharecropping: Historical Anomaly or Political Strategy?," *American Journal of Sociology* 90, no. 1 (1984): 1–29; Das, "Reconceptualizing Capitalism."

101. Mike Davis, *Planet of Slums* (Verso, 2006), 181. See also Bernstein, "Is There an Agrarian Question."

102. Prudham, *Knock on Wood*.

103. Harold D. Woodman, *King Cotton and His Retainers: Financing and Marketing the Cotton Crop of the South, 1800–1925* (University of Kentucky Press, 1968); Wells, "Resurgence of Sharecropping."

104. McMichael, *Settlers and the Agrarian Question*; Onur Ulas Ince, *Colonial Capitalism and the Dilemmas of Liberalism* (Oxford University Press, 2018); Eric Williams, *Capitalism & Slavery* (1944; University of North Carolina Press, 2021).

105. Caitlin Rosenthal, *Accounting for Slavery: Masters and Management* (Harvard University Press, 2019), 115. Although cotton plantations did not, obviously, use free labor, they were integrated into capitalism: they relied on debt to expand production and produced cotton at competitive prices. John Clegg, "A Theory of Capitalist Slavery," *Journal of Historical Sociology* 33, no. 1 (2020): 87. See also Johnson, *River of Dark Dreams*.

106. Michael Gorup, "Not Subjects of the Market, but Subject to the Market: Capitalist Slavery as Expropriation," *Political Theory* 51, no. 6 (2023): 997–98.

107. On these forms of bonded labor: Annuska Derks, "Bonded Labour in Southeast Asia: Introduction," *Asian Journal of Social Science* 38, no. 6 (2010): 839–52; Peter Vandergeest and

Melissa Marschke, "Modern Slavery and Freedom: Exploring Contradictions through Labour Scandals in the Thai Fisheries," *Antipode* 51, no. 1 (2020): 291–315; A. D. Couper, Hance D. Smith, and Bruno Ciceri, *Fishers and Plunderers: Theft, Slavery and Violence at Sea* (Pluto, 2015).

108. On the family and liberalism: Carole Pateman, "Feminist Critiques of the Public/Private Dichotomy," in *Public and Private in Social Life*, ed. S. Benn and G. Gaus (Croom Helm, 1983), 281–303.

109. Burawoy, *Politics of Production*, 93, 114n26.

110. S. Mann, *Agrarian Capitalism*, 82–83.

111. Cf. Mae Ngai, *Impossible Subjects: Illegal Aliens and the Making of Modern America* (Princeton University Press, 2004); Cindy Hahamovitch, *No Man's Land: Jamaican Guestworkers in America and the Global History of Deportable Labor* (Princeton University Press, 2011).

112. Martin Legassick and David Hemson, *Foreign Investment and the Reproduction of Racial Capitalism in South America* (Anti-Apartheid Movement, 1976), 3. On the genealogy of "racial capitalism": Robin D. G. Kelley, "Racial Capitalism: An Unfinished History," *Ethnic and Racial Studies* 43, no. 16 (2023): 3562–68; Julian Go, "Three Tensions in the Theory of Racial Capitalism," *Sociological Theory* 39, no. 1 (2021): 38–47.

113. Genevieve LeBaron, "Unfree Labour beyond Binaries: Insecurity, Social Hierarchy and Labour Market Restructuring," *International Feminist Journal of Politics* 17, no. 1 (2015): 1–19. On this phenomenon more broadly: Amy Dru Stanley, *From Bondage to Contract: Wage Labor, Marriage, and the Market in the Age of Slave Emancipation* (Cambridge University Press, 1998).

114. Jairus Banaji, "The Fictions of Free Labour: Contract, Coercion, and So-Called Unfree Labour," *Historical Materialism* 11 no. 3 (2003): 69–95.

115. On the *mir*: Kohei Saito, *Karl Marx's Ecosocialism: Capital, Nature, and the Unfinished Critique of Political Economy* (Monthly Review, 2017). On "commoning": Silvia Federici, *Re-enchanting the World: Feminism and the Politics of the Commons* (PM, 2018). Hopeful gestures to peasants as new agents of an ecological consciousness, meanwhile, are widespread. See, e.g., Jason Moore, *Capitalism in the Web of Life: Ecology and the Accumulation of Capital* (Verso, 2015); Joan Martínez-Alier, *The Environmentalism of the Poor: A Study of Ecological Conflicts and Valuation* (Edward Elgar, 2002); Pierre Charbonnier, *Affluence and Freedom: An Environmental History of Political Ideas*, trans. Andrew Brown (Polity, 2021).

116. The sociologist Vivek Chibber goes so far as to suggest that factories "solved some collective action problems" for industrial workers: Chibber, *The Class Matrix: Social Theory after the Cultural Turn* (Harvard University Press, 2022), 162. Relatedly: Mike Davis, "Old Gods, New Enigmas: Notes on Historical Agency," *Catalyst* 1, no. 2 (2017), https://catalyst-journal.com/2017/11/historical-agency-davis.

117. Marx, *Capital*, 1: 929.

118. Cf. Eric J. Hobsbawm, *Primitive Rebels: Studies in Archaic Forms of Social Movement in the 19th and 20th Centuries* (W. W. Norton, 1965); Georg Lukács, *History and Class Consciousness: Studies in Marxist Dialectics*, trans. Rodney Livingston (MIT Press, 1967), 55; see also Davis, "Old Gods, New Enigmas." For a more complex account of Marx's shifting view of the peasantry: Kevin B. Anderson, *Marx at the Margins: On Nationalism, Ethnicity, and Non-Western Societies* (University of Chicago Press, 2016).

119. On the history of American populism: Lawrence Goodwyn, *Democratic Promise: The Populist Movement in America* (Oxford University Press, 1976); Charles Postel, *The Populist Vision* (Oxford University Press, 2007). On contemporary agrarian populism in India: Amita Baviskar and Michael Levien, "Farmers' Protests in India: Introduction to the *JPS* Forum," *Journal of Peasant Studies* 48, no. 7 (2021): 1341–55. On a more recent populist movement with a climate dimension: Kai Bosworth, *Pipeline Populism: Grassroots Environmentalism in the Twenty-First Century* (University of Minnesota Press, 2022).

120. On tensions between populism and socialism: Gabriel Winant, "No Going Back: The Power and Limits of the Anti-monopoly Tradition," *Nation*, January 21, 2020, https://www

.thenation.com/article/culture/goliath-monopoly-and-democracy-matt-stoller-review/. For an intriguing suggestion that nineteenth-century labor republicans might have shared more with agrarian populists than often recognized: Jason Frank, "Theorizing the Cooperative Commonwealth," *Political Theory* 48, no. 4 (2019): 503–9.

121. Joshua Clover, *Riot. Strike. Riot: The New Era of Uprisings* (Verso, 2016); Charles Tilly, *Contentious Performances* (Cambridge University Press, 2008). For insightful commentary: Alberto Toscano, "Limits to Periodization," *Viewpoint*, September 2016; Amanda Armstrong, "Disarticulating the Mass Picket," *Viewpoint*, September 2016.

122. Without taking these as *only* materialist. See Charmaine Chua and Kai Bosworth, "Beyond the Chokepoint: Blockades as Social Struggles," *Antipode* 55, no. 5 (2023): 1301–20.

123. Timothy Mitchell, *Carbon Democracy: Political Power in the Age of Oil* (Verso, 2011).

124. My analysis here draws extensively on the research and arguments of Geoff Mann: G. Mann, "Class Consciousness and Common Property: The International Fishermen and Allied Workers of America," *International Labor and Working-Class History* 61 (2002): 141–60.

125. G. Mann, "Class Consciousness"; G. Mann, *Our Daily Bread*, 136.

126. Connections to nature are often emphasized in agrarian and peasant movements that describe themselves as "people of the land." While these movements usefully highlight the ways that work on nature can motivate care for it, designations that emphasize, first and foremost, relationships to nature can come at the cost of flattening differences in class position among those who are unified to some degree by their common relationship to natural agents, while setting up sectoral differences across workers. See Bernstein, "Is there an Agrarian Question."

127. Indeed, although tech platforms like Uber seem the opposite of a nature-based industry, the unpredictability of traffic constitutes a form of suprasumption that mimics that of many natural processes.

128. Lichtenstein, "Return of Merchant Capitalism"; Nelson Lichtenstein, ed., *Wal-Mart: The Face of Twenty-First Century Capitalism* (New Press, 2006).

129. *Manufactured Landscapes*, directed by Jennifer Baichwal, 16 mm (Foundry Films, 2006).

130. Thea Riofrancos, "Seize and Resist," *Baffler* 54 (2020): 19; see also Martín Arboleda, *Planetary Mine: Territories of Extraction under Late Capitalism* (Verso, 2020); Charmaine Chua, "Disruption from Above, the Middle, and Below: Three Terrains of Governance," *Review of International Studies* 49, no. 1 (2022): 37–52; Chua, "Logistics," in *SAGE Handbook of Marxism*, ed. Beverly Skeggs, Sarah Farris, Alberto Toscano, and Svenja Bromerg (SAGE, 2022): 1442–60.

131. Contra Gorz, *Farewell to the Working-Class*.

Chapter 4

1. Robert Heinlein, *The Moon Is a Harsh Mistress* (Berkley Medallion, 1966), 129.

2. Milton Friedman, *There's No Such Thing as a Free Lunch* (Open Court, 1975).

3. Barry Commoner, *The Closing Circle: Nature, Man & Technology* (Knopf, 1971); cf. Philip Mirowski, "Energy and Energetics in Economic Theory: A Review Essay," *Journal of Economic Issues* 22, no. 3 (1988): 811–30.

4. Kenneth Boulding, "The Economics of the Coming Spaceship Earth," in *Environmental Quality in a Growing Economy*, ed. Henry Jarrett (Johns Hopkins University Press, 1966), 3–14; see also Barbara Ward, *Spaceship Earth* (Columbia University Press, 1966); Richard Buckminster Fuller, *Operating Manual for Spaceship Earth* (Southern Illinois University Press, 1969); Sabine Höhler, *Spaceship Earth in the Environmental Age, 1960–1990* (Routledge, 2015).

5. Joachim Radkau, *Nature and Power: A Global History of the Environment* (Cambridge University Press, 2008), 239–49. On "industrial diseases": Alice Hamilton, *Exploring the Dangerous Trades* (Little, Brown, 1944); see also Samuel P. Hays, *Beauty, Health, and Permanence: Environ-*

mental Politics in the United States, 1955–1985 (Cambridge University Press, 1987); Dorceta E. Taylor, *The Environment and the People in American Cities, 1600s–1900s: Disorder, Inequality, and Social Change* (Duke University Press, 2009).

6. The problem did not escape Marx's notice altogether. In *Capital*, he makes occasional references to the effects of smoke, dust, and other industrial discharge on workers' health, as well as to the squalor of their living conditions; and in the 1844 *Manuscripts*, he decries the "universal pollution [*Vergiftung*], evident in large towns" and the conditions in which "*filth*, this stagnation and putrefaction of man—the *sewage* of civilisation (speaking quite literally)—comes to be the *element of life* for him": Karl Marx, *Capital: A Critique of Political Economy*, vol. 1, trans. Ben Fowkes (Penguin Books, 1976), 808–22; Marx, *Economic and Philosophic Manuscripts of 1844*, in *Marx & Engels Collected Works*, trans. Martin Milligan and Dirk J. Struik, vol. 3 (Lawrence and Wishart, 1975), 253, 308 (translation modified). See also John Bellamy Foster, *Marx's Ecology: Materialism and Nature* (Monthly Review, 2000). On London fog: Christine L. Corton, *London Fog: The Biography* (Harvard University Press, 2015); William M. Cavert, *The Smoke of London: Energy and Environment in the Early Modern City* (Cambridge University Press, 2016).

7. Friedrich Engels, *The Condition of the Working Class in England*, trans. W. O. Henderson and W. H. Chaloner (1845; Stanford University Press, 1958), 51, 60. On the "urban environmental crisis" of this period: Joachim Radkau, *The Age of Ecology*, trans. Patrick Camiller (Wiley, 2014), 32–36.

8. Engels, *Condition of the Working Class*, 108–9, 119–20. On social murder: Nate Holdren, "Social Murder: Capitalism's Systematic and State-Organized Killing," in *Marxism and the Capitalist State: Towards a New Debate*, ed. Rob Hunter, Rafael Khachaturian, and Eva Nanopoulos (Springer, 2023), 185–207.

9. For a partial list of significant works: Commission for Racial Justice, *Toxic Wastes and Race in the United States: A National Report on the Racial and Socioeconomic Characteristics of Communities with Toxic Waste Sites* (United Church of Christ, 1987); Robert D. Bullard, *Dumping in Dixie: Race, Class, and Environmental Quality*, 3rd ed. (1990; Routledge, 2000); Bullard, ed., *Unequal Protection: Environmental Justice and Communities of Color* (Sierra Club Books, 1994); Daniel Faber, ed., *The Struggle for Ecological Democracy: Environmental Justice Movements in the United States* (Guilford, 1998); Richard Hofrichter, ed., *Toxic Struggles: The Theory and Practice of Environmental Justice* (University of Utah Press, 2002); David N. Pellow and Robert J. Brulle, eds., *Power, Justice, and the Environment: A Critical Appraisal of the Environmental Justice Movement* (MIT Press, 2005); Julie Sze, *Noxious New York: The Racial Politics of Urban Health and Environmental Justice* (MIT Press, 2006); David Naguib Pellow, *Resisting Global Toxics: Transnational Movements for Environmental Justice* (MIT Press, 2007).

10. For engagement by political theorists: Andrew Dobson, *Justice and the Environment: Conceptions of Environmental Sustainability and Theories of Distributive Justice* (Oxford University Press, 1998); John Dryzek, *The Politics of the Earth: Environmental Discourses* (Oxford University Press, 1997), 213; David Schlosberg, *Defining Environmental Justice: Theories, Movements, and Nature* (Oxford University Press, 2007); Steve Vanderheiden, *Atmospheric Justice: A Political Theory of Climate Change* (Oxford University Press, 2008); Stephen M. Gardiner, *A Perfect Moral Storm: The Ethical Tragedy of Climate Change* (Oxford University Press, 2011); Henry Shue, *Climate Justice: Vulnerability and Protection* (Oxford University Press, 2014); Simon Caney, "Climate Change, Intergenerational Equity and the Social Discount Rate," *Politics, Philosophy & Economics* 13, no. 4 (2012): 320–42.

11. Rob Nixon, *Slow Violence and the Environmentalism of the Poor* (Harvard University Press, 2011), 2.

12. Mazzocchi quoted in Les Leopold, *The Man Who Hated Work and Loved Labor: The Life and Times of Tony Mazzocchi* (Chelsea Green, 2007), 301; United Farm Workers quoted in Laura Pulido, *Environmentalism and Economic Justice: Two Chicano Struggles in the Southwest*

(University of Arizona Press, 1996), 109–111; Pascal Marichalar, Gerald Markowitz, and David Rosner, "Sartre as Prosecutor of Occupational Murder: Notes from a People's Tribunal in a French Mine (1970)," *International Labor and Working-Class History* 99 (2021): 170. For other examples: Pulido, "Flint, Environmental Racism, and Racial Capitalism," *Capitalism Nature Socialism* 27, no. 3 (2016): 1–16; Pulido, "Geographies of Race and Ethnicity II: Environmental Racism, Racial Capitalism and State-Sanctioned Violence," *Progress in Human Geography* 41, no. 4 (2017): 524–33; Rebecca Solnit, "Call Climate Change What It Is: Violence," *Guardian*, April 7, 2014; Andreas Malm, *How to Blow Up a Pipeline: Learning to Fight in a World on Fire* (Verso, 2020); Kellan Anfinson, "Climate Change and the New Politics of Violence," *New Political Science* 44, no. 1 (2022): 138–52.

13. Judith Lichtenberg, "Negative Duties, Positive Duties, and the 'New Harms,'" *Ethics* 120, no. 3 (2010): 557–78.

14. David Wallace-Wells, "Ten Million a Year," *London Review of Books*, December 2021; Beth Gardiner, *Choked: Life and Breath in the Age of Air Pollution* (University of Chicago Press, 2019).

15. For a call to go "beyond the distributive paradigm": Luke Cole and Sheila Foster, *From the Ground Up: Environmental Racism and the Rise of the Environmental Justice Movement* (New York University Press, 2000), 64.

16. Perhaps more accurately, its use value is negative. David Bond describes a similar phenomenon in term of "negative ecologies" in *Negative Ecologies: Fossil Fuels and the Discovery of the Environment* (University of California Press, 2022). See also Nicholas Georgescu-Roegen, "The Economics of Production," *American Economic Review* 60, no. 2 (1970): 1–9.

17. Mary Douglas, *Purity and Danger: An Analysis of Concepts of Pollution and Taboo* (1966; Routledge, 1984), 36.

18. Cf. Karl Marx and Friedrich Engels, "Manifesto of the Communist Party [1848]," in *Marx & Engels Collected Works*, vol. 6 (Lawrence and Wishart, 1976), 477–519.

19. John H. Dales, *Pollution, Property and Prices: An Essay in Policy-Making and Economics* (University of Toronto Press, 1970), 6.

20. Jacques Derrida, *Given Time: I. Counterfeit Money*, trans. Peggy Kamuf (University of Chicago Press, 1992). Thanks to Andreas Folkers for this suggestion.

21. Commoner, *Closing Circle*, 42.

22. Nicholas Stern, *The Economics of Climate Change: The Stern Review* (Cambridge University Press, 2007), 27.

23. For recent work in climate economics: Gernot Wagner and Martin Weitzman, *Climate Shock: The Economic Consequences of a Hotter Planet* (Princeton University Press, 2015); William Nordhaus, *The Climate Casino: Risk, Uncertainty, and Economics for a Warming World* (Yale University Press, 2013); Gilbert E. Metcalf, *Paying for Pollution: Why a Carbon Tax is Good for America* (Oxford University Press, 2019). For moral philosophy drawing on economic analyses: John Broome, *Climate Matters: Ethics in a Warming World* (W. W. Norton, 2012); Ravi Kanbur and Henry Shue, *Climate Justice: Integrating Economics and Philosophy* (Oxford University Press, 2018); Mark Budolfson, Tristam McPherson, and David Plunkett, *Philosophy and Climate Change* (Oxford University Press, 2021). On the lack of attention to the externality itself: Melissa Lane, "Political Theory on Climate Change," *Annual Review of Political Science* 19 (2016): 107–23.

24. Arthur C. Pigou, *The Economics of Welfare* (Macmillan, 1920); published in an earlier form as *Wealth and Welfare* (Macmillan, 1912). Ronald H. Coase, "The Problem of Social Cost," *Journal of Law & Economics* 3 (1960): 1–44.

25. See Eric MacGilvray, *The Invention of Market Freedom* (Cambridge University Press, 2011); MacGilvray, *Liberal Freedom: Pluralism, Polarization, and Politics* (Cambridge 2022).

26. R. D. Collison Black, Alfred William Coats, and Craufurd Goodwin, eds., *The Marginal Revolution in Economics: Interpretation and Evaluation* (Duke University Press, 1973). Pigou wrote from the Marshallian variant of this approach then dominant at Cambridge, which was

more open to deductive empiricism and utilitarian considerations than its continental equivalents.

27. Ian Kumekawa, *The First Serious Optimist: A. C. Pigou and the Birth of Welfare Economics* (Princeton University Press, 2017); Steven G. Medema, *The Hesitant Hand: Taming Self-Interest in the History of Economic Ideas* (Princeton University Press, 2009).

28. Alfred Marshall, *Principles of Economics*, 2nd ed., vol. 1 (Macmillan, 1891), 76.

29. Pigou, *Economics of Welfare*, 11. On Pigou's notion of welfare: Philipp Lepenies, *The Power of a Single Number: A Political History of GDP* (Columbia University Press, 2016); Kumekawa, *First Serious Optimist*.

30. Pigou, *Economics of Welfare*, 32; 172–203.

31. Pigou, *Economics of Welfare*, 184.

32. Pigou, *Economics of Welfare*, 184n3.

33. Pigou, *Economics of Welfare*, 185–86.

34. Pigou, *Economics of Welfare*, 127–28. In particular, Pigou referenced Smith's argument in the *Wealth of Nations* that government should provide goods that markets would not.

35. Pigou, *Economics of Welfare*, 192.

36. Tibor Scitovsky, "Two Concepts of External Economies," *Journal of Political Economy* 62, no. 2 (1954): 143; see also Steven G. Medema, "'Exceptional and Unimportant'? Externalities, Competitive Equilibrium, and the Myth of a Pigovian Tradition," *History of Political Economy* 52, no. 1 (2020): 135–70.

37. Rachel Carson, *Silent Spring* (Houghton Mifflin, 1962); E. J. Mishan, *The Costs of Economic Growth* (F. A. Praeger, 1967); E. J. Mishan, "The Postwar Literature on Externalities: An Interpretative Essay," *Journal of Economic Literature* 9, no. 1 (1971): 1–28; Fred Hirsch, *Social Limits to Growth* (Harvard University Press, 1976). See also Chad Montrie, *The Myth of Silent Spring: Rethinking the Origins of American Environmentalism* (University of California Press, 2018).

38. Friedrich A. Hayek, *The Road to Serfdom* (1944; Routledge Classics, 2001); Milton Friedman, *Capitalism and Freedom* (University of Chicago Press, 1960). On the significance of externalities to neoliberals: Thomas Biebricher, *The Political Theory of Neoliberalism* (Stanford University Press, 2018). On neoliberalism more generally: William Callison and Zak Manfredi, *Mutant Neoliberalism: Market Rule and Political Rupture* (Fordham University Press, 2020); Wendy Brown, *Undoing the Demos: Neoliberalism's Stealth Revolution* (Zone, 2015).

39. Daniel Luban, "What Is Spontaneous Order?," *American Political Science Review* 114, no. 1 (2020): 68–80; Frank Hahn, "Reflections on the Invisible Hand," Warwick Economics Research Paper Series, University of Warwick, 1981; Medema, *Hesitant Hand*.

40. For a discussion of the harm principle and carbon emissions: Melissa Lane, *Eco-Republic: What the Ancients Can Teach Us about Ethics, Virtue, and Sustainable Living* (Princeton University Press, 2011), 66–69.

41. Hayek, *Road to Serfdom*, 40.

42. Robert Nozick, *Anarchy, State, and Utopia* (Basic Books, 1974).

43. Milton Friedman, "Adam Smith's Relevance for 1976," in *The Indispensable Milton Friedman: Essays on Politics and Economics*, ed. Lanny Ebenstein (Regnery, 2012), 45–46. This was also Friedman's most significant disagreement with Adam Smith, then being revived as a proto-Chicago School thinker. See Glory M. Liu, *Adam Smith's America: How a Scottish Philosopher Became an Icon of American Capitalism* (Princeton University Press, 2022).

44. Friedman further addressed "neighborhood effects" across a number of works: Friedman, *Capitalism and Freedom*; Friedman, *Free Lunch*; Friedman and Rose Friedman, *Free to Choose: A Personal Statement* (1980; Mariner Books, 1990).

45. Roger E. Backhouse, "Economics," in *The History of the Social Sciences since 1945*, ed. Backhouse and Philippe Fontaine (Cambridge University Press, 2010), 38–70; see also Lionel Robbins, *An Essay on the Nature and Significance of Economic Science* (Macmillan, 1932);

Robbins, "Interpersonal Comparisons of Utility: A Comment," *Economic Journal* 48, no. 192 (1938): 635–41; Nicholas Kaldor, "Welfare Propositions of Economics and Interpersonal Comparisons of Utility," *Economic Journal* 49, no. 195 (1939): 549–52; J. R. Hicks, "The Foundations of Welfare Economics," *Economic Journal* 49, no. 196 (1939): 696–712.

46. Coase, "Problem of Social Cost"; see also Steven G. Medema, "Neither Misunderstood nor Ignored: The Early Reception of Coase's Wider Challenge to the Analysis of Externalities," *History of Economic Ideas* 22, no. 1 (2014): 111–32; Donald MacKenzie, "Constructing Emissions Markets," in *Material Markets: How Economic Agents Are Constructed* (Oxford University Press, 2009), 137–76.

47. As he explained later: see R. H. Coase, "The Firm, the Market, and the Law," in *The Firm, the Market, and the Law* (University of Chicago Press, 1988), 26.

48. Coase, "Problem of Social Cost," 13.

49. Coase, "Problem of Social Cost," 2, 13, 42.

50. Coase, "Problem of Social Cost," 34.

51. Coase, "Problem of Social Cost," 42.

52. Coase, "Problem of Social Cost," 18, 41–42.

53. Coase, "Problem of Social Cost," 41.

54. Coase, "Problem of Social Cost," 44.

55. Assuming no transaction costs—a condition that Coase acknowledged was rarely met in practice. See Coase, "Notes on the Problem," 158.

56. See, e.g., Herman E. Daly, *Steady-State Economics: The Economics of Biophysical Equilibrium and Moral Growth*, 2nd ed. (1977; Island, 1991); Daly and Kenneth N. Townsend, eds., *Valuing the Earth: Economics, Ecology, Ethics* (MIT Press, 1993); Nicholas Georgescu-Roegen, *The Entropy Law and the Economic Process* (Harvard University Press, 1971); William D. Nordhaus, "World Dynamics: Measurement without Data," *Economic Journal* 83, no. 332 (1973): 1156–83; Nordhaus and James Tobin, "Is Growth Obsolete?," in *Economic Research: Retrospect and Prospect*, vol. 5, *Economic Growth* (National Bureau of Economic Research, 1972); Elinor Ostrom, *Governing the Commons: The Evolution of Institutions for Collective Action* (Cambridge University Press, 1990).

57. The Coase Theorem, per Stigler, holds that if private property rights are well defined and transaction costs are zero, it does not matter who initially holds the rights in question. See George J. Stigler, *The Theory of Price*, 3rd ed. (Macmillan, 1966). Coase himself disliked the theorem, which he thought oversimplified a complex problem: see "Notes on the Problem"; see also Deirdre McCloskey, "Other Things Equal? The So-Called Coase Theorem," *Eastern Economic Journal* 24, no. 3 (1998): 367–71; Steven G. Medema, "A Case of Mistaken Identity: George Stigler, 'The Problem of Social Cost,' and the Coase Theorem," *European Journal of Law and Economics* 31, no. 1 (2011): 11–38. On the significance of the Coase Theorem to neoliberalism: Biebricher, *Political Theory of Neoliberalism*.

58. Duncan Kennedy, "Law-and-Economics from the Perspective of Critical Legal Studies," in *The New Palgrave Dictionary of Economics and the Law*, ed. Peter Newman (Macmillan 1998), 465–74; Mark Kelman, "Misunderstanding Social Life: A Critique of the Core Premises of 'Law and Economics,'" *Journal of Legal Education* 33, no. 2 (1983): 274–84.

59. Michael Walzer, *Spheres of Justice: A Defense of Pluralism and Equality* (Basic Books, 1983).

60. Michael J. Sandel, "It's Immoral to Buy the Right to Pollute," *New York Times*, December 15, 1997; see also Sandel, *What Money Can't Buy: The Moral Limits of Markets* (Farrar, Straus, and Giroux, 2012), 73–75; Elizabeth Anderson, *Value in Ethics and Economics* (Harvard University Press, 1993), 195. For a similar argument: Robert E. Goodin, "Selling Environmental Indulgences," *Kyklos* 47, no. 4 (1994): 573–96.

61. Wilfred Beckerman and Joanna Pasek, "The Morality of Market Mechanisms to Control Pollution," *World Economics* 4, no. 3 (2003): 191–207; Simon Caney and Cameron Hepburn,

"Carbon Trading: Unethical, Unjust and Ineffective?," *Royal Institute of Philosophy Supplement* 69 (2011): 201–34.

62. Lawrence H. Summers, "Memo on 'Dirty' Industries," World Bank, December 12, 1991.

63. Pellow, *Resisting Global Toxics*, 9.

64. Summers, "Memo on 'Dirty' Industries."

65. Milton Friedman, "Playboy Interview (1973)," in *Free Lunch*, 16.

66. Milton Friedman, "Free Trade and the Steel Industry," lecture, Utah State University, 1978.

67. Debra Satz, *Why Some Things Should Not Be for Sale: The Moral Limits of Markets* (Oxford University Press 2010), 95–97.

68. See also Kennedy, "Law and Economics."

69. Elizabeth Cripps, *Climate Change and the Moral Agent: Individual Duties in an Interdependent World* (Oxford University Press, 2013); Vanderheiden, *Atmospheric Justice*; Dale Jamieson, "Climate Change, Responsibility and Justice," *Science and Engineering Ethics* 16 (2010): 431–45; Jamieson, "Ethics, Public Policy and Global Warming," *Science, Technology, and Human Values* 17 (1992): 139–53; Douglas MacLean, "Climate Complicity and Individual Accountability," *Monist* 102, no. 1 (2019): 1–21.

70. Gardiner, *A Perfect Moral Storm*, 34.

71. Lichtenberg, "Negative Duties." For further reflection, see Cripps's *Climate Change and the Moral Agent*.

72. Lichtenberg, "Negative Duties," 558.

73. Derek Parfit, *Reasons and Persons* (Clarendon, 1984), 67–86.

74. Lichtenberg, "Negative Duties," 560.

75. MacGilvray, *Invention of Market Freedom*, 103.

76. On Kapp: Sebastian Berger, *The Social Costs of Neoliberalism: Essays on the Economics of K. William Kapp* (Spokesman Books, 2017); Berger, "K. William Kapp's Social Theory of Social Costs," *History of Political Economy* 47, no. S1 (2015): 227–52.

77. Karl William Kapp, *The Social Costs of Private Enterprise* (Harvard University Press, 1950).

78. Kapp, *Social Costs*, 91. For a direct echo: Commoner, *The Closing Circle*, 268.

79. Kapp, *Social Costs*, 231.

80. Kapp, *Social Costs*, 16; echoing Karl Polanyi, *The Great Transformation: The Political and Economic Origins of Our Time* (1944; Beacon, 2001).

81. Alain Resnais, *Le chant du styrène*, 35 mm (Les Films de la Pléiade, 1958).

82. Susan Freinkel, *Plastic: A Toxic Love Story* (Mariner, 2011).

83. Barry Commoner, *The Poverty of Power: Energy and the Economic Crisis* (Knopf, 1976), 209; Freinkel, *Plastic*.

84. Robert Gordon, "'Shell No!' OCAW and the Labor-Environmental Alliance," *Environmental History* 3, no. 4 (1998): 460–87.

85. Heather Davis, *Plastic Matter* (Duke University Press, 2020).

86. See Rebecca Giggs, *Fathoms: The World in the Whale* (Simon and Schuster, 2020), 14.

87. Gabriel Winant, *The Next Shift: The Fall of Industry and the Rise of Health Care in Rust Belt America* (Harvard University Press, 2021); Gordon, "'Shell No!,'" 45. See also the discussion of the "coal-industrial complex" by Sartre: Jean-Paul Sartre, *Critique of Dialectical Reason*, ed. Jonathan Rée, trans. Alan Sheridan-Smith, vol. 1 (Verso, 2004), 196.

88. G. A. Cohen, "Are Workers Who Take Hazardous Jobs Forced to Take Hazardous Jobs?," in *History, Labour, and Freedom: Themes from Marx* (Clarendon, 1988), 239–54. For a more basic statement of this argument: Cohen, "The Structure of Proletarian Unfreedom," *Philosophy & Public Affairs* 12, no. 1 (1983): 3–33; Cohen, "Capitalism, Freedom, and the Proletariat," in *On the Currency of Egalitarian Justice, and Other Essays in Political Philosophy* (Princeton University Press, 2011), 147–65.

89. As Hayek puts it, "Even if the threat of starvation to me and perhaps to my family impels me to accept a distasteful job at a very low wage . . . I am not coerced by [my employer] or by anybody else": Friedrich A. Hayek, *The Constitution of Liberty* (University of Chicago Press, 1960), 204.

90. Cohen, "Hazardous Jobs," 252. See also Nicholas Vrousalis, *Exploitation as Domination: What Makes Capitalism Unjust* (Oxford University Press, 2023); A. J. Julius, "The Possibility of Exchange," *Politics, Philosophy & Economics* 12, no.4 (2013): 361–74.

91. Although these particular examples pertain to localized environmental harms rather than global phenomena like climate change, scalar dimensions are often interconnected. Despite some notable exceptions—Malibu mansions, Miami real estate—climate vulnerability tends to follow existing patterns of social vulnerability. See US Environmental Protection Agency, *Climate Change and Social Vulnerability in the United States: A Focus on Six Impacts* (EPA, 2021).

92. See, notably, Pellow and Brulle, *Power, Justice, and the Environment*; Liam Downey and Brian Hawkins, "Race, Income, and Environmental Inequality in the United States," *Sociological Perspectives* 51, no. 4 (2008): 759–81; Charles W. Mills, "Black Trash," in *Faces of Environmental Racism: Confronting Issues of Global Justice*, ed. Laura Westra and Bill E. Lawson (Rowman and Littlefield, 2001), 73–91. On race and residential patterns: Dorceta Taylor, *Toxic Communities: Environmental Racism, Industrial Pollution, and Residential Mobility* (New York University Press, 2014). On the legacies of colonialism: Olúfẹ́mi O. Táíwò, *Reconsidering Reparations* (Oxford University Press, 2022), 162–66.

93. G. A. Cohen, "Freedom and Money," in *On the Currency of Egalitarian Justice, and Other Essays in Political Philosophy* (Princeton University Press, 2011), 166–92.

94. Marx, *Capital*, 1: 270.

95. Pulido, "Geographies of Race and Ethnicity," 529.

96. See discussion by George Caffentzis in "The Work/Energy Crisis and the Apocalypse" (*Midnight Notes* 3 [1980]): 26.

97. Cohen, "Hazardous Jobs."

98. A similar idea underpins the ecosocialist James O'Connor's "second contradiction" thesis: O'Connor, "Capitalism, Nature, Socialism: A Theoretical Introduction," *Capitalism, Nature, Socialism*, 1, no. 1 (1988): 11–38.

99. Coase, "Problem of Social Cost," 10. At least, given the situation of no transaction costs.

100. For Kapp, this argument comes from the planning side of the socialist calculation debate, which ecological economists would later embrace in their efforts to translate biophysical costs into monetary terms. Indeed, the origins of Kapp's thought in the socialist calculation debate are notable: Ludwig von Mises, "Economic Calculation in the Socialist Commonwealth," in *Collectivist Economic Planning: Critical Studies on the Possibilities of Socialism*, ed. F.A. Hayek (George Routledge and Sons, 1935), 87–130; see also John O'Neill, "Who Won the Socialist Calculation Debate?," *History of Political Thought* 17, no. 3 (1996): 431–42; O'Neill, *Ecology, Policy, and Politics: Human Well-Being and the Natural World* (Routledge, 1993); Joan Martínez-Alier, Giuseppe Munda, and John O'Neill, "Weak Comparability of Values as a Foundation for Ecological Economics," *Ecological Economics* 26 (1998): 277–96. Daly saw himself in the tradition of the "market socialist" Oskar Lange; Martínez-Alier followed Neurath: Herman Daly and Benjamin Kunkel, "Ecologies of Scale: An Interview with Herman Daly," *New Left Review*, no. 109 (2018): 81–104; Martínez-Alier, *The Environmentalism of the Poor: A Study of Ecological Conflicts and Valuation* (Edward Elgar, 2002).

101. Simon Caney, "Climate Change, Energy Rights, and Equality," in *The Ethics of Global Climate Change*, ed. Denis G. Arnold (Cambridge University Press, 2011), 77–103. For an argument for the inalienable right to a healthy environment: Henry Shue, "Bequeathing Hazards: Security Rights and Property Rights of Future Humans," in *Global Environmental Economics*, ed. Mohammed H. I. Dore and Timothy D. Mount (Blackwell, 1999), 40–42.

102. See Pellow, *Resisting Global Toxics*; Sara Holiday Nelson, "Neoliberal Environments: Crisis, Counterrevolution, and the Nature of Value" (PhD dissertation, University of Minnesota, 2017).

103. On articulation: Stuart Hall, "Race, Articulation, and Societies Structured in Dominance [1980]," in *Essential Essays*, vol. 1, ed. David Morley (Duke University Press, 2018), 195–245.

104. Martínez-Alier, *Environmentalism of the Poor*.

105. Ulrich Beck, *Risk Society: Towards a New Modernity*, trans. Mark Ritter (SAGE, 1992), 41.

106. Beck, *Risk Society*, 36.

107. On the temporalities of "residuals": Andreas Folkers, "Fossil Modernity: The Materiality of Acceleration, Slow Violence, and Ecological Futures," *Time & Society* 30, no. 2 (2021): 223–46; Folkers, "Staying with the Rubble: Residual Reification and Reparative Critique" (unpublished manuscript); Chloe Ahmann, "It's Exhausting to Create an Event out of Nothing: Slow Violence and the Manipulation of Time," *Cultural Anthropology* 33, no. 1 (2018): 142–71.

108. Engels, *Condition of the Working Class*, 111.

109. See Georges Bataille, *The Accursed Share: An Essay on General Economy*, vol. 1, trans. Robert Hurley (Zone Books, 1991); Laura Ephraim, "Everyone Poops: Consumer Virtues and Excretory Anxieties in Locke's Theory of Property," *Political Theory* 50, no. 5 (2022): 673–99.

110. Herman E. Daly, "On Economics as a Life Science," *Journal of Political Economy* 76, no. 3 (1968): 401.

111. Joan Martínez-Alier, "Political Ecology, Distributional Conflicts, and Economic Incommensurability," *New Left Review* I/211 (1995): 70–88.

112. Sartre, *Critique of Dialectical Reason*, 164.

113. Ajay Singh Chaudhary, *Exhausted of the Earth: Politics in a Burning World* (Repeater Books, 2024), 46.

114. See, notably, Pellow and Brulle, *Power, Justice, and the Environment*; Downey and Hawkins, "Race, Income, and Environmental Inequality"; Mills, "Black Trash." On race and residential patterns: Taylor, *Toxic Communities*. On the legacies of colonialism: Táíwò, *Reconsidering Reparations*, 162–66.

115. See also Anneleen Kenis and Matthias Lievens, "Politicizing Air: On the Political Effects of Spatial Imagination," in *[Un]Grounding: Post-Foundational Geographies*, ed. Friederike Landau, Lucas Pohl, and Nikolai Roskamm (transcript Verlag, 2021), 261–78.

116. Carson, *Silent Spring*. Human bodies can also mediate pollution, as gestation and breastfeeding in particular make clear. LaDuke, *All Our Relations*, 18.

117. Though on the difficulties of assessing reproductive and sexual effects, see Heather Davis, "Toxic Progeny: The Plastisphere and Other Queer Futures," (*philoSOPHIA* 5, no. 2 2015): 231–50.

118. Sunaura Taylor, *Disabled Ecologies: Lessons from a Wounded Desert* (University of California Press, 2024), 7.

119. See Giggs, *Fathoms*, 11–15.

120. Chad Montrie, *Making a Living: Work and Environment in the United States* (University of North Carolina Press, 2008); Emily E. LB. Twarog, *Politics of the Pantry: Housewives, Food, and Consumer Protest in Twentieth-Century America* (Oxford University Press, 2017); Pulido, *Environmentalism and Economic Justice*.

121. On "new social movements": Jürgen Habermas, *Toward a Rational Society: Student Protest, Science, and Politics* (Beacon, 1970); Ronald Inglehart, *The Silent Revolution: Changing Values and Political Styles among Western Publics* (Princeton University Press, 1977); Ernesto Laclau and Chantal Mouffe, *Hegemony and Socialist Strategy: Towards a Radical Democratic Politics*, trans. Paul Cammack and Winston Moore (Verso, 1985); Ellen Meiksins Wood, *The Retreat from Class: A New "True" Socialism* (Verso, 1999); Steven M. Buechler, *Social Movements in Advanced Capitalism: The Political Economy and Cultural Construction of Social Activism* (Oxford University

Press, 1999). For a review of the literature: Nelson A. Pichardo, "New Social Movements: A Critical Review," *Annual Review of Sociology* 23 (1997): 411–30.

122. For brief observations on this point: Mancur Olson, *The Logic of Collective Action: Public Goods and the Theory of Groups* (Harvard University Press, 1971), 171–73.

123. Christopher D. Stone, "Should Trees Have Standing? Toward Legal Rights for Natural Objects," *Southern California Law Review* 45 (1972): 450–501.

124. Stone, "Should Trees Have Standing?," 474.

125. Economists tend to lump these kinds of challenges to collective action under the banner of transaction costs; the Coase theorem's assumption that they are nonexistent is one of its well-canvassed shortcomings. See Steven Medema, "The Coase Theorem at Sixty," *Journal of Economic Literature* 58, no. 4 (2020): 1045–128; Paul A. Samuelson, "Some Uneasiness with the Coase Theorem," *Japan and the World Economy* 7, no. 1 (1995): 1–7.

126. Stone, "Should Trees Have Standing?," 475.

127. Stone, "Should Trees Have Standing?," 475.

128. Stone, "Should Trees Have Standing?," 474.

129. Stone, "Should Trees Have Standing?," 474n82.

130. The relationship between Indigenous ontologies and law and the rights of nature framework is complicated; while Stone's account remains squarely within the tradition of Western law, I think there is potential for it to operate in tandem with an Indigenous critique of capitalism. For reflection: Erin O'Donnell, Anne Poelina, Alessandro Pelizzon, and Cristy Clark, "Stop Burying the Lede: The Essential Role of Indigenous Law(s) in Creating Rights of Nature," *Transnational Environmental Law* 9, no. 3 (2020): 403–27; James D. K. Morris and Jacinta Ruru, "Giving Voice to Rivers: Legal Personality as a Vehicle for Recognising Indigenous Peoples' Relationships to Water?," *Australian Indigenous Law Review* 14, no. 2 (2010): 49–62.

131. For the classic theory of collective bargaining: Sidney Webb and Beatrice Webb, "The Method of Collective Bargaining," *Economic Journal* 6, no. 21 (1896): 1–29.

132. Folkers, "Fossil Modernity."

Chapter 5

1. Randy Kennedy, "An Artist Who Calls the Sanitation Department Home," *New York Times*, September 21, 2016, https://www.nytimes.com/2016/09/22/arts/design/mierle-laderman-ukeles-new-york-city-sanitation-department.html.

2. Mierle Laderman Ukeles, "Manifesto for Maintenance Art" (1969). See Patricia C. Phillips, ed., *Mierle Laderman Ukeles: Maintenance Art* (Prestel, 2016).

3. For an overview of ecofeminism: Greta Gaard, "Ecofeminism Revisited: Rejecting Essentialism and Re-placing Species in a Material Feminist Environmentalism," *Feminist Formations* 23, no. 2 (2011): 26–53; Johanna Oksala, *Feminism, Capitalism, and Ecology* (Northwestern University Press, 2023).

4. Francis, *Laudato Si': On Care for Our Common Home* (Libreria Editrice Vaticana, 2015).

5. Robin Wall Kimmerer, *Braiding Sweetgrass: Indigenous Wisdom, Scientific Knowledge, and the Teachings of Plants* (Milkweed Editions, 2013), 103.

6. Karl Marx, *Capital: A Critique of Political Economy*, vol. 1, trans. Ben Fowkes (Penguin Books, 1976), 134.

7. Bernard Le Bovier de Fontenelle, *A Week's Conversation on the Plurality of Worlds* (1686; trans. William Gardiner, 4th. ed., C. Hitch and L. Hawes, and J. Hodges, 1757); Barry Commoner, *The Closing Circle: Nature, Man, and Technology* (Knopf, 1971), 32.

8. James O'Connor, "Capitalism, Nature, Socialism: A Theoretical Introduction," *Capitalism, Nature, Socialism*, 1, no. 1 (1988): 11–38; Nancy Fraser, "Behind Marx's Hidden Abode," *New Left Review*, no. 86 (2014): 55–72; Val Plumwood, *Feminism and the Mastery of Nature* (Routledge,

1993), 20–21; Maria Mies, *Patriarchy and Accumulation on a World Scale: Women in the International Division of Labour*, 3rd ed. (Zed Books, 2014); Jason Moore, *Capitalism in the Web of Life: Ecology and the Accumulation of Capital* (Verso, 2015); Marilyn Waring, *If Women Counted: A New Feminist Economics* (Harper and Row 1988); Nancy Folbre, *Valuing Children: Rethinking the Economics of the Family* (Harvard University Press, 2008). For discussions of reproduction in feminist political thought more generally: Wendy Brown, *Manhood and Politics: A Feminist Reading in Political Theory* (Rowman and Littlefield, 1988); Susan Moller Okin, *Justice, Gender, and the Family* (Basic Books, 1989).

9. See Plumwood, *Feminism and the Mastery of Nature*; Kate Soper, *What Is Nature? Culture, Politics, and the Non-Human* (Blackwell, 1995); Donna J. Haraway, *Simians, Cyborgs, and Women: The Reinvention of Nature* (Routledge, 1991); Carolyn Merchant, *The Death of Nature: Women, Ecology, and the Scientific Revolution* (Harper Row, 1980).

10. Shulamith Firestone, *The Dialectic of Sex: The Case for Feminist Revolution* (1970; Farrar, Straus & Giroux, 2003), 2.

11. Mies, *Patriarchy and Accumulation*, 75; Plumwood, *Feminism and the Mastery of Nature*, 32; Silvia Federici, *Revolution at Point Zero: Housework, Reproduction, and Feminist Struggle* (PM, 2012); Federici, *Caliban and the Witch: Women, the Body and Primitive Accumulation* (AK, 2004); Maria Mies, Veronika Bennholdt-Thomsen, and Claudia von Werlhof, eds., *Women: The Last Colony* (Zed, 1988), 97–99; Maria Mies and Veronika Bennholdt-Thompsen, *The Subsistence Perspective: Beyond the Globalised Economy* (Zed, 1999).

12. As Melinda Cooper and Catherine Waldby observe, "the abstract and the material (indeed, embodied) dimensions of labor cannot be theorized in isolation": Cooper and Waldby, *Clinical Labor: Tissue Donors and Research Subjects in the Global Bioeconomy* (Duke University Press, 2014), 11.

13. For a crucial intervention on this front: Maya Gonzalez and Jeanne Neton, "The Logic of Gender: On the Separation of Spheres and the Process of Abjection," in *Contemporary Marxist Theory: A Reader*, ed. Andrew Pendakis, Jeff Diamanti, Nicholas Brown, Josh Robinson, and Imre Szeman (Bloomsbury, 2004), 149–74.

14. Following other critiques of how labor is gendered: Sophie Lewis, *Full Surrogacy Now: Feminism against Family* (Verso, 2019); Emma Heaney, "Is a Cervix Cis? My Year in the Stirrups," *Aster(ix)*, February 18, 2021, https://asterixjournal.com/is-a-cervix-cis/; Diane Fuss, *Essentially Speaking: Feminism, Nature, and Difference* (Routledge, 1989); and, ultimately, Beauvoir herself. In fact, I bracket the "woman question" altogether: I don't aim to offer an account of gender at all. In this, my argument also differs from recent attempts to derive a "logic of gender" from the logic of capital. See Gonzalez and Neton, "Logic of Gender"; Amy De'Ath, "Gender and Social Reproduction," in *The SAGE Handbook of Frankfurt School Critical Theory*, ed. Beverly Best, Werner Bonefeld, and Chris O'Kane (SAGE, 2018), 1534–50.

15. On the anxieties of biological determinism: Lena Gunnarsson, "The Naturalistic Turn in Feminist Theory: A Marxist-Realist Contribution," *Feminist Theory* 14, no. 1 (2013): 3–19; Elizabeth Wilson, *Gut Feminism* (Duke University Press, 2015).

16. Aristotle, *Nicomachean Ethics*, trans. C.D.C. Reeve (Hackett, 2024); Aristotle, *Politics*, trans. C.D.C. Reeve (Hackett, 1998); William James Booth, *Households: On the Moral Architecture of the Economy* (Cornell University Press, 1993).

17. For a rare exception: Friedrich Engels, *The Origin of the Family, Private Property and the State* (1884; Penguin Books, 2010).

18. Hannah Arendt, *The Human Condition*, 2nd ed. (1958; University of Chicago Press, 1998): 94. For reflections on *The Human Condition* in particular: Patchen Markell, "Arendt's Work: On the Architecture of *The Human Condition*," *College Literature* 38, no. 1 (2011): 15–44; Hanna Fenichel Pitkin, *Attack of the Blob: Hannah Arendt's Concept of the Social* (University of Chicago Press, 1998); Seyla Benhabib, *The Reluctant Modernism of Hannah Arendt* (Rowman and Littlefield, 2003).

19. Arendt, *Human Condition*, 139.

20. Simone de Beauvoir, *The Second Sex*, trans. Constance Borde and Sheila Malovany-Chevallier (1949; Vintage, 2011). On Beauvoir's feminist thought: Toril Moi, *Simone de Beauvoir: The Making of an Intellectual Woman* (Blackwell, 1994); Lori Marso and Patricia Moynagh, eds., *Simone de Beauvoir's Political Thinking* (University of Illinois Press, 2006); Nancy Bauer, *Simone de Beauvoir, Philosophy, and Feminism* (Columbia University Press, 2001); Sonia Kruks, *Simone de Beauvoir and the Politics of Ambiguity* (Oxford University Press, 2012); Marso, *Politics with Beauvoir: Freedom in the Encounter* (Duke University Press, 2017). On Arendt's inattention to gender and complicated relationship to feminism: Benhabib, *Reluctant Modernism of Hannah Arendt*; Mary Dietz, *Turning Operations: Feminism, Arendt, and Politics* (Routledge, 2002); Bonnie Honig, ed., *Feminist Interpretations of Hannah Arendt* (Penn State University Press, 1995). On the resonance in Beauvoir and Arendt's views of labor: Andrea Veltman, "Simone de Beauvoir and Hannah Arendt on Labor," *Hypatia* 25, no. 1 (2010): 55–78.

21. Beauvoir, *Second Sex*, 55, 62.

22. Albert Camus, *The Myth of Sisyphus* (1942; Vintage, 1955); Beauvoir, *Second Sex*, 474.

23. Betty Friedan, *The Feminine Mystique* (W. W. Norton, 1963); Ti-Grace Atkinson, "Radical Feminism," in *Notes from the Second Year: Women's Liberation*, ed. Shulamith Firestone and Anne Koedt (Radical Feminism, 1970), 32–37.

24. Firestone, *Dialectic of Sex*, 8. For critiques of this reductive materialism: Haraway, *Simians, Cyborgs, and Women*, 10; Sophie Lewis, "Low-Tech Grassroots Ectogenesis," *Brand New Life*, April 2021.

25. For a useful overview of the "woman question" in socialist thought: Lise Vogel, *Marxism and the Oppression of Women: Toward a Unitary Theory* (1983; Haymarket, 2013); M. E. O'Brien, "To Abolish the Family," *Endnotes* 5 (2020): 360–417.

26. Marx, *Capital*, 1: 270. See also Karl Marx, "Wage Labour and Capital," in *Marx & Engels Collected Works*, vol. 9 (London: Lawrence and Wishart, 1977), 202–3.

27. Marx, *Capital*, 1: 274–75.

28. See Margaret Benston, "The Political Economy of Women's Liberation," *Monthly Review* 21, no. 4 (1969): 13–27; Juliet Mitchell, *Woman's Estate* (Pantheon, 1971); Zillah R. Eisenstein, ed., *Capitalist Patriarchy and the Case for Socialist Feminism* (Monthly Review, 1979); Bonnie Fox, ed., *Hidden in the Household: Women's Domestic Labour under Capitalism* (Women's Press, 1980); Ellen Malos, ed., *The Politics of Housework* (Allison and Busby, 1980).

29. For recent histories and assessments: Kathi Weeks, *The Problem with Work: Feminism, Marxism, Antiwork Politics and Postwork Imaginaries* (Duke University Press, 2011); Weeks, "Life within and against Work: Affective Labor, Feminist Critique, and Post-Fordist Politics," *Ephemera: Theory & Politics in Organization* 7 no. 1 (2007): 233–49; *Viewpoint Magazine*, no. 5: *Social Reproduction* (October 2015); Louise Toupin, *Wages for Housework: A History of an International Feminist Movement, 1972–1977* (University of British Columbia Press, 2018); Katrina Forrester, "Feminist Demands and the Problem of Housework," *American Political Science Review* 116, no. 4 (2022): 1278–92; Beverly Best, "Wages for Housework Redux: Social Reproduction and the Utopian Dialectic of the Value-Form," *Theory and Event* 24, no. 4 (2021): 896–921; Emily Callaci, *Wages for Housework: The Story of a Movement, an Idea, a Promise* (Allen Lane, 2025).

30. Selma James, introduction to *The Power of Women and the Subversion of the Community* by Mariarosa Dalla Costa and James (Falling Wall, 1972), 5. For other key works: Leopoldina Fortunati, *The Arcane of Reproduction: Housework, Prostitution, Labor, and Capital*, trans. Hilary Creek, ed. Jim Fleming (Autonomedia, 1995); Federici, *Revolution at Point Zero*; James, *Sex, Race, and Class: The Perspective of Winning; A Selection of Writings 1952–2011* (PM, 2012); Federici and Arlen Austin, eds., *Wages for Housework: The New York Committee 1972–1977; History, Theory, Documents* (Autonomedia, 2017); Dalla Costa, *Women and the Subversion of the Community: A*

Mariarosa Dalla Costa Reader, ed. Camille Barbagallo (PM, 2019). On the complicated politics of the authorship of *The Power of Women*: Katrina Forrester, "Capitalism and the Organization of Displacement: Selma James's Internationalism of the Unwaged," *Political Theory* 52, no. 4 (2024): 659–92.

31. For the classic autonomist text: Mario Tronti, *Workers and Capital,* trans. David Broder (1966; Verso, 2019). On autonomism: Steve Wright, *Storming Heaven: Class Composition and Struggle in Italian Autonomist Marxism* (Pluto, 2017). On the welfare rights movement: Guida West, *The National Welfare Rights Movement: The Social Protest of Poor Women* (Praeger, 1981); On feminism's subject question: Linda Zerilli, *Feminism and the Abyss of Freedom* (University of Chicago Press, 2005), 10–11.

32. Selma James, "Women, the Unions, and Work, or, What is Not to Be Done (1972)," in *Sex Race and Class,* 68; Silvia Federici, *The Patriarchy of the Wage: Notes on Marx, Gender, and Feminism* (PM, 2021). For an extensive discussion of the wage: Federici and Nicole Cox, "Counterplanning from the Kitchen (1975)," in Federici, *Revolution at Point Zero,* 28–40. For further discussion: Weeks, *Problem with Work.*

33. The Marxist analysis of ideology is not necessarily the view held by Marx himself. See Charles W. Mills and Danny Goldstick, "A New Old Meaning of 'Ideology,'" *Dialogue: Canadian Philosophical Review/Revue Canadienne de philosophie* 28, no. 3 (1989): 417–32; Raymond Geuss, *The Idea of a Critical Theory: Habermas and the Frankfurt School* (Cambridge University Press, 1981).

34. Stuart Hall, "The Problem of Ideology: Marxism without Guarantees [1983]," in *Selected Writings on Marxism,* ed. Gregor McLennan (Duke University Press, 2021), 134–57.

35. Marx, *Capital,* 1: 270; Marx, "Wage Labour and Capital," 204.

36. Silvia Federici, "Wages against Housework (1975)," in Federici, *Revolution at Point Zero,* 17, 35; Federici and Austin, "Theses on Wages for Housework (1974)," in *Wages for Housework,* 33.

37. Dalla Costa and James, "Women and the Subversion of the Community," 28; see also Fortunati, *Arcane of Reproduction,* 97; Federici, "Wages against Housework."

38. Geuss, *Idea of a Critical Theory;* Michael Rosen, *On Voluntary Servitude: False Consciousness and the Theory of Ideology* (Harvard University Press, 1996); Rahel Jaeggi, "Rethinking Ideology," in *New Waves in Political Philosophy,* ed. Boudewijn de Bruin and Christopher F. Zurn (Palgrave Macmillan, 2009), 63–86.

39. Federici, "Wages against Housework," 16.

40. Federici, "Wages against Housework," 17.

41. Selma James, "The Global Kitchen," in *Sex, Race, and Class,* 169.

42. Federici, "Wages against Housework," 15.

43. Federici, "Wages against Housework," 18. Italics in original.

44. Federici, "Wages against Housework," 19, 37.

45. Soper, *What Is Nature?;* Forrester, "Feminist Demands."

46. New York Wages for Housework Committee poster, in Federici and Austin, *Wages for Housework,* 124.

47. Federici, "Wages against Housework," 18–19. For discussion: Forrester, "Feminist Demands"; Weeks, *Problem with Work.*

48. William Clare Roberts, *Marx's Inferno: The Political Theory of Capital* (Princeton University Press, 2017), 172–74. For a related analysis: Sianne Ngai, *Theory of the Gimmick: Aesthetic Judgment and Capitalist Form* (Harvard University Press, 2020), 299–300.

49. Federici and Cox, "Counterplanning from the Kitchen," 37.

50. Angela Y. Davis, *Women, Race, & Class* (Random House, 1981).

51. Heidi Hartmann, "The Unhappy Marriage of Marxism and Feminism: Towards a More Progressive Union," *Capital & Class* 3, no. 2 (1979): 1–33; Barbara Ehrenreich, "Life without Father: Reconsidering Socialist-Feminist Theory," *Socialist Review* 73, no. 14.1 (1984): 48–57.

52. Mies, *Patriarchy and Accumulation*, 142.

53. Mies, *Patriarchy and Accumulation*, 118; Claudia von Werlhof, "The Proletarian Is Dead: Long Live the Housewife!," in Mies, Bennholdt-Thomsen, and Von Werlhof, *Women*, 176.

54. Von Werlhof, "Proletarian Is Dead."

55. Mies, *Patriarchy and Accumulation*; Mies, Bennholdt-Thomsen, and von Werlhof, *Women*. Housewifization theory also built on Rosa Luxemburg's *The Accumulation of Capital: A Contribution to the Economic Theory of Imperialism* ed. Peter Hudis and Paul Le Blanc, trans. Nicholas Gray, vol. 2 of *The Complete Works of Rosa Luxemburg* (1913; Verso, 2016).

56. Mies, *Patriarchy and Accumulation*, 69, 45.

57. Claudia von Werlhof, "On the Concept of Nature and Society in Capitalism," in Mies, Bennholdt-Thomsen, and Von Werlhof, *Women*, 97.

58. Mies, *Patriarchy and Accumulation*, 88.

59. Von Werlhof, "Concept of Nature," 97, 99.

60. Mies, *Patriarchy and Accumulation*, 77, 33–34.

61. Federici, *Caliban and the Witch*, 17.

62. Merchant, *The Death of Nature*, 4.

63. Plumwood, *Feminism and the Mastery of Nature*, 4.

64. As discussed by Janet Biehl in *Rethinking Ecofeminist Politics* (South End, 1991).

65. For important recent works: Tithi Bhattacharya, ed., *Social Reproduction Theory: Remapping Class, Recentering Oppression* (Pluto, 2017); Cinzia Arruzza, Bhattacharya, and Nancy Fraser, *Feminism for the 99%: A Manifesto* (Verso, 2019); Susan Ferguson, *Women and Work: Feminism, Labour, and Social Reproduction* (Pluto, 2020); Fraser, *Cannibal Capitalism: How Our System Is Devouring Democracy, Care, and the Planet—and What We Can Do about It* (Verso, 2022).

66. Johanna Brenner and Barbara Laslett, "Gender, Social Reproduction, and Women's Self-Organization: Considering the U.S. Welfare State," *Gender & Society* 5, no. 3 (1991): 314.

67. Evelyn Nakano Glenn, "From Servitude to Service Work: Historical Continuities in the Racial Division of Paid Reproductive Labor," *Signs: Journal of Women in Culture and Society* 18, no. 1 (1992): 4.

68. Iris Marion Young, "Beyond the Unhappy Marriage: A Critique of the Dual Systems Theory," in *Women and Revolution*, ed. Lydia Sargent (South End, 1981), 43–69; Seyla Benhabib and Drucilla Cornell, eds., introduction to *Feminism as Critique: On the Politics of Gender* (University of Minnesota Press, 1987), 2.

69. Vogel, *Marxism and the Oppression of Women*, 196.

70. "Notice to All Governments," in Federici and Austin, *Wages for Housework*, 44.

71. Mignon Duffy, "Doing the Dirty Work: Gender, Race, and Reproductive Labor in Historical Perspective," *Gender & Society* 21, no. 3 (2007): 313–36; see also Glenn, "From Servitude to Service Work"; Evelyn Nakano Glenn, *Forced to Care* (Harvard University Press, 2010).

72. Quoted in Judith Shulevitz, "How to Fix Feminism," *New York Times*, June 10, 2016, https://www.nytimes.com/2016/06/12/opinion/sunday/how-to-fix-feminism.html.

73. Federici, "Wages against Housework," 16–17.

74. Fraser, *Cannibal Capitalism*, 57, 60, 96; Arruzza, Bhattacharya, and Fraser, *Feminism for the 99%*, 21; Stefania Barca, *Forces of Reproduction* (Cambridge University Press, 2020), 6, 37.

75. Bhattacharya, *Social Reproduction Theory*, 2; Vandana Shiva, *Staying Alive: Women, Ecology, and Development* (Zed Books, 1988), 44; Maria Mies and Shiva, *Ecofeminism*, 2nd ed. (Zed Books, 2014); Ariel Salleh, *Ecofeminism as Politics: Nature, Marx, and the Postmodern* (Zed Books, 1997), 130; Raj Patel and Jason Moore, *A History of the World in Seven Cheap Things* (University of California Press, 2017), 158.

76. On functionalism: Weeks, *Problem with Work*; Lillian Cicerchia, "Rethinking Capitalism, Stabilizing the Critique," *Rivista Italiana di filosofia politica* 2 (2022): 63–81. For a defense: Cinzia

Arruzza, "Functionalist, Determinist, Reductionist: Social Reproduction Feminism and Its Critics," *Science & Society* 80, no. 1 (2016): 9–30. For a critique of the simplifying assumptions of Marxist feminism: Hartmann, "Unhappy Marriage."

77. Catharine MacKinnon, *Towards a Feminist Theory of the State* (Harvard University Press, 1989); Kate Phelan, "Ideology: The Rejected True," *Inquiry* 24 (2022), https://doi.org/10.1080/0020174X.2022.2152092.

78. Diane Elson and Ruth Pearson, "'Nimble Fingers Make Cheap Workers': An Analysis of Women's Employment in Third World Export Manufacturing," *Feminist Review* 7 (1981): 87–107.

79. This also speaks to problems with the ideology of gender: to explain the *globally* low value of reproductive work as a function of gender (rather than the reverse) requires a remarkably powerful and unitary theory of ideology capable of producing the same effects worldwide, such that "housewifization" can operate even in societies where the Fordist housewife has never existed. Reliance on the explanatory power of ideology can therefore have the familiar effect of collapsing differences between women, while neglecting other kinds of social identities and cultural variations in the perception of gender. For classic critiques of these broader tendencies of feminist thought: bell hooks, *Feminist Theory: From Margin to Center* (South End Classics, 2000); Chandra Talpade Mohanty, *Feminism without Borders: Decolonizing Theory, Practicing Solidarity* (Duke University Press, 2003).

80. Barbara Jeanne Fields, "Slavery, Race, and Ideology in the United States of America," *New Left Review* I/181 (1990): 95–118.

81. For a critique of the idea that gender is "merely cultural": Judith Butler, "Merely Cultural," *New Left Review* I/227 (1990): 33–44.

82. See, e.g., Johanna Brenner and Maria Ramas, "Rethinking Women's Oppression," *New Left Review* I/144 (1984): 33–71.

83. Judith Butler, *Gender Trouble: Feminism and the Subversion of Identity* (1990; Routledge, 2007), 159. On ideas of nature: Haraway, *Simians, Cyborgs, and Women*; Raymond Williams, "The Idea of Nature," in *Culture and Materialism* (1980; Verso, 2005), 70; William Cronon, ed., *Uncommon Ground: Rethinking the Human Place in Nature* (W. W. Norton, 1996).

84. Although Moore acknowledges that "Cheap Nature" is "more than intellectual and symbolic," the symbolic representation of nature, and the conceptual language used to describe it, plays a central role in his own account: Moore, *Capitalism in the Web of Life*, 63.

85. Moore, *Capitalism in the Web of Life*, 216, see also 64–65.

86. Moore, *Capitalism in the Web of Life*, 54.

87. Moore, *Capitalism in the Web of Life*, 4, 194.

88. Moore, *Capitalism in the Web of Life*, 61.

89. Gunnarsson, "Naturalistic Turn in Feminist Theory," 6.

90. Beauvoir, *Second Sex*, 46. For discussion: Sonia Kruks, "Simone de Beauvoir: Engaging Discrepant Materialisms," in *New Materialisms: Ontology; Agency, and Politics*, ed. Diana Coole and Samantha Frost (Duke University Press, 2010), 258–80; Toril Moi, *What Is a Woman? And Other Essays* (Oxford University Press, 1999), 83.

91. On feminist standpoint: Nancy Hartsock, *The Feminist Standpoint Revisited* (Routledge, 1998).

92. Angela Davis, "Women and Capitalism," in *The Angela Davis Reader*, ed. Joy James (Blackwell, 1998), 161–92. On profit rather than ideology as the motivating force for capital: Elson and Pearson, "Nimble Fingers," 92.

93. Key works in the domestic labor debates include: Caroline Freeman, "When Is a Wage Not a Wage?," *Red Rag* 5 (1973): 16–18; Wally Seccombe, "The Housewife and Her Labour under Capitalism," *New Left Review* 83 (1974): 3–24; and Seccombe, "Domestic Labour: Reply to Critics," *New Left Review* 94 (1975): 85–96; Margaret Coulson, Branka Magaš, and Hilary

Wainwright, "'The Housewife and Her Labour under Capitalism'—A Critique," *New Left Review* 89 (1975): 59–71; Jean Gardiner, "Women's Domestic Labour," *New Left Review* 89 (1975): 47–58; Maxine Molyneux, "Beyond the Domestic Labour Debate," *New Left Review* 116 (1979): 3–27; Annette Kuhn and Anne Marie Wolpe, eds., *Feminism and Materialism* (Routledge, 1978); Vogel, *Marxism and the Oppression of Women*; Davis, *Women, Race, & Class.*

94. For such criticisms: O'Brien, "To Abolish the Family," 403; Weeks, *Problem with Work*, 119; Eva Kaluzynska, "Wiping the Floor with Theory: A Survey of Writings on Housework," *Feminist Review* 6 no. 1 (1980): 27–49; Toupin, *Wages for Housework*, 40; Mies, *Patriarchy and Accumulation*, 33; Vogel, *Marxism and the Oppression of Women.*

95. Adam Smith, *An Inquiry into the Nature and Causes of the Wealth of Nations*, ed. R. H. Campbell and A. S. Skinner (Oxford University Press, 1976), 330.

96. Marx, *Capital*, 1: 16, 509; Karl Marx, *Economic Manuscript of 1861–63*, trans. Emile Burns, in *Marx & Engels Collected Works*, vol. 31 (1863; Lawrence and Wishart, 1989), 7–31.

97. See also Ian Gough, "Marx's Theory of Productive and Unproductive Labor," *New Left Review* I/76 (1972): 47–72; Michael Heinrich, *An Introduction to the Three Volumes of Karl Marx's Capital*, trans. Alex Locascio (Monthly Review, 2012), 121–23.

98. Marx, *Capital*, 1: 643–44. Marx is elsewhere scathing about efforts to valorize various forms of activity by naming them *productive labor*, decrying "the sycophantic underlings of political economy [who] felt it their duty to glorify and justify every sphere of activity by demonstrating that it was 'linked' with the production of material wealth" (*Economic Manuscript*, 31).

99. Fortunati, *Arcane of Reproduction*, 99–104; Dalla Costa and James, "Women and the Subversion of the Community," 28; Mies, *Patriarchy and Accumulation*, 31, 47.

100. Federici and Cox, "Counterplanning from the Kitchen," 29.

101. Even housework's use value is dubious, some have argued: because household tasks are not subjected to "social" evaluation of the market there is no way to gauge the usefulness of what a housewife does all day. André Gorz, *Critique of Economic Reason*, trans. Gillian Handyside and Chris Turner, 2nd ed. (1989; Verso, 2011), 140.

102. A. Smith, *Wealth of Nations*, 330. See also: Jason E. Smith, *Smart Machines and Service Work: Automation in an Age of Stagnation* (Reaktion 2020).

103. W. J. Baumol and W. G. Bowen, "On the Performing Arts: The Anatomy of Their Economic Problems," *The American Economic Review* 55, no. 1/2 (1965): 495–502; Baumol, "Macroeconomics of Unbalanced Growth: The Anatomy of Urban Crisis," *American Economic Review* 57, no. 3 (1967): 415–26; William J. Baumol, Sue Anne Batey Blackman, and Edward N. Wolff, *Productivity and American Leadership: The Long View* (MIT Press, 1989); William Baumol, *The Cost Disease: Why Computers Get Cheaper and Health Care Doesn't* (Yale University Press, 2012). For discussion, see Simon Torracinta, "The Post-Industrial Politics of Productivity: Structures and Statistics of the Service Transition in the Long 1970s," *History of Political Economy* (forthcoming).

104. Baumol, *Cost Disease*, 19.

105. Aaron Benanav and John Clegg, "Misery and Debt: On the Logic and History of Surplus Populations and Surplus Capital," *Endnotes* 2 (2012), https://endnotes.org.uk/articles/misery -and-debt. For related analysis: J. Smith, *Smart Machines and Service Work*; Gabriel Winant, *The Next Shift: The Fall of Industry and the Rise of Health Care in Rust Belt America* (Harvard University Press, 2021).

106. W. E. Burghardt Du Bois, "The Servant in the House," in *Darkwater: Voices from within the Veil* (1920; Verso, 2016), 67–69; Davis, *Women, Race, & Class*, 222–44; Firestone, *Dialectic of Sex*, 179–182.

107. Gardiner, "Women's Domestic Labour," 54; italics mine.

108. Gonzalez and Neton, "Logic of Gender," 169. Joan Tronto also briefly acknowledges this problem, though she does not fully explore its significance. See Tronto, *Caring Democracy: Markets, Equality, and Justice* (New York University Press, 2013). Cf. Ferguson, *Women and Work*, 113.

109. S. G. [Suzanne Gail], "The Housewife," *New Left Review* I/43 (1967): 45–54.

110. Beauvoir, *Second Sex*, 476.

111. "Epitaph for a Tired Housewife," in Malos, *Politics of Housework*, 6. Thanks to Sophie Smith for bringing this to my attention.

112. Beauvoir, *Second Sex*, 639. See Molyneux, "Beyond the Domestic Labour Debate," 26; Vogel, *Marxism and the Oppression of Women*; Johanna Brenner, *Women and the Politics of Class* (Monthly Review, 2000); Nancy R. Folbre, "A Patriarchal Mode of Production," in *Alternatives to Economic Orthodoxy*, ed. Randy Albelda (Routledge, 1987), 323–38.

113. Dalla Costa and James, "Woen and the Subversion of the Community," 29.

114. Merchant, The Death of Nature, xvi. See Susan Griffin's *Woman and Nature: The Roaring Inside Her* (Harper and Row, 1978), Mary Daly's *Gyn/Ecology: The Metaethics of Radical Feminism* (Women's Press, 1979), and even in places, Mies and Shiva's *Ecofeminism*. For analyses and overviews of ecofeminist traditions: Greta Gaard, *Ecological Politics: Ecofeminists and the Greens* (Temple University Press, 1998).

115. On age: Simone de Beauvoir, *A Very Easy Death*, trans. Patrick O'Brian (1964; Pantheon Books, 1965); Beauvoir, *The Coming of Age*, trans. Patrick O'Brian (1970; Norton, 1996). On disability and capitalism: Marta Russell, *Capitalism and Disability: Selected Writings by Marta Russell*, ed. Keith Rosenthal (Haymarket, 2019).

116. Gabriel Winant, "The Baby and the Bathwater: Class Analysis and Class Formation after Deindustrialization" *Historical Materialism* 32, no. 3 (2024): 3–30.

117. Joan Tronto, *Moral Boundaries: A Political Argument for an Ethic of Care* (Routledge, 1993), 110.

118. Mary Mellor, "Ecofeminism and Ecosocialism: Dilemmas of Essentialism and Materialism," *Capitalism, Nature, Socialism* 3, no. 2 (1992): 43–62; see also Mary Mellor, *Feminism and Ecology* (Polity, 1997). See also E. P. Thompson, "Time, Work-Discipline, and Industrial Capitalism," *Past & Present* 38, no. 1 (1967): 79.

119. Lewis, *Full Surrogacy Now*, 75.

120. See Emily Blumenfeld and Susan Mann, "Domestic Labour and the Reproduction of Labour Power: Towards an Analysis of Women, the Family, and Class," in Fox, *Hidden in the Household*, 267–307.

121. Cf. Will McKeithen and Sky Naslund, "Worms and Workers: Placing the More-than-Human and the Biological in Social Reproduction," *Society and Space*, November 14, 2017, https://www.societyandspace.org/articles/worms-and-workers-placing-the-more-than-human-and-the-biological-in-social-reproduction; Katie Meehan and Kendra Strauss, introduction to *Precarious Worlds: Contested Geographies of Social Reproduction*, ed. Meehan and Strauss (University of Georgia Press, 2015), 1–22.

122. Claude Levi-Strauss, *The Raw and the Cooked* (1964; University of Chicago Press, 1969); Mellor, *Feminism and Ecology*; Beauvoir, *Second Sex*, 639. On the increased burden of household labor caused by pollution: Winant, *Next Shift*.

123. Kirstin Munro, "'Social Reproduction Theory,' Social Reproduction, and Household Production," *Science & Society* 83, no. 4 (2019): 451–68.

124. Winant, "Baby and the Bathwater." Relatedly: Moore, *Capitalism*, 17.

125. Baumol, "Macroeconomics of Unbalanced Growth," 415.

126. Sheila Rowbotham, *Woman's Consciousness, Man's World* (1973; Verso, 2015), 122.

127. Alex Blanchette, *Porkopolis: American Animality, Standardized Life, and the Factory Farm* (Duke University Press, 2020).

128. Jennifer Morgan, *Laboring Women: Gender and Reproduction in the Making of New World Slavery* (University of Pennsylvania Press, 2004); Davis, *Women, Race, and Class*; Saidiya Hartman, "The Belly of the World: A Note on Black Women's Labors," *Souls* 18, no. 1 (2016): 166–73. For a discussion of this literature: Shatema Threadcraft, *Intimate Justice: The Black Female Body and the Body Politic* (Oxford University Press, 2016).

129. There are occasional exceptions to this rule too, as Davis and others have observed. Black South African miners were housed in barracks; Henry Ford managed his workers' households to ensure a supply of "quality" labor. Davis, *Women, Race, and Class*.

130. Emma Dowling, *The Care Crisis* (Verso, 2021), 137.

131. Cf. Ferguson, *Women and Work*, 113. They therefore tend to rely disproportionatelyon extracting rents from publicly funded programs, as Winant details: Winant, *Next Shift*.

132. Echoing Gonzalez and Neton in "The Logic of Gender."

133. Winant, "Baby and the Bathwater," 22.

134. Pierrette Hondagneu-Sotelo, *Doméstica: Immigrant Workers Cleaning and Caring in the Shadows of Affluence* (University of California Press, 2001); Barbara Ehrenreich and Arlie Russell Hochschild, eds., *Global Woman: Nannies, Maids, and Sex Workers in the New Economy* (Henry Holt, 2002); Rhacel Salazar Parreñas, *Servants of Globalization: Migration and Domestic Work*, 2nd ed. (Stanford University Press, 2015).

135. Thomas Hobbes, *On the Citizen*, ed. Richard Tuck and Michael Silverthorne (Cambridge University Press, 1998), 102. For a representative critique: Seyla Benhabib, *Situating the Self: Gender, Community, and Postmodernism in Contemporary Ethics* (Routledge, 1992); see also Paul Sagar, "Of Mushrooms and Method: History and the Family in Hobbes's Science of Politics," *European Journal of Political Theory* 14 no. 1 (2015): 98–117.

136. Baumol, *Cost Disease*, 43–44, 67.

137. See Alyssa Battistoni, "Living, Not Just Surviving," *Jacobin* 26 (2017): 65–71; Battistoni, "Ways of Making a Living: Revaluing the Work of Social and Ecological Reproduction," *Socialist Register* 56 (2020): 182–98.

138. Baumol, *Cost Disease*, 76. Cf. Winant, *Next Shift*. See also O'Connor, "Capitalism, Nature, Socialism"; Nancy Folbre, "Children as Public Goods," *American Economic Review* 84, no. 2 (1994): 86–90; Paula England and Folbre, "Who Should Pay for the Kids?," *Annals of the American Academy of Political and Social Science* 563 (1999): 194–207.

139. Baumol, *Cost Disease*, 54.

140. Asad Haider and Salar Mohandesi, "Making a Living," *Viewpoint Magazine*, October 28, 2015, https://viewpointmag.com/2015/10/28/making-a-living/; Nancy Fraser, "Contradictions of Capital and Care," *New Left Review* 100 (2016): 115–16; Helen Hester and Nick Srnicek, *After Work: A History of the Home and the Fight for Free Time* (Verso, 2023).

141. For instances of the uptake of Wages for Housework–type analyses in public discourse: Claire Cain Miller, "Stay-at-Home Parents Work Hard. Should They Be Paid?," *New York Times*, October 3, 2019; Gus Wezerek and Kristen R. Ghodsee, "Women's Unpaid Labor Is Worth $10,900,000,000,000," *New York Times*, May 5, 2020; Kim Brooks, "This Mother's Day, Forget Pancakes. Pay Women," *New York Times*, May 8, 2020; Jordan Kinser, "The Lockdown Showed How the Economy Exploits Women. She Already Knew," *New York Times*, February 17, 2021; Sarah Jaffe, "The Women of Wages for Housework," *Nation*, March 2018; Dayna Tortorici, "More Smiles? More Money," *n+1* 17 (2013), https://www.nplusonemag.com/issue-17/reviews/more-smiles-more-money/.

142. Gorz, *Critique of Economic Reason*, 144; Elizabeth Anderson, "Is Women's Labor a Commodity?," *Philosophy and Public Affairs* 19, no. 1 (1990): 71–92; Michael Walzer, *Spheres of Justice: A Defense of Pluralism and Equality* (Basic Books, 1983), 232.

Chapter 6

1. Rebecca Reider, *Dreaming the Biosphere: The Theater of All Possibilities* (University of Minnesota Press, 2009), 102.

2. Joel E. Cohen and David Tilman, "Biosphere 2 and Biodiversity: The Lessons So Far," *Science* 274, no. 5290 (1996): 1150–51.

3. John Avise, "The Real Message from Biosphere 2," *Conservation Biology* 8, no. 2 (1994): 328.

4. Robert Costanza, Ralph d'Arge, Rudolf de Groot, Stephen Farberll, Monica Grasso, Bruce Hannon, Karin Limburg, et al., "The Value of the World's Ecosystem Services and Natural Capital," *Nature* 387, no. 6630 (1997): 255.

5. Anna Lowenhaupt Tsing, *The Mushroom at the End of the World: On the Possibility of Life in Capitalist Ruins* (Princeton University Press, 2015), 22; for related views: Donna Haraway, *Staying with the Trouble: Making Kin in the Chthulucene* (Duke University Press, 2016); Marisol de la Cadena, *Earth Beings: Ecologies of Practice across Andean Worlds* (Duke University Press, 2015).

6. Bruno Latour, *Facing Gaia: Eight Lectures on the New Climatic Regime*, trans. Catherine Porter (Polity, 2017), 91–92; Latour, *Down to Earth: Politics in the New Climatic Regime* (Polity, 2018), 87; Latour and Peter Weibel, eds., *Critical Zones: The Science and Politics of Landing on Earth* (MIT Press, 2020). For a vital note of caution regarding Gaia theory: Leah Aronowsky, "Gas Guzzling Gaia, or: A Prehistory of Climate Change Denialism," *Critical Inquiry* 47, no. 2 (2021): 306–27.

7. David Attenborough, foreword to Partha Dasgupta, *The Economics of Biodiversity: The Dasgupta Review* (HM Treasury, 2021), 1.

8. William D. Nordhaus, "World Dynamics: Measurement without Data," *Economic Journal* 83, no. 332 (1973): 1178n1.

9. Partha Dasgupta, "It's Not a Giant Step to Introduce Nature into Economics," *Financial Times*, November 4, 2021.

10. Gretchen Daily, *Nature's Services: Societal Dependence on Natural Ecosystems* (Island, 1997), 6.

11. Quoted in Gillian Tett, "Why We Need to Put a Number on Our Natural Resources," *Financial Times*, September 23, 2020.

12. *Natural capital* is defined as the stock; *ecosystem services*, the benefits that flow from it, including the provision of usable goods like foods and fibers; regulation of temperatures, rainfall, and waste; regeneration of soil; energy capture; and nutrient cycling—plus an array of cultural benefits. For early salvos in a now-enormous literature: Daily, *Nature's Services*; Gretchen Daily and Katherine Ellison, *The New Economy of Nature: The Quest to Make Conservation Profitable* (Island, 2002). For more recent analyses: Dasgupta, *Economics of Biodiversity*; Paula DiPerna, *Pricing the Priceless: The Financial Transformation to Value the Planet, Solve the Climate Crisis, and Protect Our Most Precious Assets* (Wiley, 2023). For an important critique: Adrienne Buller, *The Value of a Whale: On the Illusions of Green Capitalism* (Manchester University Press, 2022).

13. Edward O. Wilson, *The Diversity of Life* (W. W. Norton, 1992), 283.

14. André Gorz, *Ecology as Politics* (South End Books, 1980), 65.

15. John Locke, *Two Treatises of Government*, ed. Peter Laslett (Cambridge University Press, 1988), 297.

16. James Tully, "Rediscovering America: The *Two Treatises* and Aboriginal Rights," in *Locke's Philosophy: Content and Context*, ed. G.A.J. Rogers (Clarendon, 1994), 165–96; Onur Ulas Ince, *Colonial Capitalism and the Dilemmas of Liberalism* (Oxford University Press, 2018). For a more wide-ranging consideration of the relationship between Indigenous dispossession and property relations: Robert Nichols, *Theft Is Property! Dispossession and Critical Theory* (Duke University Press, 2019). On property more generally: Jacob Blumenfeld, *The Concept of Property in Kant, Fichte, and Hegel: Freedom, Right, and Recognition* (Routledge, 2024).

17. Karl Marx, *Capital: A Critique of Political Economy*, trans. Ben Fowkes, vol. 1 (Penguin Books, 1976), 874. The term has more recently, and accurately, been translated as "so-called original accumulation": see Karl Marx, *Capital: Critique of Political Economy*, vol. 1, trans. Paul Reitter, ed. Paul North and Reitter (Princeton University Press, 2024), 651.

18. Cited in Karl Marx, "On the Jewish Question (1843)," in *Marx & Engels Collected Works*, trans. Clemens Dutt, vol. 3 (Lawrence and Wishart, 1976), 172.

19. James C. Scott, *Seeing like a State: How Certain Schemes to Improve the Human Condition Have Failed* (Yale University Press, 1998), 39.

20. For a valuable overview of this paradigm: Sara H. Nelson and Patrick Bigger, "Infrastructural Nature," *Progress in Human Geography* 46, no. 1 (2022): 86–107.

21. Haeckel, cited in Donald Worster, *Nature's Economy: A History of Ecological Ideas*, 2nd ed. (Cambridge University Press, 1994), 192.

22. On Marsh: Paul R. Ehrlich and Harold A. Mooney, "Ecosystem Services: A Fragmentary History," in Daily, *Nature's Services*, 12; on Darwin: Worster, *Nature's Economy*, 157–58; Rachel Carson, *Silent Spring* (Houghton Mifflin 1962), 251.

23. Study of Critical Environmental Problems, *Man's Impact on the Global Environment* (MIT Press, 1970), 123. On this crisis, see: Melinda Cooper, *Life as Surplus: Biotechnology and Capitalism in the Neoliberal Era* (University of Washington Press, 2008); Sara Holiday Nelson, "Neoliberal Environments: Crisis, Counterrevolution, and the Nature of Value" (PhD dissertation, University of Minnesota, 2017).

24. Walter E. Westman, "How Much Are Nature's Services Worth?," *Science* 197, no. 4307 (1977): 960–64; John P. Holdren and Paul R. Ehrlich, "Human Population and the Global Environment," *American Scientist* 62, no. 3 (1974): 282–92. For a longer history: Worster, *Nature's Economy*.

25. Herman E. Daly, "On Economics as a Life Science," *Journal of Political Economy* 76, no. 3 (1968): 397.

26. Ernst Friedrich Schumacher, *Small Is Beautiful: Economics as if People Mattered* (Harper and Row, 1973), 4; Wendell Berry, *The Unsettling of America: Culture & Agriculture* (Sierra Club Books, 1977), 183; Barry Commoner, *The Closing Circle: Nature, Man & Technology* (Knopf, 1971), 273.

27. Westman, "How Much."

28. For a useful overview of these debates: Mark Sagoff, *The Economy of the Earth: Philosophy, Law, and the Environment*, 2nd ed. (Cambridge University Press, 2007); John O'Neill, *Ecology, Policy, and Politics: Human Well-Being and the Natural World* (Routledge, 1993). On cultural value: Anna Chiesura and Rudolf de Groot, "Critical Natural Capital: A Sociocultural Perspective," *Ecological Economics* 44, no. 2–3 (2003): 219–31. On "willingness to pay": Marion Fourcade, "Cents and Sensibility: Economic Valuation and the Nature of 'Nature,'" *American Journal of Sociology* 116, no. 6 (2011): 1721–77.

29. On ways of valuing whales: Buller, *Value of a Whale*; Rebecca Giggs, *Fathoms: The World in the Whale* (Simon and Schuster, 2020); Bathsheba Demuth, *Floating Coast: An Environmental History of the Bering Strait* (W. W. Norton, 2019); Alexis Pauline Gumbs, *Undrowned: Black Feminist Lessons from Marine Mammals* (AK, 2020); Herman Melville, *Moby-Dick; or, The Whale* (Oxford University Press, 2008).

30. Ralph Chami, Thomas F. Cosimano, Connel Fullenkamp, and Sena Oztosun, "Nature's Solution to Climate Change: A Strategy to Protect Whales Can Limit Greenhouse Gases and Global Warming," *Finance & Development* 56, no. 004 (2019): 34–38. For a critique: Buller, *Value of a Whale*.

31. Steven Kelman, "Cost-Benefit Analysis: An Ethical Critique," *Regulation* 5, no. 1 (1981): 33–40.

32. Viviana A. Zelizer, *The Purchase of Intimacy* (Princeton University Press, 2007), 22; for a related defense of separate "spheres": Michael Walzer, *Spheres of Justice: A Defense of Pluralism and Equality* (Basic Books, 1983).

33. Timothy C. Weiskel, "Selling Pigeons in the Temple: The Danger of Market Metaphors in an Ecosystem," Harvard Seminar on Environmental Values, Harvard Divinity School, 1997.

34. Robin Wall Kimmerer, *Braiding Sweetgrass: Indigenous Wisdom, Scientific Knowledge, and the Teachings of Plants* (Milkweed Editions, 2013), 197; see also Kelman, "Cost-Benefit Analysis"; Sian Sullivan, "On 'Natural Capital', 'Fairy Tales' and Ideology," *Development and Change* 48, no. 2 (2017): 397–423; Arild Vatn, "The Environment as a Commodity," *Environmental Values* 9, no. 4 (2000): 493–509.

35. Arne Naess, "The Deep Ecological Movement: Some Philosophical Aspects," *Philosophical Inquiry* 8, no. 1/2 (1986): 10–31; see also Val Plumwood, *Feminism and the Mastery of Nature* (Routledge, 1993); Paul W. Taylor, *Respect for Nature: A Theory of Environmental Ethics* (1986; Princeton University Press, 2011), 142; Sharon R. Krause, "Political Respect for Nature," *Philosophy & Social Criticism* 47, no. 2 (2021): 241–66. A similar view is expressed by Aldo Leopold in *A Sand County Almanac; and Sketches Here and There* (Oxford University Press, 1949, vii).

36. Sullivan, "On 'Natural Capital,'" 398; see also Kathleen McAfee, "Selling Nature to Save it? Biodiversity and Green Developmentalism," *Environment and Planning D: Society and Space* 17, no. 2 (1999): 133–54.

37. Michael Sandel, *What Money Can't Buy: The Moral Limits of Markets* (Farrar, Straus, and Giroux, 2012), 78. For other "crowding out" arguments: George Monbiot, "The Pricing of Everything" *Ecological Citizen* 2, no. 1 (2018): 89–96; Sullivan, "On 'Natural Capital'"; Sagoff, *Economy of the Earth*; O'Neill, *Ecology, Policy, and Politics*. For a critique of the idea of "crowding out": Herbert Gintis, "Giving Economists Their Due," *Boston Review*, June 2012.

38. O'Neill, *Ecology, Policy, and Politics*, 75; Sagoff, *Economy of the Earth*; see also Jon Elster, "The Market and the Forum: Three Varieties of Political Theory," in *Foundations of Social Choice Theory*, ed. Elster and Aamund Hylland (Cambridge University Press, 1986), 103–32.

39. Gretchen Daily, "Introduction: What Are Ecosystem Services?," in *Nature's Services*, 7; L. H. Goulder and D. Kennedy, "Valuing Ecosystem Services: Philosophical Bases and Empirical Methods," in Daily, *Nature's Services*, 23–47.

40. Donella Meadows, "Nature Is More than a Commodity," *Sustainability Institute* (blog), November 21, 1991, https://donellameadows.org/archives/nature-is-more-than-a-commodity/.

41. Cited in Dempsey, *Enterprising Nature*, 33.

42. Paul Burkett, "Value, Capital and Nature: Some Ecological Implications of Marx's Critique of Political Economy," *Science & Society* 60, no. 3 (1996): 332–59; Matt Huber, "Resource Geographies I: Valuing Nature (or Not)," *Progress in Human Geography* 42, no. 1 (2018): 148–59.

43. Costanza et al., "Value of the World's Ecosystem Services."

44. Robert Costanza, Rudolf de Groot, Paul Sutton, Sander van der Ploeg, Sharolyn J. Anderson, Ida Kubiszewski, Stephen Farber, and R. Kerry Turner, "Changes in the Global Value of Ecosystem Services," *Global Environmental Change* 26 (2014): 153–54. See also Walter V. C. Reid, *Millennium Ecosystem Assessment Synthesis Report* (Millennium Ecosystem Assessment, 2005), v. For an assessment: Richard Norgaard, "Ecosystem Services: From Eye-Opening Metaphor to Complexity Blinder," *Ecological Economics* 69, no. 6 (2010): 1219–27.

45. William E. Rees, "Ecological Footprints and Appropriated Carrying Capacity: What Urban Economics Leaves Out," *Environment and Urbanization*, 4 no. 2 (1992): 121–30; Patrick Bond and Rahul Basu, "Intergenerational Equity and the Geographical Ebb and Flow of Resources: The Time and Space of Natural Capital Accounting," in *The Routledge Handbook of Critical Resource Geography*, ed. Matthew Himley, Elizabeth Havice, and Gabriela Valdivia (Routledge, 2021), 260–73; Alf Hornborg, "Towards an Ecological Theory of Unequal Exchange: Articulating World System Theory and Ecological Economics," *Ecological Economics* 25, no. 1 (1998): 127–36; Stephen Bunker, *Underdeveloping the Amazon: Extraction, Unequal Exchange, and the Failure of the Modern State* (University of Chicago Press, 1985); Rowil Aguillon, Nimmo Bassey, Elizabeth Bravo, Aurora Donoso, Festus Iyaye, Esperanza Martínez, Karin Nansen, et al., *No More Looting and Destruction! We the Peoples of the South are Ecological*

Creditors (Southern Peoples Ecological Debt Creditors Alliance, Acción Ecológica, and Instituto de Estudios Ecologistas del Tercer Mundo, 2003); Olúfẹ́mi O. Táíwò, *Reconsidering Reparations* (Oxford University Press, 2022).

46. Félix Tshisikedi, "We Are Tired of Waiting—Africa Must Be a Priority for COP26," *Financial Times*, October 25, 2021, https://www.ft.com/content/3da44d66-a1d3-4e12-8a29-b9bf6f399324. See also David Pilling, "Africa's Green Superpower: Why Gabon Wants Markets to Help Tackle Climate Change," *Financial Times*, July 20, 2021, https://www.ft.com/content/4f0579ac-409f-41d2-bf40-410d5a2ee46b.

47. Alyssa Battistoni, "Bringing in the Work of Nature: From Natural Capital to Hybrid Labor," *Political Theory* 45, no. 1 (2017): 5–31. For a related analysis: David Meyer Temin, "Wages for Earthwork," *American Political Science Review* 119, no. 1 (2025): 179–92.

48. Anjana Ahuja, "Turning Whales into Carbon-Based Assets Won't Be Easy," *Financial Times*, May 3, 2023.

49. A. C. Pigou, *The Economics of Welfare* (Macmillan, 1920), 184.

50. J. E. Meade, "External Economies and Diseconomies in a Competitive Situation," *Economic Journal* 62, no. 245 (1952): 54–67.

51. Meade, "External Economies," 61; see also uptake by Francis Bator in "Anatomy of Market Failure" *Quarterly Journal of Economics* 71, no. 3 (1958): 351–79.

52. Steven N. S. Cheung, "The Fable of the Bees: An Economic Investigation," *Journal of Law & Economics* 16, no. 1 (1973): 11–33; see also David B. Johnson, "Meade, Bees, and Externalities," *Journal of Law & Economics* 16, no. 1 (1973): 35–52.

53. "The Solution," Intrinsic Exchange Group, accessed October 20, 2024, https://www.intrinsicexchange.com/en/solution; KPMG International, *The Investment Case for Nature* (KPMG International, 2023).

54. "Why Invest in Nature, the World's Most Undervalued Asset Class," *Lombard Odier* (blog), January 18, 2024, https://www.lombardodier.com/contents/corporate-news/corporate/2024/january/let-s-invest-in-nature-the-world.html.

55. David Harvey, *The New Imperialism* (Oxford University Press, 2003); drawing on Rosa Luxemburg, *The Accumulation of Capital: A Contribution to the Economic Theory of Imperialism*, ed. Peter Hudis and Paul Le Blanc, trans. Nicholas Gray, vol. 2 of *The Complete Works of Rosa Luxemburg* (1913; Verso, 2016). For an orthogonal view: Glen Sean Coulthard, *Red Skin, White Masks: Rejecting the Colonial Politics of Recognition* (University of Minneapolis Press, 2014). For critical analyses: William Clare Roberts, "What Was Primitive Accumulation? Reconstructing the Origin of a Critical Concept," *European Journal of Political Theory* 19, no. 4 (2020): 532–52; Robert Nichols, "Disaggregating Primitive Accumulation," *Radical Philosophy*, no. 194 (2015): 18–28.

56. Harvey, *New Imperialism*, 148.

57. Neil Smith, "Nature as Accumulation Strategy," *Socialist Register* 43 (2007): 16–36; Adam Bumpus and Diana Liverman, "Accumulation by Decarbonization and the Governance of Carbon Offsets," *Economic Geography* 84, no. 2 (2008): 127–55; Bram Büscher and Robert Fletcher, "Accumulation by Conservation," *New Political Economy* 20, no. 2 (2015): 273–98; Fletcher, "Using the Master's Tools? Neoliberal Conservation and the Evasion of Inequality," *Development and Change* 43, no. 1 (2012): 295–317; John Bellamy Foster, "The Defense of Nature: Resisting the Financialization of the Earth," *Monthly Review* 73, no. 11 (2022): 5.

58. Smith, "Nature as Accumulation Strategy," 17.

59. Morgan Robertson, "Measurement and Alienation: Making a World of Ecosystem Services," *Transactions of the Institute of British Geographers* 37, no. 3 (2012): 396.

60. Nancy Fraser, "Can Society Be Commodities All the Way Down? Post-Polanyian Reflections on Capitalist Crisis," *Economy and Society* 43, no. 4 (2014): 552.

61. Jessica Dempsey and Daniel Chiu Suarez, "Arrested Development? The Promises and Paradoxes of 'Selling Nature to Save It,'" *Annals of the American Association of Geographers* 106, no. 3 (2016): 654; see also Jessica Dempsey and Patrick Bigger, "Intimate Mediations of For-

Profit Conservation Finance: Waste, Improvement, and Accumulation," *Antipode* 51 no. 2 (2019): 517–38; Stefan Ouma, Leigh Johnson, and Patrick Bigger, "Rethinking the Financialization of 'Nature,'" *Environment and Planning A: Economy and Space* 50, no. 3 (2018): 500–511.

62. Alyssa Battistoni, "Private Virtues, Public Vices: Nature, Philanthropy, and the New Fables of the Bees" (unpublished manuscript, 2024).

63. Mark Carney, "Stop Debating Carbon Markets and Start Building Them," *Financial Times*, June 17, 2024. For a discussion of the failure of the related sector of ESG (environmental, social, governance) investing, see Buller, *Value of a Whale*, 152–82.

64. Convention on Biodiversity, *Contribution to a Draft Resource Mobilization Component of the Post-2020 Biodiversity Framework as a Follow-Up to the Current Strategy for Resource Mobilization: Third Report of the Panel of Experts on Resource Mobilization* (Convention on Biodiversity, 2021), 9.

65. Andrew Deutz, Geoffrey M. Heal, Rose Niu, Eric Swanson, Terry Townshend, Zhu Li, Alejandro Delmar, Alqayam Meghji, Suresh A. Sethi, and John Tobin-de la Puente, *Financing Nature: Closing the Global Biodiversity Financing Gap* (Nature Conservancy, 2020), 8. See also: Ivo Mulder, Aurelia Blin, Justin Adams, Teresa Hartmann, Danielle Carreira, Mark Schauer, Waltraud Ederer, Robin Smale, Mateo Salazar, and Marta Simonetti, *State of Finance for Nature: Tripling Investments in Nature-Based Solutions by 2030* (United Nations Environmental Programme, 2021).

66. Neil Smith, *Uneven Development: Nature, Capital, and the Production of Space*, 3rd ed. (University of Georgia Press, 2008), 78.

67. Sandel, *What Money Can't Buy*, 8.

68. For an overview of the pollinator crisis: Dasgupta, *Economics of Biodiversity*, 405; Rebecca A. Ellis, Tony Weis, Sainath Suryanarayanan, and Kata Beilin, "From a Free Gift of Nature to a Precarious Commodity: Bees, Pollination Services, and Industrial Agriculture," *Journal of Agrarian Change* 20, no. 3 (2020): 437–59.

69. On domesticated and industrialized bees: Jake Kosek, "The Natures of the Beast," in *Global Political Ecology*, ed R. Peet (Routledge, 2010), 245; Jake Kosek, "Industrial Materials: Labor, Landscapes, and the Industrialized Honeybee," in *How Nature Works: Rethinking Labor on a Troubled Planet*, ed. Sarah Besky and Alex Blanchette (University of New Mexico Press, 2019), 149–68.

70. Gary Paul Nabhan and Stephen L. Buchmann, "Services Provided by Pollinators," in Daily, *Nature's Services*, 136.

71. Karl Marx, *Economic Manuscript of 1861–63*, trans. Emile Burns, in *Marx & Engels Collected Works*, vol. 31 (1863; Lawrence and Wishart, 1989), 467–68.

72. On rent: Romain Felli, "On Climate Rent," *Historical Materialism* 22, no. 3–4 (2014): 251–80; Diego Andreucci, Melissa García-Lamarca, Jonah Wedekind, and Erik Swyngedouw, "'Value Grabbing': A Political Ecology of Rent," *Capitalism Nature Socialism* 28, no. 3 (2017), http://dx.doi.org/10.1080/10455752.2016.1278027; Brett Christophers, *Rentier Capitalism: Who Owns the Economy, and Who Pays for It?* (Verso, 2020); Anne Haila, "The Theory of Land Rent at the Crossroads," *Environment and Planning D: Society and Space* 8, no. 3 (1990): 275–296; Callum Ward and Manuel B. Aalbers, "'The Shitty Rent Business': What's the Point of Land Rent Theory?," *Urban Studies* 53, no 9 (2016): 1760–83.

73. Karl Marx, *Capital: A Critique of Political Economy*, vol. 3, trans. Ernest Untermann, in *Marx & Engels Collected Works*, vol. 37 (1894; Lawrence and Wishart 1998), 627. See also Beverly Best, *The Automatic Fetish: The Law of Value in Marx's "Capital"* (Verso, 2024).

74. See the early description of nature's "free services" as "the ways in which the components of the system interact[,] . . . the dynamics of ecosystems": Westman, "How Much," 961. See also Dasgupta, *Economics of Biodiversity*; Robertson, "Measurement and Alienation."

75. On efforts to financialize nature: Robertson, "Measurement and Alienation"; Smith, "Nature as Accumulation Strategy"; Büscher and Fletcher, "Accumulation by Conservation."

For a detailed discussion of financialization and nature: Buller, *Value of a Whale*. For a critique of the financialization of nature model: Brett Christophers, "The Limits to Financialization," *Dialogues in Human Geography* 5, no. 2 (2015): 183–200.

76. Patrick Bigger and Jessica Dempsey, "Reflecting on Neoliberal Natures: An Exchange," *Environment and Planning E: Nature and Space* 1, no. 1–2 (2018): 25–75. See also Donald MacKenzie, "Social Connectivities in Global Financial Markets," *Environment and Planning D: Society and Space* 22, no. 1 (2004): 98; Donald MacKenzie, Fabian Muniesa, and Lucia Siu, eds., *Do Economists Make Markets? On the Performativity of Economics* (Princeton University Press, 2008). On exclusion: Blumenfeld, *Concept of Property*.

77. Cited in Samuel C. Wiel, "Natural Communism: Air, Water, Oil, Sea, and Seashore," *Harvard Law Review* 47, no. 3 (1934): 425.

78. Hugo Grotius, *The Free Sea (Mare Liberum)*, trans. Richard Hakluyt (1609; Liberty Fund, 2004), 26; John H. Dales, *Pollution, Property, and Prices: An Essay in Policy-Making and Economics* (University of Toronto Press, 1970), 61–62.

79. Wiel, "Natural Communism," 425; see also reference in Andreas Malm, *Fossil Capital: The Rise of Steam Power and the Roots of Global Warming* (Verso, 2016).

80. Jean-Baptiste Say, *A Treatise on Political Economy, or The Production, Distribution and Consumption of Wealth* (1803; 4th ed., 1819), trans. C. R. Prinsep (Claxton, Remsen and Haffelfinger, 1880; repr. Augustus M. Kelley, 1971), 360.

81. The lighthouse has often been a paradigmatic example, though one also disputed by Coase: John Stuart Mill, *Principles of Political Economy* (1870; Longmans, Green, 1909), 976; for a challenge: R. H. Coase, "The Lighthouse in Economics," *Journal of Law & Economics* 17, no. 2 (1974): 357–76.

82. Dieter Helm, *Natural Capital: Valuing Our Planet* (Yale University Press, 2015), 12.

83. See discussion in Steven Vogel's *Thinking Like a Mall: Environmental Philosophy after the End of Nature* (MIT Press, 2015), 199–238.

84. Elinor Ostrom, *Governing the Commons: The Evolution of Institutions for Collective Action* (Cambridge University Press, 1990); Silvia Federici, *Re-enchanting the World: Feminism and the Politics of the Commons* (PM, 2018); Peter Linebaugh, *Stop, Thief! The Commons, Enclosures, and Resistance* (PM, 2014).

85. J. R. McNeill and Peter Engelke, *The Great Acceleration: An Environmental History of the Anthropocene Since 1945* (Harvard University Press, 2014). Moishe Postone argues in *Time, Labor, and Social Domination: A Reinterpretation of Marx's Critical Theory* that capitalism has restructured "all spheres of social life in the modern world" (Cambridge University Press, 1993), 391.

86. For examples: William Cronon, *Nature's Metropolis: Chicago and the Great West* (W. W. Norton, 1991), 266; Walter Johnson, *River of Dark Dreams: Slavery and Empire in the Cotton Kingdom* (Harvard University Press, 2013), 156.

87. Troy Vettese, "A Marxist Theory of Extinction," *Salvage* 7 (2020), https://salvage.zone /a-marxist-theory-of-extinction/. On extinction more generally: Ashley Dawson, *Extinction: A Radical History* (OR Books, 2016); Lynne Huffer, *These Survivals: Autobiography of an Extinction* (Duke University Press, 2025).

88. Troy Vettese and Drew Pendergrass, *Half-Earth Socialism: A Plan to Save the Future from Extinction, Climate Change and Pandemics* (Verso, 2022); McNeill and Engelke, *Great Acceleration*; Thea Riofrancos, "What Green Costs," *Logic* 9 (2019): 161–71. While Martha Nussbaum attributes responsibility for these indirect effects to "humans" in general, then, it is better located with capitalism. Nussbaum, *Justice for Animals: Our Collective Responsibility* (Simon and Schuster, 2023).

89. Gumbs, *Undrowned*, 101.

90. Adam Smith, *An Inquiry into the Nature and Causes of the Wealth of Nations*, ed. R. H. Campbell and A. S. Skinner (Oxford University Press, 1976), 1: 27.

91. Tania Murray Li, "To Make Live or Let Die? Rural Dispossession and the Protection of Surplus Populations," *Antipode* 41, no. s1 (2010): 66–93; Michael Denning, "Wageless Life," *New Left Review*, no. 66 (2010): 79–97; Endnotes Collective, "Misery and Debt," *Endnotes* 2 (2010): 20–51. On "surplus" in the context of biodiversity: Jessica Dempsey, *Enterprising Nature: Economics, Markets, and Finance in Global Biodiversity Politics* (John Wiley and Sons, 2016), 29.

92. Demuth, *Floating Coast*, 70.

93. Keeanga-Yamahtta Taylor, *Race for Profit: How Banks and the Real Estate Industry Undermined Black Homeownership* (University of North Carolina Press, 2019), 254.

94. Ruth Wilson Gilmore, *Golden Gulag: Prisons, Surplus, Crisis, and Opposition in Globalizing California* (University of California Press, 2007), 178.

95. A. Smith, *Wealth of Nations*, 2: 724–32. For exceptions: see Coase, "Lighthouse in Economics"; James Buchanan, "Public Goods in Theory and Practice: A Note on the Minasian-Samuelson Discussion," *Journal of Law and Economics* 10 (1967): 193–97; see also Thomas Biebricher, *The Political Theory of Neoliberalism* (Stanford University Press, 2018).

96. Friedrich A. Hayek, *The Road to Serfdom* (1944; Routledge Classics, 2001), 40.

97. Including, potentially, in the United States: Jane Lubchenco, Heather Tallis, and Eli Fenichel, "Accounting for Nature on Earth Day 2022," White House, April 14, 2022, https://www.whitehouse.gov/ostp/news-updates/2022/04/24/accounting-for-nature-on-earth-day-2022/.

98. Daily and Ellison, *The New Economy of Nature*.

99. Dempsey and Suarez, "Arrested Development?"; Bigger and Dempsey, "Reflecting on Neoliberal Natures."

100. Felli, "On Climate Rent"; Morgan Robertson, "Before Neoliberal Natures," in Bigger and Dempsey, "Reflecting on Neoliberal Natures," 43–46.

101. Nelson and Bigger, "Infrastructural Nature"; Ashley Carse, "Nature as Infrastructure: Making and Managing the Panama Canal Watershed," *Social Studies of Science* 42, no. 4 (2012): 539–63; Sara H. Nelson, Leah L. Bremer, Kelly Meza Prado, and Kate A. Brauman, "The Political Life of Natural Infrastructure: Water Funds and Alternative Histories of Payments for Ecosystem Services in Valle Del Cauca, Colombia," *Development and Change* 51, no. 1 (2020): 26–50. On infrastructure more generally: Susan Leigh Star, "The Ethnography of Infrastructure," *American Behavioral Scientist* 43 (1999): 377–91.

102. Nor is infrastructure necessarily public: it too can be an "asset class." Nelson and Bigger, "Infrastructural Nature"; Brett Christophers, *Our Lives in Their Portfolios: Why Asset Managers Own the World* (Verso, 2022).

103. James O'Connor, "Capitalism, Nature, Socialism: A Theoretical Introduction," *Capitalism Nature Socialism*, 1, no. 1 (1988): 34; Winona LaDuke and Deborah Cowen, "Beyond Wiindigo Infrastructure," *South Atlantic Quarterly* 119, no. 2 (2020): 245. For a related though distinct discussion of "public things," see also Bonnie Honig's *Public Things: Democracy in Disrepair* (Fordham University Press, 2017). For a related discussion of the differences between infrastructure oriented toward colonial commerce and popular well-being: Walter Rodney, *How Europe Underdeveloped Africa* (1972; Verso, 2018). The prospects for the provision of "means of life" depend to some degree on one's analysis of the relation between capital and the state, which I cannot address here; for analysis: Alyssa Battistoni, "State, Capital, Nature: State Theory for the Capitalocene," in *Marxism and the Capitalist State: Towards a New Debate*, ed. Rob Hunter, Rafael Khachaturian, Eva Nanopoulos (Palgrave Macmillan, 2023), 31–51.

104. Nelson et al., "Political Life of Natural Infrastructure"; Karen Bradshaw, *Wildlife as Property Owners: A New Conception of Animal Rights* (University of Chicago Press, 2020).

105. O'Connor, "Capitalism, Nature, Socialism," 24.

106. Alfred Sohn-Rethel, *Intellectual and Manual Labour: A Critique of Epistemology*, trans. Martin Sohn-Rethel (1970; Haymarket Books, 2020), 17.

107. By *artificial abstraction* I mean something different from Jason Moore's idea of *abstract social nature*, which describes the process of making nature legible in abstract terms—what we might call, riffing on James Scott, "seeing like capital." In my view, Moore mistakenly equates his concept of abstract social nature with the real abstraction, as explored in chapters 2 and 5. Moore, *Capitalism in the Web of Life*; Scott, *Seeing like a State*.

108. The "artificial man" is of course Hobbes's term for the state: Thomas Hobbes, *Leviathan*, ed. Edwin Curley (Hackett, 1994).

109. Giorgos Kallis and Erik Swyngedouw, "Do Bees Produce Value? A Conversation between an Ecological Economist and a Marxist Geographer," *Capitalism Nature Socialism* 29, no. 3 (2018): 42.

110. Dempsey and Bigger, "Intimate Mediations."

111. Katie Kedward, Sophus O.S.E. zu Ermgassen, Josh Ryan-Collins, and Sven Wunder, "Nature as an Asset Class or Public Good? The Economic Case for Increased Public Investment to Achieve Biodiversity Targets," *SSRN* (2022), http://dx.doi.org/10.2139/ssrn.4306836.

112. Jacob Blumenfeld, "The Socialization of Nature," ICI Politics of Nature Conference, Berlin, October 20, 2022.

113. On pleasure: Lida Maxwell, "Queer/Love/Bird Extinction: Rachel Carson's *Silent Spring* as a Work of Love," *Political Theory* 45, no. 5 (2017): 682–704.

114. Cf. Simone de Beauvoir, *The Second Sex*, trans. Constance Borde and Sheila Malovany-Chevallier (1949; Vintage, 2011), 46. Or, per the resource scholar Erich Zimmermann, "Resources *are* not; they *become*": Zimmermann, *World Resources and Industries* (Harper, 1951), 15.

115. The Red Nation, *The Red Deal: Indigenous Action to Save Our Earth* (Common Notions, 2021), 92; Coulthard, *Red Skin, White Masks*.

116. Nick Estes, "Indigenous People Are Already Working 'Green Jobs'—but They're Unrecognized and Unpaid," *Intercept*, September 23, 2019; Ariel Salleh, "From Metabolic Rift to 'Metabolic Value': Reflections on Environmental Sociology and the Alternative Globalization Movement," *Organization & Environment* 23, no. 2 (2010): 205–19. For related ideas: Battistoni, "Bringing in the Work of Nature"; Latour, *Down to Earth*; Mierle Laderman Ukeles, "Manifesto for Maintenance Art" (1969); Stefania Barca, *Workers of the Earth: Labour, Ecology and Reproduction in the Age of Climate Change* (Pluto, 2024).

117. Joshua Farley and Robert Costanza, "Payments for Ecosystem Services: From Local to Global," *Ecological Economics* 69, no. 11 (2010): 2060–68; Sven Wunder, "Revisiting the Concept of Payment for Ecosystem Services," *Ecological Economics* 117 (2015): 234–43.

118. Neera M. Singh, "Payments for Ecosystem Services and the Gift Paradigm: Sharing the Burden and Joy of Environmental Care," *Ecological Economics* 117 (2015): 53–61.

119. Benjamin Neimark, Sango Mahanty, Wolfram Dressler, and Christina Hicks, "Not Just Participation: The Rise of the Eco-Precariat in the Green Economy," *Antipode* 52, no. 2 (2020): 496–521; Nelson and Bigger, "Infrastructural Nature."

120. On housing and transit as ecological demands: Kate Aronoff, Alyssa Battistoni, Daniel Aldana Cohen, and Thea Riofrancos, *A Planet to Win: Why We Need a Green New Deal* (Verso, 2019); Cohen, *Street Fight: Climate Change and Inequality in the 21st Century City* (Princeton University Press, forthcoming); Nancy Fraser, "Climates of Capital: For a Trans-environmental Eco-socialism," *New Left Review* 127 (2021): 94–127. On public energy infrastructures: Brett Christophers, *The Price Is Wrong: Why Capitalism Won't Save the Planet* (Verso, 2023).

121. On undoing infrastructure: Andreas Malm, *How to Blow Up a Pipeline: Learning to Fight in a World on Fire* (Verso, 2020); Vettese and Pendergrass, *Half-Earth Socialism*.

122. Sharon Krause, *Eco-Emancipation: An Earthly Politics of Freedom* (Princeton University Press, 2023). On the complicated use and potential co-optation of *buen vivir/sumak kawsay*: Thea Riofrancos, *Resource Radicals: From Petro-Nationalism to Post-Extractivism in Ecuador* (Duke University Press 2019), 177–79.

123. Marx, *Capital*, 3: 763; see also Best, *The Automatic Fetish*; Kohei Saito, *Karl Marx's Eco-socialism: Capital, Nature, and the Unfinished Critique of Political Economy* (Monthly Review, 2017).

124. Donna J. Haraway, "A Manifesto for Cyborgs: Science, Technology, and Socialist-Feminism in the Late Twentieth Century," in *Simians, Cyborgs, and Women: The Reinvention of Nature* (Routledge, 1991), 181.

125. Táíwò, *Reconsidering Reparations*.

Chapter 7

1. Richard Buckminster Fuller, "World Energy," *Fortune*, February 1940.

2. Andrew Nikiforuk, *The Energy of Slaves: Oil and the New Servitude* (Greystone Books, 2012).

3. On similar grounds Donella Meadows, coauthor of *Limits to Growth*, accused herself of being a slaveholder no less than Thomas Jefferson: Meadows, "Thomas Jefferson and Donella Meadows, Slaveowners," *Sustainability Institute* (blog), November 12, 1998, https://donella meadows.org/archives/thomas-jefferson-and-donella-meadows-slave-owners/.

4. Nikiforuk, *Energy of Slaves*, 9.

5. Dipesh Chakrabarty, "The Climate of History: Four Theses," *Critical Inquiry* 35, no. 2 (2009): 208; see also Chakrabarty, "Climate and Capital: On Conjoined Histories," *Critical Inquiry* 41 no. 1 (2014), 1–23; Chakrabarty, *The Climate of History in a Planetary Age* (University of Chicago Press, 2021).

6. Arguments to this effect are widespread in the literature on modern growth, particularly but not exclusively that written from an environmental perspective. See Vaclav Smil, *Energy in Nature and Society: General Energetics of Complex Systems* (MIT Press, 2008); Smil, *Transforming the Twentieth Century: Technical Innovations and Their Consequences* (Oxford University Press, 2006); J. R. McNeill, *Something New under the Sun: An Environmental History of the Twentieth-Century World* (W. W. Norton, 2000); McNeill and Peter Engelke, *The Great Acceleration: An Environmental History of the Anthropocene Since 1945* (Harvard University Press, 2014). For more explicit arguments that energy use has expanded freedom: John Asafu-Adjaye, Linus Blomqvist, Stewart Brand, Barry Brook, Ruth de Fries, Erle Ellis, Christopher Foreman, et al., "An Eco-modernist Manifesto," Breakthrough Institute, April 1, 2015, https://thebreakthrough.org /manifesto/manifesto-english; Leigh Phillips, *Austerity Ecology and the Collapse-Porn Addicts: A Defense of Growth, Progress, Industry, and Stuff* (Zero Books, 2015).

7. Pierre Charbonnier, *Affluence and Freedom: An Environmental History of Political Ideas* (Polity, 2021), 9.

8. Chakrabarty, "Climate of History," 210.

9. On the anxieties and ambivalences of freedom: Wendy Brown, *States of Injury: Power and Freedom in Late Modernity* (Princeton University Press, 1995). On the story of modern emancipation with respect to ecology: Bruno Latour, "Love Your Monsters: Why We Must Care for Our Technologies as We Do Our Children," *Breakthrough Journal*, no. 2 (2011), https:// thebreakthrough.org/journal/issue-2/love-your-monsters.

10. Elisabeth Anker, *Ugly Freedoms* (Duke University Press, 2022).

11. Sharon Krause, *Eco-Emancipation: An Earthly Politics of Freedom* (Princeton University Press, 2023).

12. Linda Zerilli, *Feminism and the Abyss of Freedom* (University of Chicago Press, 2005).

13. I'm grateful to Fred Neuhouser and Will Roberts for suggesting this frame. See also Sharon R. Krause, "Plural Freedom," *Politics & Gender* 8, no. 2 (2012): 238–45.

14. Karl Marx, *Capital: A Critique of Political Economy*, vol. 3, trans. Ernest Untermann, in *Marx & Engels Collected Works*, vol. 37 (1894; Lawrence and Wishart 1998), 807.

15. It has often been read as a call for the mastery of nature, for example, but for an ecological reading, see Kohei Saito's *Karl Marx's Ecosocialism: Capital, Nature, and the Unfinished Critique of Political Ecology* (Monthly Review, 2017), 214.

16. Aristotle, *Politics*, trans. C.D.C. Reeve (Hackett, 1998), 6.

17. Karl Kautsky, *The Class Struggle (Erfurt Program)*, trans. William E. Bohn (1892; C. H. Kerr, 1910), 153. On Kautsky's legacy: Jukka Gronow, *On the Formation of Marxism: Karl Kautsky's Theory of Capitalism, the Marxism of the Second International and Karl Marx's Critique of Political Economy* (Brill, 2016). For a discussion of Kautsky's views of nature and humanity: Leszek Kolakowski, *Main Currents of Marxism: Its Rise, Growth, and Dissolution*, vol. 2, *The Golden Age* (Clarendon, 1978), 34–40.

18. Kautsky, *Class Struggle*, 158.

19. Marshall Sahlins, *Stone Age Economics* (Aldine, 1972).

20. G. A. Cohen, *Karl Marx's Theory of History: A Defence* (1978; Princeton University Press, 2000), 61.

21. Cohen, *Karl Marx's Theory of History*, 23. Cohen would later admit that his own reading of this point, and of the "conquest of nature" in particular, was influenced as much by the Marxism of his youth as by Marx himself: see the fascinating aside in his *Self-Ownership, Freedom, and Equality* (Cambridge University Press, 1995), 133n39.

22. Cohen, *Self-Ownership, Freedom, and Equality*, 10–11.

23. Cohen, *Karl Marx's Theory of History*, 323.

24. Cohen, *Self-Ownership, Freedom, and Equality*, 6, 10.

25. Matthew T. Huber, *Lifeblood: Oil, Freedom, and the Forces of Capital* (University of Minnesota Press, 2013), 157–58.

26. Huber, *Lifeblood*, 215; see also David Schwartzman, "Solar Communism," *Science and Society* 60, no. 3 (1996): 307–31.

27. Matthew T. Huber, "Fossilized Liberation: Energy, Freedom, and the 'Development of Productive Forces,'" in *Materialism and the Critique of Energy*, ed. Brent Ryan Bellamy and Jeff Diamanti (MCM', 2018), 517.

28. Phillips, *Austerity Ecology*, 237.

29. Aaron Bastani, *Fully Automated Luxury Communism: A Manifesto* (Verso, 2019). For further discussion: Alyssa Battistoni, "Disrupting the Future: Review, *Fully Automated Luxury Communism*, by Aaron Bastani," *Nature Sustainability* 2 (2019): 651.

30. Bastani, *Fully Automated Luxury Communism*, 119.

31. Mary Mellor, *Feminism and Ecology* (Polity, 1997), 190; see also Maria Mies and Vandana Shiva, *Ecofeminism*, 2nd ed. (Zed Books, 2014).

32. Dipesh Chakrabarty, "Baucom's Critique: A Brief Response," *Cambridge Journal of Postcolonial Literary Inquiry* 1, no. 2 (2014): 248.

33. For illustrative examples: Chakrabarty, "Climate and Capital," 15–16; Robert Gordon, *The Rise and Fall of American Growth: The U.S. Standard of Living since the Civil War* (Princeton University Press, 2016), 322. For the counterpoint: Ruth Schwarz Cowan, *More Work for Mother: The Ironies of Household Technology from the Open Hearth to the Microwave* (Basic Books, 1983).

34. As argued decades ago: William Ophuls, *Ecology and the Politics of Scarcity: Prologue to a Political Theory of the Steady State* (W. H. Freeman, 1977).

35. Sebastiano Timpanaro, *On Materialism*, trans. Lawrence Garner (Verso, 1980), 20, 62.

36. Timpanaro, *On Materialism*, 20. Here he draws on the Italian poet Giacomo Leopardi, whose experience of scoliosis and poor health, Timpanaro claims, had made him attentive to physical conditions that Marxists have tended to ignore. He locates Leopardi's own inspiration in the Italian philosopher Pietro Verri, who had chastised the physiocrats for failing to recognize what would later be understood as the second law of thermodynamics. Timpanaro's immediate inspiration is Engels's late materialism in *Dialectics of Nature* (1883).

37. Timpanaro, *On Materialism*, 20. For a useful analysis and critique: Raymond Williams, "Problems of Materialism," *New Left Review* I/109 (1978): 3–17.

38. Shulamith Firestone, *The Dialectic of Sex: The Case for Feminist Revolution* (1970; Farrar, Straus, & Giroux, 2003)—a book published, strikingly, the same year as Timpanaro's. Firestone's view is not so far from Cohen's as it might seem: it is ultimately reliant on Engels's forces-relations argument in *Origins of the Family, Private Property, and the State*. Despite this resonance, feminist and Marxist engagements with bodily materialism have proceeded on largely parallel tracks.

39. Firestone, *Dialectic of Sex*, 184.

40. Versions of the call to realize "freedom within necessity" are widespread in feminist and ecological thought: Robyn Eckersley, *Environmentalism and Political Theory: Toward an Ecocentric Approach* (State University of New York Press, 1992), 87; Wendy Brown, *Manhood and Politics: A Feminist Reading in Political Theory* (Rowman and Littlefield, 1988); Maria Mies, *Patriarchy and Accumulation on a World Scale: Women in the International Division of Labour*, 3rd ed. (Zed Books, 2014); Nancy Hartsock, *Money, Sex, and Power: Towards a Feminist Historical Materialism* (Northeastern University Press, 1985), 244; Ariel Salleh, *Ecofeminism as Politics: Nature, Marx, and the Postmodern* (Zed Books, 1997); Ariel Salleh and Martin O'Connor, "Eco-socialism/Ecofeminism," *Capitalism, Nature, Socialism* 2, no. 1 (1991): 129–37; Val Plumwood, *Feminism and the Mastery of Nature* (Routledge, 1993), 43.

41. Mies and Shiva, *Ecofeminism*, 8.

42. Mies, *Patriarchy and Accumulation*, 216.

43. Mies, *Patriarchy and Accumulation*, 217, 216. Italics in the original.

44. Mies, *Patriarchy and Accumulation*, 218. Italics in the original.

45. Mies and Shiva, *Ecofeminism*, 19.

46. Mies and Shiva, *Ecofeminism*, 227. For critiques of this stance toward technology: Donna Jeanne Haraway, *Simians, Cyborgs, and Women: The Reinvention of Nature* (Routledge, 1991); Laboria Cuboniks, *The Xenofeminist Manifesto: A Politics for Alienation* (Verso, 2018).

47. Mies and Shiva, *Ecofeminism*, 138. Indeed, while Mies's socialist feminism began with a close attention to working conditions and an analysis of the global division of labor, she would eventually become fixated on technology, cofounding the organization Feminist International Network of Resistance to Reproductive and Genetic Engineering (FINRRAGE) to contest biotechnology, surrogacy, and reproductive technologies. For discussion of Mies's position on reproduction in particular: Helen Hester, *Xenofeminism* (Polity, 2018), 16–17; Sophie Lewis, *Full Surrogacy Now: Feminism against Family* (Verso, 2019).

48. On this view of nature: Kate Soper, *What Is Nature? Culture, Politics, and the Non-Human* (Blackwell, 1995); Andrew Collier, *Critical Realism* (Verso, 1994); Lena Gunnarsson, "The Naturalistic Turn in Feminist Theory: A Marxist-Realist Contribution," *Feminist Theory* 14, no. 1 (2013): 3–19. Mies's position is in this sense the opposite of xenofeminism, for which a "normative anti-naturalism has pushed us towards an unflinching ontological naturalism": Cuboniks, *Xenofeminist Manifesto*, 0x11.

49. David James, *Practical Necessity, Freedom, and History: From Hobbes to Mark* (Oxford University Press, 2021); John Bellamy Foster, *The Return of Nature: Socialism and Ecology* (New York University Press, 2020), 20.

50. Philip Pettit, "Freedom in the Market," *Politics, Philosophy & Economics* 5, no. 2 (2006): 132–33.

51. Philip Pettit, *Republicanism: A Theory of Freedom and Government* (Oxford University Press, 1997), 117–19, 158–65. See also Quentin Skinner, *Liberty before Liberalism* (Cambridge University Press, 1998).

52. Texts in this burgeoning tradition include: K. Sabeel Rahman, *Democracy against Domination* (Oxford University Press, 2017); James Muldoon, "A Socialist Republican Theory of

Freedom and Government," *European Journal of Political Theory* 21, no. 1 (2022): 47–67; Alex Gourevitch, *From Slavery to the Cooperative Commonwealth: Labor and Republican Liberty in the Nineteenth Century* (Cambridge University Press, 2014); Bruno Leipold, Karma Nabulsi, and Stuart White, eds., *Radical Republicanism: Recovering the Tradition's Popular Heritage* (Oxford University Press, 2020).

53. William Clare Roberts, *Marx's Inferno: A Political Theory of Capital* (Princeton University Press, 2017), 237.

54. Daniel Luban, "In Marx's Republic," *Nation*, April 4, 2018, https://www.thenation.com /article/archive/in-marxs-republic/. On the history of republican ideas of freedom across time: J. A. Pocock, *The Machiavellian Moment: Florentine Political Thought and the Atlantic Republican Tradition* (Princeton University Press, 1975); Annelise de Dijn, *Freedom: An Unruly History* (Harvard University Press, 2020).

55. Reading taken on October 24, 2024, from Mauna Loa Observatory, Hawaii, as reported by the National Aeronautics and Space Administration.

56. Elizabeth Anderson, *Private Government: How Employers Rule Our Lives (and Why We Don't Talk about It)* (Princeton University Press, 2017), 52.

57. Alex Gourevitch, "Labor Republicanism and the Transformation of Work," *Political Theory* 41, no. 4 (2013): 596–97; Tom O'Shea, "Socialist Republicanism," *Political Theory* 48, no. 5 (2020): 13.

58. Cf. Gourevitch, *From Slavery to the Cooperative Commonwealth*.

59. Let alone, as Jasper Bernes points out, the rest of the apparatus of capitalism, including technologies and practices of circulation. Jasper Bernes, "The Belly of the Revolution: Agriculture, Energy, and the Future of Communism," in *Materialism and the Critique of Energy*, ed. Brent Ryan Bellamy and Jeff Diamanti (MCM', 2018), 331–75. See also: Moishe Postone, *Time, Labor, and Social Domination: A Reinterpretation of Marx's Critical Theory* (Cambridge University Press, 1993), 14, 337, 352; Postone, "Rethinking Marx (in a Post-Marxist World)," in *Reclaiming the Sociological Classics: The State of the Scholarship*, ed. Charles Camic (Blackwell, 1997), 45–80.

60. Postone, *Time, Labor, and Social Domination*, 27.

61. Moishe Postone, "Necessity, Labor, and Time: A Reinterpretation of the Marxian Critique of Capitalism," *Social Research* 45, no. 4 (1978): 778.

62. As of 2020, anthropogenic mass has surpassed all biomass, human and nonhuman alike—in other words, the mass of objects produced by human beings has come to exceed the mass of all living things on Earth: Jedediah Purdy, "The World We've Built," *Dissent Magazine*, July 2018; Emily Elhacham, Liad Ben-Uri, Jonathan Grozovski, Yinon M. Bar-On, and Ron Milo, "Global Human-Made Mass Exceeds All Living Biomass," *Nature* 588, no. 7838 (2020): 442–44.

63. David S. Landes, *The Unbound Prometheus: Technological Change and Industrial Development in Western Europe from 1750 to the Present*, 2nd ed. (1969; Cambridge University Press, 2003); Karen Bakker and Gavin Bridge, "Material Worlds? Resource Geographies and the 'Matter of Nature,'" *Progress in Human Geography* 30, no. 1 (2006): 5–27; Karl Marx, *Capital: A Critique of Political Economy*, vol. 1, trans. Ben Fowkes (Penguin Books, 1976), 505–7.

64. Postone, *Time, Labor, and Social Domination*, 382.

65. Aaron Benanav, *Automation and the Future of Work* (Verso, 2019): 81–93. A similar tendency is apparent in at least some republican texts: for example, Alex Gourevitch, "Post-Work Socialism?," *Catalyst* 6, no. 2 (2022), https://catalyst-journal.com/2022/09/post-work-social-ism; O'Shea, "Socialist Republicanism," 13.

66. Martin Hägglund, *This Life: Secular Faith and Spiritual Freedom* (Pantheon Books, 2019).

67. Hägglund, *This Life*, 303. See Benjamin Kunkel's related critique: Kunkel, "Free Time and Paid Work," *Los Angeles Review of Books*, July 15, 2020, https://lareviewofbooks.org/article/free -time-and-paid-work/.

68. Hägglund, *This Life*, 256.

69. On "real wealth" and the production of beautiful things under communism: Kye Barker, "The Cause of Labour Is the Hope of the Earth: William Morris and Regrowth Communism," presentation, American Political Science Association, Philadelphia, September 7, 2024; see also William Morris, "Useful Work versus Useless Toil," in *News from Nowhere and Other Writings* (1884; Penguin Books, 1998), 285–306.

70. Roberts, *Marx's Inferno*, 151, 154; italics mine.

71. Roberts, *Marx's Inferno*, 165.

72. For work that confronts similar challenges: Lucas Stancyzk, "Productive Justice," *Philosophy and Public Affairs* 40, no. 2 (2012): 144–64.

73. Simone de Beauvoir, *The Ethics of Ambiguity*, trans. Bernard Frechtman (1947; Open Road, 2018), 6. For a discussion of the significance of ambiguity to Beauvoir's work: Sonia Kruks, *Simone de Beauvoir and the Politics of Ambiguity* (Oxford University Press, 2012).

74. Beauvoir, *Ethics of Ambiguity*, 5–6. Beauvoir's concept of ambiguity was strongly influenced by phenomenology of Maurice Merleau-Ponty, which led her to adopt a less strict division between object and subject than Sartre typically affirmed. See, for example, Beauvoir, "A Review of *The Phenomenology of Perception*," in *Philosophical Writings*, ed. Margaret A. Simons (University of Illinois Press, 2004), 151–64. On Beauvoir's view of embodiment: Judith Butler, "Sex and Gender in Simone de Beauvoir's *Second Sex*," *Yale French Studies*, no. 72 (1986): 35–49; Penelope Deutscher, "Bodies, Lost and Found: Simone de Beauvoir from *The Second Sex* to *Old Age*," *Radical Philosophy*, no. 96 (1999): 6–16; Sonia Kruks, "Simone de Beauvoir: Engaging Discrepant Materialisms," in *New Materialisms: Ontology, Agency, and Politics*, ed. Diana Coole and Samantha Frost (Duke University Press, 2010), 258–80.

75. Beauvoir, *Ethics of Ambiguity*, 8.

76. On Beauvoir's potential to help feminist theory navigate between biological essentialism and social constructivism: Toril Moi, *What Is a Woman? And Other Essays* (Oxford University Press, 1999); Kruks, "Simone de Beauvoir: Engaging Discrepant Materialisms," 276.

77. Jean-Paul Sartre, *Being and Nothingness: An Essay in Phenomenological Ontology*, trans. Sarah Richmond (1943; Washington Square, 2018), 630–31.

78. Sartre, *Being and Nothingness*, 629; see also David Detmer, *Freedom as a Value: A Critique of the Ethical Theory of Jean-Paul Sartre* (Open Court, 1986).

79. Beauvoir, *Ethics of Ambiguity*, 41.

80. Simone de Beauvoir, *The Second Sex*, trans. Constance Borde and Sheila Malovany-Chevallier (1949; Vintage, 2011), 46.

81. For the ethical significance of this account of human beings: Daniela Dover and Jonathan Gingerich, "Towards an Existentialist Metaethics," in *Analytic Existentialism*, ed. Berislav Marušić and Mark Schroeder (Oxford University Press, 2024): 180–205.

82. Beauvoir, *Second Sex*, 5.

83. Thanks to Kye Barker for this framing. For a discussion of Beauvoir's departure in *The Second Sex* from Sartre's initial view of freedom: Sonia Kruks, "Simone de Beauvoir and the Limits to Freedom," *Social Text*, no. 17 (1987): 111–22; Kate Kirkpatrick, "Beauvoir and Sartre's 'Disagreement' about Freedom," *Philosophy Compass* 18, no. 11 (2023). Frantz Fanon takes up a similar project from a different angle in *Black Skin, White Masks* (trans. Richard Philcox [1952; Grove 2008]). On the resonances between Fanon and Beauvoir: Robyn Marasco, *The Highway of Despair: Critical Theory after Hegel* (Columbia University Press, 2015), 214n101; Toril Moi, *Simone de Beauvoir: The Making of an Intellectual Woman* (Blackwell, 1994).

84. Firestone dedicates the *Dialectic* to Beauvoir—but she also criticizes Beauvoir as overly "sophisticated" for failing to recognize the basic truth that "woman is a womb"; Mies, meanwhile, condemns her as an advocate of "self-mutilation" in service of transcending nature. Firestone, *Dialectic of Sex*, 8; Maria Mies, "Self-Determination: The End of a Utopia?," in Mies and

Shiva, *Ecofeminism*, 226. The ecofeminist Ariel Salleh similarly decries Beauvoir as a "masculine-identified feminist" who advocates total control over an "impoverished" nature: Salleh, *Ecofeminism as Politics*, 67, 204. For discussion of similar critiques of Beauvoir, see also Manon Garcia, "Thinking with Simone de Beauvoir Today," *Analyse & Kritik* 45, no. 2 (2023): 195–214.

85. Simone de Beauvoir, "Pyrrhus and Cineas (1944)," in *Philosophical Writings*, 129.

86. Julie Livingston and Andrew Ross, *Cars and Jails: Freedom Dreams, Debt, and Carcerality* (O/R Books, 2022).

87. Beauvoir, *Ethics of Ambiguity*, 97.

88. Indeed, Beauvoir's discussion of age as an embodied state is vastly underdiscussed relative to her analysis of gender in *The Second Sex*. Simone de Beauvoir, *The Coming of Age*, trans. Patrick O'Brian (1972; Norton, 1996); see also Kruks, "Simone de Beauvoir: Engaging Discrepant Materialisms"; Kate Kirkpatrick, "Past Her Prime? Simone de Beauvoir on Motherhood and Old Age," *Sophia* 53, no. 2 (2014): 275–87. On mortality and finitude: Beauvoir, *All Men Are Mortal*, trans. Leonard Friedman (1946; W. W. Norton 1992); Beauvoir, *A Very Easy Death*, trans. Patrick O'Brian (1964; Pantheon Books, 1965). See also Sartre, *Being and Nothingness*, 460.

89. On temperature: Chakrabarty, *Climate of History*, 95–113. On water contamination: Laura Pulido, "Flint, Environmental Racism, and Racial Capitalism," *Capitalism Nature Socialism* 27, no. 3 (2016): 1–16.

90. On fishing in Marx's famous imagination of communism: Marx and Friedrich Engels, *The German Ideology* in *Marx & Engels Collected Works*, vol. 5 (Lawrence & Wishart, 1975), 47. On birds as an element of human relationships: Lida Maxwell, "Queer/Love/Bird Extinction: Rachel Carson's *Silent Spring* as a Work of Love," *Political Theory* 45, no. 5 (2017): 682–704.

91. David Wallace-Wells, *The Uninhabitable Earth: Life after Warming* (Tim Duggan Books, 2019), 34.

92. Sartre, *Being and Nothingness*, 440.

93. Thea Riofrancos, "What Green Costs," *Logic* 9 (2019): 161–71.

94. Chiara Cordelli discusses a similar aim in terms of "reconciliation": Cordelli, "Socialism as Reconciliation" (unpublished manuscript, 2024).

95. Beauvoir, "Pyrrhus and Cineas," 140.

96. Beauvoir, *Ethics of Ambiguity*, 88. Or, in other words, how the free development of each might be the condition for the free development of all. Karl Marx and Friedrich Engels, "Manifesto of the Communist Party [1848]," in *Marx & Engels Collected Works*, vol. 6 (Lawrence and Wishart, 1976), 506; see also Jan Kandiyali, "What Makes Communism Possible? The Self-Realisation Interpretation," *Politics, Philosophy, and Economics* 23, no. 3 (2024): 273–94.; Kandiyali, "The Importance of Others: Marx on Unalienated Production," *Ethics* 130, no. 4 (2020): 555–87.

97. Beauvoir, *Ethics of Ambiguity*, 172. Sartre takes a similar position with respect to Kantian ethics, suggesting that ethics must always be concrete: Jean-Paul Sartre, *Notebooks for an Ethics*, trans. David Pellauer (1983; University of Chicago Press, 1992).

98. David Scott, *Conscripts of Modernity: The Tragedy of Colonial Enlightenment* (Duke University Press, 2004), 20.

99. Ursula LeGuin, *The Dispossessed* (Harper and Row, 1974); Jasper Bernes, "Communism Might Last a Million Years," *Commune* 1 (2018), https://communemag.com/the-shield-of-utopia/.

100. Stuart Hall, "For a Marxism without Guarantees," *Australian Left Review* 84 (1983): 43; see also Hall, "The Problem of Ideology: Marxism without Guarantees [1983]," in *Selected Writings on Marxism*, ed. Gregor McLennan (Duke University Press, 2021), 134–57.

101. Beauvoir, "Pyrrhus and Cineas," 139.

102. Beauvoir, *Ethics of Ambiguity*, 129.

103. Beauvoir, *Ethics of Ambiguity*, 7–8.

104. Dover and Gingerich, "Towards an Existentialist Metaethics," 182.

105. On the irreversibility of climate change: Andreas Malm and Wim Carton, *Overshoot: How the World Surrendered to Climate Breakdown* (Verso, 2024). On the challenge of lasting residuals: Andreas Folkers, "Staying with the Rubble: Residual Reification and Reparative Critique" (unpublished manuscript, 2024). On time and climate change: Andreas Malm, *The Progress of This Storm: Nature and Society in a Warming World* (Verso, 2018).

106. On "fossil fascism": Andreas Malm and The Zetkin Collective, *White Skin, Black Fuel: On the Danger of Fossil Fascism* (Verso, 2021). On climate authoritarianism: Ross Mittiga, "Political Legitimacy, Authoritarianism, and Climate Change," *American Political Science Review* 116, no. 3 (2022): 998–1011. For the "lifeboat": Garrett Hardin, "Lifeboat Ethics: The Case against Helping the Poor," *Psychology Today* 8 (1974): 38–43. On "climate barbarism": Jacob Blumenfeld, "Climate Barbarism: Adapting to a Wrong World," *Constellations* 30, no. 2 (2023): 162–78.

107. Simone de Beauvoir, "Moral Idealism and Political Realism (1945)," in *Philosophical Writings*, 190; cf. Bruno Latour, *Down to Earth: Politics in the New Climatic Regime* (Polity, 2018).

108. Beauvoir, *Ethics of Ambiguity*, 35.

Epilogue

1. Shel Silverstein, *The Giving Tree* (Harper and Row, 1964). Gendered pronouns in the original.

2. Robin Wall Kimmerer, "Returning the Gift," *Humans and Nature*, October 1, 2013, https://humansandnature.org/earth-ethic-robin-kimmerer/.

3. Robin Wall Kimmerer, *Braiding Sweetgrass: Indigenous Wisdom, Scientific Knowledge, and the Teachings of Plants* (Milkweed Editions, 2013), 151; see also Kimmerer, "The Serviceberry: An Economy of Abundance," *Emergence*, October 26, 2022. On the contradiction of the "free gift" see also Mary Douglas, introduction to *The Gift: The Form and Reason for Exchange in Archaic Societies* by Marcel Mauss, trans. W. D. Halls (1966; Routledge, 1990): vii–xviii.

4. Winona LaDuke, "Traditional Ecological Knowledge and Environmental Futures," in *The Winona LaDuke Reader: A Collection of Essential Writings* (Voyageur, 2002), 78–88; Leanne Betasamosake Simpson, *As We Have Always Done: Indigenous Freedom through Radical Resistance* (University of Minnesota Press, 2017); Glen Sean Coulthard, *Red Skin, White Masks: Rejecting the Colonial Politics of Recognition* (University of Minnesota Press, 2014); Marisol de la Cadena, *Earth Beings: Ecologies of Practice across Andean Worlds* (Duke University Press, 2015). For concepts of multispecies reciprocity inspired by Indigenous ethics: Deborah Bird Rose, "Connectivity Thinking, Animism, and the Pursuit of Liveliness," *Educational Theory* 67, no. 4 (2017): 491–508; Rose, "Multispecies Knots of Ethical Time," *Environmental Philosophy* 9, no. 1 (2012): 127–40; James Tully, "Reconciliation Here on Earth," in *Resurgence and Reconciliation*, ed. Michael Asch, John Borrows, and Tully (University of Toronto Press, 2018), 83–132. On the gift and the commodity: Mauss, *Gift*; Karl Polanyi, *Primitive, Archaic, and Modern Economies: Essays of Karl Polanyi*, ed. George Dalton (Anchor Books, 1968); J. K. Gibson-Graham, *The End of Capitalism (as We Knew It): A Feminist Critique of Political Economy* (University of Minnesota Press, 2006); David Graeber, *Debt: The First 5,000 Years* (Melville House, 2011); Wendell Berry, *The Gift of Good Land: Further Essays Cultural and Agricultural* (North Point, 1981); Michel Serres, *The Natural Contract*, trans. Elizabeth MacArthur and William Paulson (University of Michigan Press, 1995); Donna Haraway, *Staying with the Trouble: Making Kin in the Chthulucene* (Duke University Press, 2016).

5. Christine Korsgaard, *Fellow Creatures: Our Obligations to the Other Animals* (Oxford University Press, 2018); Martha Nussbaum, *Justice for Animals: Our Collective Responsibility* (Simon and Schuster, 2023); Sharon Krause, *Eco-Emancipation: An Earthly Politics of Freedom* (Princeton

University Press, 2023); Alice Crary and Lori Gruen, *Animal Crisis: A New Critical Theory* (Polity, 2022); Sue Donaldson and Will Kymlicka, *Zoopolis: A Political Theory of Animal Rights* (Oxford University Press, 2011).

6. Kimmerer, "Returning the Gift."

7. Rob Nixon, "The Less Selfish Gene: Forest Altruism, Neoliberalism, and the Tree of Life," *Environmental Humanities* 13, no. 2 (2021): 348–71.

8. Pyotr Kropotkin, *Mutual Aid: A Factor in Evolution* (McLure Phillips, 1902). For a discussion of mutualist metaphors in fungi research, which does not quite avoid repeating them: Merlin Sheldrake, *Entangled Life: How Fungi Make Our Worlds, Change Our Minds, and Shape Our Futures* (Random House, 2020), 210–13.

9. Georges Bataille, *The Accursed Share: An Essay on General Economy*, vol. 1, trans. Robert Hurley (Zone Books, 1991); Jacques Derrida, *Given Time Vol I: Conterfeit Money*, trans. Peggy Kamuf (University of Chicago Press, 1992). For discussion of Bataille in particular: Nigel Clark, *Inhuman Nature: Sociable Life on a Dynamic Planet* (SAGE, 2011), 128–30.

10. Lorraine Daston, *Against Nature* (MIT Press, 2019), 60. For a similar point: Raymond Williams, "Ideas of Nature," in *Problems in Materialism and Culture* (Verso, 1980), 69–85.

11. Iris Marion Young, "Asymmetrical Reciprocity: On Moral Respect, Wonder, and Enlarged Thought," *Constellations* 3, no. 3 (1997): 340–63.

12. Thanks to Sharon Krause for suggesting this framing.

13. On natural freedom: Martin Hägglund, *This Life: Secular Faith and Spiritual Freedom* (Pantheon, 2019), 174; Krause, *Eco-emancipation*; Robyn Eckersley, *Environmentalism and Political Theory: Toward an Ecocentric Approach* (State University of New York Press, 1992).

14. In this I think existentialism is resonant with the view put forward by Sharon R. Krause in "Bodies in Action: Corporeal Agency and Democratic Politics" *Political Theory* 39, no. 3 (2011): 299–324.

15. Steven Vogel, *Against Nature: The Concept of Nature in Critical Theory* (State University of New York Press, 1996), 164.

16. John O'Neill is right to compare these debates to the "socialist calculation debates": O'Neill, *Ecology, Policy, and Politics: Human Well-Being and the Natural World* (Routledge, 1993).

17. For institutional proposals: Krause, *Eco-Emancipation*.

18. Anna Lowenhaupt Tsing, *The Mushroom at the End of the World: On the Possibility of Life in Capitalist Ruins* (Princeton University Press, 2015), 17, viii; see also Laura Ephraim, "Save the Appearances! Toward an Arendtian Environmental Politics," *American Political Science Review* 116, no. 3 (2022): 985–97; Lida Maxwell, "Queer/Love/Bird Extinction: Rachel Carson's *Silent Spring* as a Work of Love," *Political Theory* 45, no. 5 (2017): 682–704. For analysis of the political uses of wonder: Kye Barker, "A Political Theory of Wonder: Feelings of Order in Modern Political Thought" (PhD dissertation, University of California, Los Angeles, 2019).

19. Nussbaum, *Justice for Animals*, 12; Rebecca Giggs, *Fathoms: The World in the Whale* (Simon and Schuster, 2020).

20. Nayanika Mathur, *Crooked Cats: Beastly Encounters in the Anthropocene* (University of Chicago, 2021); Giggs, *Fathoms*.

21. Albert O. Hirschman, *The Passions and the Interests: Arguments for Capitalism before Its Triumph* (Princeton University Press, 1977).

22. Herman Melville, *Moby-Dick; or, The Whale* (1851; Oxford University Press, 2008), 189.

23. Melville, *Moby-Dick*, 145, 189.

24. Thus the voyage begins with the negotiation of the "lay"—the fraction of the total that each crew member will receive: Melville, *Moby-Dick*, 68–70. On the ship as industrial workplace populated by racialized proletarians: C.L.R. James, *Mariners, Renegades, and Castaways: The Story of Herman Melville and the World We Live In* (Dartmouth College Press, 1953).

25. Melville, *Moby-Dick*, 145.

26. Melville, *Moby-Dick*, 341–42; 346–48.

27. Melville, *Moby-Dick*, 347.

28. Melville, *Moby-Dick*, 348.

29. As described by Bathsheba Demuth in *Floating Coast: An Environmental History of the Bering Strait* (W. W. Norton, 2019), 29.

30. "For God's sake, be economical with your lamps and candles! not a gallon you burn, but at least one drop of man's blood was spilled for it" (Melville, *Moby-Dick*, 184)—to say nothing of the oceans of whale blood.

31. Minor whale-watching revenues aside. See chapter 6 for a discussion of the IMF valuation of whales; see also Adrienne Buller, *The Value of a Whale: On the Illusions of Green Capitalism* (Manchester University Press, 2022).

32. Jean-Paul Sartre, *Nausea*, trans. Lloyd Alexander (New Directions, 1964), 124.

33. Sartre, *Nausea*, 126.

34. Sartre, *Nausea*, 126.

35. Sartre, *Nausea*, 133–34.

36. Sartre himself, Beauvoir wrote, "detests the country," plants, insects, and nature; he was happy only "at the heart of a universe constructed and populated with fabricated objects": Simone de Beauvoir, "Jean-Paul Sartre," in *Philosophical Writings*, ed. Margaret A. Simons (University of Illinois Press, 2004), 230. Beauvoir herself loved the country.

37. Iris Murdoch, *Sartre: Romantic Rationalist* (1953; Bowes and Bowes, 1987), 59.

38. Sartre, *Nausea*, 131.

39. Cf. Ephraim, "Save the Appearances!," 996; Hannah Arendt, *The Human Condition*, 2nd ed. (1958; University of Chicago Press, 1998), 2–3.

40. Sartre, *Nausea*, 131. For a different but not incompatible comment on Roquentin: Bruno Latour and Timothy Lenton, "Extending the Domain of Freedom, or Why Gaia Is So Hard to Understand," *Critical Inquiry* 45, no. 3 (2019): 659–80.

41. Ed Yong, *An Immense World: How Animal Senses Reveal the Hidden Realms around Us* (Random House, 2022).

42. Rachel Carson, *The Sea around Us* (Oxford University Press, 1951). For other encounters with sea life: Alexis Pauline Gumbs, *Undrowned: Black Feminist Lessons from Marine Mammals* (AK, 2020); Augusta Foote Arnold, *The Sea-Beach at Ebb-Tide: A Guide to the Study of the Seaweeds and the Lower Animal Life Found between Tide-Marks* (Century, 1901).

43. Sophie Lewis, "My Octopus Girlfriend," *n+1* 39 (2021), 219.

INDEX

abdication, 87, 98, 104–6, 120, 135, 164, 173–76, 192, 197–98

absence of price, 2–3

absorption power, 134–35

abstraction. *See* real abstraction

abstract labor, 45

abstract time, 101–3

abundance: capitalism and, 71, 110, 131, 207; freedom and, 212–15, 218, 222–23, 230–31; of natural gifts, 8, 23, 30–31

actants, 29. *See also* practico-actant

Adorno, Theodor, 11, 19, 186

agency: fragmented, 129; moral responsibility and, 129–30; nature and, 29

agriculture, 86, 100–106, 271n92. *See also* nature

akrasia, 71

alienation: and freedom, 57, 66, 69, 74, 76; from nature, 14, 53, 74, 216–17, 239, 253n6; and property, 48–49, 182, 193, 195

ambiguity, 149, 210, 223–29

Anarchy, State, and Utopia (Nozick), 124

Anderson, Elizabeth, 126, 219

animals, 1–2, 8, 13, 23–24, 38, 44, 73, 100–103, 147, 194–96, 220, 233–34; animal labor, 171; animal laborans, 150–51; costs to, 138, 140. *See also* livestock; wildlife

Anker, Elisabeth, 61, 209

Arendt, Hannah, 19, 150–51, 169, 202

Aristotle, 150, 212

artificial abstraction, 200–201

axiarchy, 62

Babbage, Charles, 43

bad faith, 78–81, 224

Banaji, Jairus, 99, 109, 272n93

Bastani, Aaron, 214

Bataille, Georges, 9, 234

Baumol, William J., 167–69, 173, 177

Beauvoir, Simone de, 15, 55, 66, 149, 151, 164, 169, 210, 223–29, 231, 240, 303n74, 303n76, 303n83, 304n88, 305n86

Beck, Ulrich, 136–37

bees, 38–40, 189–90, 192

Benanav, Aaron, 168, 221

Berry, Wendell, 9, 184

biological time, 171

Biosphere 2, 179–80

Blanchette, Alex, 103

Blumenfeld, Jacob, 202

the body, 42, 149, 164, 169–72, 215, 217, 225–26

Bolivia, 146

Braverman, Harry, 42–44, 93, 220, 257n92

Brenner, Johanna, 158

Brewster, John, 86

Burawoy, Michael, 94, 97

Burkett, Paul, 49

Burtynsky, Edward, 115

byproduction, 119–20, 137, 139–41

Caffentzis, George, 134

capital: abdication and, 98, 104–6, 174; accumulation and, 17, 47, 71, 92, 98–99, 104, 168, 190–91, 200; authority and, 59–60, 87; byproduction and, 119–20,

309

A NOTE ON THE TYPE

This book has been composed in Arno, an Old-style serif typeface in the classic Venetian tradition, designed by Robert Slimbach at Adobe.